HEALTH AND HUMAN RIGHTS IN EUROPE

HEALTH AND HUMAN RIGHTS IN EUROPE

Brigit Toebes, Mette Hartlev,
Aart Hendriks and
Janne Rothmar Herrmann
(eds.)

intersentia
Cambridge – Antwerp – Portland

Intersentia Publishing Ltd.
Trinity House | Cambridge Business Park | Cowley Road
Cambridge | CB4 0WZ | United Kingdom
Tel.: +44 1223 393 753 | Email: mail@intersentia.co.uk

Distribution for the UK:
Hart Publishing Ltd.
16C Worcester Place
Oxford OX1 2JW
UK
Tel.: +44 1865 517 530
Email: mail@hartpub.co.uk

Distribution for the USA and Canada:
International Specialized Book Services
920 NE 58th Ave. Suite 300
Portland, OR 97213
USA
Tel.: +1 800 944 6190 (toll free)
Email: info@isbs.com

Distribution for Austria:
Neuer Wissenschaftlicher Verlag
Argentinierstraße 42/6
1040 Wien
Austria
Tel.: +43 1 535 61 03 24
Email: office@nwv.at

Distribution for other countries:
Intersentia Publishing nv
Groenstraat 31
2640 Mortsel
Belgium
Tel.: +32 3 680 15 50
Email: mail@intersentia.be

Health and Human Rights in Europe
Brigit Toebes, Mette Hartlev, Aart Hendriks and Janne Rothmar Herrmann (eds.)

ISBN 978-94-000-0151-0
NUR 828

British Library Cataloguing in Publication Data. A catalogue record for this book is available from the British Library.

PREFACE AND ACKNOWLEDGEMENTS

Increasingly, scholars from various disciplines are addressing the interfaces between health and human rights. As a legal scholar interested in this area, I started to teach a course entitled 'Health and Human Rights' at the University of Aberdeen School of Law in 2006. Finding this an important and developing area of law, I tried to identify its legal contours and its most important topics.

While I decided that there was an urgent need for a book, I struggled to cover all the areas of this broad and developing field. I am therefore utterly grateful to co-editors Mette Hartlev, Aart Hendriks and Janne Rothmar Herrmann for their excellent input and collaboration in this project. Many thanks also go the other authors for their valuable contributions and for their confidence in this project. Without them we would never have been able to cover so many perspectives of this new field and to demonstrate such knowledge and insight.

Altogether, the book is the result of much interaction and debate between the editors and authors of the book, scholars who together cover the wide areas of health law and human rights law from four different countries in Northern Europe. The aim of our project has been to write a truly coherent and comprehensive work with a number of interconnected chapters. These chapters roughly cover the scope of the area of health and human rights in Europe.

A few people have helped us at different stages in the writing and/or editorial process, including Sofia Gruskin and Daniel Tarantola, Herman Nys, Catherine Jacqueson, Dabney Evans, Maria Green, Simone Wijte, Tom Scheirs (Intersentia Publishing), and Fiona McGrath (for editing). Thanks also go to the School of Law of the University of Aberdeen, for extending my affiliation, and to the Faculty of Law of the University of Copenhagen, for enabling us to 'test' several chapters of the book by teaching a course entitled 'Health and Human Rights' in 2011. Lastly, I am grateful to the Research Department of the Danish Institute for Human Rights for granting me a temporary visiting research position, which enabled me to set the stage for this book.

Brigit Toebes, Managing Editor
Groningen, January 2012

CONTENTS

Preface and Acknowledgements v
About the Editors and Contributors xv
List of Abbreviations xvii

Introduction: Health and Human Rights in Europe
Brigit Toebes 1

1. Rationale and aim of this book 1
2. Historical introduction to 'health and human rights' 3
   2.1. Introduction 3
   2.2. The human rights movement 3
   2.3. Medical law, health law, medical and bioethics, and patients' rights .. 5
   2.4. The public health movement 7
3. Theoretical approach 9
   3.1. Main theoretical questions underpinning this research 9
   3.2. Conceptual grounding of human rights law 10
   3.3. Conceptual grounding and analysis of economic, social and cultural rights 12
   3.4. Identification of main concepts and principles underpinning this study 13
4. Method and chapter outline 16

PART I.
HEALTH AND HUMAN RIGHTS: THE EUROPEAN INSTITUTIONS

Chapter 1. The Council of Europe and Health and Human Rights
Aart Hendriks 23

1. Introduction 23
2. European Convention on Human Rights 24
   2.1. European Convention on Human Rights 24
   2.2. Rights and case-law 26
      2.2.1. General 27
      2.2.2. Health and human rights topics 30
         a. Right to health 30
         b. Right to life (Article 2) 31

c. Right to care (Article 3) 34
d. Patients' rights (Article 8) 36
2.3. Conclusions 43
3. European Social Charter 44
4. European Convention for the Prevention of Torture 47
5. Convention on Human Rights and Biomedicine 48
6. Conclusions 50

Chapter 2. The European Union and Health and Human Rights
Janne Rothmar Herrmann and Brigit Toebes 51

1. Introduction 51
1.1. The aim of this chapter 51
1.2. The EU, its institutions and functioning 52
2. EU, health and human rights 53
3. Specific responsibilities for health in the EU 57
3.1. Focus on human health in the new TFEU 57
3.2. EU engagement with public health 60
4. Free movement & health 63
4.1. Introduction 63
4.2. Free movement of services: cross-border healthcare services 63
4.2.1. The legal framework 63
4.2.2. Cross-border healthcare and issues of morality 66
4.2.3. Evaluation 68
4.3. Free movement of persons: healthcare professionals 69
4.4. Free movement of goods: pharmaceuticals 72
4.5. Free movement of goods: blood (safety) 75
4.6. Free movement of goods: cells and tissues (safety, standards and quality) 76
4.7. Data protection 77
5. Conclusions 78

PART II.
HEALTH AND HUMAN RIGHTS: AN EXPLORATION OF THE FIELD

Chapter 3. The Right to Health and Other Health-Related Rights
Brigit Toebes 83

1. Introduction 83
2.1. The right to health 86
2.1.1. Introduction 86
2.1.2. The right to health at the UN level 87
2.1.3. The right to health at the European level 89
2.1.4. Constitutional provisions 91

2.1.5. The scope of the right to health ... 92
2.1.6. Elements of the right to health ... 93
2.1.7. Guiding principles for the right to health ... 94
2.1.8. Vulnerable groups ... 96
2.1.9. Legal obligations ... 97
a. Respect, protect, fulfil ... 97
b. International obligations ... 99
c. Core obligations ... 99
2.1.10. The right to health: responsible actors ... 100
2.1.11. The right to health and public health ... 101
2.1.12. Justiciability of the right to health ... 102
3. Other health-related rights ... 103
3.1. Introduction ... 103
3.2. The right to life ... 104
3.3. The right to liberty and security of the person ... 106
3.4. The right to privacy and family life ... 107
3.5. Freedom of expression and the right to information ... 107
3.6. The right to marry and found a family ... 108
3.7. The rights to benefit from scientific progress ... 109
3.8. Economic, social and cultural rights, and the protection of health ... 109
4. Conclusions ... 110

Chapter 4. Patients' Rights
Mette HARTLEV ... 111

1. Introduction ... 111
2. Definition and development of patients' rights ... 112
2.1. Concept of patients' rights ... 112
2.2. Development of patients' rights ... 114
3. Patients' rights in international law: general principles and legal instruments ... 117
3.1. Legal instruments ... 117
3.2. General legal principles ... 119
4. Right to self-determination ... 122
4.1. Autonomy, self-determination and consent ... 122
4.2. Patients' right to self-determination in human rights and patients' rights law ... 123
4.3. Restriction on right to self-determination in patients' rights law ... 125
5. Patients' right to information ... 130
5.1. Patients' interest in information ... 130
5.2. Right to information in medical decision-making ... 130
5.3. Right not to know ... 132

5.4. Access to medical files. 133
5.5. General information 133
6. Patients who are not competent to give consent. 134
7. Medical research 136
8. Privacy and confidentiality 138
8.1. Confidential relationships and informational self-determination. . . 138
8.2. Processing of health data in connection with medical treatment . . . 140
8.3. Use of health data for purposes other than medical care 142
9. Concluding remarks 144

Chapter 5. Reproductive Health
Janne ROTHMAR HERRMANN 145

1. Introduction 145
2. Women's reproductive health and human rights 146
2.1. Introduction 146
2.2. Reproductive autonomy 147
2.3. Right to respect for privacy and family life 149
2.4. The prohibition of discrimination 149
3. Family planning. 149
3.1. Abortion 150
3.1.1. The UN Conventions. 150
3.1.2. The European Convention on Human Rights. 152
a. The balancing of interests between woman and foetus . . 152
b. The balancing of interests between woman and state . . . 155
c. The balancing of interests between woman and man . . . 158
3.2. Contraception 160
4. Procreative healthcare services 161
4.1. Fertility treatment 162
4.1.1. A privacy issue? 162
4.1.2. Access to treatment? 164
4.2. Embryo and foetus selection 169
5. Pregnancy, health and autonomy 174
5.1. Maternal and foetal health. 174
5.2. Forced treatment of pregnant women 175
6. Concluding remarks 176

Chapter 6. Euthanasia and Physician-Assisted Suicide from a Human Rights Perspective
Jozef DORSCHEIDT. 177

1. Introduction 177
2. Terminology 178

3. End-of-life decisions and human rights. 181
3.1. End-of-life decisions and the right to life 181
3.2. End-of-life decisions and freedom from inhuman or degrading treatment. 185
3.3. End-of-life decisions and the right to privacy. 187
4. National legislation on euthanasia and PAS 189
4.1. The Netherlands. 190
4.2. Belgium 194
4.3. Switzerland 197
5. Strasbourg jurisprudence on end-of-life decisions. 201
5.1. *Pretty v. United Kingdom*. 201
5.2. *Haas v. Switzerland* 204
5.3. *Koch v. Germany*. 205
6. A human right to die?. 206
7. Final remarks 209

PART III.
VULNERABLE GROUPS, HEALTH INEQUALITIES, AND THE SOCIAL DETERMINANTS OF HEALTH

Chapter 7. Health Inequalities and the Social Determinants of Health
Brigit Toebes, Aart Hendriks and Karien Stronks 213

1. Introduction 213
2. The human rights framework 215
3. Human rights and the social determinants of health 217
3.1. Availability, accessibility, acceptability, quality, accountability and participation: 'AAAQ-AP' 218
3.2. Vulnerable groups and non-discrimination 219
3.3. Definition of legal state obligations 220
3.4. Progressive realisation and core obligations. 221
3.5. Indicators and benchmarks 222
3.6. Obligations of non-state actors 223
4. Linking the rights framework with the CSDH goals on the social determinants 224
5. Towards accountability for the social determinants of health. 225

Chapter 8. Children and the Right to Health Protection
Henriette Sinding Aasen 227

1. Introduction 227
2. Legal sources and starting points 228
3. Public health issues relating to children 229

4. Health inequalities affecting children 231
5. State obligations to provide equitable access to healthcare for children .. 232
5.1. The Biomedicine Convention 232
5.2. The Charter of Fundamental Rights of the European Union....... 234
5.3. Special focus on children and accessibility of healthcare services and information 235
6. Health protection and promotion.............................. 238
6.1. The European Social Charter (ESC).............................. 238
6.1.1. Overview.............................. 238
6.1.2. General provisions.............................. 239
6.1.3. Child-specific provisions 241
6.2. EU regulation.............................. 242
6.2.1. The Charter of Fundamental Rights.............................. 242
6.2.2. The Treaty on the Functioning of the European Union 243
7. Implementation of the right to health for children: challenges and strategies 244
8. Conclusion: human rights not a matter of choice but of legal requirement 246

Chapter 9. The Rights of Persons with Disabilities in the Context of Healthcare
Oddný Mjöll Arnardóttir.............................. 249

1. Introduction.............................. 249
2. Disability and health.............................. 250
3. Non-discrimination and accessibility 253
4. Mental disability and autonomy.............................. 257
4.1. Placement in institutions 258
4.2. Treatment 263
4.2.1. General principles 263
4.2.2. Compulsory medical treatment.............................. 265
4.2.3. The protection of persons not able to consent............. 268
5. Concluding remarks 271

Chapter 10. The Right to Health Protection for the Elderly: Key Elements and State Obligations
Henriette Sinding Aasen 273

1. Introduction.............................. 273
2. Legal sources and starting points 276
3. Other important instruments 277
4. Health concerns and 'ageism' 279
5. Maltreatment and serious neglect: application of Article 3 ECHR....... 281

6. Right to health protection for older persons: State obligations 283
6.1. Overview 283
6.2. The Biomedicine Convention and equitable access to appropriate healthcare 283
6.2.1. Starting points 283
6.2.2. 'Equitable access' 284
6.2.3. 'Appropriate healthcare' 288
6.2.4. Respect, protect, fulfil: recommendations for actions 290
6.3. The European Social Charter and health protection for the elderly 292
6.3.1. General provisions: Article 11 292
6.3.2. General provision: Article 13 293
6.3.3. General provisions: Articles 14, 30 and 31 295
6.3.4. Provisions directed towards older persons 295
6.4. The EU Charter of Fundamental Rights and the right to health protection 297
7. Final remarks 298

PART IV.
CONCLUSIONS, CHALLENGES AND RECOMMENDATIONS

Conclusions
Brigit Toebes 303

ABOUT THE EDITORS AND CONTRIBUTORS

Oddný Mjöll Arnardóttir (PhD) is a Professor in human rights law at Reykjavik University, Iceland. Her main research interests are human rights jurisprudence, non-discrimination law, disability rights and health law. Her publications include Equality and Non-Discrimination under the European Convention on Human Rights (Martinus Nijhoff 2003), The UN Convention on the Rights of Persons with Disabilities – European and Scandinavian Perspectives (ed., with Gerard Quinn and Martinus Nijhoff 2009), and numerous edited book chapters and articles. She currently holds the post of President of the Board of the Icelandic Human Rights Centre.

Jozef Dorscheidt (PhD) is a senior lecturer in health law, Faculty of Law, University of Groningen, the Netherlands, and board member of the Groningen Centre for Children's Rights in Health Care. Furthermore, he is an alternate judge at the District Court in Groningen, and alternate legal member of the Dutch Central Commission on Research involving Human Subjects. His research interests involve the legal position of the child in healthcare, health law matters at the beginning and the end of life, and the regulation of medical research on humans.

Mette Hartlev (PhD and LL.D) is a Professor in health law at the University of Copenhagen, Denmark. Her main research interests are health law and patients' rights, with a special focus on right to health in EU law and international law. She has also researched and published in the field of biolaw and bioethics and law, science and technology studies. She has participated in a number of EU-funded cross-disciplinary research projects, and is a member of the editorial board of European Journal of Health Law.

Aart Hendriks (PhD) is a Professor in health law at Leiden University/Leiden University Medical Centre (LUMC); a health law advisor to the Royal Dutch Medical Association (KNMG); a substitute judge at the District Court of Rotterdam; a Member of the Group of specialists on predictivity, genetic testing and insurance of the Council of Europe; a board member of various national and international non-governmental organisations (NGOs) working in the field of health, disability and human rights law; and an editor of several academic journals. He obtained his Ph.D. from the University of Amsterdam (UvA) on a dissertation concerning the right of persons with disabilities to equal access in the employment market, and has written extensively on such issues as human rights, health law, minority rights and patients' rights.

Janne Rothmar Herrmann (PhD) is an Associate Professor in biolaw at the Faculty of Law of Copenhagen University. Her research interests include biolaw & bioethics, reproductive rights, conscientious objections, beginning and ending of life, and privacy & technology. She is a Member of the Nordic Committee on Bioethics by appointment by the Nordic Council of Ministers, and is currently an elected Member of the Board of Directors of the European Association of Health Law.

Henriette Sinding Aasen (dr. juris) is professor at the Faculty of Law at the University of Bergen, Norway. She is currently the coordinator of the University of Bergen's research programme on the Rule of Law and Democracy. Her current research activities are in the area of health and human rights, vulnerable groups (children, immigrants, women), constitution and welfare state. She has participated in several national law commissions in the area of health, human rights and biomedical research, and is currently leading three interdisciplinary research projects funded by the Norwegian Research Council (Juridification and social citizenship; Constitution, welfare state and citizenship; Health promotion, dignity and human rights: the improvement of maternal health in Tanzania).

Karien Stronks (PhD) is professor of social medicine at the Academic Medical Center (AMC) /University of Amsterdam (UvA), and head of the department of Public Health of the AMC. Her main research interests are inequalities in health caused by socioeconomic status, as well as ethnic background, and the effectiveness of interventions and policies tackle these inequalities.

Brigit Toebes (PhD) is a lecturer in international law at the Faculty of Law of the University of Groningen. She previously worked as a lecturer at the University of Aberdeen School of Law, after which she was based as an external lecturer and consultant in Copenhagen. Her PhD research, which she conducted at Utrecht University, involved the definition of health as a human right (Intersentia 1999). Her research interests are public international law, human rights law, economic, social and cultural rights and the definition of health as a right, health law, and medical ethics. She is a Board Member of the International Federation of Health and Human Rights Organisations (IFHHRO).

LIST OF ABBREVIATIONS

'Biomedicine Convention'	Convention on Human Rights and Biomedicine (CoE)
CAT	Convention against Torture and Other Cruel, Inhuman or Degrading Treatment or Punishment (UN, 1984)
CEDAW	Convention on the Elimination of All forms of Discrimination Against Women (UN, 1979)
CIE	Committee of Independent Experts (ESC, CoE)
CoE	Council of Europe
CPT	European Convention for the Prevention of Torture (CoE, 1987)
CRC	Convention on the Rights of the Child (UN, 1989)
CRPD	Convention on the Rights of Persons with Disabilities (UN, 2006)
CSDH	Committee on the Social Determinants of Health (WHO)
EC Treaty	Treaty establishing the European Community (EU, 1993)
ECFR	Charter of Fundamental Rights of the European Union (EU, 2000)
ECHR	Convention for the Protection of Human Rights and Fundamental Freedoms (CoE, 1950)
ECJ	European Court of Justice
EComHR	European Commission of Human Rights
ECSR	European Committee of Social Rights (ESC, CoE)
ECtHR	European Court of Human Rights (CoE)
ESC	European Social Charter (CoE, 1961)
EU	European Union
GC	Grand Chamber (of the ECtHR)
GC 14	General Comment 14 to the ICESCR (on the right to health) (UN, 2000)
HIV	Human immunodeficiency virus
ICCPR	International Convention on Civil and Political Rights (UN, 1966)

ICERD	International Convention on the Elimination of All Forms of Racial Discrimination (UN, 1965)
ICESCR	International Covenant on Economic, Social and Cultural Rights (UN, 1966)
ICF	International Classification of Functioning, Disability and Health
ILO	International Labour Organization
MIPAA	Madrid Political Declaration and International Plan of Action on Ageing (UN)
MWC	International Convention on the Protection of the Rights of All Migrant Workers and Members of their Families (UN, 1990)
OECD	Organisation for Economic Co-Operation and Development
'Oviedo Convention'	Convention on Human Rights and Biomedicine (CoE)
PAS	Physician assisted suicide
(Revised) ESC	(Revised) European Social Charter (CoE, 1996)
TEU	Treaty of the European Union (EU, 1992)
TFEU	Treaty on the Functioning of the European Union (EU, 2007)
UDHR	Universal Declaration of Human Rights (UN, 1948)
UN	United Nations
UNECE	UN Economic Commission of Europe
UNESCO	UN Educational, Scientific and Cultural Organisation
WHO	World Health Organization
WMA	World Medical Association

INTRODUCTION: HEALTH AND HUMAN RIGHTS IN EUROPE

Brigit Toebes*

1. RATIONALE AND AIM OF THIS BOOK

The area of 'health and human rights' is a newly emerging area under international and European human rights and health law. While previously mostly an area of public health, legal scholars and practitioners are now increasingly engaged with the interfaces between health and human rights law. Taking a 'health and human rights approach' means using international, European and national human rights law in relation to a wide range of health issues, including access to healthcare, health insurance policies, patients' rights, health data protection, reproductive health, the quality of pharmaceutical drugs, as well as embryo selection, abortion, and environmental health. Human rights law can be used to enrich other areas of law that engage with health issues, including national medical law, health law, biolaw and bioethics, and environmental law. It creates a new and often more international, as well as a moral dimension, to existing legal analyses of health issues. This is essential in an increasingly interconnected and internationalised world in which health issues can no longer be addressed solely at a domestic level. There is, however, still very little understanding of the various and multiple legal interfaces between 'health' and 'human rights', and of the implications of this approach for legal research and practice.

This book focuses on the legal interfaces between 'health' and 'human rights' in Europe. The European context raises specific questions in terms of health and human rights. Such specific questions arise not only in terms of health issues and health outcomes, but also from a political and legal perspective, Europe is a region *sui generis*. In response to a legacy of wars and massive human rights violations it has established two exceptionally strong regional organisations, the Council of Europe and the European Union, both of which aim to promote

* The author wishes to thank Mette Hartlev, Aart Hendriks, Janne Rothmar Herrmann and Dabney Evans for their valuable comments to an earlier version of this chapter.

human rights and well-being. The case law of the European Court of Human Rights (ECtHR) of the Council of Europe increasingly touches upon health-related issues. Furthermore, as a result of the (revised) European Social Charter, the mandate of the Council of Europe has increased significantly with regard to health rights. In addition, within the context of the Council of Europe the Convention on Human Rights and Biomedicine ('Biomedicine Convention') was adopted, which has been complemented with various protocols (see Chapters 2 and 4 of this study). And while the European Union was originally established as a regional organisation to promote the economic integration of its Member States, it has become increasingly clear that its work, including the legal standards, also impact upon issues falling within the realm of health and human rights. The recently-adopted Lisbon (Reform) Treaty expands the mandate of the EU and emphasises the importance of individual and public health (see Chapter 2 of this study). This makes a study on the relationship between health and human rights from a European perspective all the more important and topical.

Looking at the topic from a health and societal perspective, we see that the interfaces between health and human rights are important in light of the current health status of the Europeans, and the current demographic and economic situation in Europe. According to the World Health Organization (WHO), Europe faces a widening health gap between Western and Eastern countries and between socioeconomic groups within countries (see, also, Part III of this book).[1] Demographically speaking, population ageing is currently the most outstanding feature in Europe, while migration is the other, and increasingly dominant, population growth factor. Due to the growing number of elderly people amongst Europe's population (see Chapter 10), the number of citizens of working age is declining.[2] Under these circumstances it is to be expected that healthcare costs will increase rapidly. In order to make health systems more efficient and affordable, European governments are increasingly resorting to the privatisation of (certain branches of) their healthcare systems. From a human rights and health law perspective, the question arises as to what extent health services will remain accessible and of good quality to an increasingly elderly and migrant population.[3] These and other vulnerable groups may have specific health needs, while they may not always be able to voice such needs, or to afford the necessary healthcare services (see Chapters 7–10). Human rights law is a useful framework for assessing these and other questions in the health field, as it couples such health problems with a legal and moral dimension.

---

1 See WHO, The European Health Report 2005 (and also addressed in its later reports), Copenhagen, 2005, available at www.euro.who.int/__data/assets/pdf_file/0004/82435/E87325.pdf accessed September 2011.

2 Council of Europe, *Demograpic Yearbook, 2004 Ed.*, available at www.coe.int, accessed September 2011.

3 See, also, Elisabeth Rynning, 'The ageing populations of Europe – Implications for Health Systems and Patients' Rights', *EJHL*, 2008 (3), pp. 297–306.

2. HISTORICAL INTRODUCTION TO 'HEALTH AND HUMAN RIGHTS'

2.1. INTRODUCTION

As with any discipline, it is difficult to point out when exactly it all started. When it comes to the area of 'health and human rights', several key historical moments and trends can be mentioned that were important for the development of this field. While the term 'health and human rights' has increasingly been used since the 1980s, the underlying fields of human rights, bioethics and patient rights were gradually introduced, in particular, since the Second World War.

During the aftermath of the Second World War there was a general sense of awareness that the atrocities committed during and preceding this war should not be repeated, and that mechanisms should be established to offer protection against such abuses. Initiatives were taken, both in the field of human rights law and in the field of bioethics. While the Universal Declaration of Human Rights (UDHR) marked the beginning of a phase of standard-setting in the area of human rights law, the Nuremberg Code was a milestone in the area of health law, as well as bioethics and medical ethics. As such, both the Universal Declaration and the Nuremberg Code have been called 'post-Holocaust documents'.[4]

The decennia after the Second World War were marked by a phase of standard-setting in both the areas of human rights and bioethics. While the two fields developed separately, they were also intertwined and they influenced each other mutually. As part of these developments, the cross-cutting area of health and human rights gradually emerged. These subsequent developments will be discussed below.

2.2. THE HUMAN RIGHTS MOVEMENT

As mentioned, since the Second World War a large number of human rights treaties and other documents have gradually been adopted. Many of these documents have a relevance to the area of health (see, also, more elaborately, Chapter 3). The first important international landmark for the area of 'health and human rights' was the recognition of the 'right to the highest attainable standard of health' in the preamble to the Constitution of the newly-established WHO (1946). After that, a set of general human rights documents were gradually adopted which contain many references to health: the so-called 'International Bill of Human Rights', which embraces the Universal Declaration of Human

4 Robert Baker, 'Bioethics and Human Rights: A Historical Perspective', (2001) 10 *Cambridge Quarterly of Healthcare Ethics* 241–252, p. 243.

Rights (UDHR 1948); the International Covenant on Civil and Political Rights (ICCPR,1966); and the International Covenant on Economic, Social and Cultural Rights (ICESCR 1966). The UDHR, which contains both civil and political rights and economic, social and cultural rights, recognises a right to an adequate standard of living (Article 25), which includes a right to medical care and necessary social services. While the ICCPR contains a number of health-related civil and political human rights, including the right to life and the prohibition of torture, the ICESCR recognises, in Article 12, the 'right to the highest attainable standard of health'. Subsequently, a number of UN human rights treaties were gradually adopted that integrate civil and political rights and economic, social and cultural rights, the most important of which are the Convention on the Elimination of all forms of Discrimination Against Women (CEDAW 1979), the Convention on the Rights of the Child (CRC 1989), the Convention on the Protection of All Migrant Workers and Members of Their Families (MWC 1990), and the Convention on the Rights of Persons with Disabilities (CRPD 2006). Each of these documents contains a specific provision on the 'right to health' and several health-related rights (see, also, Chapter 3).[5]

A similar trend took place at a European level: within the framework of the Council of Europe a number of regional human rights treaties were gradually adopted, which reflect a similar split between civil and political rights and economic, social and cultural rights. While the rights in the European Convention on Human Rights and Fundamental Freedoms (ECHR 1950) and the European Convention for the Prevention Against Torture and Inhuman or Degrading Treatment or Punishment (1987) have a relevance to health in many ways, the (Revised) European Social Charter (ESC,1961/1996) recognises a 'right to protection of health' in Article 11 and a 'right to social and medical assistance' in Article 13 (see, also, Chapters 1 and 3).[6]

From the 1980s onwards human rights scholars began to analyse the meaning and implications of economic, social and cultural rights, which had remained undeveloped and undefined in comparison with civil and political rights. Courts and policymakers had so far been very reluctant to apply economic, social and cultural rights, as they feared the financial consequences for governments once a socioeconomic right was granted.[7] Scholars attempted to prove and underline

---

5 Articles 12 CEDAW, 24 CRC, 28 Migrant Workers' Convention, and Article 25 of the Disability Convention. See, also, for example, Article 25 of ILO Convention 169 on Indigenous Peoples, and Rules 22 to 26 of the Standard Minimum Rules for the Treatment of Prisoners.

6 Convention for the Protection of Human Rights and Fundamental Freedoms, 4 November 1950; European Social Charter, 26 February 1965, and revised in 1996; European Convention for the Prevention of Torture and Inhuman and Degrading Treatment or Punishment, 26 November 1987.

7 Brigit C.A. Toebes, *The right to health as a human right in international law*, Oxford/Antwerp: Intersentia/Hart, 1999, p. 169.

that economic and social rights were more equal to civil and political rights than had been previously assumed. The so-called 'interdependence' of all human rights was confirmed by the Vienna Declaration and Programme of Action, which underlines that all human rights are 'universal, indivisible and interdependent and interrelated'.[8] Scholars also started to explore the specific meaning of economic, social and cultural rights, including the right to health. A range of General Comments was gradually adopted by the Committee on Economic, Social and Cultural Rights, which, *inter alia*, address the meaning and implications of the substantive economic, social and cultural rights. The General Comment on the Right to the Highest Attainable Standard of Health in Article 12 ICESCR was adopted in 2000.[9] From then onwards, the 'right to health' was addressed by many forums and from many angles, not in the least by the then Special Rapporteur on the Right to Health, Paul Hunt.[10]

The European human rights discourse followed this trend. As will be explored more elaborately in Chapter 1, the right to protection of health is increasingly addressed by the European and Social Rights' Committee of the Council of Europe. In addition, the ECtHR has ruled on a wide variety of health issues on numerous occasions (see Chapter 1).

2.3. MEDICAL LAW, HEALTH LAW, MEDICAL AND BIOETHICS, AND PATIENTS' RIGHTS

Patients' rights are often considered as an elaboration of human rights law in the field of healthcare. Before we can focus on the definition of patients' rights and further embark on an analysis of these rights, we need to define the underlying areas of medical law, health law, and the medical-ethical and bioethical movements. First, a distinction needs to be made between the terms 'medicine' and 'public health'. As will also be highlighted in Chapter 3, while 'medicine' is mainly focused on the individual and often aimed at secondary and tertiary care, 'public health' is population based, and largely preventive in its orientation. Related to this, some confusion may arise regarding the difference between 'medical law' and 'health law'. Some see these as two distinct disciplines where

---

8 Article 5 Vienna Declaration and Programme of Action (UN Doc. A/Conf.157/23), 12 July 1993 (World Conference on Human Rights, Vienna, 14–25 June 1993).

9 UN Committee on Economic, Social and Cultural Rights (CESCR), General Comment 14 on the Right to the Highest Attainable Standard of Health, UN Doc. E/C.12/2000/4, August 11, 2000.

10 See the website of the former Special Rapporteur on the Right to the Highest Attainable Standard of Health, Paul Hunt, www2.essex.ac.uk/human_rights_centre/rth/, accessed September 2011. The current Special Rapporteur is Arnand Grover (India); see www2.ohchr.org/english/issues/health/right/, and also www.lawyerscollective.org/, accessed September 2011.

medical law is associated with issues such as medical doctors' duties, professional standards and autonomy, and medical negligence, while health law would place more emphasis on prevention, the provision of healthcare (including healthcare insurance) and the rights of the patient. Others do not make this distinction, and use the terms interchangeably, or use one of the two to refer to the field as a whole. Sometimes, and this is the approach we take in this book, 'medical law' is seen as a narrower area of 'health law', primarily focused on the legal standards applying to healthcare providers.[11] Furthermore, it is important to note that there is an increasing emphasis the so-called underlying or social determinants of health - conditions which are decisive for people's health (see Chapters 7, 8 and 10). Such conditions are considered to be essential components of the 'right to health' and they blur the line between medical law, health law and other forms of law since they are inter-sectoral.

Medical ethics and bioethics have served as an important source of inspiration for health law. With medical ethics, reference is made to a system of moral principles that apply to the practice of medicine, and tends to be understood as being concerned with professional ethics. Bioethics, which is closely connected to medical ethics, is generally more concerned with ethical questions brought about by advances in biology and medicine. As such, bioethics can be broader than medical ethics, addressing the philosophy of science and issues of biotechnology. Given the substantive overlap between the two fields, the terms are used interchangeably in this study. For the purposes of our study it is important to note that medical ethics and bioethics have increasingly incorporated rights-based approaches.

Altogether, we can say that patients' rights are rooted in health law and have been influenced by medical ethics, bioethics, and human rights law. As Mette Hartlev describes in Chapter 4, the developments towards the creation of patient rights started many centuries ago. An important landmark was the above-mentioned Nuremberg Code, which constitutes of a set of ethical principles for human experimentation, which were formulated as a result of the subsequent Nuremberg Trials at the end of the Second World War. This document was

11 In the UK, the term 'medical law' is still often used, while it seems that on the Continent there has been a shift towards the use of the term 'health law'. For the UK perspective, see Mason & McCall Smith's *Law and Medical Ethics*, Seventh ed., Oxford: Oxford University Press, 2006 (which also focuses on 'health law'); and Shaun D. Pattinson, *Medical Law and Medical Ethics*, London: Sweet & Maxwell, 2006. For more on these distinctions see, *inter alia*, Margaret Brazier and Nicola Glover, 'Does Medical Law Have a Future?', in David Hayton (eds.), *Law's Future*, Oxford: Hart, 2000, pp. 371–388; and see also Tamara K. Hervey and Jean V. McHale, *Health Law and the European* Union, Cambridge: Cambridge University Press, 2004, pp. 7–19; and, for example, the approach taken in the *European Journal of Health Law, inter alia*, Sjef Gevers, 'Health Law in Europe: From the Present to the Future, *European Journal of Health Law* 15 (2008), pp. 261–272.

followed by two documents adopted by the World Medical Association (WMA),[12] which focused on the role of the physician: a short 'Physician's Oath' in the Declaration of Geneva (1948), and a more elaborate document on the duties of doctors in general in the International Code of Medical Ethics (1949).[13] It is observed that this short-lived phase of 'post-war idealism' was replaced by a phase of 'realism' during the Cold War era. During this era politicians treated human rights as barriers to foreign policy, while research policy also shifted to 'realism', for example, with the introduction of a restricted informed consent in relation to experiments involving therapeutic benefit.[14]

In chapter 4, Mette Hartlev recounts that patient rights were really placed on the agenda in the 1970s.[15] Gradually, a body of (bio) medical law came to existence, which further extended the focus on the individual and on individual rights that had begun the aftermath the Second World War. An important landmark in Europe was the adoption of the Convention on Human Rights and Biomedicine (Biomedicine Convention 1997), which addresses a wide range of biomedical issues, but also contains patient rights and a general right to healthcare (see Chapters 1 and 4). Also worth mentioning is the EU patient rights Directive (2009), which is, to some extent, based on the Biomedicine Convention (see Chapter 2).

As will become clear in this book, 'human rights' and 'patients' rights' both play an important role in the area of 'health and human rights'. Patients' rights and human rights are, to a considerable extent, overlapping, and there is an increasing congruence between the two. However, although human rights have been a powerful source of inspiration for the development of patients' rights, it is important to recall that patients' rights have various roots, and as such, they are not a mere branch of human rights law. We will come back to the connections between human rights and patients' rights in the conclusions to our book.

2.4. THE PUBLIC HEALTH MOVEMENT

The public health movement started to pay attention to the specific links between health and human rights in the 1980s. The main impetus for these activities were the HIV/AIDS pandemic and the reproductive and sexual health concerns,

12 The WMA is an international non-governmental organisation representing physicians. The organisation was founded in 1947.

13 See www.cirp.org/library/ethics, accessed November 2011. WMA standards are accessible through www.wma.net.

14 Baker, 2001, see note 4, p. 245.

15 *Ibid.*

which have, in fact, been instrumental in clarifying the ways that health and rights connect.[16]

The first global health and human rights strategy was launched in the late 1980s, and addressed the problem of AIDS. It was the 'Global Programme on AIDS' that was directed by the late Jonathan Mann at the WHO.[17] The main motivation to take a human rights approach to HIV/AIDS was because it showed that discrimination was undermining people's access to prevention and care programmes.[18] Gradually, a public health approach to 'health and human rights' emerged, which was led by a number of important scholars in this area, including Jonathan Mann, Lawrence Gostin, Sofia Gruskin, and Daniel Tarantola.[19] By taking a human rights approach, the focus in the public health movement shifted from merely focusing on the health of society as a whole to a more integrated approach, where the health and human rights of individuals are balanced against the interests of society at large.[20]

By the end of 1994, the first issue of the Journal *Health and Human Rights* came out, in which the links between (public) health and human rights were discussed. In one of the contributions to this issue, a three-part framework is proposed for considering linkages between health and human rights. According to the authors, the linkages between health and human rights are as follows: 1) the notion that health policies, programmes and practices impact on human rights; 2) the understanding that human rights violations have health impacts; and 3) the notion that protection of human rights and protection of health are fundamentally linked.[21] This thinking about 'health and human rights' has been pivotal for the further development of this field.

As a subsequent development governmental, as well as non-governmental, organisations increasingly started to embed 'health and human rights' approaches in their strategies and policies. Such activities were undertaken, *inter alia*, by the WHO, and civil society organisations such as the Open Society

16 Sofia Gruskin, Edward J. Mills and Daniel Tarantola, 'History, principles and practice of health and human rights', *The Lancet*, Vol. 370, August 4, 2007, pp. 449–455, p. 449.

17 WHO, Global Strategy for the prevention and control of HIV/AIDS, Res. WHA40.26, World Health Assembly, 40th Sess., 1987.

18 J.M. Mann and D. Tarantola, 'Responding to HIV/Aids: a historical perspective', 2 *Health and Human Rights* 1998; pp. 5–8, at p. 5.

19 Gruskin, Mills and Tarantola, 2007, see note 16, pp. 449–455, at p. 449.

20 For 'public health' developments in Europe see the website of the European Public Health Organisation at www.eupha.org, which pays attention to issues like health disparities but not from a human rights perspective. Furthermore, the European Public Health Alliance pays attention to the intersection between health and human rights, see www.epha.org, accessed September 2011.

21 Jonathan M. Mann, Lawrence Gostin, Sofia Gruskin, Troyen Brennan, Zita Lazzarini, and Harvey Fineberg, 'Health and Human Rights', *Health and Human Rights*, Vol. 1, no. 1, pp. 6–23, at p. 12.

Institute (OSI), national doctors for human rights organisations, and the – overlapping – International Federation of Health and Human Rights Organisations (IFHHRO).[22]

All these developments form an important starting point for our analysis of the legal perspectives of 'health and human rights'. Health lawyers and human rights lawyers are all increasingly focusing on the intersections between health and human rights, and they are increasingly recognising 'health and human rights' as a new field of the law. However, as mentioned above, there is a lack of clarity regarding the implications and scope of this new area of the law, and a lack of interfacing between the various movements that deal with this emerging area of the law. It is important to clarify what we mean with 'health and human rights' from a legal perspective: how have the international and national judicial bodies dealt with these interfaces; which human rights are relevant, and in what way; how the international human rights laws affect health law; how patient rights and human rights are intertwined; and what are the core topics in this field.[23]

3. THEORETICAL APPROACH

3.1. MAIN THEORETICAL QUESTIONS UNDERPINNING THIS RESEARCH

The starting point for the research is a set of health-related human rights that are recognised in various international and European human rights treaties. At the core of these health-related rights lies the 'right to health', which functions as key right that connects to a set of other rights which are relevant to the protection and promotion of human health. These other rights include both civil and political rights, as well as economic, social and cultural rights, including the rights to life, privacy and family life, information, and the prohibition of torture. Hence, an important point of departure for this study is that all human rights are indivisible, interdependent and interrelated, as confirmed in various human

22 See, *inter alia*, the WHO's Health and Human Rights publication series, available at www.who.int/hhr/activities/publication_series/en/; and see, also, for example, the work of the International Federation of Health and Human Rights Organisations (IFHHRO), available at www.ifhhro.org, accessed October 2011; and, for example, the 'Law and Health Initiative' of the Open Society Institute (OSI), available at www.soros.org/initiatives/health, accessed October 2011.

23 Regarding the intersections between human rights and bioethics/patients' rights, see Richard E. Ashcroft, 'Could Human Rights Supersede Bioethics?' *Human Rights Law Review*, 10:4 (2010), pp. 639–660; and T.A. Faunce, 'Will International Human Rights Subsume Medical Ethics?' Intersections in the UNESCO Universal Bioethics Declaration', (2004), 31 *Journal of Medical Ethics* 173.

rights forums.[24] Taking such an approach raises a number of intricate theoretical questions, which will be addressed below:

- What is the conceptual grounding of human rights law, and what is the rationale for using them in a European context?
- What is the conceptual grounding of economic, social and cultural or 'welfare' rights more specifically?
- What are the main principles or concepts underlying the area of 'health and human rights'?

3.2. CONCEPTUAL GROUNDING OF HUMAN RIGHTS LAW

As mentioned, human rights law consists of a set of international treaties that were gradually adopted after the Second World War. Through these treaties, rights are guaranteed to individuals, and correlative duties fall upon states to guarantee these rights. Critics of human rights law have pointed at the lack of conceptual grounding of human rights. They have questioned the origins and soundness of rights, in particular, the economic and social rights or 'welfare rights', and the collective rights.[25] We need to address such criticism in our study, as such criticism may question our approach of taking human rights law as a starting point for assessing health issues in a European legal setting.

Generally, such criticism goes against the idea that people can have rights unconditionally, simply by virtue of their humanity.[26] This concerns, in fact, a rebuttal of the idea that human rights derive from natural law.[27] Over the course of the past decades legal scholars have moved away from the idea that human rights should have a basis in natural law, and they have sought for more practical bases.[28] Our study will be founded on such more practical theories of human

---

24 Article 5 Vienna Declaration and Programme of Action (UN Doc. A/Conf.157/23), 12 July 1993 (World Conference on Human Rights, Vienna, 14–25 June 1993). For a critical analysis, see Ida Elisabeth Koch, *Human Rights as Indivisible Rights*, Leiden: Martinus Nijhoff Publishers, 2009, *inter alia* pp. 2–3.

25 One of the first critics of human rights was Jeremy Bentham, who argued that natural rights are 'nonsense upon stilts'. Jeremy Bentham, *Anarchical Fallacies: Being an Examination of the Declaration of Rights Issued during the French Revolution* (1972); republished in *The Works of Jeremy Bentham* (1792), Vol. II, (ed). J. Bowring (Edinburgh: William Tait, 1843), p. 501. His theory on 'legal positivism' was refined later by other scholars, including H.L.A. Hart.

26 Amartya Sen, 'Elements of a Theory of Human Rights', *Philosophy & Public Affairs* 32, no. 4 (2004), pp. 315–356.

27 Natural law: the law of nature; law as the emanation of the Divine providence and rooted in the nature and reason of man. (*Osborn's Concise Law Dictionary*, London: Sweet & Maxwell, 2005).

28 See Ronald Dworkin's study, *Taking Rights Seriously*, Bath: Duckworth 1977. See, also, Beitz, see note 30; and Sen, see note 26.

rights. We will not look for a basis for human rights law in natural law or naturalist theories. Nor will we look for a basis for human rights in 'agreement theories', which conceptualise human rights as standards over which people from dissimilar cultures agree and which argue that human rights express a 'common core' or an 'intercultural agreement'.[29] Rather, in line with the approach of the scholar Beitz,[30] we will look for the sources of human rights law in an *emergent practice* where human rights are increasingly applied. In line with Beitz' approach, we will take as a starting point that a human rights practice is emerging in Europe, reflecting, to some extent, a 'common European standard'. We also argue that while where there are different ethical standpoints, rights can still be rights, as they have been recognised as legally binding entitlements.

We will study human rights practice by conducting a thorough study of European human rights law in relation to health at a European institutional and at a state level. As such, to quote Beitz, we will attempt to 'grasp the concept of a human right as it occurs within an existing practice.'[31] Beitz defines human rights as:

> '(...) an emergent discursive practice consisting of a set of norms for the regulation of the conduct of governments and a range of actions open to various agents for which a government's failure to abide by these norms supplies reasons.'[32]

As such, Beitz develops a model in which he distinguishes between two levels:

- governments as primary duty holders under human rights law; and
- other 'agents' or institutions that address failures to comply with human rights by states.

As such, while states are the primary duty holders under international human rights law, they are not the only entities that carry out this responsibility.[33] There are 'agents' outside the state that may take action when states fail to realise human rights. In this study we identify the Council of Europe and the EU as important 'agents' outside the state. The health and human rights practice of these European institutions will be the starting point of our study (Chapters 1 and 2 of the book). Where relevant, subsequent state practice will be discussed throughout the book (e.g. in relation to euthanasia in Chapter 4).

---

29 Beitz, 2009, see note 30, pp. 73–74. The study builds upon a study by John Rawls. John Rawls, *The Law of Peoples*, Cambridge: MA: Harvard University Press, 1999. In Beitz, 2009, see note 30, pp. 96–98.

30 Charles R. Beitz, *The Idea of Human Rights*, Oxford: Oxford University Press, 2009.

31 Beitz, see note 30, p. 102.

32 *Ibid.*, p. 44.

33 *Ibid.*, p. 114.

3.3. CONCEPTUAL GROUNDING AND ANALYSIS OF ECONOMIC, SOCIAL AND CULTURAL RIGHTS

A more specific point of criticism of human rights concerns the character of the so-called 'second generation rights', also called 'second generation rights' or 'welfare rights'. It is maintained that given their presumed 'positive' or programmatic nature they are 'costly' for governments and interfere with a margin of appreciation that governments have in relation to their social policies. Altogether, some authors maintain that they are not enforceable before a court of law.[34]

Under human rights law, governments are distinguished as the primary duty holders under human rights. As the entities that have ratified and become parties to the treaties, they have legal responsibilities to recognise and realise the rights of individuals. To clarify the character of the state duties, scholars have tried to specify the human rights obligations of state actors (and increasingly, also of other duty holders). In the 1980s, human rights scholar Asbjørn Eide presented a tripartite typology of state obligations, which is now well-established and frequently used in human rights law and practice. This approach takes as a starting point that inherent in *all* human rights are state obligations to:

- 'respect' the underlying interests;
- 'protect' the underlying interests against threats from non-state agents; and
- 'aid' or 'assist' those who are non-voluntarily victims of deprivation.[35]

This approach makes it clear that both positive and negative state undertakings may result from all human rights, economic, social and cultural, as well as civil and political ones, as both 'positive' and 'negative' obligations are inherent in all human rights ('respect' being a 'negative' obligation to refrain from action, while 'protect and fulfil' implying positive actions). For example, while a right to a fair trial may have positive or 'costly' implications for states (e.g. to establish a legal system), so may a right to health imply negative duties (e.g. not to harm individual health). As such, this approach goes in defence of the moral weight and legal grounding of economic, social and cultural rights. It rebuts the above-mentioned assertion that civil and political rights carry more weight and are more readily enforceable before a court of law than economic, social and cultural

34 *Inter alia*, E.W. Vierdag, 'The Legal Nature of the Rights Granted by the International Covenant on Economic, Social and Cultural Rights', *Netherlands Yearbook of International Law*, Vol. 9, 1987, pp. 69–105.

35 A. Eide, UN Doc. E/CN.4/Sub.2/1987. For a similar analysis, see Henry Shue, *Basic Rights, Subsistence, Affluence and U.S. Foreign Policy*, New Jersey: Princeton, 1980. For a discussion, see, also, Brigit Toebes, 1999, see note 7, pp. 307–311, and Chapters 3 and 9 of this book.

rights. This underlines the notion that all human rights are 'indivisible, interdependent and 'interrelated', as proclaimed by the Vienna Declaration and Programme of Action in 1993.[36]

However, the approach of the tripartite typology has been criticised more recently for being too rigid, as states' duties cannot always easily be classified into obligations to respect, protect or fulfil respectively.[37] An additional argument is that the ECtHR is not occupied with fitting a certain obligation into a certain category, and it has therefore been suggested to speak of 'waives of duties' rather than of specific obligations to respect, protect and to fulfil (see Chapter 3).[38] In our study we will take a flexible approach towards the identification of states' duties, and will use the tripartite typology where we consider this useful.

3.4. IDENTIFICATION OF MAIN CONCEPTS AND PRINCIPLES UNDERPINNING THIS STUDY

In Beitz' model, human rights are described as 'urgent individual interests', as opposed to 'universal' human interests, understood as those necessarily shared by all human beings as 'such'.[39] In relation to his identification of 'urgent interests' Beitz develops a scheme for identifying the strength of a human rights claim. He states that the interests protected must be *sufficiently important* when reasonably regarded from the perspective of those protected; while it would be *advantageous* to protect the underlying interest by means of legal policy instruments available to the state; and a failure to protect this interest would be a *matter of international concern.*

Several of such important interests or principles play a role in our study, which derive from human rights law as well as from the area of patients' rights. The most important principles are (human) dignity, health, autonomy, integrity, privacy, confidentiality, and non-discrimination (see, also, Chapters 3 and 4). In addition, the so-called 'AAAQ' plays an important role in this study: the notion that all necessary health services have to be available, accessible, acceptable and of good quality (Chapters 3, 7, 8 and 10). Lastly, in relation to human rights, the notions of 'participation' in the human rights decision-making process and

36 Vienna Declaration and Programme of Action, UN Doc. A/Conf. 157/23, 12 July 1993 (World Conference on Human Rights, Vienna, 14–25 June 1993).

37 Ida Elisabeth Koch, *Human Rights as Indivisible Rights*, Leiden, the Netherlands: Martinus Nijhoff Publishers, 2009, pp. 14–28.

38 Koch, 2009, see note 37.

39 Beitz, see note 30, p. 109. There is some similarity with Dworkin's study *Taking Rights Seriously*, which argued that rights have a dimension that rules do not have: the dimension of 'weight and importance'. Ronald Dworkin, *Taking Rights Seriously*, Bath: Duckworth 1977.

'accountability' for human rights violations are increasingly mentioned (see Chapters 3 and 7). We identify these principles as important interests which merit protection under health and human rights law and which are matters of international concern.

A few additional words need to be devoted to the principle of *'(human) dignity'*, which is often referred to as the core principle underlying human rights law, and which plays an important role in the area of patients' rights. Human dignity is mentioned in the Preamble and in Article 1 of the Universal Declaration of Human Rights (UDHR), in the Preambles to the UN Covenants on Civil and Political Rights and Economic, Social and Cultural Rights (ICCPR and ICESCR), as well as the Preamble and Article 1 of the Charter of Fundamental Rights of the European Union (ECFR 2000).[40] Article 1 UDHR stipulates that 'all human beings are born free and equal in dignity of rights', whereas the ECFR simply states 'Human dignity is inviolable. It must be respected and protected.' Hartlev observes that as Article 1 UDHR mentions dignity before rights, it might be regarded as more fundamental within the rights thinking than the human rights and correlated freedoms.[41] In this respect, it should be noted that human dignity not only calls for respect of human rights, but also imposes restrictions on the use of human rights by individuals, for example, by prohibiting the financial exploitation of the human body, even with the consent of the individual concerned. But while this concept plays an important role in the legal human rights discourse, there is little clarity and agreement over its meaning and interpretation.[42] The concept of human dignity has deep roots in theology, philosophy and anthropology.[43] Such analyses often go back to the philosophy of Immanuel Kant, who sees human dignity as being inviolable and unconditional. Kant's approach is often discussed when it comes to the distinction between human dignity and autonomy, and as such, the question of whether persons unable to take autonomous actions possess dignity.[44] While in Kant's view dignity and autonomy are interrelated, others argue that dignity can be broader,

---

40 See, also, Articles 10 ICCPR and 13 ICESCR.

41 Mette Hartlev, Coercive Treatment and Human Dignity, in Henriette Sinding Aasen, Rune Halvorsen and António Barbosa da Silva (eds.), *Human Rights, Dignity and Autonomy in Health Care and Social Services: Nordic Perspectives*, Antwerp-Oxford-Portland: Intersentia, 2009, pp. 129–144, at p. 131.

42 See also Eckart Klein and David Kretzmer, 'Foreword' to *The Concept of Human Dignity in Human Rights Discourse* (Klein and Kretzmer eds.), The Hague/London/New York: Kluwer Law International, 2002, pp. v-vii, at p. vi. For specific studies on human dignity, see Deryck Beyleveld and Roger Brownsword, *Human Dignity in Bioethics and Biolaw, Oxford: Oxford University Press, 2001*; and Henriette Sinding Aasen, Rune Halvorsen and António Barbosa da Silva (eds.), *Human Rights, Dignity and Autonomy in Health Care and Social Services: Nordic Perspectives*, Antwerp-Oxford-Portland: Intersentia, 2009.

43 Klein and Kretzmer, see note 42, p. vi.

44 See, also, António Barbosa da Silva, 'Autonomy, Dignity and Integrity in Health Care Ethics – A Moral Philosophical Perspective', in Sinding Aasen *et al.*, see note 41, pp. 13–52.

and can encompass all human beings, including those who do not have the capacity for autonomous actions.[45] Based on this broader approach, Hartlev identifies three dimensions of dignity: dignity in the way it relates to *human freedom and personal autonomy*, dignity relating to the *intrinsic worth of every human being*, and dignity associated with *conditions essential to living a life with dignity*.[46] The first two dimensions will be touched upon in Chapter 4 (Hartlev). While the right to self-determination that is discussed in this chapter reflects the importance of the link between *autonomy* and dignity, the connection between *intrinsic worth* and dignity is reflected in rules restricting individual autonomy to avoid individuals compromising their own dignity. The third dimension of dignity identified by Mette Hartlev (*conditions essential to living a life with dignity*) refers to the conditions that are provided or accepted for individuals. For example, if a psychiatric patient does not want to be treated, but is obviously not capable of living a life in dignity, it may be justified to intervene (and infringe the person's right to self-determination) to ensure dignified living conditions. This dimension is also relevant with regard to the cases where prisoners in need of medical care are not provided with access to healthcare services, or where psychiatric patients are kept in poor condition in institutions or hospitals. This notion will come to the fore in Chapter 6 on euthanasia and physician assisted suicide (Dorscheidt), as this touches upon the notion of 'dying with dignity'. It also plays a role in Chapters 8–10, which the position of vulnerable groups (children, persons with disabilities, and the elderly) in healthcare settings is discussed (Sinding Aasen and Mjöll Arnardóttir).

Furthermore, it is obvious that the notion of '*health*' plays an important role in this study. 'Health' can be defined and interpreted in many different ways. As was raised by Aart Hendriks during our preparatory discussion for this book, we need to make a distinction between the definition of health as a *concept* as such, and the definition of health as a *right*.[47] When it comes to the definition of the term health as a standalone *concept*, a distinction can be made between the broad definition of health and a definition of health in a medical sense. We find the broad definition of health in the preamble to the Constitution of the WHO, where it is defined as 'complete, physical, mental and social well-being'. While this definition can be criticised for being too vague and absolute in nature, it illustrates effectively that health is not only about the absence of disease, and that our socioeconomic circumstances are pivotal to our health. Hendriks adds

---

45 See, more elaborately, Mette Hartlev, 'Coercive Treatment and Human Dignity', in Henriette Sinding Aasen, Rune Halvorsen and António Barbosa da Silva (eds.), *Human Rights, Dignity and Autonomy in Health Care and Social Services: Nordic Perspectives*, Antwerp-Oxford-Portland: Intersentia, 2009, pp. 129–144, at p. 130. Hartlev refers to Ronald Dworkin's study *Life's Dominion*, London: Harper/Collins, 1993, p. 236.

46 Hartlev, see note 45, p. 132.

47 See unpublished concept note by Aart Hendriks, February 2010.

to this that it is important to take into account by whom the term is defined, e.g. by a medical specialist or professional body, or by a legal entity such as a legislature or judge. Furthermore, we need to look into the terminology that is being used, e.g. human health, safety, care, medical assistance, public health, and disability.[48]

When it comes to the definition of health as a *right*, Aart Hendriks suggests that we need to identify firstly the definition of health as a human right under international and European human rights law (Chapters 1–3). Secondly, we can look at health as a general principle, safety concern or goal that needs to be taken into account when making policies or interpreting rights that have an effect on human rights and the right to health (Chapter 3). Thirdly, health can appear as an interest or value restricting the enjoyment of human rights, and fourthly, it can appear as an interest or value expanding the interpretation of human rights (see, in particular, Chapter 3).[49] This typology of health concepts underlies the analysis of health and human rights in the various chapters of this book.

4. METHOD AND CHAPTER OUTLINE

In *Part I* of this work we will analyse the emergent health and human rights practice of the European institutions. We identify the European Institutions as important 'agents' for the realisation of health-related human rights.[50] In these chapters, we will take an integrated approach to human rights, based on the notion that human rights are interdependent and interrelated. The two major European institutions that are relevant to human rights are the Council of Europe and the EU. It should be mentioned at the outset that there are some differences between EU and Council of Europe law. With its 47 Member States, the Council of Europe has a broader regional scope of application than the EU, which has 27 Member States. As such, EC law applies to a smaller set of states. It should also be taken into account that while states enjoy a certain liberty to opt in and out of the obligations derived from the human rights conventions, this is generally not the case with regard to the obligations imposed upon them by community law.[51] While the Council of Europe can only 'shape' laws by means of treaties and legal decision-making and states are free to ratify, the EU is a legal order *sui generis* which prevails above national law. It should also be noted that the EU is not primarily a human rights organisation. Yet even where a particular

48 Aart Hendriks, February 2010.

49 Aart Hendriks, February 2010.

50 See above, the analysis of Beitz, see note 30.

51 Janne Rothmar Herrmann, Janne and Malene Rowlandson, 'The Role of Ethics and Morality in EU Law', *JIBL*, Vol. 05 I 2008, pp. 241–251, at p. 241.

piece of EU legislation is not, strictly speaking, a human rights law, it may still have implications for a human rights and health context. For example, the possibility of seeking cross-border health services under EU law may have an impact on the right to access to healthcare services (Chapter 2).

Chapter 1 (Hendriks) focuses on the protection of human rights within the Council of Europe: The instruments that are addressed are the European Convention and Human Rights (and the case law of the ECtHR), the European Social Charter (and its Committee), the European Convention for the Prevention of Torture (and the CPT), and the Biomedicine Convention. Chapter 2 (Rothmar Herrmann and Toebes) discusses the way in which the EU influences the area of health and human rights. *Inter alia*, attention will be paid to the Charter of Fundamental Rights of the European Union (ECFR 2000); the specific responsibilities for health in the EU, including the EU's engagement with public health and clinical research; and free movement and health (cross-border healthcare services, pharmaceuticals, blood and cells and tissues).

Subsequently in *Part II*, the study will focus on a number of important topics in the area of health and human rights. Given the broad range of topics that can potentially be addressed, the study will limit itself to a selection of topics. But by demonstrating how a certain health issue can be addressed, the study will provide an exemplary demonstration of how a similar 'health and human rights' approach can be taken in relation to other health topics. For example, the discussion of embryo selection in Chapter 5 illustrates how other human rights issues relating to the status of the embryo can be taken up in a similar fashion.

Building on Chapters 1 and 2, Chapter 3 (Toebes) describes the meaning and scope of the health-related rights, with particular emphasis on the definition of the right to health. For example, it is asserted that a 'right to health' has two dimensions: access to healthcare and securing the underlying conditions for health. This gives recognition to the broad character of the 'right to health', which embraces not only a right to 'healthcare', but also covers the so-called underlying conditions for health (e.g. health information, preventive care and environmental health). Subsequently, a shorter description is provided of the other health-related rights, so as to provide an overview of the field. Chapter 4 of the book (Hartlev) focuses on patients' rights. The chapter defines patients' rights and describes its development and codification. A number of general legal principles are discussed which are of pivotal importance in this area: dignity, integrity, autonomy, privacy and confidentiality, and equal treatment and non-discrimination. Subsequently, attention is paid to a few specific issues that arise under patient rights: patients' rights to self-determination, information and confidentiality. Chapter 5 (Rothmar Herrmann) focuses on the protection of reproductive rights in a European setting. Attention is paid to a number of important underlying principles, i.e. reproductive autonomy, respect for privacy and family life, and prohibition of discrimination. Subsequently, a number of the important reproductive health issues come to the fore, i.e. family planning, including abortion and contraception; procreative healthcare services, including (access to) fertility treatment, embryo and foetus selection; and pregnancy, including the pregnant woman's lifestyle and forced treatment of pregnant women. Chapter 6 (Dorscheidt) of the book focuses on euthanasia and physician assisted suicide from a human rights perspective. The chapter discusses the rights that are relevant when it comes to end-of-life decisions. The legislation in the Netherlands and Belgium is discussed elaborately, as well as the case law of the ECtHR. The question of whether a 'right to die' exists is subsequently raised.

Part III of the book focus on health inequalities and on the health-related rights of vulnerable groups. Chapter 7 (Toebes, Hendriks and Stronks) is a short chapter that analyses the human rights perspectives of the 'social determinants of health' – socioeconomic conditions which impact upon people's health, and which are an important trigger for the increasing health inequalities across Europe. Chapters 8–10 pay attention to several groups in society that are vulnerable when it comes to their health, and when it comes to accessing health services. In these chapters we focus on children, persons with disabilities and the elderly. We are fully aware that the selection of 'vulnerable groups' is limited; for example, we could also have paid specific attention to women, ethnic minorities, and/or migrants. Yet the position of women will, to some extent, be discussed in Chapter 5 on reproductive health, while the position of migrants is implicitly at issue in Chapter 7 on the social determinants of health, as migrants in Europe are, to some extent, affected by poor socioeconomic living conditions.

In Chapter 8 of Part III, Sinding Aasen discusses children's right to protection of health from a public health perspective. An important starting point for this chapter is the notion that there are widening health inequalities in Europe, as is also discussed in Chapter 7. Hence, poverty is identified as the largest threat to children in Europe. In this light, children's right to protection of health is defined by identifying a set of state obligations based on the international and European human rights law. Chapter 9 (Mjöll Arnardóttir) discusses the rights of persons with disabilities in the context of healthcare. The starting point for this chapter is the notion that due to the increasing prevalence of chronic diseases, the growth and ageing of the world's population, and advances in medical science, there is an increasing prevalence of disability. The Convention on the Rights of Persons with Disabilities (CRPD 2006) plays an important role in this chapter, hence demonstrating that both UN and European human rights law are important for this vulnerable group in Europe. Attention is paid to the links between disability and health, and to the important underlying principles of non-discrimination and accessibility. Subsequently, attention is paid to mental disability and autonomy, raising issues regarding the placement in institutions, forced treatment, and the protection of persons not able to consent. In Chapter 10 (Sinding Aasen), attention is paid to the right to protection of health of the elderly. While this is a growing group in society, little attention has as of yet been paid to the definition of a right to (protection of) health of older persons. This chapter discusses the particular health vulnerabilities of the elderly, and establishes a link with international and European human rights law, as such, presenting a legal human rights framework for assessing the health needs of the elderly.

Part IV. In the last chapter of this book (Toebes), some concluding observations are drawn on the scope and implications of the area of 'health and human rights' in Europe.

PART I

HEALTH AND HUMAN RIGHTS: THE EUROPEAN INSTITUTIONS

CHAPTER 1
THE COUNCIL OF EUROPE AND HEALTH AND HUMAN RIGHTS

Aart HENDRIKS

1. INTRODUCTION

The Council of Europe, founded in the aftermath of the Second World War, is an intergovernmental organisation seeking to create a common democratic and legal area throughout the whole of the European region, ensuring respect for human rights, democracy and the rule of law. Or, according to Article 1 (a) of the Statute of the Council of Europe (1949): 'The aim of the Council of Europe is to achieve a greater unity between its members for the purpose of safeguarding and realising the ideals and principles which are their common heritage and facilitating their economic and social progress.' The membership of the organisation gradually grew from 10 (1949) to 47 (since 2007) States. In addition, there are five States formally affiliated to the Council with the status of observer (Canada, Holy See, Japan, Mexico and United States) while two applications for full membership are still pending (Belarus and Montenegro). It can therefore be said that the organisation covers the entire European continent, even though some States currently are not yet full members.

The Council of Europe is particularly well-known for its standard-setting activities in the field of human rights.[1] The most famous achievement in this respect is the adoption, in 1950, of the European Convention on Human Rights. This treaty entails various rights – and corresponding obligations for contracting States – on the interface of health and human rights. In this chapter the most relevant Articles of the Convention and related case law of the European Court of Human Rights, an inexhaustible source of information and inspiration for all interested in health and human rights law, will be examined (§2). This analysis will be followed by an examination of the health and human rights standards

1 All treaties, incl. those referred to in this chapter, can be downloaded as follows: go to http://conventions.coe.int/ > treaties > full list. You will not only find the full name and text of the treaties, but also other relevant information.

protected by three other monumental treaties adopted within the context of the Council of Europe, being the European Social Charter (§3), the European Convention for the Prevention of Torture (§4) and the Convention on Human Rights and Biomedicine (§5).

2. EUROPEAN CONVENTION ON HUMAN RIGHTS

2.1. EUROPEAN CONVENTION ON HUMAN RIGHTS

The Convention for the Protection of Human Rights and Fundamental Freedoms (henceforth: European Convention on Human Rights or ECHR) sets forth a number of rights and freedoms pertaining to the domain of civil and political rights (life, liberty, privacy, freedom of speech etc.). The Convention was adopted in 1950 and entered into force in 1953. Additional Protocols, adopted as from 1952, grant more rights or contain changes with respect to the ECHR's enforcement mechanism.[2]

The ECHR is considered the Council of Europe's crown jewel, also distinguishing this organisation from the European Union. Nowadays a State cannot become a member of the Council of Europe or accede to the European Union without signing and ratifying this treaty. Ratification of the ECHR not only means that the State is bound to observe its provisions and shall secure that everyone within its jurisdiction can enjoy the rights and freedoms laid down in the Convention, but also implies that the State is subjected to the ECHR's exceptionally powerful enforcement mechanism. This basically means that a contracting State accepts that individuals whose rights as protected by the ECHR, allegedly have been violated by or on account of this State can petition a body established under the Convention. Not only (groups of) individuals claiming to be victims of human rights violation (Article 34), but also States that feel that a contracting State has breached its ECHR obligations can file complaints against such a contracting State (Article 33 ECHR).

The investigation of such complaints is, nowadays, solely performed by the Strasbourg-based European Court of Human Rights (henceforth: Court of ECtHR). This is an independent body composed of full-time judges and instituted on a permanent basis. The number of judges is equal to the number of contracting States, thus at the moment 47. All judges are elected with respect to a contracting State by the Council of Europe's Parliamentary Assembly. They do not necessarily have to have the nationality of the contracting State by which they have been nominated; knowledge and impartiality are the most important requirements for judges.

---

2 At present that Convention has been supplemented / amended by 14 Protocols.

In 1998, the currently operating Court replaced the former and non-permanent European Commission of Human Rights, established in 1954, and the European Court of Human Rights, created in 1959. Until 1994, individuals could only petition the Court indirectly. It was for the European Commission to decide on the admissibility of complaints, depending on which case was forwarded to the Court. The abolition of the Commission not only implies that individuals can invoke the Court directly, but also that there is no longer a separate body determining the admissibility of the complaints. The filtering – as it is often perceived – of admissible complaints now has to be performed by the Court itself (more than 90% of the petitions are declared inadmissible or concern striking-out cases), which lays a considerable burden on the Court. It is hoped that Protocol XIV, which entered into force on 1 June 2010, will allow the Court to perform this task more efficiently.

The jurisprudence of the Court is not confined to the interpretation of the Convention; the Court is also authorised to decide upon matters of application (Article 32 ECHR). The jurisdiction of the Court therefore goes even further than that of the Court of Justice of the European Union which – under the Treaty on the Functioning of the European Union (TFEU) – has the power to interpret the EU treaties, to measure the interpretation of these treaties by certain others and to judge a limited number of conflicts within the realm of EU law.[3]

Judgements of the Court are legally binding (Article 46 para. 2 ECHR), thus attaching additional importance to them. The judgements adopted by a Chamber of the Court become final, and therewith binding, basically three months after the date of the judgement, unless the judgement was referred to the so-called Grand Chamber (GC). Judgements of the Grand Chamber are final and binding once they have been published (Article 44 ECHR). The execution of the judgements of the Court is monitored by the Committee of Ministers of the Council of Europe (Article 46 para. 2 ECHR).

Whereas the judgements of the Court are, officially, only binding on the respective contracting States, they have a bearing that reaches much further. In fact, due to the authority the Court has gained throughout the years, its case law is closely followed by courts, governments and legal scholars both from within and outside the Council of Europe. References to the ECtHR's jurisprudence can be found in the opinions of other human rights bodies, including the UN Human Rights Committee, and in the judgements of the highest judicial bodies of various countries, including Canada, Germany, South Africa and the United States of America.

Through its case law the Court has articulated the meaning of the various ECHR rights which turned out to be of particular relevance from a health and human rights perspective. But before looking at these judgements in greater detail, it should be emphasised that the Court does not pretend to operate in a

[3] Articles 267–279 TFEU.

normative vacuum. In fact, the Court seeks to interpret the ECHR 'in harmony with the general principles of international law'.[4] In doing so, the Court takes into account the rules of international law, (emerging) European standards and practices, and the opinions of other judicial and human rights bodies.[5]

When it comes to the interpretation of health-related rights protected by the ECHR, the Court regularly refers to the European Social Charter, the European Convention for the Prevention of Torture, the Convention on Human Rights and Biomedicine and the work or the bodies authorised to monitor compliance with these treaties.[6] This is another reason why separate attention will be paid to these conventions below.

2.2. RIGHTS AND CASE-LAW[7]

As mentioned before, the ECHR contains various rights that are highly relevant from a health and human rights perspective. This may come as a surprise, considering the fact that the ECHR and its additional Protocols almost exclusively contain civil and political rights. These rights – including the right to life (Article 2), the prohibition of torture (Article 3) and the right to private and family life (Article 8), which will be examined in greater detail below – typically impose negative obligations on contracting States, that is to say: duties to refrain from taking measures that interfere with the rights and freedoms of individuals. It was for this very reason that it was acceptable to the contracting States to subject themselves to an enforcement mechanism that provided for the right of individual petition with binding judgements of the ECtHR. Notably through the dynamic case law of the ECtHR it has become widely accepted that most rights and freedoms protected by the ECHR entail both negative and positive

---

4 ECtHR 6 July 2010, *Neulinger & Shuruk v. Switzerland* (GC), no. 41615/07, §131.

5 ECtHR 21 November 2001, *Al-Adsani v. the UK* (GC), no. 35763/97 and ECtHR 28 February 2008, *Saadi v. Italy*, (GC), no. 37201//06, §62.

6 For references to the European Social Charter see e.g. ECtHR 2 July 2002, *Wilson v. the UK*, no. 30668/96; 30671/96 & 30678/96; ECtHR 11 January 2006, *Sørensen & Rasmussen t. Denmark* (GC), no. 52562/99 & 52620/99 and ECtHR 12 November 2008, *Demir & Baykara t. Turkey* (GC), no. 34503/97, §103, for references to the European Convention for the Prevention of Torture see e.g. ECtHR 10 October 2000, *Akkoç v. Turkey*, no. 22947/93 & 22948/93; ECtHR 19 April 2001, *Peers v. Greece*, no. 24888/94; ECtHR 13 September 2005, *Ostrovar v. Moldova*, no. 36536/02; ECtHR 5 April 2007, *Todor Todorov v. Bulgaria*, no. 50765/99 and ECtHR 29 April 2008, *Petrea v. Romania*, no. 4792/03 for references to the Convention on Human Rights and Biomedicine see e.g. ECtHR 10 May 2001, *Cyprus v. Turkey* (GC), no. 25781/94; ECtHR 9 March 2004, *Glass v. the UK*, no. 61827/00; ECtHR 8 July 2004, *Vo v. France* (GC), no. 53924/00; ECtHR 7 March 2006, *Evans v. the UK*, no. 6339/05; ECtHR 10 April 2007, *Evans v. the UK* (GC), no. 6339/05; ECtHR 6 May 2008, *Juhnke v. Turkey*, no. 20817/04 and ECtHR 7 October 2008, *Bogumil v. Portugal*, no. 35228/03.

7 This paragraph is partially based on A.C. Hendriks, 'De betekenis van het EVRM voor het gezondheidsrecht', in: A.C. Hendriks, J.W. van de Gronden & J.J.M. Sluijs, *Gezondheidszorg en Europees recht, Preadvies VGR 2009*, The Hague: Sdu publishers 2009, p. 7–102.

obligations for States.[8] As a result, the meaning of these human rights, which sometimes also resemble social and economic rights,[9] cannot be correctly understood without taking into account the case law of the ECtHR. Therefore, before turning to some of the most relevant provisions of the ECHR and the way the Court elaborated on their meaning in the field of health and human rights law, a few features of the interpretation methods of the ECtHR will be described first.

2.2.1. General

In the first decades after its creation, the Court relied heavily upon *traveaux préparatoires* when interpreting the various treaty provisions.[10] As of 1978, the Court took a slightly different approach. When confronted with a question as to how to read a right in a concrete situation it started by underlining that the Court is a living instrument that 'must be interpreted in the light of present-day conditions'.[11] As a result of the latter the case law of the Court evolved, for example with respect to transsexuality it keeps a close eye on 'medical and scientific considerations.'[12] The Court recognises that the treatment an individual should receive is a decision to be taken by the medical authorities on the basis of their professional standards.[13] It is therefore reluctant to impose its own view, particularly with regard to sensitive moral and ethical issues. However, the Court does require States to stay within the margins of human rights law and to comply with emerging standards. As a result of the latter, the Court has come out with far-reaching judgements in the fields of health law and medicine.[14] In this respect it is important that the Court has reiterated that healthcare represents an important value in a democratic society.[15] According to the Court 'the very purpose of the medical profession' is 'to protect the health and life of patients'.[16] These principles serve as a yardstick against which acts of commission and acts of omission by a State can be measured.

---

8 All judgements can be found on www.echr.coe.int/echr/Homepage_EN > case-law > hudoc.

9 A.C. Hendriks, 'The close connection between classical rights and the right to health, with special reference to the right to sexual and reproductive health', *Medicine and Law* 1999, p. 225–242 and E. Palmer, 'Protecting socio-economic rights through the European Convention on Human Right: trends and developments in the European Court of Human Rights', *Erasmus Law Review* 2009, p. 397–425.

10 The official records of the negations preceding the adoption of the ECHR.

11 ECtHR 25 April 1978, *Tyrer v. the UK*, no. 5856/72, §31.

12 ECtHR 11 July 2002, *Christine Goodwin v. the UK* (GC), no. 28957/95.

13 ECtHR 24 September 1992, *Herczegfalvy v. Austria*, no. 10533/83, §82; ECtHR 18 December 2007, *Dybeku v. Albania*, no. 41153/06, §47 and ECtHR 28 February 2006, *Wilkinson v. the VK* (dec.), no. 14659/02.

14 Cf ECtHR 8 July 2004, *Vo v. France* (GC), no. 53924/00, §82 and ECtHR 1 April 2010, *S.H. et al. v. Austria*, no. 57813/00.

15 ECtHR 29 January 2008, *Villnow v. Belgium* (dec.), no. 16938/05.

16 ECtHR 16 December 2008, *Frankowicz v. Poland*, no. 53025/99.

According to the case law of the ECtHR, the rights and freedoms guaranteed by the ECHR do not merely impose duties to respect and to refrain from interfering with the rights and freedoms of individuals (negative obligations) on contracting States, but also duties to take adequate measures to protect and ensure the full enjoyment of the rights concerned (positive obligations). This already follows from Article 1 of the ECHR: 'The High Contracting Parties shall *secure* to everyone within their jurisdiction the rights and freedoms ...' This duty to ensure the enjoyment of Convention rights holds true with respect to everyone finding himself or herself within the jurisdiction of a contracting State, even if this is geographically in another country.[17]

The Court's doctrine on positive obligations has strengthened the bonds between health and human rights, and provides guidance for the interpretation of health-related human rights. The doctrine of positive obligations is essential for health law because it is on on this basis that the Court imposes various duties of care on the State. The doctrine of positive obligations as developed by the ECtHR is characterized by a contextual approach[18], in which the distinction between negative and positive obligations is not always clear-cut. Or, as the Court observed in the *Dickson* case: 'The boundaries between the State's positive and negative obligations under Article 8 do not lend themselves to precise definition.'[19] Also the difference between civil and political rights on the one hand and economic and social rights on the other become blurred as a result of this doctrine. Irrespective of this, the Court recalls that it does not seek to become a court of fourth instance or to otherwise try to substitute the role of national authorities: 'In so doing it [the Court – AH] cannot assume the rôle of the competent national authorities, for it would thereby lose sight of the subsidiary nature of the international machinery of collective enforcement established by the Convention.'[20] It naturally follows from this that the Court allows the national authorities a certain margin to make their own assessment on how human rights can be best protected given the particular context. This so-called *margin of appreciation* corresponds with the strictness of the test applied by the Court to determine whether one of the ECHR's rights has been violated. In the absence of common standards within Europe with respect to the issue at stake, such as the legal status of a fetus, the Court leaves a broad margin of appreciation for the national authorities to regulate this issue as inclined:

> '...the issue of when the right to life begins comes within the margin of appreciation which the Court generally considers that States should enjoy in this sphere ... The reasons for that conclusion are, firstly, that the issue of such protection has not been

---

17 ECtHR 2 March 2010 *Al-Saadoon & Mufdhi v. the UK*, no. 61498/08.

18 E.g. ECtHR 26 March 1985, *X & Y v. Netherlands*, no. 8978/80, §23 and ECtHR 21 June 1988, *Plattform 'Ärzte für das Leben' v. Austria*, no. 10126/82, §32.

19 ECtHR 4 December 2007, *Dickson v. the UK* (GC), no. 44362/04, §70.

20 ECtHR 23 July 1968, *Belgian Linguistic Case*, no. 1474/62, §10.

> resolved within the majority of the Contracting States themselves, in France in particular, where it is the subject of debate (...) and, secondly, that there is no European consensus on the scientific and legal definition of the beginning of life (...).'[21]

For the Court, it is also important to what extent an impugned measure interferes with a person's rights and freedoms: the more intrusive a measure, the stricter the safeguards applied by the Court against abuse.[22]

Before turning to the rights and freedoms guaranteed by the ECHR that are of particular relevance from a health and human rights perspective, it should be mentioned that only a few of these rights are absolute, allowing no exceptions, justifications or limitations, irrespective of the circumstances of the case or the conduct of the person concerned. This holds true, for example with respect to the right to life (Article 2), the prohibition of torture (Article 3) and the prohibition of slavery and forced labour (Article 4). Most of the rights and freedoms allow, however, for a balancing of interests which could result in a restriction of the right concerned. As regards the rights protected by Articles 8–11 ECHR the conditions under which such a restriction can be deemed justified are exhaustively listed in the second paragraphs of these Articles. Basically these clauses stipulate that the restriction should be a) prescribed by law, b) necessary in a democratic society, and c) aimed at achieving one of the listed general interests.

The protection of health is one of the grounds on the basis of which most rights and freedoms guaranteed by the ECHR can be restricted. What is meant by this criterion? From the Court's case law it can be learned that the Court largely leaves it to the national health authorities to determine whether there is an individual or public health justification to interfere with the rights and freedoms set forth by the ECtHR: '... it is for the medical authorities to decide, on the basis of the recognised rules of medical science, on the therapeutic methods to be used ...'.[23] Compliance with this standard implies that a contested measure 'cannot in principle be regarded as inhuman and degrading'.[24] The Court also attaches more weight to the therapeutic necessity of a form of treatment than the right to physical and moral integrity.[25] This does not mean that patients should always accept interventions with their personal integrity to avoid (further) damage to the individual's health; the Court fully acknowledges the right to refuse medical treatment, even if such a refusal may have a fatal

---

21 ECtHR 8 July 2004, *Vo v. France* (GC), no. 53924/00, §82.

22 ECtHR 2 September 2010, *Uzun v.Germany*, no. 35623/05.

23 ECtHR 24 September 1992, *Herczegfalvy v. Austria*, no. 10533/83, §82 and ECtHR 18 December 2007, *Dybeku v. Albania*, no. 41153/06, §47 and ECtHR 28 February 2006, *Wilkinson v. the VK* (dec.), no. 14659/02.

24 ECtHR 11 July 2006, *Jalloh v. Germany* (GC), no. 54810/00, §69.

25 ECtHR 7 October 2008, *Bogumil v. Portugal*, no. 35228/03, §89–90.

outcome for the individual concerned: 'the imposition of medical treatment without the consent of a mentally competent adult patient would interfere with his or her right to physical integrity and impinge on the rights protected under Article 8 of the Convention.'[26]

Intervening in the rights and freedoms guaranteed by the ECHR can also be justified in view of the health interests of others, notably children. A father who may pose a health risk to his children cannot object to child protection measures which interfere with his private life, including necessary and proportionate assessments of his medication consumption.[27]

From these and other judgements it follows that the Court is inclined to accept quite rapidly that a measure was necessary for the protection of health, and that interference with one of the rights or freedoms guaranteed by the ECHR was justified.

2.2.2. Health and human rights topics

a. Right to health

The ECHR does not guarantee the right to the highest attainable standard of health, however defined. In spite of this, the Court clearly holds the opinion that States have a special responsibility to protect, respect and promote the health of persons. This can be illustrated with a judgement of the Court in which it concurs with the European Commission of Human Rights and holds that the authorities are required to provide adequate medical care to persons deprived of their liberty.[28] The failure to live up to this requirement can lead to State liability: 'The Court acknowledges that the assumption of responsibilities by the authorities of a Contracting State for the health of an individual may in certain defined contexts engage their liability under the Convention with respect to that individual (...) as well as with respect to third parties (...).'[29] This does not suggest that a judgement by a medical professional which retrospectively turns out to be incorrect automatically results in liability: '... mistaken judgements or assessments by professionals do not *per se* render child-care measures incompatible with the requirements of Article 8. The authorities, medical and social, have duties to protect children and cannot be held liable every time genuine and reasonably-held concerns about the safety of children *vis-à-vis* members of their family are proved, retrospectively, to have been misguided.'[30]

The responsibility of States to protect the health of individuals is not confined to the vertical relations. States are, for example, obliged to formulate adequate

---

26 ECtHR 10 June 2010, *Jehova's Witnessess of Moscow v. Russia*, no. 302/02, §135.
27 ECtHR 5 January 2006, *K.T. v. Norway* (dec.), no. 26664/03/03.
28 ECtHR 28 January 1994, *Hurtado v. Switzerland*, no. 17549/90, §79.
29 ECtHR 11 September 2001, *Clunis v. the UK* (dec.), no. 45049/98.
30 ECtHR 30 September 2008, *R.K. & A.K. v. the UK*, no. 38000/05, §36.

legislation to protect the life and physical, mental and sexual integrity of individuals against threats from other individuals.[31] The Court interprets the right to integrity broadly:

> 'even a minor interference with the physical integrity of an individual must be regarded as an interference with the right to respect for private life under Article 8 if it is carried out against the individual's will.'[32]

The Court is fully aware of the threat for the health of individuals stemming from sexual violence.[33] To the extent possible, States are obliged to prevent and combat sexual and other forms of violence detrimental to human health. However, the States' responsibility for the prevention and protection of the health of individuals is not endless. In the case concerning the forced return of a woman with AIDS to Uganda, the Court considered as follows:

> 'Article 3 does not place an obligation on the Contracting State to alleviate such disparities [between the level of treatment available in the Contracting State and the country of origin] through the provision of free and unlimited health care to all aliens without a right to stay within its jurisdiction.'[34]

b. Right to life (Article 2)

Article 2 of the ECHR stipulates that 'everyone's right to life shall be protected by law'. The right to life is one of 'the most fundamental provisions in the Convention'.[35] For the authorities this implies a prohibition (negative obligation) to deliberately take people's lives and the (positive) obligation to protect the lives of all human beings within their national jurisdiction.[36] In several cases the Court decided that this right also imposes positive obligations on the authorities to protect the lives of persons receiving care. For example, the authorities have to make sure that healthcare institutions have an effective system, both for establishing the cause of death of patients and for examining the possible liability of the carers concerned.[37]

The positive obligations enshrined in Article 2 ECHR require States to make regulations compelling hospitals, whether public or private, to adopt appropriate measures for the protection of their patients' lives. They also require States to set up an effective independent judicial system so that the cause of death of patients

31 ECtHR 26 March 1985, *X & Y v. Netherlands*, no. 8978/80, §23.
32 ECtHR 16 June 2005, *Storck v. Germany*, no. 61603/00.
33 ECtHR 12 June 2008, *Bevacqua & S. v. Bulgaria*, no. 71127/0, §65.
34 ECtHR 27 May 2008, *N. v. the UK* (GC), no. 26565/05, §44.
35 ECtHR 27 September 1995, *McCann et al. v. the UK*, no. 18984/91, §147.
36 ECtHR 9 June 1998, *L.C.B. v. the UK*, no. 23413/94, §36 and ECtHR 28 October 1998, *Osman v. the UK* (GC), no. 23452/94, §115.
37 Since ECtHR 26 October 1999, *Erikson v. Italy* (dec.), no. 37900/97.

in the care of the medical profession, whether in the public or the private sector, can be determined and those responsible made accountable.[38]

On the basis of Article 2 ECHR States are required, pursuant to the case law of the ECtHR, to take the necessary measures to prevent individuals from committing suicide[39], from endangering their lives by going on hunger strike[40] or from dying prematurely in any other way[41] for reasons of illness or under pressure from others. As regards force-feeding hunger strikers the Court recognised from the start that force-feeding contains elements that suggest degrading treatment and, in certain circumstances, could result in a violation of Article 3 ECHR (the prohibition of inhuman and degrading treatment). The European Commission of Human Rights already acknowledged that in case a detained person persists in a hunger strike, a tension emerges between the (negative) obligation to respect a person's integrity, covered by Article 8, and the (positive) obligation to protect the person's life, covered by Article 8, for which the ECHR does not provide a clear-cut solution.[42] In this respect the Court proceeds on the basis that 'as a general rule, a measure which is of therapeutic necessity cannot be regarded as inhuman or degrading.'[43] 'This can be said, for instance, about force-feeding that is aimed at saving the life of a particular detainee who consciously refuses to take food.'[44]

The Court interprets the requirement of 'therapeutic necessity' considerably broader than 'life saving'.[45] Similarly the Court has repeatedly ruled that a therapeutically necessary (forced) treatment – whether or not in the case of a hunger strike – doet not constitute a violation of Article 3 ECHR.[46] In the case of *Nevmerzhitsky* the Court formulated additional requirements to justify forced feeding in case of a hunger strike.[47]

The right to life also imposes procedural obligations on the authorities, among which the obligation to conduct a diligent investgation of any deaths.[48] 'The essential purpose of such an investigation is to secure the effective

---

38 ECtHR 17 January 2002, *Calvelli & Ciglio v. Italy* (GC), no. 32967/96, §49.

39 ECtHR 3 April 2001, *Keenan v. the UK*, no. 27229/95; EHRM 7 June 2005, *Kılınç et al. v. Turkey*, no. 40145/98 and ECtHR 2 March 2010, *Lütfi Demirci et al. v. Turkey*, no. 28809/05.

40 ECtHR 5 April 2005, *Nevmerzhitsky v. Ukraine*, no. 54825/00.

41 ECtHR 23 May 2006, *Taïs v. France* (GC), no. 39922/03.

42 ECommissionHR 9 May 1984, *X v. Germany*, no. 10565/83.

43 ECtHR 24 September 1992, *Herczegfalvy v. Austria*, no. 10533/83, §82 and ECtHR 19 June 2007, *Ciorap v. Moldova*, no. 12066/02, §77.

44 ECtHR 11 July 2006, *Jalloh v. Germany* (GC), no. 54810/00, §69.

45 ECommissionHR 26 February 1997, *Buckley v. the UK*, no. 28323/95 and ECtHR 28 February 2006, *Wilkinson v. the UK* (dec.), no. 14659/02.

46 ECtHR 24 September 1992, *Herczegfalvy v. Austria*, no. 10533/83, §82 and ECtHR 10 February 2004, *Gennadi Naoumenko v. Ukraine*, no. 42023/98, §112.

47 ECtHR 5 April 2005, *Nevmerzhitsky v. Ukraine*, no. 54825/00, §94. See also ECtHR 19 June 2007, *Ciorap v. Moldova*, no. 12066/02.

48 ECtHR 27 September 1995, *McCann et al. v. the UK*, no. 18984/91; ECtHR 19 February 1998, *Kaya v. Turkey*, no. 22729/93 and ECtHR 15 May 2007, *Ramsahai et al. v. Netherlands* (GC), no. 52391/02.

implementation of the domestic laws which protect the right to life and, in those cases involving State agents or bodies, to ensure their accountability for deaths occurring under their responsibility.'[49] This duty also applies to situations in which it is highly unlikely that the death is to be attributed to unlawful violence on the part of the authorities. Furthermore, this duty also holds true irrespective of whether or not next of kin have requested this.[50] However, this duty applies *a fortiori* in cases of suspected unnatural death.[51]

Abortion

The Court has repeatedly been asked to rule on whether the right to life interferes with providing pregnant women with the possibility to have an abortion. The Court is of the opinion that it is for the contracting State to find a balance between the necessity of protecting the fetus and the woman's interests.[52] In this respect the Court allows the contracting States a wide margin of appreciation. Therefore the sole fact that abortion is legal in a country does not in itself constitute a violation of Article 2 ECHR.[53]

In 2010 the situation is such that abortion is permitted in all contracting States under certain – divergent – conditions. Moreover, in *Tysiąc* the Court decided that if the national legislation provides for the right of women to have an abortion, they should also be able to exercise this right.[54]

Euthanasia

In *Pretty* the Court considered that the right to life does not confer on individuals the right to terminate their lives. 'Article 2 cannot, without a distortion of language, be interpreted as conferring the diametrically opposite right, namely a right to die; nor can it create a right to self-determination in the sense of conferring on an individual the entitlement to choose death rather than life.'[55] This case concerned the request of a terminally ill woman who wanted to be certain that her husband would not be prosecuted if he were to help her commit suicide.

Although the Court made it clear with this ruling that the ECHR does *not* contain the right to die, in my opinion this does not mean that the ECHR forbids

---

49 ECtHR 4 May 2001, *Kelly et al. v. the UK*, no. 30054/96, §94.

50 ECtHR 8 November 2005, *Gongadze v. Ukraine*, no. 34056/02, §175 and ECtHR 7 February 2006, *Scavuzzo-Hager et al. v. Switzerland*, no. 41773/98, §75.

51 ECtHR 13 November 2008, *Khaylo v. Ukraine*, no. 39964/02, §62 and ECtHR 18 December 2008, *Kats et al. v. Ukraine*, no. 29971/04, §115–116.

52 ECommissionHR 13 May 1980, *Paton v. the UK*, no. 8416/79 and ECommissionHR 19 May 1992, *Hercz v. Norway*, no. 17004/90.

53 ECtHR 5 September 2002, *Boso v. Italy* (dec.), no. 50490/99.

54 ECtHR 20 March 2007, *Tysiąc v. Poland*, no. 5410/03, §124.

55 ECtHR 29 April 2002, *Pretty v. the UK*, no. 2346/02, §39.

contracting States to offer individuals the possibility to terminate their lives (or have their lives terminated) under certain circumstances. Above all, the Court declared that the right to life and the possible claim to a dignified death are two different matters. It can be maintained that, though indirectly, this also follows from a later case concerning Article 8 (right to private and family life). According to the Court this right was violated, now that a son had not been given the opportunity to bid farewell to his father who had died by means of euthanasia.[56]

c. Right to care (Article 3)

Article 3 ECHR prohibits torture as well as inhuman or degrading treatment or punishment. The Court has repeatedly found that depriving a person of necessary care may constitute a violation of Article 3 and/or Article 2 ECHR, two provisions complementing each other.[57] Indeed, given that failing to render the necessary care could lead to a person's death and/or severe suffering, the authorities have a duty of care.

For the same reason Article 3 ECHR, precludes, in 'exceptional circumstances', the extradition of an individual with a life-threatening disease to a country lacking the necessary care facilities.[58] Withholding adequate care can also violate a person's dignity in another way and thus be in contravention of Article 3 ECHR.[59] According to the Court such a situation could occur when the authorities fail to transfer a detainee with complex care needs to a specialised hospital.[60]

The manner and the circumstances in which care is given can also be in contravention of the right to private life as protected by Article 8 ECHR. Indeed, according to settled case law this right includes the right to physical and moral integrity.[61]

The duty of care holds particularly true *vis-à-vis* individuals who have been deprived of their freedom by the State. In 2002 the Court held that the prison authorities have to ensure that due account is taken of a detainee's health and well-being, more specifically by providing medical care.[62] Furthermore, this care must be tailored to the medical need of the individual: giving equal care to all could constitute a violation of Article 3 ECHR.[63]

---

56 ECtHR 6 December 2007, *Lind v. Russia*, no. 25664/05.

57 ECtHR 10 May 2001, *Cyprus v. Turkey* (GC), no. 25781/94, §219.

58 ECtHR 2 May 1997, *D. v. the UK*, no. 30240/96, §53.

59 ECtHR 24 May 2007, *Gorodnichev v. Russia*, no. 52058/99, §83.

60 ECtHR 11 July 2006, *Rivière t. Frankrijk*, no. 33834/03 and ECtHR 22 December 2008, *Aleksanyan v. Russia*, no. 46468/06.

61 ECtHR 26 March 1985, *X & Y v. Netherlands*, no. 8978/80, §22; ECtHR 29 April 2002, *Pretty v. the UK*, no. 2346/02, §61–63 and ECtHR 9 March 2004, *Glass v. the UK*, no. 61827/00, §70.

62 ECtHR 14 November 2002, *Mouisel v. France*, no. 67263/01, §40.

63 ECtHR 20 January 2009, *Slawomir Musial v. Poland*, no. 28300/06.

The Government's responsibility for people's health also calls for the protection of detainees with mental health problems, including psychiatric patients:

> 'the assessment of whether the treatment or punishment concerned is incompatible with the standards of Article 3 has, in the case of mentally ill persons, to take into consideration their vulnerability and their inability, in some cases, to complain coherently or at all about how they are being affected by any particular treatment'.[64]

The authorities' duty of care *vis-à-vis* these persons includes the guarantee of continued psychiatric care.[65] The authorities also have a responsibility with regard to the suitability of the establishment where mentally-ill people are accommodated: 'having the applicant detained in establishments not suitable for incarceration of the mentally-ill, raises a serious issue under the Convention'.[66]

In several cases the Court has been called on to consider the access to artificial procreation techniques.[67] The ECtHR allows the authorities a wide margin of appreciation in determining the eligibility and treatment criteria. In a 2010 judgement, the Court acknowledged the wide margin of appreciation the national authorities enjoy, also due to the lack of common ground between the approach adopted by the various contracting States. The Court added, however, that these differences 'do not, as such, make any solution reached by a legislature acceptable. It does not absolve the Court from carefully examining the arguments discussed in the legislative process and from examining whether the arguments advanced by the Government for justifying the difference of treatment in issue are relevant and sufficient'.[68] On the basis of a rather strict assessment of all the arguments put forward, the Court concluded that the prohibition of heterologous artificial procreation techniques for *in vitro* fertilisation, as laid down in the Austrian Artificial Procreation Act, violated the ECHR.

Through its case law the Court made it clear that care does not only have to meet quality requirements, but also that it must be provided *in time* and *safely*. If the necessary care fails to be provided, this could, according to the Court, be regarded as a violation of the ECHR.[69] The requirement of safe care follows from the authorities' positive obligation under Article 2 ECHR. On the basis thereof the authorities must take the proper measures to protect life. 'The aforementioned positive obligations therefore require States to make regulations compelling hospitals, whether public or private, to adopt appropriate measures

64 ECtHR 24 September 1992, *Herczegfalvy v. Austria*, no. 10533/83, §82; ECtHR 30 July 1998, *Aerts v. Belgium*, no. 25357/94, §66; ECtHR 3 April 2001, *Keenan v. the UK*, no. 27229/95, §111.
65 ECtHR 29 April 2008, *Petrea v. Romania*, no. 4792/03.
66 ECtHR 20 January 2009, *Slawomir Musial v. Poland*, no. 28300/06, §94.
67 ECtHR 4 December 2007, *Dickson v. the UK* (GC), no. 44362/04.
68 ECtHR 1 April 2010, *S.H. et al. v. Austria*, no. 57813/00, §69.
69 ECtHR 10 March 2009, *Paladi v. Moldova* (GC), no. 39806/05.

for the protection of their patients' lives.'[70] However, if a patient dies as a consequence of a medical error[71] this does not necessarily mean that Article 2 ECHR has been violated, as long as an effective and independent investigation of the cause of death is provided for.[72]

Consequently, on the basis of Articles 2, 3 and 8 ECHR the authorities have a duty of care subject to provisos. This duty of care also includes quality elements (adequacy, safety and speed) and has to be provided in a manner appropriate to the rights and dignity of individuals. Detainees cannot invoke the principle of equivalence. If care is medically necessary – even if the intervention is extremely radical and no *informed consent* has been obtained – there is no violation of Article 3 or 8 ECHR, provided that it has been been shown convincingly that treatment was necessary, proportionate and performed adequately.[73]

d. Patients' rights (Article 8)

As mentioned before, Article 8 guarantees the right to respect for private and family life. This right forms the basis of various patients' rights, even though patients' rights are also grounded in other rights protected by the ECHR.

Right to information

The ECHR contains a separate provision with regard to the right of freedom of expression (Article 10). This right includes the freedom to receive or disseminate information. In an Irish case the Court held that the ban on the dissemination of information regarding the possibilities of having an abortion in another country could be justified in view of the protection of public morals, namely 'profound moral values concerning the nature of life'.[74] Nonetheless, eventually the Court decided that Article 10 ECHR had been violated. In the situation at hand the ban constituted a disproportionate breach of the freedom of expression as protected by Article 10 ECHR.[75]

Therefore this violation can be qualified as impermissible interference with the freedom of expression on the part of the authorities. Those assuming that Article 10 ECHR does not only impose negative obligations on States but also similar positive obligations are mistaken. According to settled case law of the Court this right of freedom cannot be 'construed as imposing on a State ...

70 ECtHR 17 January 2002, *Calvelli & Ciglio v. Italy* (GC), no. 32967/96, §49.
71 ECtHR 27 June 2006, *Byrzykowski v. Poland*, no. 11562/05, §104.
72 ECtHR 26 October 1999, *Erikson v. Italy* (dec.), no. 37900/97 and ECtHR 4 May 2000, *Powell v.t he UK* (dec.), no. 45305/99.
73 ECtHR 7 October 2008, *Bogumil v. Portugal*, no. 35228/03.
74 ECtHR 29 October 1992, *Open Door & Dublin Well Woman v. Ireland*, no. 14234/88 & 14235/88, §63.
75 *Idem*, §80.

positive obligations to collect and disseminate information of its own motion.'[76] Due to the absence of a general duty of information under Article 10 ECHR this separate provision is of secondary importance for the right to *informed consent* or other patients' rights.

Nonetheless, in several cases the Court did underline the importance of adequate information as a prerequisite for authorising a violation of an individual's physical integrity. The Court bases this (positive) duty of information on the right to private life as protected by Article 8 ECHR.[77] According to settled case law the contracting States have the positive obligation to make certain that physicians discuss the possible effects of a treatment with patients, and this in such a way that the requirement of *informed consent* is complied with. In the Court's opinion, failing to provide patients with adequate information harms the self-determination of the person concerned and could constitute a violation of Article 8 ECHR[78]

According to the Court's case law the medical professionals' duty of information also applies with regard to the parents and carers of minors. On the basis of the right to family life, also protected by Article 8 ECHR, parents are in principle entitled to be informed on and involved in the treatment of their child.[79] However, an exception to this rule is possible, notably when this is deemed necessary with a view to the child's interests. The authorities are allowed a wide margin of appreciation in determining this necessity.[80]

Many people applied to the Court because, at least in their view, the authorities were not sufficiently cooperative in helping them obtain information about their (biological) parents. In these cases too the applicants invoke the right to private life as protected by Article 8 ECHR. This raises the question of whether a person has the right to know his/her origins or genetic descent.

In *Gaskin* the Court approvingly quoted the EComHR, which had held that 'respect for private life requires that everyone should be able to establish details of their identity as individual human beings and that in principle they should not be obstructed by the authorities from obtaining such very basic information without specific justification.'[81] Building on this line of thought, the Court decided in a Croation case that the right to private life refers to 'a person's physical and psychological integrity and can sometimes embrace aspects of an individual's physical and social identity.'[82] In doing so the Court acknowledged

76 ECtHR 19 February 1998, *Guerra et al. v. Italy*, no. 14967/89, §53.
77 ECtHR 5 October 2006, *Trocellier v. France* (dec.), no. 75725/01.
78 ECtHR 12 July 2007, *Testa v. Croatia*, no. 20877/04, §52.
79 ECtHR 17 December 2002, *Venema v. Netherlands*, no. 35731/97 and ECtHR 17 July 2008, *X. v. Croatia*, no. 11223/04.
80 ECtHR 7 February 2007, *Köhler & Köhler v. Germany* (dec.), no. 1638/03 and ECtHR 12 February 2008, *D. et al. v. the UK* (dec.), no. 38000/05.
81 ECtHR 7 July 1989, *Gaskin v. the UK*, no. 10454/83, §39.
82 ECtHR 7 February 2002, *Mikulic v. Croatia*, no. 53176/99, §53.

that, in principle, knowledge of one's origins is protected by the ECHR, in the sense that the person concerned must be able to gain access to the relevant information: 'In the Court's opinion, persons in the applicant's situation have a vital interest, protected by the Convention, in receiving the information necessary to uncover the truth about an important aspect of their personal identity.'[83] This may include information about biological parenthood.[84]

The Court acknowledges that providing information about biological parenthood also affects the private life of the biological parent(s). This issue came up in *Odièvre,* where the Grand Chamber held that 'the two private interests with which the Court is confronted in the present case are not easily reconciled'.[85]

Right to consent

The ECHR does not contain any provisions on the basis of which obtaining consent is required to be able to treat a person or to place him/her in a care institution. Also in respect of other acts possible within the framework of healthcare – such as making photographs – the ECHR does not explicitly stipulate that this is only allowed in the case of voluntary consent.[86] However, from the ECHR system it follows that, in principle, an individual can only give up the enjoyment of an ECHR right after he/she has voluntarily and unambiguously consented to this and this consent is not contrary to an important public interest.[87] The Court extended this principle to the right to private life (Article 8 ECHR) and the right to liberty and security (Article 5 ECHR). However, regarding the enjoyment of these rights the rule still is that a person cannot consent lawfully to treatments which are at odds with the norms and values of the ECHR, such as in the case of dwarf tossing[88] or otherwise subjecting oneself to treatments incompatible with human dignity.[89]

Violating a person's private life, including his/her physical, mental or sexual integrity[90], in the context of healthcare is, in principle, only permitted after the

83 *Idem*, §64.

84 ECtHR 13 February 2003, *Odièvre v. France* (GC), no. 42326/98, §29 and ECtHR 13 July 2006, *Jäggi v. Switzerland*, no. 58757/00, §25.

85 ECtHR 13 February 2003, *Odièvre v. France* (GC), no. 42326/98, §44.

86 ECtHR 15 January 2009, *Reklos & Davourlis v. Greece*, no. 1234/05.

87 ECtHR 27 February 1980, *Deweer v. Belgium*, no. 6903/75, §51; ECtHR 25 February 1992, *Pfeifer & Plankl v. Austria*, no. 10802/84, §37 and ECtHR 18 October 2006, *Hermi v. Italy* (GC), no. 1855/02, §73.

88 ECommissionHR 16 October 1996, *Wackenheim v. France*, no. 29961/96.

89 ECtHR 19 February 1997, *Laskey, Jaggard & Brown v. the UK*, no. 21627/93; 21826/93 & 21974/93.

90 ECtHR 26 March 1985, *X & Y v. Netherlands*, no. 8978/80, §23 and ECtHR 28 October 1998, *Osman v. the UK* (GC), no. 23452/94, §128–130 and ECtHR 4 December 2003, *M.C. v. Bulgaria*, no. 39272/98, §152.

voluntary, explicit and informed consent of the person concerned.[91] To answer the question of whether there has indeed been *voluntary* consent the Court engages in a critical appraisal of the context in which the person concerned found himself/herself. In the case of detention or if the person concerned is suspected of having committed a serious offence it is not possible to assume without question that the consent to an invasive examination was genuinely voluntary.[92] Similar problems with regard to free decision-making may occur when a person is confined to a psychiatric institution[93] and when, in the case of psychological need, decisions are taken that could have a major impact on the person's private and family life.[94]

However, from the above it does not follow that voluntary and informed consent on the part of the person in question or his/her representative is required in order to proceed to treatment. Indeed, enjoyment of the right to private life as protected by Article 8 ECHR, or as the case may be integrity, can be limited in view of health, national security, public safety or the protection of the rights and freedoms of others.

The Court is inclined to regard the failure to comply with the requirement of consent as justified when this involves 'therapeutic necessity' for treatment[95], a criterion which the Court interprets broadly.[96] Furthermore, the Court's case law shows that forced treatment can also be justified without this being in the interests of (the health of) the person concerned.[97]

Just like forced treatment, involuntary confinement in a care institution constitutes a far-reaching infringement of a person's personal freedom. Therefore the rule is that in principle this admission is only lawful if the person concerned consents to this. Indeed, consenting to treatment does not mean consenting to deprivation of freedom.[98] Consent for admission should be given voluntarily, explicitly and on the basis of prior information. If the person concerned is deemed not to be capable of this, it would be appropriate to examine whether his or her ECHR rights can be guaranteed in another way.[99] In determining whether these conditions have been fulfilled the Court will have a critical look at the context in which the person concerned found himself/herself.[100]

---

91 ECtHR 9 March 2004, *Glass v. the UK*, no. 61827/00, §82.

92 ECtHR 6 May 2008, *Juhnke v. Turkey*, no. 20817/04, §77 resp. ECtHR 7 October 2008, *Bogumil v. Portugal*, no. 35228/03, §58& 71 etc.

93 ECtHR 16 June 2005, *Storck v. Germany*, no. 61603/00, §103.

94 ECtHR 13 January 2009, *Todorova v. Italy*, no. 33932/06, §75.

95 *Herczegfalvy/Oostenrijk*, no. 10533/83 en ECtHR 7 October 2008, *Bogumil v. Portugal*, no. 35228/03.

96 ECommissionHR 26 February 1997, *Buckley v. the UK*, no. 28323/95 and ECtHR 28 February 2006, *Wilkinson v. the UK* (dec.), no. 14659/02.

97 ECtHR 11 July 2006, *Jalloh v. Germany* (GC), no. 54810/00, §70.

98 ECtHR 6 November 2008, *Gulub Atanasov v. Bulgaria*, no. 73281/01, §65.

99 ECtHR 5 October 2004, *H.L. v. the UK*, no. 45508/99, §90.

100 *Idem*, §91.

Article 5 ECHR calls for very strict material and procedural requirements with regard to involuntary deprivation of freedom. The general purpose of Article 5 ECHR is the prevention of arbitrariness of arrests and detention.[101] The procedural rights include the right to take proceedings by which the lawfulness of the detention shall be decided speedily by a court (Article 5 para 4 ECHR)[102] and the right to compensation in case of an arrest or detention in contravention of the ECHR (Article 5 para 5 ECHR).[103]

The term deprivation of liberty is interpreted autonomously by the Court.[104] The basis is not so much the (national) legal qualification but rather all circumstances pertaining to the case. That way the Court guarantees all contracting States an equal level of legal protection. According to the established case law of the Court a person cannot be considered to be of 'unsound mind' (Article 5 para 1(e) ECHR) and deprived of his or her liberty unless the following three minimum conditions are satisfied:

a) he or she must reliably be shown to be of unsound mind;
b) the mental disorder must be of a kind or degree warranting compulsory confinement;
c) the validity of continued confinement depends upon the persistence of such a disorder.[105]

In the *Varbanov* case the Court held that the first requirement was not met unless the authorities had tried to obtain an expert medical opinion establishing the mental disorder prior to the deprivation of liberty of the individual concerned.[106] Furthermore, the Court later on emphasised that there must be some relationship between the ground of permitted deprivation of liberty relied on and the place and conditions of detention. In principle, the 'detention' of a person as a mental health patient is only considered 'lawful' for the purposes of Article 5 paragraph 1 sub-paragraph (e) if effected in a hospital, clinic or other appropriate institution.[107]

Until now there is only one judgement of the ECtHR on the deprivation of liberty to prevent the spreading of infectious diseases. In this case (*Enhorn*) the Court held that more or less the same criteria should be applied to justify the deprivation of liberty of individuals with an infectious disease, as compared to persons with a mental disorder. These requirements are the following:

101 ECtHR 13 June 2002, *Anguelova v. Bulgaria*, no. 38361/97, §154.
102 ECtHR 7 March 2006, *Van Glabeke v. France*, no. 38287/02 and ECtHR 16 January 2007, *Menvielle v. France (No. 2)*, no. 97/03.
103 ECtHR 25 October 2005, *Fedotov v. Russia*, no. 5140/02 and ECtHR 15 December 2005, *Georgiev v. Bulgaria*, no. 47823/99.
104 ECtHR 28 May 1985, *Ashingdane v. the UK*, no. 8225/78, §46.
105 ECtHR 24 October 1979, *Winterwerp v. Netherlands*, no. 6301/73, §39.
106 ECtHR 5 October 2000, *Varbanov v. Bulgaria*, no. 31365/96.
107 ECtHR 28 May 1985, *Ashingdane v. the UK*, no. 8225/78, §46.

a) it must be reliably shown that the individual concerned has an infectious disease;
b) the disease must be of a kind or degree warranting compulsory confinement;
c) the validity of continued confinement depends upon the persistence of the disease;
d) the deprivation of liberty is effected in a hospital, clinic or other appropriate institution; and
e) the deprivation of liberty must be necessary in the given circumstances, with no other, less severe measures available to safeguard the individual or public interest.[108]

Access to personal data

In the healthcare system patient information is stored with a view to guaranteeing continuity and quality of care. These forms of data processing affect the patient's private life, as protected by Article 8 ECHR. The Court has repeatedly pointed out that data processing with regard to the private life of a person falls within the scope of Article 8 ECHR.[109] The Court gives a broad interpretation to the concept of private life and related information. According to the Court this concept does not only refer to video footage[110], but, where appropriate, includes photographs as well.[111] It also follows from the case law of the EctHR that there are certain requirements with regard to the collection, recording, storage and dissemination of personal data.

With respect to healthcare, the Court has never explicitly considered that Article 8 ECHR entails a (positive) obligation to store a patient's health and other personal data in a medical file. Nonetheless, some judgements do tend in that direction. In *Powell* the parents of the deceased Robert declared, inter alia, that the medical file was incomplete and had been tampered with. The Court's decision of admissibility is no reason to conclude that the authorities are compelled to guarantee completeness and accuracy of medical files.[112] Yet, the Court does set store by good documentation, which is also illustrated by the significance attributed to data recorded in medical files in numerous other judgements.[113] The absence of full and detailled records of the health status of a

---

108 ECtHR 25 January 2005, *Enhorn v. Sweden*, no. 56529/00, §42–46.

109 ECtHR 26 March 1987, *Leander v. Sweden*, no. 9248/81, §48 and ECtHR 4 May 2000, *Rotaru v. Romania* (GC), no. 28341/95, §43.

110 ECtHR 28 January 2003, *Peck v. the UK*, no. 44647/98, §57.

111 ECommissionHR 7 December 1992, *Lupker et al. v. Netherlands*, no. 18395/91; ECtHR 31 January 1995, *Friedl v. Austria*, no. 15225/89 and ECtHR 15 January 2009, *Reklos & Davourlis v. Greece*, no. 1234/05.

112 ECtHR 4 May 2000, *Powell v.t he UK* (dec.), no. 45305/99.

113 See e.g. ECtHR 13 October 2005, *Mogoş v. Romania*, no. 20420/02; ECtHR 23 May 2006, *Taïs v. France* (GC), no. 39922/03; ECtHR 18 December 2007, *Dybeku v. Albania*, no. 41153/06 and ECtHR 15 June 2010, *Ashot Harutyunyan v. Armenia*, no. 34334/04.

patient can, according to the Court, undermine the effectiveness of any monitoring or supervision process.[114] Moreover, judging by the critical remarks made by the Court in various cases, the file has to comply with certain quality requirements:

> '69. According to a one-page document that presumably forms part of a medical record, on 11 February 2005 the applicant visited a doctor and complained that he had been infected with hepatitis C in UF-91/15. The applicant, who had refused to take anti-tuberculosis treatment, was prescribed with essenciale, vitamin B6 and two more medicines, the names of which are illegible.
> 70. The case file contains a barely legible one-page document from which it transpires that the applicant spent some time in an unspecified medical institution with a diagnosis of recurrence of tuberculosis concurrent with viral hepatitis C with zero activity. The document contains no information concerning the treatment prescribed to the applicant.'[115]

The Court has repeatedly stated to attach great weight to the confidentiality of medical data:

> 'The protection of personal data, in particular medical data, is of fundamental importance to a person's enjoyment of his or her right to respect for private and family life as guaranteed by Article 8 of the Convention. Respecting the confidentiality of health data is a vital principle in the legal systems of all the Contracting Parties to the Convention. It is crucial not only to respect the sense of privacy of a patient but also to preserve his or her confidence in the medical profession and in the health services in general.'[116]

In the same line the Court places weight on the physician's duty to respect the confidentiality of medical data.[117] In case of a breach of the secrecy of medical data it will be necessary to examine on a case-by-case basis whether, and if so, for how long, further infringements of the private life of the person concerned will have to be prevented. In a French case, where the authorities had prohibited a publishing company to publish a book written by former President Mitterand's personal physician for an indefinite period, the Court found that this was a disproportionate violation of the freedom of expression.[118]

---

114 ECtHR 3 April 2001, *Keenan v. the UK*, no. 27229/95, §114. See also ECtHR 16 December 2008, *Rupa v. Romania*, no. 58478/00.

115 ECtHR 7 February 2008, *Mechenkov v. Russia*, no. 35421/05. See also ECtHR 24 May 2007, *Gorodnichev v. Russia*, no. 52058/99, §87 and ECtHR 11 October 2005, *Tarariyeva v. Russia* (dec.), no. 4353/03.

116 ECtHR 25 February 1997, *Z. v. Finland*, no. 22009/93, §95; ECtHR 10 October 2006, *L.L. v. France*, no. 7508/02, §44; ECtHR 17 July 2008, *I. v. Finland*, no. 20511/03, §38 and ECtHR 25 November 2008, *Armoniene t. Lithuania*, no. 36919/02, §40.

117 ECtHR 10 October 2006, *L.L. v. France*, no. 7508/02, §23.

118 ECtHR 18 May 2004, *Plon (Société) v. France*, no. 58148/00.

Of course the physician's duty not to disclose medical data does not imply an absolute ban on handing over details from a patient's file. In the social security case *M.S.*, where details from the applicant's medical file had been released following her application for incapacity benefits, the Court's conclusion was that all conditions justifying a violation of the right to private life had been satisfied. The circumstance that 'the medical records in question contained highly personal and sensitive data about the applicant, including information relating to an abortion' did not alter this.[119] As long as there are enough guarantees, handing over information from a father's medical records to child protection authorities can also be justified.[120]

On the presumption that information kept in a medical file lies at the core of Article 8 ECHR[121], it is obvious that the person concerned is also entitled to access to the file. Access can only be refused in exceptional circumstances.[122]

According to the Court's settled case law access should also be possible with a view to correcting mistakes or preventing abuse of information relating to the person concerned[123] or with a view to obtaining information on the individual's origins and identity.[124] Individuals whose personal data have been stored (data subjects) should not be obliged to specifically justify a request to be provided with a copy of their personal data files. It is, according to the Court, rather for the authorities to show that there are compelling reasons for refusing this facility.[125]

Even though the Court considers that people should be able to have access to stored information, the ECHR does not extend to access to a file which only contains professional information not related to the identity or personal history of individuals.[126]

2.3. CONCLUSIONS

Despite the fact that the ECHR does not set forth a right to health or healthcare, it can be learned from an analysis of the Court's case law that the Convention imposes various (notably, positive) obligations on contracting States relevant to health protection and the prevention of health risks. These obligations do not

119 EctHR 27 August 1997, *M.S. v. Sweden*, no. 20837/92, §35.

120 ECtHR 5 January 2006, *K.T. v. Norway* (dec.), no. 26664/03.

121 ECtHR 17 July 2008, *I. v. Finland*, no. 20511/03, §35.

122 ECommissionHR 28 February 1996, *Martin v. the UK* (dec.), no. 27533/95 resp. ECtHR 20 January 2009, *Uslu v. Turkey (no. 2)*, no. 23815/04.

123 ECtHR 4 May 2000, *Rotaru v. Romania* (GC), no. 28341/95.

124 ECtHR 7 July 1989, *Gaskin v. the UK*, no. 10454/83, §39 and ECtHR 7 February 2002, *Mikulic v. Croatia*, no. 53176/99, §54.

125 ECtHR 28 April 2009, *K.H. et al. v. Slowakia*, no. 32881/04, §48. See also ECtHR 15 October 2009, *Tsourlakis v. Greece*, no. 50796/07.

126 *Smith/VK* (ontv.besl.), no. 39658/05.

confine themselves to the vertical relations, but also entail duties for the horizontal relations. From the wealth of case law of the Court it can further be concluded that various patients' rights (also) are protected by the ECHR, thus strengthening their basis in the national legal order.

3. EUROPEAN SOCIAL CHARTER

The European Social Charter (henceforth: Charter or ESC) was adopted in 1961 and entered into force in 1965. It is the counterpart of the ECHR, that is to say 'a human rights instrument envisaged to complement the European Convention on Human Rights'.[127] Since the ECHR almost exclusively protects civil and political rights, the need was felt to also introduce legal guarantees for the enjoyment of social and economic rights. At the same time, the supervision mechanism established under the ECHR, notably the possibility for individuals and States to file complaints, was deemed less appropriate when it comes to promoting compliance with social and economic rights. In the 1960s, social and economic rights were generally considered to lack justiciability.[128] It was claimed that these rights, including the right to health, above all reflected (vague) political intentions that could not be enforced by courts.[129] It was exclusively for governments to decide how they wanted to progressively realise the aspirations enshrined in these rights, also given the large sums of money involved.

The ESC 1961[130] entails various rights that are of imminent importance from a health and human rights perspective. First of all, Article 11 explicitly recognises the right to protection of health. According to these provisions, contracting States are, amongst others, required to take appropriate measures to remove the causes of ill-health; to provide facilities for the promotion of health and to prevent epidemic, endemic and other diseases. The ESC 1961 also recognises the right to safe and healthy working conditions (Article 3), the right of children and young persons to protection (Article 7) and the right to social and medical assistance (Article 13).

Since it was nevertheless thought that States should somehow be held accountable for their policies to achieve these aspirations, the 1961 ESC foresees in periodic reporting procedures. When it comes to monitoring compliance, the European Committee of Social Rights (henceforth: Committee or ECSR) plays a key role. The ECSR, previously known as the Committee of Independent Experts

127 ECSR 7 November 2004, *FIDH v. France*, no. 14/2003, §27. Idem, ECSR 27 October 2009, *DCI v. Netherlands*, no. 47/2008, §34.

128 Ch. Courtis, 'Standards to make ESC rights justiciable: a summary exploration', *Erasmus Law Review* 2009, p. 379–395.

129 B.C.E. Toebes, *The Right to Health as a Human Right in International Human Rights Law*, Antwerp / Oxford: Intersentia / Hart 1999.

130 The text of the ESC as well as the Additional Protocols can be found at www.coe.int/t/dghl/monitoring/socialcharter/Presentation/TreatiesIndex_en.asp.

(CIE), is composed of 15 experts, elected by the Council of Europe's Committee of Ministers. Contracting States are required to report to this committee every two years on their implementation of the ESC and the problems they may have come across. After an examination of these reports by the ECSR, the reports together with the ECSR's views on them ('conclusions') are considered by the Governmental Committee (a body of national senior civil servants) and the Committee of Ministers. The latter may make recommendations to contracting States that do not fully comply with the ESC's rights. The ECSR's conclusions and the Committee of Ministers' recommendations provide useful insights as to the interpretation and correct application of the ESC.

In the 1990s the need was felt to revitalise the ESC.[131] This led to a revision of the ESC in 1996, and the adoption of two Additional Protocols. The revised ESC, which entered into force in 1999, did not substantially change the rights most relevant from a health and human rights perspective. The numbering of the Articles also remained the same. However, new provisions were added as well, like the right of children and young persons to social, legal and economic protection (Article 17) and a general provision prohibiting discrimination in the enjoyment of the rights set forth by the ESC, including discrimination on grounds of 'health' (Article E).

The overwhelming majority of the Member States of the Council of Europe has signed and ratified the revised ESC, if not the 1961 ESC. Only a few States have failed to ratify both treaties.

Of much greater importance for health and human rights in Europe was the introduction of the Additional Protocol which provided a system of collective complaints and was adopted in 1995. On the basis of this protocol, which came into force in 1998, a number of national and international non-governmental organisations can now lodge complaints with the ECSR. In case the ECSR finds the complaint admissible, it will submit a report with its findings and its conclusions on the merits of the case.[132] These mostly well reasoned reports, followed by a resolution adopted by the Committee of Ministers deciding on whether the complaint is upheld, are very authoritative even though they do not have the same status as legally binding decisions.

In 2004, the ECSR found that the reforms in France of the 'Aide médicale de l'Etat' (State medical assistance) and the 'Couverture maladie universelle' (Universal sickness cover), due to which a large number of adults and children with insufficient resources were deprived of medical assistance, resulted in a violation of Article 17 of the revised ESC (the right of children and young persons to social, legal and economic protection). A (narrow) majority of the

---

131 R.R. Churchill & U. Khaliq, 'The Collective Complaints System of the European Social Charter: An Effective Mechanism for Ensuring Compliance with Social and Economic Rights?', *European Journal of International Law* 2004, p. 417–456.

132 All reports can be found on: www.coe.int/t/dghl/monitoring/socialcharter/Complaints/Complaints_en.asp.

ECSR ruled that Article 17 protects, in a general manner, the right of children and young persons, including unaccompanied minors, to care and assistance, and that the French law reforms undermined this entitlement.[133]

In 2006, the ECSR found that Greece had violated the ESC by not responding adequately to the health hazards caused by lignite that was mined in certain areas of Greece. The main provision Greece failed to adhere to was Article 11 ESC, the provision on the right to health. According to the ECSR, 'Under Article 11 of the Charter, everyone has the right to benefit from any measures enabling him to enjoy the highest possible standard of health attainable. The Committee sees a clear complementarity between Article 11 of the Charter and Article 2 (right to life) of the European Convention on Human Rights, as interpreted by the European Court of Human Rights (...). Measures required under Article 11 should be designed, in the light of current knowledge, to remove the causes of ill-health resulting from environmental threats such as pollution (...).'[134]

In 2008, the ECSR found that the Bulgarian health insurance legislation discriminated against particular groups, notably Roma. The ECSR concluded that the way this body of legislation was framed constituted a violation of Article 11 (right to health) in conjunction with Article E (non-discrimination).[135]

In 2009, the ECSR came out with a report on sexual and reproductive health information as delivered in Croatian schools. In its report the ECSR formulated the following criteria for this type of health information:

States must ensure

- that sexual and reproductive health education forms part of the ordinary school curriculum;
- that the education provided is adequate in quantitative terms, i.e. in respect of the time and other resources devoted to it (teachers, teacher training, teaching materials, etc.);
- that the form and substance of the education, including curricula and teaching methods, are relevant, culturally appropriate and of sufficient quality, in particular that it is objective, based on contemporary scientific evidence and does not involve censoring, withholding or intentionally misrepresenting information, for example as regards contraception and different means of maintaining sexual and reproductive health; and
- that a procedure is in place for monitoring and evaluating the education with a view to effectively meeting the above requirements; and
- that it is delivered in time limited fragments through general school subjects, through occasional lectures by doctors.

---

133 ECSR 7 November 2004, *International Federation of Human Rights Leagues (FIDH) v. France*, no. 14/2003.

134 ECSR 6 December 2006, *Marangopoulos Foundation for Human Rights (MFHR) v. Greece*, no. 30/2005.

135 ECSR 3 December 2008, *European Roma Rights Centre v. Bulgaria*, no. 46/2007.

The ESCR unanimously found that the health information provided in Croatian schools did not meet these criteria and that the information conveyed was discriminatory towards homosexuals, thus finding a violation of Article 11 in conjunction with Article E of the revised ESC.[136]

So obviously the ESC and the work of the ECSR are of major importance when it comes to interpreting the interrelationships between health and human rights law in Europe.

4. EUROPEAN CONVENTION FOR THE PREVENTION OF TORTURE

Another Council of Europe treaty that merits mentioning in the matter of analysing the bonds between health and human rights law is the European Convention for the Prevention of Torture and Inhuman or Degrading Treatment or Punishment (henceforth: European Convention for the Prevention of Torture or CPT). This treaty was adopted in 1987 and entered into force in 1989. In 1993 two Protocols amending the CPT were adopted and became effective as of 2002. The CPT has been ratified by all Member States of the Council of Europe. Apart from that, its ratification is nowadays a precondition for joining the Council of Europe.

The CPT, which does not have any material provisions, seeks to reinforce the right not be subjected to torture or to inhuman or degrading treatment or punishment, as laid down in Article 3 of the ECHR. It was assumed that the – above all retrospective – protection offered by Article 3 of the ECHR could benefit from proactive measures aimed at 'strengthening, if necessary, the protection of such persons (deprived of their liberty – AH) from torture and from inhuman or degrading treatment or punishment' (Article 1 CPT). Thereto, the CPT foresees in the establishment of an independent committee, the European Committee for the Prevention of Torture and Inhuman or Degrading Treatment or Punishment, composed of members with different professional backgrounds. Their number is equal to that of the States party to the CPT. The members of this committee, nominated by the contracting States, are required to be independent and impartial. They are elected by the Council of Europe's Council of Ministers.

The Committee is permitted to visit and inspect all 'places of detention' of the Council of Europe's Member States without prior announcement or approval by the authorities. Places of detention, as defined by the CPT, are all places in which people are deprived of their liberty by a public authority, including psychiatric institutions and (other) care institutions where people are held against their will.

---

136 ECSR 30 March 2009, *Interights v. Croatia*, no. 45/2007.

After a visit, the Committee prepares a report with its findings and recommendations and sends this to the government of the respective State. Officially, these reports are only made public with the consent of the government concerned, but in actual practice all reports are published accompanied by the government's response.[137]

The reports of the Committee contain useful information on the detention situations in Member States and provide insights in how the Committee defines torture, inhuman or degrading treatment or punishment with respect to persons detained of their liberty. These reports and the standards applied by the Committee are frequently used by the ECtHR in cases where applicants claim that Article 3 ECHR has been violated. Examples of two reports are given here.

In 2009, the Committee published its report following a visit to the Czech Republic in 2008. In this report, the Committee made a number of critical remarks on the treatment of sentenced sex-offenders. After examining the situation, the Committee recommended the Czech authorities to review the treatment offered and to revise its legislation to ensure their compatibility with the CPT.[138]

That same year the Committee published a report following a country visit to Spain. In this report, the Committee addresses – amongst others – the issue of force-feeding. According to the Committee, a decision to force-feed a prisoner should be based upon medical necessity and should be carried out under suitable conditions reflecting the medical nature of the measure. Moreover, the Committee considered that the methods used to execute force-feeding should not be unnecessarily painful and should be applied with skill and minimum force. It can therefore be concluded that, in principle, the Committee does not reject force-feeding, but considers this only acceptable once strict requirements are met.[139]

5. CONVENTION ON HUMAN RIGHTS AND BIOMEDICINE

In 1996, the Council of Ministers of the Council of Europe adopted a framework convention laying down the main human rights principles and some general standards for the protection of human rights and human dignity in areas concerning the application of biology and medicine. This treaty, the Convention for the Protection of Human Rights and Dignity of the Human Being with regard to the Application of Biology and Medicine (henceforth: Convention on Human Rights and Biomedicine or Biomedicine Convention), elaborates some of

137 See www.cpt.coe.int/en/.

138 CPT 5 February 2009, Report Czech Republic, CPT/Inf (2009) 8.

139 CPT 2 March 2009, Report Spain, CPT/Inf (2009) 10.

the principles and rights enshrined in the European Convention on Human Rights. In fact, the Biomedicine Convention can be considered as an addition to – or a *lex specialis vis-à-vis*[140] – the ECHR with a view to the rapid developments in biology and medicine.

The Biomedicine Convention was opened for signature and ratification in Oviedo (Spain) on 4 April 1997. This Convention – since then also known as the Oviedo Convention – entered into force on 1 December 1999. As from 1998, four Additional Protocols were adopted: on the prohibition of cloning human beings (1998), on transplantation of organs and tissues of human origin (2002), on biomedical research (2005) and on genetic testing for health purposes (2008). By the year 2010 the Biomedicine Convention was ratified by 26 Member States of the Council of Europe. All but the genetic testing protocol had meanwhile entered into force.

As mentioned before, the Biomedicine Convention is a framework convention.[141] It only sets out a number of principles, rights and standards upon which there was clarity and consensus amongst the drafters. Other issues have been or will be dealt with in Additional Protocols, like the four mentioned before, provided that the drafters can agree. With respect to such issues as abortion and euthanasia, it seems very unlikely that this will occur in the near future.

The Biomedicine Convention itself consists of 'principles', 'rights' and 'standards' applying to specific fields of biology and medicine. The principles the Biomedicine Convention recognises include the protection of human dignity and identity (Article 1); the protection of the integrity of human beings (Article 1); equitable access to health care and the prohibition of discrimination (Articles 3 and 1); the primacy of the human being (Article 2); and the prohibition of financial gain and disposal of the human body (chapter VII).

The Biomedicine Convention further contains more specific rights and standards with respect to consent (chapter II); private life and information (chapter III); the human genome (chapter IV); scientific research (chapter V) and organ and tissue removal from living human beings (chapter VI). Basically the rights laid down in these chapters are an elaboration of the rights and freedoms protected by the ECHR.

Different from the ECHR, the Biomedicine Convention does not foresee in a strong enforcement mechanism. In fact, the Convention does not even impose a duty on contracting States to regularly report on the progress made with respect to the implementation of the Convention, an obligation quite common under human rights treaties. The Convention does, however, authorise the Secretary General of the Council of Europe to ask a contracting State to 'furnish an

140 E. Roucounas, 'The Biomedicine Convention in relation to other international instruments', in: J.K.M. Gevers, E.H. Hondius & J.H. Hubben (eds.), *Health Law, Human Rights and the Biomedicine Convention*, Leiden: Brill 2005, p. 23–34 (26).

141 H.D.C. Roscam Abbing, 'The Convention on Human Rights and Biomedicine: An Appraisal of the Council of Europe Convention', *European Journal of Human Rights* 1998, p. 377–387.

explanation of the manner in which its internal law ensures the effective implementation of any of the provisions of the Convention' (Article 30). Moreover, a government as well as the Steering Committee on Bioethics may request the ECtHR to give an *advisory* opinion (Article 29), i.e. they are not legally binding. Until 2010, no use was made of either one of these possibilities.

As mentioned before, the ECtHR does sometimes refer to provisions of the Biomedicine Convention in cases concerning the application of techniques or forms of treatment in the field of medicine.[142] This occurs, seemingly, in a haphazard manner. In the majority of cases touching upon biomedical questions the Court does not see a need to invoke the more elaborated provisions of the Biomedicine Convention to judge the case.

6. CONCLUSIONS

Although the Council of Europe may be less strong than the European Union in terms of powers and also may have less economic and political significance in our global village, this organisation embracing 47 States has come forward with four very important treaties in the field of health and human rights law. The European Convention of Human Rights is by far the most significant of these treaties, even though this treaty focuses on the protection of civil and political rights. Thanks to the case law of the European Court of Human Rights, the ECHR provisions also have great relevance in the field of health and human rights law. The European Social Charter has enormous potentials, particularly now that the European Committee on Social Rights can receive collective complaints. Under the system of the European Convention for the Prevention of Torture, a specially appointed independent and impartial committee can visit and inspect all places of detention in an effort to strengthen the prohibition of torture. The reports produced and standards developed by this committee have an impact that goes far beyond the CPT. Last but not least, the Biomedicine Convention is a framework convention with elaborated principles, rights and standards in view of the developments in biology and medicine. The number of ratifications to this Convention is still relatively low and the Convention lacks an effective enforcement mechanism. Once more States have ratified this Convention and more Additional Protocols have been adopted, this Convention has the potential to acquire the place its deserves in the European area of health and human rights law.

---

142 ECtHR 10 May 2001, *Cyprus v. Turkey* (GC), no. 25781/94; ECtHR 9 March 2004, *Glass v. the UK*, no. 61827/00; ECtHR 8 July 2004, *Vo v. France* (GC), no. 53924/00; ECtHR 7 March 2006, *Evans v. the UK*, no. 6339/05; ECtHR 10 April 2007, *Evans v. the UK* (GC), no. 6339/05; ECtHR 6 May 2008, *Juhnke v. Turkey*, no. 20817/04; ECtHR 7 October 2008, *Bogumil v. Portugal*, no. 35228/03; ECtHR 23 March 2010, *M.A.K. & R.K. v. the UK*, no. 45901/05 & 40146/06 and ECtHR 1 April 2010, *S.H. et al. v. Austria*, no. 57813/00.

CHAPTER 2

THE EUROPEAN UNION AND HEALTH AND HUMAN RIGHTS

Janne Rothmar Herrmann and Brigit Toebes*

1. INTRODUCTION

1.1. THE AIM OF THIS CHAPTER

In this section we will explore the ways in which EU law has a bearing on health and human rights. The European Union is still predominantly an economic organisation, and as such its primary focus is economic integration rather than issues such as human rights, health protection and promotion. Nonetheless, with the entering into force of the European Charter on Fundamental Rights (ECFR) through the adoption of the Lisbon Treaty, the EU has become increasingly engaged with human rights. Furthermore, while the main responsibility for health protection and promotion lies primarily with national authorities,[1] EU laws and policies can have a substantial impact on the health protection and promotion of Europeans. It is one of the Union's explicit aims to raise the standard of living and quality of life.[2] This aim has resulted in various policies and strategies relevant for the protection and promotion of health. Finally, the rules of the internal market impact upon national health systems, as various aspects of healthcare can be caught by the free movement rules.

EU law does not, however, provide for a comprehensive framework in the area of health and human rights. Rather, one finds a patchwork of rules, which may, in one way or another, affect the area of health and human rights. As such, it will be impossible to provide a complete and comprehensible overview of all the EU regulation that is potentially relevant to this study.

* We thank Catherine Jacqueson (University of Copenhagen, Denmark) and Aart Hendriks (Leiden University, the Netherlands) for their useful comments to an earlier version of this chapter. An adjusted version of this chapter has been published in *European Human Rights Law Review* 4(2011), pp. 419–436.

1 Article 168 TFEU.

2 Article 9 TFEU.

Below, an attempt will be made to describe and discuss the most important aspects of the field. First, attention will be paid to the way in which the EU engages with health and human rights directly, through the recognition of health and human rights (Section 2). Subsequently, the focus will be on a number of specific responsibilities of the EU in the area of health, based on Article 168 of the Treaty on the Functioning of the European Union (Section 3). Then, the concept of free movement is discussed in relation to health and human rights (Section 4). In this regard, attention will be paid to the free movement of patients, healthcare professionals, pharmaceuticals, blood, and cells and tissues, as well as the issue of data protection, which, besides being connected to the creation of a free internal market for data flow, is also strongly connected to the right to privacy under the European Charter (Section 6).

1.2. THE EU, ITS INSTITUTIONS AND FUNCTIONING

The European Union as we know it today is the further development of an agreement between France, Germany, Italy, Belgium, the Netherlands and Luxemburg in the aftermath of World War II to collaborate on the production of coal and steel. To overcome the repercussions of the War and to avoid warfare between the European nations, these countries agreed, in the 1951 Treaty of Paris, to give up part of their national sovereignty, thus establishing the European Coal and Steel Community. In time, the Community expanded not only in numbers, as the circle of Member States widened, but also in substance, with the adoption of the subsequent treaties of Rome, Maastricht, Amsterdam and Lisbon. The aim of the European Union is to create an ever-closer union among the peoples of Europe, implying that the Union has a wider aim than the traditional international collaboration.[3]

On 1 December 2009, the Treaty of Lisbon entered into force, establishing one European Union instead of a pillar-based organisation with different governing structures and rules for the European Community and the European Union. At the same time, the Lisbon Treaty (or Reform Treaty) does not replace, but only amends, the current EU and EC Treaties. Among other issues, it provides for a strengthened role of the European Parliament and national parliaments, simplified methods and voting rules, and stronger human rights protection through the reference in Article 6 of the Treaty on the European Union (TEU) to the above-mentioned European Charter of Fundamental Rights (ECFR). Altogether, throughout this section on EU law reference will be made to two important EU Treaties: the TEU (Treaty of the European Union) and the TFEU (Treaty on the Functioning of the European Union). In addition, reference will be made to the ECFR (the European Charter on Fundamental Rights).

3 Article 1 TEU.

The Treaties form the legal basis for the various legal measures the Union can take. Each measure has a distinct set of legal implications, and the Treaty will usually include directions on which legal instrument to use, depending on the area of regulation in question. *Regulations* can implicate both rights and duties for the European citizens and do not need any implementing measures, therefore making them directly applicable. *Directives*, on the other hand, need to be transposed into the Member States' national laws, and therefore provide the Member States with some leeway as to the interpretation and the means by which the required results are to be achieved. *Decisions* are binding for those to whom the Decision is addressed, and do not leave any leeway in the implementation. Unless otherwise stated, Regulations enter into force 20 days after publication. Most Directives also require publication to enter into force. Member States can file an annulment claim before the Court of First Instance e.g. if there is, in their view, no legal basis in the Treaty for implementing the proposed EU Regulation.

The European Court of Justice (ECJ), including the lower Court of First Instance, is one of the core bodies of the European Union. Its role is to make sure that EU legislation is interpreted and applied in the same way in all EU countries. It ensures, for example, that national courts do not give different rulings on the same issue regarding EU law. The Court has the power to settle legal disputes between EU Member States, EU institutions, businesses and individuals.

2. EU, HEALTH AND HUMAN RIGHTS

This section will focus on the way the EU institutions deal with health and human rights. As mentioned, in December 2009 the Lisbon Treaty entered into force. This Treaty has important implications for the way in which the EU engages with human rights law.

Firstly, with the entry into force of the Lisbon Treaty there is now a legal basis for the EU to accede to the ECHR.[4] Once acceded to the ECHR, the EU will be able submit its actions to external judicial review. This implies that acts by the EU that involve or infringe on a human rights issue may be the subject of scrutiny by the ECtHR. As was shown in Chapter 1 on the Council of Europe, the ECtHR increasingly engages with health issues. As such, the future scenario may be that the ECtHR scrutinises an act by the EU that involves a health and human rights issue just as it may be possible that the ECJ will assess and enforce the human rights adopted in the ECFR.

---

4 Article 6(2) TEU.

Furthermore, with the entry into force of the Lisbon Treaty, the European Charter on Fundamental Rights (ECFR) was given binding legal effect equal to the Treaties.[5] As will be clarified below, this document brings together a number of rights previously recognised in a variety of legislative instruments, including the Treaty, various Directives, as well as Council of Europe instruments, so as to make a comprehensive overview. The ECFR contains seven Chapters (dignity, freedoms, equality, solidarity, citizens' rights, justice, and general provisions). Taking a closer look at the rights in these Chapters, we see that several rights throughout these Chapters can be relevant to the promotion and protection of health, and to the area of health and human rights.

Firstly, in Chapter I ('dignity'), we find a general right to dignity, the right to life, the right to integrity of the person, and the prohibition of torture and inhuman and degrading treatment.[6] Article 1 on the right to dignity can be seen as the core right underlying all the other health-related rights. As will also be demonstrated in Chapter 3, the right to life in Article 2 can also be relevant when it comes to health-related matters. Potentially, therefore, looking at the case law of the ECtHR, this right can play a role when it comes to the status of the foetus, end-of-life decision-making, and possibly, in connection with the right to healthcare, in situations where a denial of access to healthcare has lead to life-threatening situations.[7]

Article 3 on the integrity of the person also merits some special attention. The second paragraph of this provision refers to informed consent and prohibits eugenic practices (in particular the 'selection of persons'), the sale of body parts and reproductive cloning. It remains uncertain what the scope of these provisions will be. It is likely that they will be interpreted in light of the more elaborate and more specific international human rights provisions on which the Charter is based, including the Biomedicine Convention.[8] For example, in line with the approach taken in the Biomedicine Convention, it is likely that the

5 Article 6(1) TEU. Europa, summaries of legislation at http://europa.eu/legislation_summaries/justice_freedom_security/citizenship_of_the_union/l33501_en.htm#, accessed September 2010 and http://europa.eu/rapid/pressReleasesAction.do?reference=IP/10/1348&format=HTML&aged=0&language=EN&guiLanguage=en, accessed November 2010.

6 Human dignity (Article 1), the right to life (Article 2), integrity of the person (Article 3), torture and inhuman and degrading treatment (Article 4).

7 See, also, McHale, 2010, see note 15, p. 10. The ECtHR discussed the right to life of the foetus in Vo. v. France, application no. 53924/00, judgment of 08/07/2004. Whether the right to life embraces a right to die was addressed in ECtHR, *Pretty v. UK*, 29 April 2002, no. 2346/02, and access to healthcare and the right to life came to the fore in ECtHR, *Cyprus v. Turkey*, 6 December 2001 (GC), no. 25781/94.

8 Council of Europe, Convention on Human Rights and Biomedicine (1997, adopted in 2009, not ratified by, e.g., the UK), which sets out the fundamental principles applicable in day-to-day medicine, as well as those applicable to new technologies in human biology and medicine.

selection of the sex of embryos will be prohibited, except where serious hereditary sex-related disease is to be avoided.[9]

Chapter II of the Charter ('freedoms') contains, *inter alia*, the rights to respect for private and family life and the protection of personal data.[10] These provisions can play a role when it comes to the protection of medical data, the patients' entitlement to view their medical records, and the protection of data with respect to medical research. It is important to note that Article 8 on the protection of personal data is not part of the ECHR,[11] although the ECtHR case law demonstrates that the protection of personal data is encompassed in Article 8 of the ECHR.

Chapter III ('equality') stresses the non-discrimination principle (Article 21), which draws from Article 14 ECHR.[12] This provision could become of relevance when addressing matters relating to equal access to healthcare services, and as such, it could reinforce the right to healthcare in Article 35.

The 'right to healthcare' is contained in Article 35 ECFR in Chapter IV ('solidarity') of the Charter:

> 'Everyone has the right of access to preventive health care and the right to benefit from medical treatment under the conditions established by national laws and practices. A high level of human health protection shall be ensured in the definition and implementation of all Union policies and activities.'[13]

This provision has two dimensions: it recognises the right to healthcare of Europeans, and it establishes a duty to ensure the protection of health within the policies and activities of the Union. The second part of the provision is a repetition of the 'mainstreaming' obligation in Article 168 TFEU (see below). It has been observed that the entitlement to healthcare in the first sentence may actually encompass the broader 'right to health' as the term 'preventive health care' may potentially encompass the notion of the pre-conditions for health.[14]

---

9 On sex selection see, *inter alia*, Brigit Toebes, 'Sex selection under international human rights law', *Medical Law International*, vol. 9(3), 2008, pp. 197–225.

10 Privacy: Article 7; data protection: Article 8.

11 As Hervey and McHale indicate, this provision could apply to national measures implementing the Data Protection Directive (see Tamara K. Hervey and Jean V. McHale: *Health Law and the European Union*, Cambridge University Press, 2004, chapter 5 and p. 409).

12 See, also, Tamara K. Hervey, 'The Right to Health in European Union Law', in Tamara K. Hervey, Jeff Kenner (eds.), *Economic and social rights under the EU Charter of Fundamental Rights: a legal perspective*, Oxford: Hart Publishing, 2003, pp. 127–150, at pp. 202–203.

13 EUFCR.

14 Hervey, 2003, see note 12, p. 202. See, also, T. Hervey, 'We don't see a connection: "the right to health" in the EU Charter and European Social Charter', in G. de Búrca and B. de Witte (eds.), *Social Rights in Europe*, Oxford: Oxford University Press, 2005, pp. 305–355.

The provision may only have limited implications for Member States, as it binds them only to the extent that they are implementing EU law. Also limiting the scope of the provision may be the phrase 'under the conditions established by national laws and practices'. Yet McHale suggests that Article 35 may, in the future, be used by individuals travelling to another Member State to receive treatment, then claiming reimbursement for the cost of such treatment[15] McHale highlights an interesting reference to the right to healthcare in the Charter in an opinion of the Advocate General.[16] The case concerned the question of whether the Greek authorities could refuse the reimbursement of the cost of treatment in a private hospital abroad. The Advocate General stated hat:

> 'However, although the case law takes as the main point of reference the fundamental freedoms established in the Treaty, there is another aspect which is becoming more and more important in the Community sphere, namely the right of citizens to health care, proclaimed in Article 35 of the Charter of Fundamental Rights of the European Union, (24) since, "being a fundamental asset, health cannot be considered solely in terms of social expenditure and latent economic difficulties". This right is perceived as a personal entitlement, unconnected to a person's relationship with social security, and the Court of Justice cannot overlook that aspect.'

Here, the right to healthcare was mentioned in support of a 'free movement' claim to healthcare. The question then arises, whether such claims actually construe a right to healthcare, or whether they are essentially free movement claims. Furthermore, they may lead to concerns about resource allocation at the national level.[17]

Furthermore, Chapter IV on solidarity rights contains a number of other rights that are of importance for the protection and promotion of health, including social security and social assistance, and environmental protection.[18] There is a growing amount of research indicating that the social determinants of health (i.e. the way people are raised and educated, and the way people live and work) are decisive for people's health.[19] Based on this notion, there have been increasing calls on governments to enhance the so-called 'social determinants of

15 Jean McHale, 'Fundamental rights and health care', in Elias Mossialis *et al*, *Health Systems Governance in Europe*, European Observatory on Health Systems and Policies, Cambridge: Cambridge University Press, 2010, pp. 282–314, at p. 303.

16 AG Opinion (Ruiz-Jarabo Colomer), Case C-444/05, *Stamatelaki* [2007] ECR I-3185.

17 McHale, 2010, see note 15, p. 305.

18 Social security: Article 34 (including in the event of maternity and illness), environmental protection: Article 37.

19 *Inter alia*, World Health Organization/Commission on the Social Determinants of Health, *Closing the gap in a generation, Health equity through action on the social determinants of health*, WHO 2008, available at www.who.int/social_determinants/thecommission/finalreport/en/index.html.

health'.[20] Rights that guarantee such conditions to health, such as the ones included in the Charter, can potentially play a role in strengthening these calls on governments. It is also possible that these rights encourage the EU institutions to prioritise the emphasis on the social determinants of health in their laws and policies

Lastly, the question arises as to what the scope of application of the Charter will be. This is defined by Article 51 ECFR: the Charter is addressed to the bodies and institutions of the Union with due regard for the principle of subsidiarity, and to Member States only when they are implementing Union law. As such, the Charter does not create new competencies, but rather imposes certain restrictions on the Union's institutions in exercising the competencies allocated to them by the Treaties. It also imposes certain restrictions on States when acting within the scope of Union law, i.e. when implementing Union law or applying it.[21]

Generally speaking, the provisions of the Charter have the potential to provide a normative framework when it comes to judicial review of EU legislation and administrative acts. Furthermore, the provisions of the Charter may become reference points for the interpretation of provisions of EU law, also for Member States when they are implementing EU law.[22] The fact that the wording of the provisions is rather general in nature may be problematic. However, as McHale suggests, these provisions are likely to be qualified in practice when they are interpreted and applied.[23]

3. SPECIFIC RESPONSIBILITIES FOR HEALTH IN THE EU

3.1. FOCUS ON HUMAN HEALTH IN THE NEW TFEU

The EU institutions now have a significant impetus to focus more on human health in their policies and activities with the adoption of the new Article 9 TFEU, which focuses on policy-making within the EU. This provision contains a 'social clause' stating that the activities of the Union have to take into account a number of social objectives, including the protection of human health.

20 WHO/CSDH, 2008.

21 EU Network of Independent Experts in Fundamental Rights (CFR-CDF), Report on the Situation of Fundamental Rights in The European Union and its Member States in 2002, p. 11.

22 Hervey and McHale, 2004, see note 11, pp. 406–410.

23 McHale, 2010, see note 15, p. 298.

Furthermore, with the adoption of the Treaty of Lisbon, the previous public health Article (152 TEC) has been replaced by the new Article 168 of the Treaty on the Functioning of the European Union (TFEU). The new Article reads as follows:

1. A high level of human health protection shall be ensured in the definition and implementation of all Union policies and activities. Union action, which shall complement national policies, shall be directed towards improving public health, preventing physical and mental illness and diseases, and obviating sources of danger to physical and mental health. Such action shall cover the fight against the major health scourges, by promoting research into their causes, their transmission and their prevention, as well as health information and education, and monitoring, early warning of and combating serious cross-border threats to health. The Union shall complement the Member States' action in reducing drugs-related health damage, including information and prevention.
2. The Union shall encourage cooperation between the Member States in the areas referred to in this Article and, if necessary, lend support to their action. It shall in particular encourage cooperation between the Member States to improve the complementarity of their health services in cross-border areas. Member States shall, in liaison with the Commission, coordinate among themselves their policies and programmes in the areas referred to in paragraph 1. The Commission may, in close contact with the Member States, take any useful initiative to promote such coordination, in particular initiatives aiming at the establishment of guidelines and indicators, the organisation of exchange of best practice, and the preparation of the necessary elements for periodic monitoring and evaluation. The European Parliament shall be kept fully informed.
3. The Union and the Member States shall foster cooperation with third countries and the competent international organisations in the sphere of public health.
4. By way of derogation from Article 2(5) and Article 6(a) and in accordance with Article 4(2)(k) the European Parliament and the Council, acting in accordance with the ordinary legislative procedure and after consulting the Economic and Social Committee and the Committee of the Regions, shall contribute to the achievement of the objectives referred to in this Article through adopting in order to meet common safety concerns:
   (a) measures setting high standards of quality and safety of organs and substances of human origin, blood and blood derivatives; these measures shall not prevent any Member State from maintaining or introducing more stringent protective measures;
   (b) measures in the veterinary and phytosanitary fields which have as their direct objective the protection of public health;

(c) measures setting high standards of quality and safety for medicinal products and devices for medical use.

5. The European Parliament and the Council, acting in accordance with the ordinary legislative procedure and after consulting the Economic and Social Committee and the Committee of the Regions, may also adopt incentive measures designed to protect and improve human health and in particular to combat the major cross-border health scourges, measures concerning monitoring, early warning of and combating serious cross-border threats to health, and measures which have as their direct objective the protection of public health regarding tobacco and the abuse of alcohol, excluding any harmonisation of the laws and regulations of the Member States.
6. The Council, on a proposal from the Commission, may also adopt recommendations for the purposes set out in this Article.
7. Union action shall respect the responsibilities of the Member States for the definition of their health policy and for the organisation and delivery of health services and medical care. The responsibilities of the Member States shall include the management of health services and medical care and the allocation of the resources assigned to them. The measures referred to in paragraph 4(a) shall not affect national provisions on the donation or medical use of organs and blood.

Article 168 TFEU differs to some extent from the previous Article 152 TEC.[24] However, the general idea of EU action in the field of health remains the same, i.e. that it shall be directed towards improving public health, preventing illness and obviating sources of danger to health. Added to this provision has been the statement that such action should cover monitoring, early warning of, and combating, serious cross-border diseases. As a result, the range of possible actions available to the fight against the major health scourges has now been expanded.[25]

Furthermore, the primary responsibility for the organisation and delivery of healthcare is still left to each Member State. Like in the old provision 152 TEC, the Union has competency to regulate within the specific areas of public health policies mentioned in subparagraph 4, sections (a)-(e), which includes setting minimum standards for quality and safety in relation to organs and tissues of human origin, blood and blood products, measures in the veterinary field which have as their direct objective the protection of public health, and general incentives designed to protect and improve human health, as long as these incentives do not require any harmonisation of national laws and regulations.

---

24 For a discussion of (the old) Article 152 TEC, see Hervey and McHale, 2004, see note 11, pp. 76–81.

25 European Health Management Association, *EU Briefing: The Impact of the Treaty of Lisbon on EU Health Law*, available at www.ehma.org, accessed September 2010.

New to the provision is that the EU shall encourage cooperation between the Member States to improve health services in cross-border areas. In addition, the Commission may take initiatives to promote the coordination between Member States so as to establish guidelines and indicators, to organise the exchange of best practices, and to prepare the necessary elements for periodic monitoring and evaluation (paragraph 2). This text seems to expand the EU's ability to operate in these areas and to enable the EU to play a more proactive role when it comes to cross-border health services, for example.

Finally, while the principle of subsidiarity has been maintained (paragraph 7), this has been expanded with a reference to the responsibility of Member States for the management of health services and medical care and the allocation of the resources assigned to them. In addition, the new paragraph 5 refers to the possibility for the European Parliament and the Council to adopt incentive measures designed to combat serious cross-border threats to health and measures regarding tobacco and the use of alcohol.

Altogether, with the adoption of the Lisbon Treaty, the scope of operation of the EU in the area of health has expanded to some extent. Although it remains as yet unclear how this will take effect in practice, there is an intention to play a more proactive role in this area, while this provision can also form a legal basis for addressing the role of the EU in such areas.

3.2. EU ENGAGEMENT WITH PUBLIC HEALTH

Public health is, by nature, an issue that often requires transnational measures. As such, the specialised UN organisation, the World Health Organization (WHO) is especially engaged with the promotion, safeguarding and regulation of international public health. However, regional cooperation is equally important when addressing and combating, e.g. contagious diseases affecting populations regionally, or even globally.

Public health touches on a number of fundamental human rights. On the one hand, an adequate protection of public health offers some protection at the individual level in terms of the right to health. On the other hand, state measures that seek to secure public health may also infringe on other rights, e.g. the right to freedom of person, privacy and physical integrity.[26]

As explained above, the EU has competence (Article 168 TFEU) to complement national action on health. This mainly provides the legal scope for protecting

[26] See e.g. the International Health Regulations (WHO) 2005, www.who.int/ihr/en/, accessed February 11, 2011.

people against health threats and disease, for promoting healthy lifestyles, and for helping national authorities in the EU cooperate on health issues. In other words, the EU is required by its founding Treaty to ensure that human health is protected as part of all its policies, and to work with the EU countries to improve public health, to prevent human illness, and to eliminate sources of danger to physical and mental health.

The EU's strategy for protecting and improving human health is chiefly implemented through the Commission's health programmes, currently the Programme of Community action in the field of public health 2008–2013, which came into force on 1 January 2008 and followed the first programme (2003–2008) which financed over 300 projects[27] and an EU Health Strategy (2008–2013).[28]

The EU Health Strategy is a strategic approach to EU health policy for the period 2008–2013. It aims at providing an overarching framework that covers not only core European health issues, but also broader aspects, such as health in all policies and global health. One of the objectives of the Strategy is strengthening the EU's voice in global health. This includes responding to health threats in Third World countries and strengthening coordination between international organisations. As such, the human rights values that are enshrined in the Treaty are also meant to be emphasised and promoted in the EU's relations with the global community. Within the EU the main objective of the Strategy is to ensure health and to control future health expenses in the face of the ageing populations of the Member States of the EU. Public health relating to poor diet physical activity and the consumption of alcohol, tobacco and drugs is a key area of action in this respect. The protection of human health is a Treaty obligation, as mentioned *supra*. Improving safety and security and protecting citizens against health threats have therefore always been at the heart of Community health policy. The Strategy stresses that the Commission will continue its work within this classic area of EU health policy, but also points to other emerging issues to be dealt with, including pandemics, biological incidents, bioterrorism, food safety, climate change, workers' safety and patient safety.[29]

The Programme of Union action in the field of public health is an instrument that helps bring the EU's Health Strategy to life. The Programme has three overarching objectives. It seeks to *improve citizens' health security* by promoting actions relating to patient safety through high quality and safe healthcare, scientific advice and risk assessment, safety and quality of organs and blood; to

27 See http://ec.europa.eu/health/, accessed 10 February 2011.

28 See http://ec.europa.eu/health-eu/doc/whitepaper_en.pdf, accessed 10 February 2011.

29 Objective 2 of the Strategy.

promote health by reducing health inequalities, increasing healthy life years, and promoting healthy ageing; and finally, to *generate and disseminate health information* and knowledge by facilitating the exchange of knowledge and best practice on health issues.

As mentioned *supra*, measures on public health often cross national and regional borders. Whereas the EU, as such, is not a member of the WHO, each EU Member State is. In the International Health Regulations, which is the only binding international instrument addressing epidemic diseases, Article 57(3) addresses the legal challenges that may arise for the EU Member States in this respect, as the provision stipulates that state parties that are members of a regional economic integration organisation shall apply, in their mutual relationships, the common rules in force in that regional economic integration organisation. Any measures imposed by the WHO – such as refusing certain goods into the country – that affect any area of competency falling within the scope of EU law must thus be addressed on the initiative of the European Commission, even though it is the Member States and not the Union as such that are duty bound by WHO regulations. As such, the Union may interact in the area of public health in various ways, and thus, may also correspondingly interact with human rights in various ways.

Clinical research

One area that has seen EU engagement in the area of health has been the achievements in harmonising the regulation of clinical trials. Clinical trials are investigations in humans intended to discover or verify the effects of one or more investigational medicinal products. As such, it is a necessary part of the development and improvement of healthcare, while, at the same time, touching upon human rights values such as autonomy, physical integrity and privacy.

Requirements for the conduct of clinical trials in the EU are provided for in Directive 2001/20/EC of the European Parliament, and of the Council of 4 April 2001, on the approximation of the laws, regulations and administrative provisions of the Member States relating to the implementation of good clinical practice in the conduction of clinical trials in medicinal products for human use (the Clinical Trials Directive). The Clinical Trials Directive was concretised further by Directive 2005/28/EC of 8 April 2005, laying down principles and detailed guidelines for good clinical practice as regards investigational medicinal products for human use, as well as the requirements for authorisation of the manufacturing or importation of such products (the Good Clinical Practice Directive).

At first glance, the EU involvement in the regulation of clinical research appears to be driven by a harmonisation-based rationale;[30] by harmonising the administrative provisions for the conduction of clinical trials, the effective conduction of such trials is not only secured, but it also helps to build a 'single market culture' around pharmaceutical products for the benefit of pharmaceutical companies and patients alike, but also around research, as cross-community research is seen as benefiting industry, employment and the ability to compete on a global market. However, the Clinical Trials Directive also contains a number of provisions which regulate the rights of the research subjects and which contain particular references to human rights values, such as the right to physical and mental integrity and privacy. As such, the EU legal framework complements the international and regional regulatory instruments also addressing clinical research, e.g. the Helsinki Declaration, the WHO regulations, and most importantly in Europe, the Council of Europe's Convention on Human Rights and Biomedicine.

4. FREE MOVEMENT & HEALTH

4.1. INTRODUCTION

The *raison d'être* of the European Union is the creation of the single market. To that end, four fundamental freedoms form the core of European Union law, i.e. the free movement of persons, goods, capital and services. The four freedoms have important implications for a wide spectre of health law, ranging from patients, healthcare professionals and medicines The four freedoms, as we will elaborate on *infra*, have had a substantial impact on the development of cross-border issues in health law.

4.2. FREE MOVEMENT OF SERVICES: CROSS-BORDER HEALTHCARE SERVICES

4.2.1. The legal framework

A distinction can be made here between two legal regimes. Firstly, there is the mechanism of Regulation 883/2004/EC (the previous 1408/71/EEC), on the co-ordination of social security systems.[31] This Regulation provides social

30 See also Hervey and McHale, 2004, see note 11, pp. 237–239.

31 The new Regulation aims to modernise and simplify the co-ordination of Member States' social security systems by allowing posted workers to remain insured in their home country for a period of two years (Article 21-1 of the Regulation).

security coverage, including in the field of healthcare, to certain groups (roughly speaking, insured persons in Europe) exercising the right to free movement.

The second route is based on Article 56 TFEU (the previous 49 TEC), which prohibits restrictions on the freedom to provide services within the EU. This provision implies an enforceable right of patients to travel abroad to access healthcare services.[32]

Triggered by the restrictive pre-authorisation policies that Member States applied, this right has been addressed in a number of cases before the ECJ.[33] The decisions of the ECJ reflect a gradual widening of the possibility of seeking medical services paid by the state or insurance of origin in other Member States. For an evaluation of this case law, a distinction needs to be made between extramural (non-hospital or outpatient) and intramural (hospital or inpatient) care. When it comes to extramural care, the ECJ is of the opinion that prior authorisation is not justified. In principle, therefore, based on the Court's case law, Member States have to reimburse the costs of such treatments. In this regard, the ECJ is of the opinion that the removal of the requirement of prior authorisation for such services would not result in a risk of seriously undermining the financial balance of national social security systems. As a result, this removal would not jeopardise the overall level of protection of public health.[34]

However, the ECJ is more cautious when it comes to inpatient care. Here the Court takes the position that Member States should have more freedom to decide how to organise this form of healthcare.[35] Central in the Court's approach is the requirement of planning: national authorities should have sufficient opportunities to plan healthcare in their hospitals. In this regard, the Court stresses that 'the public health' and 'the survival of the population' are at issue'.[36] Free movement of intramural care may, therefore, be restricted through a system of prior authorisation. There are, however, two requirements: the required care has to be available, and the necessity of the care should be determined on the basis of international criteria.[37] In the *Watts* case, for

32 Hervey and McHale, 2004, see note 11, p. 124.

33 Willy Palm and Irene A. Glinos, 'Enabling patient mobility in the EU: between free movement and coordination', in Mossialis et al, 2010, see note 15, pp. 509–560, at p. 517.

34 Case C-385/99 *Müller-Fauré and van Riet* [2003] ECR I-4509, paragraphs 93–98 (dental treatment of a Dutch person in Germany). See, also, J.W. Van de Gronden and J.J.M. Sluijs, 'De betekenis van het EG-Verdrag voor het reguleren van de zorgmarkt' [The implications of the EC Treaty for the regulation of the healthcare market], *Gezondheidszorg en Europees Recht, Preadvies 2009*, The Hague: SDU, 2009, pp. 103–181, at p. 110.

35 Van de Gronden and Sluijs, 2009, see note 34, p. 110.

36 Case C-157/99 *Geraets-Smits and Peerbooms* [2001] ECR I-5473, paragraph 74. See also Van de Gronden and Sluijs, 2009, see note 34, at p. 110.

37 Smits & Peerbooms, see note 36, paragraphs 107 and 97. See, also, Van de Gronden and Sluijs, 2009, see note 34, at pp. 110–111.

example, the ECJ found that in order to refuse authorisation to go abroad for treatment, the Member State must establish that the waiting time in the domestic healthcare system does not exceed the period which is acceptable on the basis of an objective medical assessment of the clinical needs of the patient.[38]

This case-by-case approach has been consolidated in a Directive, which was presented by the Commission in July 2008 and accepted – with amendments – by the European Parliament in December 2010, and subsequently adopted by the Council in February 2011.[39] According to its Preamble, the Directive is intended to ensure a more general and effective application of principles developed by the ECJ (paragraph (8)). Its aim is to establish rules for facilitating access to safe and high-quality cross-border healthcare in the Union and to ensure patient mobility (Preamble, paragraph (10)). The preamble also stresses the overarching rules of 'universality, access to good quality care, equity, and solidarity' (paragraph 21), and it stresses that all patients 'are to be treated equitably on the basis of their healthcare needs' (paragraph 21). The Preamble also indicates that cross-border healthcare is still the exception, by stating that the 'vast majority of patients in the Union receive healthcare in their own country and prefer to do so' (para. 39).

Like the case law of the ECJ, starting point for the Directive is that Member States may not make the reimbursement of costs of cross-border healthcare subject to prior authorisation. However, contrary to the Court's case law, the Directive does not make a clear-cut distinction between intra- and extramural care. In other words, prior authorisation is not merely limited to hospital (intramural) care. Based on Article 8, prior authorisation is limited to healthcare which is made subject to planning requirements, and which either involves an overnight stay in a hospital or requires the use of highly specialised and cost-intensive medical infrastructure or medical equipment. In addition, it may involve treatments that present a particular risk to the patient or to the population, or when there are doubts about the quality or safety of care provided by the healthcare provider concerned.[40] Prior authorisation may not be refused when the necessary healthcare cannot be provided on its territory within a reasonable time limit.[41]

---

38 Case C-372/04 *Watts* [2006] ECR I-4325.

39 European Parliament legislative resolution of 19 January 2011 on the Council position at first reading with a view to the adoption of a directive of the European Parliament and of the Council on the application of patients' rights in cross-border health care (11038/2010 – C7–0266/2010 – 2008/0142 (COD)). Council of the European Union, Directive on cross-border health care adopted, Brussels, 28 February 2011 (7056/11).

40 Article 8 paragraphs 1–2 of the Directive.

41 Article 8–5 of the Directive.

Furthermore, the Directive seeks to ensure that patients seeking healthcare services in another country have access to information about the possibility and conditions of seeking these services. For this, the Directive provides for the establishment of national contact points for cross-border healthcare. These bodies are to facilitate the exchange of information on healthcare providers, patients' rights, complaints procedures, and mechanisms for seeking remedies.[42]

The Directive seems an important step in securing cross-border healthcare. Yet, from a patient and human rights perspective a few words of caution should be made. Firstly, the remark in the Preamble that patients are to be treated 'based on healthcare needs' needs to be considered with some caution: are cross-border healthcare providers truly able to adequately assess the healthcare needs of foreign patients? Furthermore, what will the role of the national contact points be? Will these bodies succeed in providing reliable information on cross-border healthcare services? In this regard, to what extent will hospitals and other healthcare providers be willing, and financially able, to share information in a transparent fashion? Altogether, to what extent will the quality of healthcare services across borders be guaranteed? More generally, the question arises as to who, and how many patients, will benefit from this legislation: will it be well-informed patients who are able to travel abroad, or will it also benefit the population as a whole?

4.2.2. Cross-border healthcare and issues of morality

A major incentive for mobile patients to cross borders in the field of healthcare is in cases where the provision of the treatment in question is unlawful in the country of residence. This scenario is especially well-known in connection with reproductive healthcare, and consequently there is a considerable traffic in this respect, of e.g. Irish women travelling to England to get legal terminations of pregnancies. The question of abortion was, unsurprisingly, the first controversial medical procedure to be exposed to the EU law perspective. The fact that EU law provides the right to shop for healthcare services, including those that are prohibited or otherwise unavailable in a patient's home country, was established in *SPUC v. Grogan*,[43] as this was the first case to establish that a controversial medical procedure (abortion) had the status of a *service* within the meaning of the EC Treaty when performed legally in the Member State in question. In the case which was referred to the ECJ as a prejudicial question, and which dealt with an Irish student organisation's dissemination of information regarding abortion

42 Article 6 of the Directive.
43 ECJ, C-159/90 – 4 October 1991: *The Society for the Protection of Unborn Children Ireland Ltd. v. Stephen Grogan*, para. 21.

clinics in England, the Society for the Protection of Unborn Children (SPUC) argued that a termination could not be regarded as a service within the meaning of the Treaty because abortion was immoral and resulted in the destruction of the unborn child. The Court noted that a termination of a pregnancy, as lawfully practised in several Member States, was a medical activity which is normally provided for remuneration and may be carried out as part of a professional activity, and in any event, the Court had already held in the judgment in *Luisi and Carbone*[44] that medical activities fell within the scope of the Treaty. Whatever the merits of SPUC's arguments on the moral plane, they could not influence the answer to the question now before the ECJ. The Court noted that it was not for the Court to substitute its assessment for that of the legislature in those Member States in which the activities in question are practised legally.[45] The fact that the moral issues at stake could not alter the classification of abortion as a service means that controversial medical procedures are part of the market. Consequently, the individual now has other options besides adapting to the values enforced in national legislation. To the extent that other jurisdictions subscribe to different moral convictions, as implemented in the law, the individual may seek out offers more in keeping with her own notions of right and wrong by relying on the right to move freely within the EU.

This fact has created healthcare rights across the spectrum of morally sensitive healthcare services. Swedish women travel to Denmark in order to receive fertility treatment with *anonymous* donor sperm, Danish women travel to the Czech Republic in order to buy eggs for fertility treatment, *etc.* The divergence in national healthcare regulation and the EU based right to move has given rise to various legal disputes. In the English case of *Diane Blood*,[46] a woman wished to export the sperm of her deceased husband to another Member State in order to begin fertility treatment. The use of the deceased husband's sperm was unlawful in the country of residence because written consent from the husband had not been obtained prior to his death.[47] The British Human Fertilisation and Embryology Authority, which initially refused the woman, was later directed by the Court to take into account EU law, and consequently as a result of her rights under the free movement paradigm, Diane Blood subsequently gave birth to a son, Liam, after receiving fertility treatment using the sperm of her deceased husband.

---

44 Joined Cases 286/82 and 26/83 *Luisi and Carbone v. Ministero del Tesoro* [1984] ECR 377, para. 16.

45 ECJ, *SPUC v. Grogan*, see note 43, paras. 18 and 20.

46 *R v. Human Fertilisation and Embryology Authority*, ex parte Blood [1997] 2 All ER 687 Attorney-General's Reference (No. 3 of 1994) [1998] AC 245.

47 See more in depth Derek Morgan & Robert G. Lee: 'In the Name of the Father? Ex parte Blood: Dealing with Novelty and Anomaly', *Modern Law Review* 1997, 60:6, pp. 840–856.

4.2.3. *Evaluation*

Looking at the notion of free movement of healthcare from a health and human rights perspective, it seems that two opposing interests are at stake, which can both impact upon a right to healthcare services. While on the one hand, the possibility to seek cross-border healthcare services may enable the individual to realise his or her right to healthcare, it has also been suggested that it may undermine the financial stability and coherence of Member States.

Regarding the first perspective, for the European citizen it has been an uphill struggle to gain cross-border rights in healthcare. It is obvious from the case law and the Directive that healthcare is going to be increasingly framed to fit a single market. It has become clear (see above) that the marketisation of healthcare has increased freedom of choice and may also increase the level of quality of healthcare services for those seeking healthcare abroad. Thus, the rationale of market and competition law, according to which monopolies are to be avoided and competition is to be increased in order to increase consumer welfare, is gaining ground in the field of healthcare. Consequently, the impact of EU law has also focused more attention on individual rights in relation to the freedom to seek healthcare services abroad. This is especially relevant for women and couples who have the freedom to move and seek out reproductive healthcare in other countries with different legal regimes.

Even countries with publicly financed healthcare systems, which traditionally need to prioritise their limited funding carefully, and thus, which tend to focus on striking a balance between individual patients' rights and societal needs to control public spending, cannot evade the principle of free movement by restricting individual rights in this regard. The patient's country of residence may, however, still retain some control over public spending, as prior permission has to be obtained in most cases if the healthcare provided abroad is to be paid by the patient's country of residence.

Furthermore, as outlined *supra*, the framing of healthcare as a service has also made that morally sensitive healthcare services are being regarded from a market perspective. This development, through which sensitive ethical issues are, in terms of EU law, framed as services, has acted as a generator of rights - especially for women, whose reproductive privacy has traditionally been very closely scrutinised by the state.

On the other hand, it has been argued that the possibility of seeking healthcare abroad may undermine the financial stability and coherence of health systems within the Member States.[48] While it may put a financial strain on the 'receiving'

[48] Hervey, 2003, see note 12, p. 206.

country, it may also disadvantage the country of origin, when it has to reimburse the costs of cross-border care that had not been anticipated, or when this country has made investments in healthcare that are not being used. One only needs to look at the supporting comments from other Member States in the case law which developed the rights in relation to cross-border healthcare to realise that national governments are concerned about the potential national costs of cross-border care, as the lack of control over the cost associated with caring for the patients seems to be viewed as incompatible with a publicly funded healthcare system.

Looking at these matters from a health and human rights perspective, those managing to receive healthcare abroad are realising their 'right to health (care)', as guaranteed under international human rights law. However, this can only be a small component of the right to health, as most people will continue to make use of healthcare services nationally. The primary responsibility for realising a right to health(care) lies with national governments, and such free movement claims can never replace this responsibility. Being able to travel abroad to make use of healthcare services is one thing, but the main essential part of the right to health implies that individuals can enjoy good quality and accessible health services in their own country.

4.3. FREE MOVEMENT OF PERSONS: HEALTHCARE PROFESSIONALS

While patients increasingly cross borders to use healthcare services, there is a similar trend among healthcare professionals[49] moving abroad to provide healthcare services. It is a matter of efficiency that healthcare providers can work in the most appropriate facilities, wherever they are situated.[50] There are, however, also dangers and challenges, such as a brain drain from Eastern European countries, and a lack of continuity of care where healthcare professionals cross borders intermittently.[51] The increasing mobility of healthcare professionals in Europe also demands that similarly high standards of practice are upheld across Europe.

---

49 Healthcare professionals are doctors and other health workers. EU law makes a distinction between regulated and non-regulated professions. For a definition of this group of professionals, see Hervey and McHale, 2004, see note 11, p. 190. They argue in favour of the 'regulatory approach', based on which healthcare professionals are identified on the basis of the regulatory control by which they are supervised.

50 Miek Peeters, Martin McKee and Sherry Merkur, 'EU law and health professionals', in Mossialos *et al*, 2010, see note 15, pp. 589–634.

51 Peeters *et al*, 2010, see note 50, p. 590.

While EU employment law and EU law on the provision of services have a limited impact on the position of healthcare professionals,[52] the most important area in which EU law has affected healthcare professionals concerns the mutual recognition of qualifications in the context of the free movement of services.

As mentioned in the introduction, the aim of the European Union is the creation of the single market. One of the four freedoms in creating the single market is the freedom of persons working within the EU. In order to ensure the free movement of persons, EU law and jurisprudence seek to prohibit restrictions on the freedom of establishment. The freedom establishment is based on Article 43 EC (the former Article 52). This provision forms the basis for the freedom of movement of healthcare professionals. Article 47(3) EC Treaty mentions the need to coordinate the health professions, which was previously taken care of by a series of sectoral Directives as well as a general Directive. The sectoral Directives covered seven professions, including five medical ones: doctor, general nurse, midwife, dental surgeon, and pharmacist. The general Directive applied to all the other regulated health professionals that were not covered by the sectoral Directives.[53]

Following a consultation exercise in 2002, the Commission produced a draft consolidation Directive, which sought to revise and replace the sectoral Directives and the general Directive on mutual recognition.[54] This resulted in Directive 2005/36/EC on the *recognition* of professional qualifications, covering all of the above-mentioned professions.[55] Both the old and the new regime regulate all forms of mobility of health professionals. This regulatory system is broader than the mere regulation of the entry to the profession, as it also coordinates the *pursuit* or exercise of the profession, such as the presentation of documents and the applicability of national (disciplinary) measures.[56]

The new 'sectoral' regime largely follows the old regime. Like the old regime, it is based on the principle of mutual recognition. This obliges every Member State to respond positively to every request for recognition once the person concerned contains the necessary diplomas listed in Annex V of the Directive. When it comes to specialist qualifications, the system of mutual recognition only applies when the speciality exists in either all, or in at least two, Member States. In addition, the 'sectoral' regime sets minimum requirements for the training of

52 Hervey and McHale, 2004, see note 11, pp. 194–197. For example, on the Working Time Directive, see Peeters *et al*, 2010, see note 50, at pp. 623–629.
53 See also Peeters *et al*, 2010, see note 50, p. 598.
54 COM (2002) 119, amended COM (2004) 317 final.
55 Directive 2005/36/EC, 7 September 2005, OJ L 255, 30.9.2005, p. 22.
56 See also Peeters *et al*, 2010, see note 50, p. 592.

the healthcare providers mentioned above.[57] The Directive also provides for the establishment of a comitology committee, which is supposed to monitor and propose periodic revisions to the Directive.[58]

The new 'general' regime allows host Member States to decide each case on its own merits. Based on Article 14, the host Member State can, under certain circumstances, impose compensating measures, implying further training to ensure that the applicant meets the national criteria. Such measures may, however, no longer concern the provision of services, as this would potentially infringe upon the free movement of services.[59]

The above-mentioned rules concerned the *recognition* of a migrant health professional in another country. Another important element concerns the granting of permission for *establishment*, which can be regulated by national law to the extent that the national law does not infringe the right of establishment. This has been the subject of several cases before the ECJ.[60] Furthermore, the *establishment* of a health professional is difficult to distinguish from the *provision of services* by health professionals: while the establishment is more strictly regulated, there is more freedom when it comes to the provision of a service, which has led to so-called 'masked establishments'. According to Peeters *et al*, the new Directive fails to set a more concrete time limit for establishment, as was suggested in an earlier proposal for the Directive.[61]

Experts have voiced concerns on the current regulatory system in cross-border healthcare. Peeters *et al* point to several shortcomings in this regulatory framework. They argue that Directive 2005/36/EC fails to coordinate disciplinary measures and professional development systems. They also point, *inter alia*, to the lack of a clear definition of 'services' in relation to 'establishment' (leading to masked establishments), and the exclusion of telemedicine from the scope of application. It will not be easy to overcome these difficulties because, as explained by Peeters *et al*, the relationship between the state and the health professional is perceived differently across the EU countries.[62] Countries with strong traditions of liberal professions would not consider it acceptable to have high levels of state control.[63] According to Peeters *et al*, 'the principle of free

---

57 Articles 24–5, 31, 34–6, 44 and 46 of the Directive.

58 European Commission, *The EU Single Market*, available at http://ec.europa.eu/internal_market/qualifications/specific-sectors_en.htm (accessed November 2010). See, also, Peeters *et al*, 2009, see note 50, p. 598.

59 Peeters *et al*, 2010, see note 50, p. 609.

60 See also Peeters *et al*, 2010, see note 50, p. 610, who refer to several decisions of the ECJ in this respect.

61 Peeters *et al*, 2010, see note 50, p. 612.

62 Peeters *et al*, 2010, see note 50, p. 633.

63 Peeters *et al*, 2010, see note 50, p. 633.

movement will only be accepted by European citizens when they can overcome mistrust and when the remaining legal issues [...] are resolved.'

From a health and human rights perspective, it is important that basic standards of care are guaranteed across Europe and that the quality of care is constantly being promoted and improved. In this respect it is also important that there is a strong system of professional accountability.

4.4. FREE MOVEMENT OF GOODS: PHARMACEUTICALS

Access to medicines is an essential component of the right to health. However, from a human rights perspective, difficult issues also arise, mainly regarding the risks that medicines pose, and in relation to that, regarding their testing and administration.[64] This may compromise the quality component of the right to health. States can be said to have a 'duty to protect' the health of individuals through the adoption of legislation that regulates the pharmaceutical industry.[65]

European regulation is increasingly important in relation to the licensing and marketing of pharmaceuticals. While on the one hand, it is aimed at facilitating the free movement of goods, on the other hand, it seeks to harmonise consumer protection regimes, and as such, to prevent the above-mentioned concerns regarding the testing and administration of drugs.[66] As such, the EU is also taking on such a 'duty to protect' the health of individuals in the EU Member States.

Other problematic issues concern the availability and affordability of medicines in the developing world, as drugs are patented and cheap alternatives are often not available.[67] Similarly, research and production of medicines are often directed towards 'profitable diseases' – diseases that affect people who can afford to buy the necessary medicines – rather than towards 'neglected diseases' – those

64 Hervey and McHale give the example of the drug Thalidomide, which was given to pregnant women in the late 1950s and was linked to the development of major congenital disabilities. See Hervey and McHale, 2004, see note 11, p. 282. See, also, J. Abraham and G. Lewis, *Regulating Medicines in Europe: Competition, expertise and public health*, London/New York: Routledge, 2000.

65 See the definition of the tri-partite typology, see Chapter 3.

66 See Emily Jackson, *Medical Law, Text, Cases and Materials*, Oxford: Oxford University Press: 2006, p. 542.

67 Among the many publications and information on this issue, see, for example, the Business and Human Rights website at www.business-humanrights.org/, and for a comprehensive overview of the issues at stake see *Report of the Special Rapporteur, Mission to the World Trade Organization*. UN Document E/CN.4/2004/49/Add.1 (1 March 2004). Available at www.ohchr.ch, accessed October 2010.

that occur in the developing world.[68] In this regard, the question is increasingly raised as to whether pharmaceutical companies themselves bear a certain responsibility under human rights law for supplying affordable drugs to developing countries.[69] While these questions are most pertinent in the developing world, it has also been reported that several European nations have difficulties in ensuring the availability of affordable medicines for their populations.[70]

EU law provides for a complex regulatory system regarding the manufacture, marketing, surveillance and advertising of pharmaceuticals, and liability for harmful effects of such products.[71] Without discussing this area in detail, we will pay some attention here to the labelling and marketing of pharmaceutical products, the surveillance system, and product liability.

EU law contains a number of rules regarding the way medicinal products are to be presented to patients and consumers. The labelling, packaging and insertion of leaflets of medicinal products is currently regulated by Directive 2001/83/EC.[72] This Directive states, for example, that specific information is mandatory on the labels of medicines, while particulars have to be given in the official language or languages of the Member State.[73] The aim of providing such information is to ensure patient safety, to satisfy consumer choice, and to realise patients' rights.[74] Given the growing availability of over-the-counter medicines, this information becomes increasingly important.[75] Advertising of medicines is now also regulated by Directive 2001/83/EC.[76] For example, while over-the-counter products may be advertised to the public as a whole, prescription-only products may be advertised only to health professionals.[77]

Furthermore, there is a European system for the authorisation of medicinal products. The European Medicines Evaluation Agency (EMEA) was established in 1993 (since 2010 called European Medicines Authority (EMA)). A new system

---

68 See, *inter alia*, Paul Hunt *et al*, *Neglected diseases, A human rights analysis*, in World Health Organization, SEB Research, Special topics No. 6, 2007.

69 Right to Health Unit of the Essex University Human Rights Centre, *Draft Human Rights Guidelines for Pharmaceutical Companies in Relation to Access to Medicines*, available at www.essex.ac.uk/human_rights_centre/research/rth/projects.aspx, accessed May 2010.

70 See, for example, The Greens / European Free Alliance in the European Parliament, at www.greenmediabox.eu/archive/2010/11/18/innovation/, accessed February 2011.

71 More elaborately, see Hervey and McHale, 2004, see note 11, in Chapter 8.

72 Which has replaced Directive 92/27/EEC.

73 Articles 54–57 and 63(1) of Directive 2001/83/EC.

74 Hervey and McHale, 2004, see note 11, p. 302.

75 Hervey and McHale, 2004, see note 11, p. 302.

76 Previously regulated by Directive 92/28/EEC.

77 Article 88 of the Directive.

for the authorisation of medicinal products was established in 1995, which provides for two routes for the licensing of medicinal products:

1) a centralised procedure with applications made to the Committee for Medicinal Products for Human Use (CHMP), which is compulsory for products derived from biotechnology and optional for other innovative medicinal products;[78] and
2) a decentralised procedure or 'mutual recognition procedure', which is applicable to the majority of conventional medicinal products.

Altogether, Europe has chosen for a two-pronged approach, which supervises some drugs centrally, whereas applications for most conventional drugs are made through the licensing procedure in individual Member States. It has been noted that the number of centralised marketing authorisations is growing steadily, and that as a result, the EU institutions are playing an increasing role in the marketing authorisation of pharmaceuticals.[79] The centralised procedure has some advantages for the manufacturer: there is less bureaucracy and less national control.[80] But commentators have also pointed at a loss of control over the process at a national level, and at a lack of transparency in the EMA's system, which may lead to undue influence on the part of the pharmaceutical industry.[81] More importantly, from a human rights perspective it has been argued that the system favours the interests of the industry over those of patients or national health services.[82] From a human rights perspective, for which we can also look at the rights laid down in the EUCFR, it is important that the rights of patients are strongly embedded in the authorisation decisions of the CHMP.

When it comes to the decentralised procedure, issues arise that may also have a potential impact on the protection of the health and human rights of patients. Like the centralised procedure, the decentralised procedure has been criticised for representing the interests of the pharmaceutical industry, rather than those of patients. An important concern is that the procedure allows companies to 'cherry pick' the state with the least rigorous assessment. Companies will seek the most speedy and least demanding procedure, which may not be in the best interest of patients.[83]

---

78 As defined in the Annex (parts A and B) to Regulation 2309/93/EC.

79 Hervey and McHale, 2004, see note 11, pp. 294–295.

80 Jackson, 2006, see note 66, p. 543.

81 In Hervey and McHale, 2004, see note 11, pp. 295–296.

82 Hervey and McHale, 2004, see note 11, p. 296, referring to the view of the International Society of Drug Bulletins, cited in E. Mossialos and M. McKee, *EU Law and the Social Character of Health Care*, Brussels: PIE Peter Lang, 2002, p. 114.

83 Hervey and McHale, 2004, see note 11, p. 297.

A final important issue concerns product liability and the possibility of bringing actions before courts. Directive 85/374/EEC establishes the principle that the producer of a product is liable for damages caused by a defect in his product, including medicinal products. As such, the Directive gives consumers the right to compensation for defective medicines.[84] Triggered by the tragic thalidomide case,[85] liability is granted on the basis of the notion of 'strict liability', meaning liability regardless of negligence or culpability.[86] This is weakened, to some extent, by an optional measure in the Directive entitled 'development risks defence'. Based on Article 7(e), the producer will not be liable under the Directive if, at the time of putting the product into circulation, the state of scientific and technical knowledge was such that the risk of harm was not foreseeable. The interpretation and desirability of this principle is an issue of debate, and has also been addressed by the ECJ.[87] While on the one hand its abolition may have damaging consequences for manufacturers, on the other hand, it could benefit consumers.[88] This debate is important from a health and human rights perspective, as it balances the interests of consumers or patients against the rights of the manufacturing industry. The human rights framework, including Article 35 ECFR, could be used in defense of a strong(er) liability regime that does not allow for a 'development risks defence'.

4.5. FREE MOVEMENT OF GOODS: BLOOD (SAFETY)

As part of the EU's effort to promote and safeguard public health, it was only natural that the Union, in the wake of the spread of HIV/AIDS took action concerning the safety of blood. The whole concept of dealing in blood is potentially controversial from a human rights perspective, as Article 21 of the Convention on Biomedicine and Human Rights prohibits the commercialisation of human materials. Consequently, this provision and the viewpoint taken also by the WHO have influenced the EU measures on blood safety.[89]

The donation of blood touches on the right to health in the sense that a sufficient supply of safe blood is a prerequisite for the delivery of many healthcare services, including successful operations, optimum maternal health during child birth,

---

84 Directive 85/374/EEC, Article 2, as amended by Directive 99/34/EC, Article 1, OJ L 210, 7.8.1985, p. 29. See, also, Hervey and McHale, 2004, see note 11, p. 308.

85 As mentioned, thalidomide was introduced as a sedative drug in the late 1950s, and found to be the cause of birth defects.

86 See, also, C.J. Miller and R.S. Goldberg, *Product Liability*, Second ed., Oxford: Oxford University Press, 2004, Chapter II, in particular under section 9B(5).

87 ECJ, Case C-183/00 *Maria Victoria Gonzales Sanchez v Medicina Asturiana* SA [2002] ECRI I-3901. Hervey and McHale, see note 11, p. 312, note 174.

88 For a discussion, see Hervey and McHale, 2004, see note 11, pp. 311–312.

89 For a more in-depth discussion, Hervey and McHale, 2004, see note 11, pp. 343–348.

etc. Blood that has been tested to ensure that it is free of disease thus has the potential to save lives, whereas untested blood infected with disease has the potential to take life away from the receiving patient.

The Blood Safety Directive (Directive 2002/98/EC setting standards of quality and safety for the collection, testing, processing, storage and distribution of human blood and blood components) was adopted in 2003, and places a strong emphasis on the voluntary and unpaid use of blood donations, cf. Article 20 of the Directive.

4.6. FREE MOVEMENT OF GOODS: CELLS AND TISSUES (SAFETY, STANDARDS AND QUALITY)

For the protection of public health, and to prevent the transmission of infectious diseases by human cells and tissues used for therapeutic purposes, the EU has adopted special regulation on safety, quality and standards in cells and tissues.

Directive 2004/23/EC of the European Parliament and of the Council of 31 March 2004 sets standards of quality and safety for the donation, procurement, testing, processing, preservation, storage and distribution of human tissues and cells, ensuring that human tissues and cells, whatever their intended use, are of comparable quality and safety. Thus, the Directive aims at bringing about the same level of protection for patients, ensuring a compatible and uniform quality. The establishment of such standards was meant to reassure the public that human tissues and cells that are procured in another Member State carry the same guarantees as those in their own country. The Directive applies to a variety of human tissues and cells, including reproductive cells, stem cells and foetal cells. Regulation of this nature helps to create a transparent market for healthcare services within the Union, further strengthening patient mobility as well as the mobility of tissues and cells used for treatment purposes across the Union.

The Directive contains several provisions that are in accordance with the principles expressed in the Council of Europe's Convention. First of all, Article 1 of the Directive stipulates that Member States shall endeavour to ensure voluntary and unpaid donations of tissues and cells. This provision thus reflects the prohibition of financial gain from the human body in Article 21 of the Convention, as well as the general rule on consent in Article 5 of the Convention, according to which an intervention in the health field may only be carried out after the person concerned has given free and informed consent to it. The emphasis on informed consent is further noted in Article 13 of the Directive, requiring that all mandatory consent and authorisations requirements in force in the Member State concerned must be met. Finally, the Directive contains safeguard requirements in relation to data protection and confidentiality in Article 14.

4.7. DATA PROTECTION

Informational privacy relates to a wide range of information related to an individual, however health information is at the core of informational privacy because of its perceived inherent sensitivity.

The right to privacy is protected in both the European Charter of Fundamental Rights and Freedoms, Articles 6 and 8, and in the Data Protection Directive (95/46/EC).[90] Moreover, the ECJ has repeatedly emphasised the duty to respect this right when taking measures seeking to achieve other aims.[91] The Directive aims at creating a common European level of privacy protection, thus facilitating the movement of personal data within the EU as part of the single market.[92] The strong emphasis on data protection in the EU means that the Council of Europe's Convention for the Protection of Individuals with regard to Automatic Processing of Personal Data (1981) has no real legal impact on the Member States of the EU, with the Directive having absorbed and developed further the main principles of data protection law. The Directive safeguards informational privacy in general, and as such, is also relevant to the regulation of health information.

The Data Protection Directive operates with different categories of personal data, and those that are particularly sensitive are subject to stricter protective measures. Article 8 states that processing of personal data concerning health is prohibited, and may only be processed with the informed consent of the subject of the data. This does not, however, apply if the processing of data is *necessary* for the purposes of preventive medicine, medical diagnosis, the provision of care or treatment, or the management of healthcare services, and where the data are processed by a health professional who is bound by a professional obligation of secrecy, or by an equivalent duty of confidentiality. According to Article 13 (2), health data may also be processed for the purposes of research. This means that there is no requirement to obtain informed consent to the use of medical records for research purposes, provided that there is no possibility of identifying the patients.

---

90 The Data Protection Directive is particularised in Directive 2002/58/EC on privacy and electronic communication.

91 Case C-465/00 *Rechnungshof* [2003] ECR 49837 *Jur.* 2003, p. I-498 and cases C-92/09 and C-93/09 *Volker and Markus Schecke* [2010] ECR (not yet published).

92 See recital 3 of the Directive.

The safeguards embedded in the Directive are meant to implement and uphold the fundamental rights, as protected in, *inter alia*, the European Convention on Human Rights, cf. recital 1 and 3 of the Directive. As far as the EUCFR is concerned, the Charter seems to reaffirm the principles that are already enshrined in the Directive, and the development of data protection in the EU must thus be expected to be developed and strengthened further, not through the EUCFR, but through the Directive and the Council of Europe's Convention on Data Protection, which are both currently in the process of being updated and renegotiated.

5. CONCLUSIONS

The aim of this chapter was to analyse how EU law has a bearing on health and human rights. To some extent, the EU engages directly with the area of health and human rights. By including a right to health (care) and other health-related rights in the EUFC, the EU has committed itself to submitting its laws and policies, and those of Member States, to the protection of health-related rights. At this point in time it is unclear how, and to what extent, these provisions will offer protection to Europeans. Whereas the ECJ, in the above-mentioned case of *SPUC v. Grogan*, refused to address the human rights aspect relating to the right to receive and impart information, thus causing this issue to be dealt with in the separate case of *Open Doors v. Ireland* before the ECtHR, the ECJ may prove less reluctant to test the human rights merits of a particular case in future. Furthermore, once the EU has acceded to the ECHR, acts that involve a health and human rights issue may become the subject of scrutiny by the ECtHR.

As was demonstrated above, EU law also increasingly regulates health issues in the context of its overall commitment to establish a single market, including in relation to pharmaceuticals, blood products, and healthcare providers. When it comes to such matters, there is an ongoing tension between the wish to enhance the free movement of goods, persons and services, and the importance of protecting health-related interests (the quality of pharmaceuticals, blood safety, and the qualification of healthcare providers). For example, while on the one hand the EU seeks to create a competitive European pharmaceutical market, on the other hand, the quality, safety and affordability of pharmaceutical products are at stake.

This tension is most pertinent when it comes to the recognition of a right to seek medical services in another EU Member State. On the one hand, this possibility can create a tension with health-related rights, for example, where the push towards the free movement of services may compromise the state's obligation to ensure a right to healthcare and access to healthcare on its territory. In this regard, it should be noted that the majority of the population will continue to seek healthcare services nationally. On the other hand, the possibility of seeking access to healthcare services abroad may enhance people's access to good-quality healthcare services – an essential component of the right to healthcare. A precondition here is that the quality of healthcare providers and services is guaranteed across borders. While EU law is continuously being strengthened in this regard, there are many challenges ahead.

PART II

HEALTH AND HUMAN RIGHTS: AN EXPLORATION OF THE FIELD

CHAPTER 3
THE RIGHT TO HEALTH AND OTHER HEALTH-RELATED RIGHTS

Brigit TOEBES

1. INTRODUCTION

In the previous chapters attention was focused on how the European institutions engage with health and human rights. Building on these chapters, this chapter will analyse the normative framework of health-related rights. As mentioned in the introduction, a wide range of human rights is, in one way or another, connected to health. Box 1 gives an overview of the most important health-related rights.[1]

Box 1. Rights and principles relevant to the protection and promotion of health

Right/principle	UN provisions	European provisions	Health topics involved
Dignity	1 UDHR 10 ICCPR 3 CRPD	1 Biomedicine Convention Section 1 (Art. 1) ECFR	'Core notion' and, *inter alia*, protection of persons with disabilities Dying with dignity
Life	3 UDHR 6 ICCPR 6 CRC 9 MWC 10 CRPD	2 ECHR 2 ECFR	Abortion, maternal mortality, protection of the foetus Euthanasia, positive obligations to protect health
Autonomy, Liberty and security of the person Integrity	1, 3 UDHR 9 ICCPR 5(b) CERD 37(b)-(d) CRC 12, 14, 17 CRPD	8 and 5 ECHR 1 and 7 Biomedicine Convention Rec (2004) 10 CoE 3 and 6 ECFR	Abortion, forced sterilisation, female genital mutilation Confinement of persons with mental disabilities Legal capacity (re disability)

[1] For a useful overview of the rights related to reproductive health see also Rebecca J. Cook and Mahmoud F. Fathalla, 'Advancing Reproductive Rights Beyond Cairo and Beijing', *International Family Planning Perspectives*, Volume 22, Number 3, September 1996, p. 116.

Right/principle	UN provisions	European provisions	Health topics involved
Prohibition of torture and inhuman and degrading treatment	5 UDHR CAT 7 ICCPR 15, 16 CRPD	3 ECHR ECPT 4 ECFR	Confinement of persons with mental disabilities Access to healthcare for prisoners Rape, sexual abuse
Privacy and family life	12 UDHR 17 ICCPR 10 ICESCR 16 CEDAW 16 CRC 22, 23 CRPD	8 ECHR 7, 10 Biomedicine Convention 7–8 ECFR	Physical and psychological integrity, including personal autonomy in the context of medical interventions Protection of personal data Involuntary placement in an institution Prohibition of compulsory use of contraceptives, non-voluntary sterilisation or abortion
Marry and found a family	16 UDHR 23 ICCPR 5(d)(iv) CERD 16 CEDAW 8, 9 CRC	12 ECHR 9 ECFR	Prohibition of compulsory use of contraceptives, non-voluntary sterilisation or abortion
Information and participation	19 UDHR 19 ICCPR 13 and 17 CRC 13 MWC 21, 29, 30 CRPD	8 and 10 ECHR 5–9 Biomedicine Convention 11 ECFR	Access to health-related information, including on reproductive health Informed consent
Access to a remedy	8 UDHR 13 CRPD	13 ECHR	'Accountability' for failures or abuses in the health sector
Non-discrimination	1, 2, 6 UDHR 2(1), 3, ICCPR 2(2), 3 ICCPR CERD 1–5 CEDAW 2 CRC 5 CRPD	14 ECHR; Protocol 12 to the ECHR 3 (Revised) ESC 1, 11 and 14 Biomedicine Convention 20–26 ECFR	Non-discrimination in access to healthcare services and other health-related services
Health, including reproductive health	12 ICESCR 12 CEDAW 24 CRC 5 CERD 28, 43, 45 MWC 24 CSR 25 ILO 169 9, 25, 26 CRPD	11 and 13 ESC 3 Biomedicine Convention 35 ECFR	Access to healthcare and other health-related services Access to reproductive health services Protection of health Reproductive health Environmental health Occupational health Rehabilitation (re disability)
Adequate standard of living	25 UDHR 11 ICESCR 27 CRC 28 CRPD	30 (Revised) ESC	Adequate standard of living Food, clothing, housing

Right/principle	UN provisions	European provisions	Health topics involved
Benefits of scientific progress	27(2) UDHR 15(2)(b) and 15(3) ICESCR WMA Declaration of Helsinki	–	Promotion of health research, including for vulnerable groups Development of affordable treatments
Social security	9 ICESCR 13 CEDAW 26 CRC 24 CSR 27 MWC	12, 14, 16 and 23 (Revised) ESC	Social security as a social determinant of health
Protection of mothers, children and of the family	10 ICESCR	7, 8, 16, 17 (Revised) ESC 24 ECFR	Paid and sufficient maternity leave Social and family benefits Protection against violence against children
Food	11 ICESCR	11 (Revised) ESC (not explicitly)	Safe and nutritious food Food as a social determinant of health
Housing	11 ICESCR 21 CSR 19 CRPD	8 ECHR 31 ESC	Housing as a social determinant of health Independent living and choice of residence (re disability)
Education	13 ICESCR 10 CEDAW 28 and 29 CRC 30, 43 and 45 MWC 24 CRPD	Protocol 1 to the ECHR (as amended by Protocol 11) 14 ECFR	Education as a social determinant of health Schooling of pregnant women Sex education at schools
Employment	6 and 7 ICESCR 11 CEDAW 17 and 18 CSR 27 CRPD ILO Conventions 25, 38–71 MWC	1–4, 7–10 and 18–22, and 24–29 (Revised) ESC 15 ECFR	Occupational health Employment as a social determinant of health

At the core of our health and human rights analysis lies the international 'right to health'. As the right to health is so important to our analysis, in this chapter we will start with an elaborate explanation of the meaning and implications of this human right. Subsequently a shorter overview is provided of the scope of the other most important health-related rights. It should be born in mind that while the right to health is the core or key right in this debate, it should not be seen as an umbrella right that covers the normative framework of the other health-related rights. While such an approach would make the right to health immensely broad and intangible, it would also deny the specific meaning of the other health-related rights.

2.1. THE RIGHT TO HEALTH

2.1.1. Introduction

A right to health, or a right to healthcare, suggests that states bear a certain responsibility for the health of their inhabitants. A sense of state responsibility, or at least community responsibility, for the health of the public has existed since the time of ancient civilisations. The public health concerns during earlier centuries were, however, mainly utilitarian in character. It was recognised that without government interference serious public health problems, including the spread of infectious diseases, were likely to arise. Gradually, the concerns became more geared towards individual well-being, which eventually led to the recognition of health as a right in the various human rights instruments adopted after World War II.[2]

Currently, it is generally recognised that government interference in the maintenance and promotion of public health is required to prevent health disparities and other threats to people's health. There is a general acceptance that the provision of health cannot be left solely to private parties. Although private healthcare providers may be very capable of providing good quality health-related services, they do not have an interest in improving the health of the population as a whole, or of certain marginalised groups. It is therefore accepted that government interference is required to prevent the selection of customers on the basis of, for example, health criteria, income, or geographic conditions.[3]

Government intervention is also necessary because individuals themselves are not always capable of looking after their own health completely, due to factors such as financial resources, a lack of information, and impaired decision-making capacities. They may carry a certain personal responsibility for their own health, but governments have to provide for a health infrastructure and create conditions under which the availability, accessibility, and quality of health services are guaranteed.[4]

---

2 Brigit Toebes, Right to Health and Health Care, *Encyclopaedia for Human Rights*, Volume I, Oxford University Press: 2009, pp. 365–376, at p. 365.

3 Toebes, 2009, pp. 365–366.

4 Toebes, 2009, p. 366.

It is one step to recognise governmental responsibility for the health of the population, however, to recognise a right of the individual to health services goes yet one step further. Health may be an important social good, but the recognition of health as a human right creates problems regarding the distribution of health services. As such, the 'right to health' is a controversial right that has led to much confusion and debate. It is difficult to define 'health', and it is challenging to indicate the boundaries of entitlements to health-related services. As a result, the 'right to health' is difficult to delineate, while it is problematic to enforce such a right before a court of law.[5] However, over the past fifteen years, much progress has been made regarding the definition of the right to health.

The most important provision on the right to health at the European level is Article 11 of the (Revised) European Social Charter (ESC). While this provision contains a right to protection of health, several other provisions in the ESC also contain health-related claims. Before discussing these provisions more elaborately, we need to look at global definitions of the right to health, as such provisions have set the stage for the adoption of the European definitions of the right to health.

2.1.2. The right to health at the UN level

The first instrument to lay down a right to health was the Constitution of the World Health Organization, adopted in 1946.[6] The preamble to the Constitution, which defines 'health' and recognises health as a right was a breakthrough in the field of international health and human rights law. It created an important point of departure for the further elaboration of a right to health in human rights documents. It is also interesting that this text defines both 'health' and 'health as a right', a distinction that was also made in the introduction of this book. The text of the preamble defines 'health' as 'a state of complete physical, mental and social well-being and not merely the absence of disease'. It is striking that this provision contains an absolute and broad definition of health, which not only embraces physical, but also mental and social, well-being. Furthermore, as mentioned, the preamble recognises health as an individual human right. In connection to this, the text refers to the relationship between health problems and the gap in development between countries,, to the importance of the healthy development of the child, and to the importance of the informed opinion and active co-operation of the public. This approach did not get the approval of everyone; for example, the American Medical Association stressed that the provision of healthcare services should be considered a concern of the individual nation rather than of an international health organisation.[7]

---

5 Toebes, 2009, p. 366.
6 Constitution of the World Health Organization, 22 July 1946, entry into force: 7 April 1948.
7 B.C.A. Toebes, *The Right to Health as a Human Right in International Law*, Antwerp-Oxford: Intersentia, 1999, p. 32.

In spite of such objections, the text was adopted and has clearly inspired the right to health provisions that were drafted at a later stage, in particular Article 12 of the UN International Covenant on Economic, Social and Cultural Rights (ICESCR). Article 12 ICESCR contains a provision along the lines of the WHO Constitution. This provision is broader than the previously adopted Article 25 of the Universal Declaration of Human Rights, which embeds a right to health into a broader provision on a right to an adequate standard of living.[8]

An issue that was heavily debated during the drafting process of Article 12 ICESCR was the question of whether the provision should contain a definition of health. Several drafters objected to the insertion of a definition of health on the basis of the argument that such a definition is not appropriate in a legal instrument. The final text of Article 12 ICESCR, therefore, does not contain a definition of health.[9] What has not been deserted is the broad approach to health – the notion that health is not merely the 'absence of disease'. Although the concept of 'social well-being' has been deleted from the text of Article 12 ICESCR during the drafting process, the steps mentioned in the Article reflect the interpretation of health as a broad concept, in referring also to environmental hygiene, preventive healthcare, and occupational diseases.[10]

The provisions that followed were Article 12 of the Convention on the Elimination of all forms of Discrimination Against Women (CEDAW, 1979) and Article 24 of the Convention of the Rights of the Child (CRC, 1989). While 12 CEDAW focuses primarily on access to healthcare for women, Article 24 CRC covers the broader right to health of children, in referring not only to healthcare facilities, but also to adequate food, drinking water, and the prohibition of harmful traditional practices. As a result, whereas Article 12 CEDAW is aimed at providing women with additional protection where this is needed, Article 24 purports to restate the principles of the WHO Constitution and of Article 12 ICESCR with respect to children.

In addition to the above-mentioned provisions, a number of other UN Treaties and Declarations exist that refer to a right to health. Some of these provision focus on equal access to medical services. For example, the Convention on the Protection of the Rights of All Migrant Workers and Members of their Families (MWC, 1990) puts emphasis on equal access to medical care for migrant

8 Toebes, 1999, p. 43.
9 Article 10 of the Protocol of San Salvador (Additional Protocol to the American Convention on Human Rights) on the right to health was the first human rights provision to explicitly use the terms 'right to health' and 'physical, mental and social well-being', as done in the WHO Constitution.
10 Toebes, 1999, pp. 40–52.

workers.[11] Article 5(e)(iv) of the Convention on the Elimination of All Forms of Racial Discrimination (CERD, 1965) is slightly more elaborate, in that it provides, in general terms, that States Parties are to prohibit and eliminate racial discrimination in the enjoyment of public health, medical care, social security and social services. Also worth mentioning are Rules 22 to 26 of the Standard Minimum Rules for the Treatment of Prisoners (1957), which lay down a number of principles for the treatment of sick prisoners. Finally, the Conventions of the ILO contain numerous references to a specific area of health, namely, occupational health. Different in character is Article 25 of ILO Convention No. 169 (1989), which explicitly recognises a right to health of indigenous and tribal peoples. Lastly, worth mentioning is the Convention on the Rights of Persons with Disabilities (CRPD, 2006), which contains several references to the health of disabled persons, including Article 25 on the right to health of disabled persons (see, also, Chapter 9).

2.1.3. *The right to health at the European level*

In addition to such global provisions, the right to health is set out in a number of regional human rights instruments. Given the scope of this book, we will focus on the relevant European provisions.[12] The European Social Charter, adopted in 19651, contains a 'right to protection of health' in Article 11. An initial draft, which was similar in several ways to Article 12 ICESCR, was eventually narrowed after objections made by several states against such a far-going text. The final text of Article 11 ESC defines three general state undertakings, which will be more elaborately discussed below. It tries to bring the responsibility of governments into perspective by referring to the individual responsibility in matters of health and to co-operation with public and private organisations. The text does not refer to child health and environmental health, yet these matters are raised within the framework of the reporting procedure.[13]

In 1996, a revised text of the ESC was adopted by the Committee of Ministers (the 'Revised ESC'). Apart from a reference to the prevention of accidents in

---

11 It should be noted that the Migrant Workers Convention only grants an equal right to healthcare services to *documented* migrant workers, while *all* migrant workers have a right to emergency medical care.

12 Other regional right to health provisions: the American Declaration of the Rights and Duties of Man (ADHR, 1948) contains a general provision in Article XI that has similarities with Article 25 of the UDHR; the 'Protocol of San Salvador' (1988), which forms an Additional Protocol to the American Convention on Human Rights (ACHR), contains a right to health in Article 10 and a right to a healthy environment in Article 11; the African Charter on Human and Peoples' Rights (1981) contains a right to health in Article 16; the Universal Islamic Declaration of Human Rights (adopted by the Islamic Council in 1981) mentions the right to medical care as part of the right to social security (Article XVIII). The Arab Charter of Human Rights (1994, not yet ratified) does not contain a reference to health.

13 Toebes, 1999, pp. 63–69.

paragraph 3, Article 11 ESC was left unchanged. The (Revised) ESC recognises several other health-related rights, the most important of which are Articles 3 (safety at work), 12 (social security), 13 (social and medical assistance), 7 and 17 (protection of mothers and children). 19 (protection and assistance to migrant works and their families), and 23 (social protection of the elderly).[14]

As was also mentioned in Chapter 1, the European Committee on Social Rights monitors compliance with the European Social Charter. Organisations entitled to submit a so-called 'collective complaint' regarding alleged violations of the rights in the Charter can lodge their complaint with the Committee. So far, the Committee has handed down more than 40 decisions. As of September 2011, three of these decisions had led to the conclusion that there was a breach of the right to protection of health under Article 11 of the Charter. Interestingly, these three decisions each concerned a different aspect of the right to protection of health. The first decision concerned the right to a healthy living environment and healthy working conditions (*Marangopoulos*), the second concerned the access to healthcare services of the Roma population in Bulgaria (*ECCR v. Bulgaria*), and the third decision concerned the right to access sexual and reproductive health education in schools in Croatia (*INTERIGHTS v. Croatia*).[15]

The Convention on Human Rights and Biomedicine (Biomedicine Convention) formulates a duty on the part of Member States to provide 'equitable access to health care of appropriate quality'.[16] The terms 'equitable access' and 'appropriate quality' are comparable to the principles formulated under the 'AAAQ' in General Comment 14 (see below). Given the scope of the Treaty, i.e. areas concerning the application of biology and medicine, this provision focuses on the narrower area of healthcare, and not on the underlying determinants of health.

The Charter of Fundamental Rights of the European Union (ECFR, 2000) contains, in Article 35, a provision on healthcare. Contrary to the Biomedicine Convention, the first sentence of this provision recognises an individual *right* to preventive as well as curative healthcare, albeit under the conditions established by national laws and practices. The second sentence expresses a 'mainstreaming'

---

14 It should be noted here that not all Contracting States have ratified the Revised Charter; to them, the (old) text of the ESC applies. www.coe.int/t/dghl/monitoring/socialcharter/Presentation/TreatiesIndex_en.asp, accessed March 2011.

15 European Committee of Social Rights, *Maragopoulous Foundation for Human Rights (MFHR) v Greece*, No. 30/2005, 6 February 2007, and *European Roma Rights Centre (ERRC) v. Bulgaria*, No. 46/2007, 3 December 2008, *INTERIGHTS v. Croatia*, No. 45/2007, for a comment see Brigit Toebes, *Sex education at schools is compulsory and must not give evidence of discrimination of homosexuals*, available at www.interights.org/view-document/index.htm?id=579, accessed March 2011.

16 Adopted by the Council of Ministers of the Council of Europe in 1996, opened for signature and ratification in 1997, and entered into force on 1 December 1999.

state obligation of health protection by providing that a high level of human health protection has to be ensured in the definition and implementation of all Union policies and activities (see, also, Chapters 2 and 9).

2.1.4. *Constitutional provisions*

The right to health is also firmly embedded in national constitutional law. According to the former UN Special Rapporteur on the Right to Health, Paul Hunt, over 100 national constitutional provisions now include the right to health, the right to healthcare, or health-related rights such as a right to a healthy environment.[17] A distinction can be made between common law and civil law countries.[18] Common law countries generally do not have an explicit right to health in their constitutions.[19] The Constitution of the Republic of Ireland, for example, contains no reference to health. Many civil law countries, on the other hand, have an explicit or implicit right to health in their constitutions. The Constitution of the Netherlands, for example, does not contain an individual right to health, but defines the duty of the Dutch Government to take steps to promote the health of the population.[20] More explicit recognitions of a right to health can be found in the constitutions of the former Socialist Republics. The Charter of fundamental rights and basic freedoms of the Czech Republic, for example, contains the following provision in Article 31:

> 'Everyone has the right to the protection of his health. Citizens shall have the right, on the basis of public insurance, to free medical care and to medical aids under conditions provided for by law.'[21]

This provision contains an explicit right to protection of health, which is made subject to public insurance and national legal conditions.

---

17 Paul Hunt, 'The human right to the highest attainable standard of health: new opportunities and challenges', *Transactions of the Royal Society of Tropical Medicine and Hygiene* (2006) 100, pp. 603–6007, at p. 6003.

18 Pan American Health Organisation (PAHO), *The Right to Health in the Americas*, Washington, D.C.: PAHO, 1989, pp. 27–521 and 607–625.

19 Yet, a reference to health is sometimes made in the preamble to the constitution, or couched in terms of a state policy. An example is India, where a state duty to improve health is stipulated as one of the 'Directive Principles of State Policy'. Interestingly, this provision has been used by the Indian Supreme Court to broaden the scope of the right to life in the Indian Constitution so as to give it a health dimension. See, also, Toebes, 1999, pp. 79–84.

20 Article 22-1 of the Constitution of the Netherlands.

21 Charter of fundamental rights and basic freedoms, which forms an integral part of the Constitution of the Czech Republic, adopted 1 January 1993. See, *inter alia*, www.wipo.int/wipolex/en/details.jsp?id=7330, accessed September 2011.

2.1.5. *The scope of the right to health*

The right to protection of health in Article 11 ESC is a broad right covering both healthcare and the underlying conditions for health. This broad approach to the definition of health as a right has been influenced by the approach taken at the UN level. An important landmark concerned the adoption of General Comment No. 14 on the 'right to the highest attainable standard of health' in Article 12 ICESCR, adopted in 2000 (General Comment 14), after consultation with NGOs and the WHO.[22] A General Comment is a document drawn up by a UN treaty monitoring body that explains the meaning and implications of a certain aspect of the Treaty concerned and that seeks to assist States Parties to fulfil their reporting obligations. While General Comments are not, strictly speaking, legally binding ('soft law instruments'), General Comments are increasingly being referred to in legal scholarship and practice. As such, they can be considered as influential and authoritative documents that can supersede the status of mere soft law.

General Comment 14 reflects the debate about the right to health that took place in the years leading up to the adoption of this text. It is an influential document that gives an authoritative explanation of the meaning and implications of the right to health. General Comment 14 recognises the somewhat absolute wording of the term 'right to health', by stating that the right to health is not a right to be healthy.[23] As such, it confirms the notion expressed by Leary, that the right to health is to be used as a 'shorthand expression', which refers to the more elaborate Treaty texts.[24] At the international level, therefore, the term 'right to health' is used, instead of the narrower term 'right to healthcare'. The term 'right to healthcare' is, however, suitable and more specific where it concerns discussions regarding access to health*care* services.

Furthermore, it is important to note that General Comment 14 takes a broad approach to the definition of health as a human right. It recognises that the right to health in Article 12 ICESCR is not confined to the right to health*care*, but extends to the underlying determinants of health, such as food and nutrition, housing, access to safe and potable water and adequate sanitation, safe and healthy working conditions, and a healthy environment.[25] This reinforces the notion that underlying determinants of health are at least as important for

---

22 UN Committee on Economic, Social and Cultural Rights (CESCR), General Comment 14 on the Right to the Highest Attainable Standard of Health, UN Doc. E/C.12/2000/4, August 11 2000.

23 General Comment 14, paragraph 8.

24 V.A. Leary, 'Implications of a Right to Health', in: K.E. Mahoney and P. Mahoney (eds.), *Human rights in the Twenty-first Century*, Deventer: Kluwer, 1993, pp. 481–493.

25 General Comment 14, paragraph 4.

people's health as access to healthcare services. There is a growing amount of research indicating that the circumstances under which people live and work are decisive for their health and well-being.[26] It is increasingly argued that the growing health inequalities (that also exist in Europe) should be addressed by trying to improve people's living conditions and their lifestyles (see, also, Chapter 7 of this book).[27]

2.1.6. Elements of the right to health

As was mentioned, the right to health covers access to healthcare services as well as a number of determinants of health. Access to such services is formulated as state duties or undertakings. The second paragraph of Article 12 ICESCR mentions the following state undertakings:

- the provision for the reduction of the stillbirth rate and of infant mortality, and for the healthy development of the child;
- the improvement of all aspects of environmental and industrial hygiene;
- the prevention, treatment and control of epidemic, endemic, occupational and other diseases;
- the creation of conditions which would assure to all medical service and medical attention in the event of sickness

Along similar lines, Article 11 (Revised) ESC contains the following state undertakings:

- to remove, as far as possible, the causes of ill-health;
- to provide advisory and educational facilities for the promotion of health and the encouragement of individual responsibility in matters of health;
- to prevent, as far as possible, epidemic, endemic and other diseases, as well as accidents.

Although both provisions focus on different health-related issues, it is clear that the range of state undertakings goes further than providing mere healthcare services. In a comprehensive report, the secretariat of the ESC explained that Article 11 covers numerous issues relating to public health, such as food safety, protection of the environment, vaccination programmes, and alcoholism.[28]

---

26 J.P. Mackenbach *et al*, 'Socioeconomic Inequalities in Health in 22 European Countries', *The New England Journal of Medicine* 385; 23, June 5 2008, pp. 2468–2481.

27 For example, World Health Organization/Commission on the Social Determinants of Health, *Closing the gap in a generation*, 2008.

28 Secretariat of the ESC, *The right to health and the European Social Charter*, March 2009, available at www.coe.int/T/DGHL/Monitoring/SocialCharter/Theme%20factsheets/FactsheetHealth_en.pdf, accessed September 2011, (not binding on the European Committee of Social Rights).

Within the framework of its reporting procedure, this European Committee of Social Rights focused on a wide range of health-related issues that go beyond the mere 'provision of healthcare services'. Attention was paid, *inter alia*, to the reduction of environmental risks, food safety, health education in schools, measures to combat smoking, tobacco control, and accidents.[29] As was illustrated in Chapter 1, the case law of the Economic Committee of Social Rights has addressed not only access to healthcare, but also access to sex education and environmental health under the umbrella of the right to protection of health in Article 11 (Revised) ESC.

2.1.7. Guiding principles for the right to health

General Comment 14 mentions a set of principles that is widely used for the definition of the general framework of the right to health (paragraph 12). Similar principles can be found in the General Comments on the right to food, housing, and education. This set of principles relates not merely to healthcare services, but to the broad range of 'functioning public health and healthcare facilities, goods and services'.[30] This set of principles can be useful for assessing health-related rights in a policy framework, for example. For example, it can be a helpful tool when analysing the impact of planned healthcare commercialisation trends. Countries could be asked to use this framework for so-called 'human rights impact assessments' of planned healthcare reforms.[31]

This set of principles, also referred to as the 'AAAQ', reads as follows:

- *Availability* of health-related services does not refer so much to the distribution of health services, but rather to the general availability of health services. It requires that 'functioning public health and healthcare facilities, goods and services, as well as programmes, are available in sufficient quantity within the State party'.
- *Accessibility* implies that 'health facilities, goods and services have to be accessible to everyone without discrimination, within the jurisdiction of the State party'. According to the General Comment, accessibility has four overlapping dimensions:
  1) *non-discrimination*: 'health facilities, goods and services must be accessible to all, especially the most vulnerable or marginalized sections

29 European Committee of Social Rights, *European Social Charter (Revised), Conclusions 2009 – Volume 1*, available at www.coe.int/t/dghl/monitoring/socialcharter/Conclusions/Year/2009Vol1_en.pdf, accessed March 2011.

30 General Comment 14, paragraph 12.

31 In this regard, see, for example, Brigit Toebes, 'Taking a human rights Approach to Healthcare Commercialization', in Patricia A. Cholewka and Mitra M. Motlagh (eds.), *Health Capital and Sustainable Socioeconomic Development*, Taylor & Francis, 2008, pp. 441–459.

of the population, in law and in fact, without discrimination on any of the prohibited grounds';

2) *physical accessibility*: 'health facilities, goods and services must be within safe physical reach for all sections of the population, especially vulnerable or marginalized groups, such as ethnic minorities and indigenous populations, women, children, adolescents, older persons, persons with disabilities and persons with HIV/AIDS';
3) *economic accessibility* (affordability): 'health facilities, goods and services must be affordable for all. Payment for healthcare services, as well as services related to the underlying determinants of health, has to be based on the principle of equity, ensuring that these services, whether privately or publicly provided, are affordable for all, including socially disadvantaged groups'; and
4) *information accessibility*: 'the right to seek, receive and impart information and ideas concerning health issues'. As also mentioned by Mette Hartlev in Chapter 4, this undertaking embraces the duty to provide information about community health problems (e.g. epidemics).

- *Acceptability* requires that 'all health facilities, goods and services are respectful of medical ethics and culturally appropriate, i.e. respectful of the culture of individuals, minorities, peoples and communities, sensitive to gender and life-cycle requirements, as well as being designed to respect confidentiality and improve the health status of those concerned.'
- *Quality* implies that 'health facilities, goods and services are scientifically and medically appropriate and of good quality.' This requires, *inter alia*, 'skilled medical personnel, scientifically approved and unexpired drugs and hospital equipment, safe and potable water, and adequate sanitation.'

Two principles are increasingly being referred to in a right to health context: accountability and participation (and as such, we can refer to a broader set of principles which can be abbreviated to 'AAAQ-AP'):

- *Accountability*[32] has been described by Potts as a broad process that requires governments to show, explain and justify how they have discharged their obligations regarding the right to health. An effective accountability process comprises the following essential elements according to Potts: monitoring, accountability mechanisms, remedies, and participation.[33] Monitoring is aimed at providing governments with the information that they need to create transparent health policies, as well as providing rights holders with

---

32 Helen Potts, *Accountability and the Right to the Highest Attainable Standard of Health*, University of Essex Human Rights Centre, available at www.essex.ac.uk/human_rights_centre/research/rth/projects.aspx, accessed September 2011.

33 Potts, pp. 13–17.

essential health-related information.[34] 'Accountability mechanisms' can be judicial or quasi-judicial (for example, a health ombudsman or other independent complaint mechanism), as well as administrative, political or social in character.[35] States should establish supervisory bodies that monitor the actions and decisions of all actors in the health sector, be they public or private actors, ranging from hospitals to health equipment providers, and where necessary, impose sanctions upon them.

- *Participation*[36] requires that the public has a say in important decisions concerning the health sector, for example, the decision to privatise or decentralise (parts of) the health sector. States should ensure political participation in the decision-making regarding the organisation of the health sector. Political participation is not only realised through a democratic system of elections, but also by providing for public consultation into planned health sector reform. When it comes to the health budget, it has been pointed out that the public and/or civil society can be actively included in all stages of the budget cycle for the health sector. Public budget hearings can be held at the local level to involve citizens in the way public services are delivered.[37]

2.1.8. Vulnerable groups

Another important notion underlying the right to health concerns the emphasis on 'vulnerable groups' when it comes to accessing health services (see Chapters 7–10). UN General Comment 14 focuses on the position of vulnerable groups. It stipulates, in paragraph 19, that states have a special obligation to provide those who do not have sufficient means with the necessary health insurance and healthcare facilities, and to prevent any discrimination on internationally prohibited grounds in the provision of healthcare and health services. Those singled out as vulnerable groups include women, children and adolescents, older people, persons with disabilities, and indigenous peoples. In addition, several UN Treaties guarantee the health rights of specific vulnerable groups, including the Women's Convention (CEDAW), the Children's Convention (CRC) and the Convention on the Rights of Persons with Disabilities (CRPD).

The (Revised) ESC contains several rights that focus on vulnerable groups: Articles 17 (protection of mothers and children), 19 (protection of, and assistance

---

[34] Potts, pp. 13–17.

[35] Potts, pp. 17–27.

[36] Helen Potts, *Participation and the Right to the Highest Attainable Standard of Health* available at www.essex.ac.uk/human_rights_centre/research/rth/projects.aspx, accessed September 2011.

[37] U4, Anti-corruption resource centre, *Corruption in the health sector*, p. 23, available at www.u4.no/document/u4-issue/u4_issue1_2006_health.pdf, accessed September 2011.

to, migrant workers and their families), and 23 (social protection of the elderly).[38] As was discussed in Chapter 1, the case law of the European Committee on Social Rights has, *inter alia*, addressed the position of the Roma and of undocumented migrants.[39]

2.1.9. Legal obligations

a. Respect, protect, fulfil

As a legal human right, the right to health imposes binding obligations on states that have ratified the treaties in which the right to health is set out. The question arises as to what these legal obligations look like. An important concept that is elaborated in General Comment 14 concerns the distinction between three types of state obligations. The General Comment explains that the right to health, like all human rights, imposes three types or levels of obligations on States Parties: the obligations 'to respect', 'to protect' and 'to fulfil'.

The obligation to *respect* is a negative state obligation, and requires states to refrain from interfering directly or indirectly with the enjoyment of the right to health. Examples of violations of these obligations are, according to General Comment 14: denying or limiting equal access to health services; enforcing discriminatory practices as a state policy; unlawfully polluting air, water and soil, e.g. through industrial waste from state-owned facilities, or through using or testing nuclear, biological or chemical weapons, if such testing results in the release of substances harmful to human health.[40]

The obligations to *protect* and to *fulfil* are positive state obligations, requiring states to take measures to prevent third parties from interfering with Article 12 guarantees (protect), and to adopt appropriate legislative, administrative, budgetary, judicial, promotional and other measures with a view to the full realisation of the right to health (fulfil). Violations of the obligation to protect may occur, for example, when states decline to adopt legislation or to take other measures ensuring equal access to healthcare and health-related services provided by third parties, or when states fail to ensure that harmful social or traditional practices do not interfere with access to pre- and post-natal care and family planning.[41]

---

38 It should be noted here that not all Contracting States have ratified the Revised Charter; to them, the (old) text of the ESC applies, which contains similar guarantees. See www.coe.int/t/dghl/monitoring/socialcharter/Presentation/TreatiesIndex_en.asp, accessed March 2011.

39 *Inter alia*, *ECCR v Bulgaria* (46/2007) and *DCI v the Netherlands* (47/2008). See, also, Chapter 1.

40 General Comment 14, paragraph 34.

41 General Comment 14, paragraph 35.

With regard to the obligation to fulfil, a distinction is made between obligations to facilitate (taking positive measures to enable and assist individuals and communities to enjoy the right to health), to provide (when individuals or a group are unable, for reasons beyond their control, to realise that right themselves by the means at their disposal), and the obligation to promote (undertaking actions that create, maintain and restore the health of the population).[42] Violations of the obligation to fulfil may, according to General Comment 14, occur when insufficient recognition is given to the right to health in the national political and legal systems; when states decline to adopt a national health policy with a detailed plan for realising the right to health; or decline to ensure provision of healthcare, including immunisation programmes against the major infectious diseases, and to ensure equal access for all to the underlying determinants of health, such as nutritious and safe food and potable drinking water, basic sanitation, and adequate housing and living conditions.[43]

As is also explained by Sinding Aasen in Chapter 10, this so-called 'tri-partite typology of state obligations' was first introduced into the human rights debate by Asbjørn Eide in 1981, later refined by several other scholars, and subsequently introduced into the UN human rights regime.[44] It is generally considered to be a useful tool for analysing positive as well as negative obligations inherent in all rights, and as such, for underlining the equality and interdependence of all human rights. However, the usefulness of this tool has also been questioned. Koch, for example, argues that the distinction between the three categories is blurred and that it is very difficult to fit certain obligatory measures into the tripartite typology She argues that 'confronted with the complexities of real life the various obligations are hard to distinguish from one another', and '(...) the adequate metaphor would rather be a slope, not divided into levels (...).'[45] Koch also notes that the case law of the ECtHR does not apply the tripartite typology According to Koch: 'The Court is not preoccupied with the issue of fitting a certain obligation into a certain category (...).'[46] While we should not overstate

42 General Comment 14, paragraph 37.

43 General Comment 14, paragraph 36.

44 Sinding Aasen in Chapter 10, *supra*, note 20, and see, also, A. Eide, 'Economic, Social and Cultural Rights as Human Rights', in *Economic. Social and Cultural Rights: A Textbook*, Dordrecht/Boston/London: Martinus Nijhoff Publishers, 2001, pp. 21–41, and G.J.H. van Hoof, 'The Legal Nature of Economic, Social and Cultural Rights: a Rebuttal of Some Traditional Views', in Ph. Alston and K. Tomaševski (eds.), *The Right to Food* (Utrecht: SIM, 1984), 97–111 and G.J.H. van Hoof, 'The Legal Nature of Economic, Social and Cultural Rights: a Rebuttal of Some Traditional Views', in Ph. Alston and K. Tomaševski (eds.), *The Right to Food* (Utrecht: SIM, 1984), 97–111. See, also, Shue's comparable categorisation in H. Shue, *Basic Rights, Subsistence, Affluence and U.S. Foreign Policy*, (New Jersey: Princeton, 1980).

45 Ida Elisabeth Koch, 'Dichotomies, Trichotomies or Waves of Duties?', *Human Rights Law Review* 5:1 (2005), 81–103, pp. 91–93.

46 Koch, 2005, p. 21.

the usefulness of the typology, it can be a helpful tool when it comes to the identification of the legal obligations resulting from economic, social and cultural rights, including the right to health.

b. International obligations

Furthermore, General Comment 14 mentions the international obligations of states with regard to the right to health, which are also stipulated in Article 2(1) of the ICESCR. States are to respect the right to health in other countries, and to prevent third parties from violating the right in other countries. For example, this obligation is of importance with regard to the tension between patent protection and the accessibility of drugs in developing countries.[47] In addition, this international obligation contains a reference to providing development aid where necessary. The General Comment refers to the obligation to facilitate access to essential health facilities, goods and services in other countries, wherever possible, and to provide the necessary aid when required.[48]

c. Core obligations

Finally, General Comment 14 refers, in paragraphs 43–44, to the definition of core obligations, which implies that States Parties have certain minimum obligations to ensure, under all circumstances, the delivery of minimum basic levels of, in this case, essential health services. For the further definition of these core obligations, the General Comment draws from the Programme of Action of the International Conference on Population and Development (UNDP, Cairo 1994), and the Primary Health Care Strategy, as set out in the Alma-Ata Declaration (WHO, 1978). As such, the core obligations include, among other things, the obligation to provide access to health facilities on a non-discriminatory basis, in particular, reproductive, maternal and child healthcare, immunisation against the major infectious diseases, prevention, treatment and control epidemic and endemic diseases, education and access to information concerning the main health problems in the community, and appropriate training for health personnel, including education on health and human rights. It should be noted that national courts have so far rejected the existence of an immediately enforceable core content in the right to health.[49] We can also doubt whether the definition of core obligations is useful in a European context, where

---

47 See also Chapter 2.

48 General Comment 14, paragraph 39.

49 For example, in the decision in *Minister of Health and Others v. Treatment Action Campaign and Others* (2005), the South-African Constitutional Court argued that 'all that can be expected from the state is that it act reasonably to provide access to the socio-economic rights (...) on a progressive basis' (paragraph 35). On the reasonableness approach, see, also, Koch, 2005, p. 287.

generally accessible healthcare packages go beyond the scope of the core obligations mentioned above. The notion of a 'core' could possibly be of some use in the debate on the issue of what healthcare services should be available to deprived or uninsured persons or population groups, including undocumented migrants.

2.1.10. The right to health: responsible actors

It is increasingly argued that other actors besides states have obligations under human rights law. International (human rights) law provides several bases for this assumption.[50] For example, the preamble to the Universal Declaration of Human Rights recognises the human rights responsibilities of 'all organs of society'; and, important for our purposes, Article 11 (Revised) ESC refers to the collaboration between the state and public and private organisations in the realisation of the right to protection of health. Even at the time of the drafting of this provision, there was awareness of the role that private organisations play in the provision of medical care.[51] Nonetheless, recognition of the human rights obligations of other actors besides states should never undermine the primary responsibility of states under international law.

One could argue that non-state actors have a so-called derived or indirect responsibility for ensuring those elements of human rights that lie within their scope of influence. This means, for example, that corporations have obligations to safeguard the health of their employees, and that factories need to ensure the environmental health of the area in which they are based. Hospitals need to respect the privacy of their patients, and doctors need to respect the patients' 'informed consent'.[52]

As health service provision is increasingly privatised and put into the hands of private providers, it is important to consider the (human rights) responsibilities of all the actors in the health sector. While governments remain ultimately responsible for human rights violations, it is important to develop the tools to address the responsibilities of private actors directly. Furthermore, health sectors are very complex in character, due to the fact that many actors engage with each

50 In this regard, reference is often made to the body of international humanitarian law, and to the Genocide Convention, which both contain references to the human rights responsibilities of non-state actors. For this debate see, *inter alia*, Nicola Jägers, *Corporate responsibility for human rights violations*, Antwerp/ Oxford: Intersentia/HART, 2000.

51 Draft report examined by the Committee on General Affairs relating to a preliminary draft recommendation, submitted by Mr Toncic (6 August 1956) – AS/AG (8) 16, *Collected 'Travaux Préparatoires'*, Vol III, 1956, p. 507, in Toebes, 1999, p. 65.

52 On this, see, also, Jernej Letnar and Brigit Toebes, 'Corporate Human Rights Violations under Economic, Social and Cultural Rights', forthcoming in T. Chowdhury, *Globalization, International Law and Human Rights*, OUP/Asia Publications, 2011.

other in multiple relationships. This makes health sectors extremely vulnerable to abuse and corruption, hence the importance of addressing abuse and corruption by all the actors in the health sector.[53]

It is one of the major issues in modern human rights law to define the human rights responsibilities of all the actors in the health sector, varying from health ministries, social security organisations, public and private insurers, hospitals, doctors, pharmacists, to pharmaceutical companies, producers of medical equipment, and patients. For example, the perceived responsibility of the pharmaceutical industry to produce and provide affordable and good quality drugs geared towards the health needs of the population at large has been the subject of intense debate. However, the role of healthcare providers, hospitals, medical research and patients can also potentially be addressed under international human rights law.

2.1.11. The right to health and public health

A distinction can be drawn between 'medicine' and public health'. While medicine is more concerned with the health and rights of the individual (e.g. creating conditions enabling a particular individual access to care), public health is more aimed at the protection of collective health interests.[54] Since the right to health represents individual claims to health *vis-à-vis* governments, it clearly represents the concept of 'medicine'. The question arises as to whether, and if so, to what extent, the right to health also contains claims to 'public health'. Meier and Mori argue that the concept of a 'right to health' insufficiently reflects this perspective. They point at the escalation of endemic diseases and the rapid proliferation of infectious and chronic diseases, and to the uneven distribution of wealth and the increase in poverty. They claim that the current definition of a right to health is no longer applicable to a globalising world, which requires a renewed focus on the societal factors that facilitate the spread of disease.[55]

According to Gruskin and Tarantola, both 'medicine' and 'public health' ideally seek to ensure every person's right to fulfil the right to the highest attainable standard of health, and both have a strong focus on the individual. As such, the right to health would both contain a 'medicine' component, in the sense that it is

---

53 Brigit Toebes, 'Human Rights and Health Sector Corruption', in J. Harrington *et al.* (eds.), *Global Health and Human Rights: Legal and Philosophical Perspectives*, Routledge, 2010, pp. 102–134.

54 Sofia Gruskin and Daniel Tarantola, *Health and Human Rights*, FXB Center Working Paper No. 10, 2000, p. 16.

55 Benjamin Mason Meier and Larisa M. Mori, 'The Highest Attainable Standard: Advancing a Collective Human Right to Public Health', *Columbia Human Rights Law Review*, 37 (2005), pp. 101–121, at p. 102.

aimed at protecting the individual's right to medical care, as well as a 'public health component', in the sense that it obliges governments to effectuate a national health policy and to enhance the health of the public.[56]

There can be a certain tension between public health component of the right to health and the civil and political rights of individuals, including the rights to physical integrity and privacy.[57] For example, while the public at large has an interest in being protected against the spread of infectious diseases, individuals have a right to be protected against unnecessary interference in their privacy Clearly, caution should be exercised if the right to health is used to justify certain types of governmental health measures. Although, as mentioned above, the state has an obligation to protect the right to health, it cannot take such measures to the extent that they violate the rights of others. According to WHO, restrictions to rights are only allowed as a last resort and should meet the so-called 'Siracusa Principles' – a set of UN principles on the limitations of human rights (see, also, Chapter 4).[58]

2.1.12. Justiciability of the right to health

Justiciability refers to the enforceability of a norm before a judicial or quasi-judicial body. The justiciability of the right to health and of other economic, social and cultural rights has been the subject of much debate.[59] There is generally great reluctance on the part of the judiciary to assess cases on the basis of economic, social and cultural rights, not only because the wording of these rights is often general and open-ended, but also because the judiciary does not want to interfere too much with the margin of appreciation of the legislature. To find evidence of the justiciability of economic and social rights, scholars have gone in search of examples of cases in which such rights were deemed justiciable. In fact, international and domestic courts have increasingly enforced access to health-related services.[60]

---

56 Gruskin and Tarantola, 2000, p. 16.

57 See, also, Article 8(2) ECHR, which stipulates under what conditions an interference with the right to private and family life is allowed; it includes restrictions 'for the protection of health and morals.'

58 United Nations, Economic and Social Council, U.N. Sub-Commission on Prevention of Discrimination and Protection of Minorities, Siracusa Principles on the Limitation and Derogation of Provisions in the International Covenant on Civil and Political Rights, Annex, UN Doc E/CN.4/1984/4 (1984). See WHO, '25 Questions & Answers on Health & Human Rights', *Health and Human Rights Publication Series*, Issue No. 1, July 2002, available at www.who.int/hhr/information/25%20Questions%20and%20Answers%20on%20Health%20and%20Human%20Rights.pdf, accessed September 2011.

59 Generally, see Fons Coomans (ed.), *Justiciability of Economic, Social and Cultural Rights*, Antwerp-Oxford: Intersentia, 2006.

60 For a recent analysis on the justiciability [see previous comments on this] of the right to health, see Alicia Yamin 'Beyond compassion: The central role of accountability in applying a

However, most of the examples of enforceability of the right to health have materialised in lower and middle-income countries where more dramatic cases have been heard in the courts.[61] Due to the absence of the minimum social service flours in many countries, violations of the rights are clear and persistent. In the developed world, where the debate is much more about the sufficiency of benefits, there is more reluctance towards the enforceability or so-called 'justiciability' of economic and social rights, including the rights to health, education, and employment. When it comes to Europe, some of the most illustrative decisions have been produced by the European Committee of Social Rights, which were discussed in Chapter 1. While such cases address a wide range of health-related topics, a recurrent theme is the socio-economic protection of vulnerable groups, including the Roma and undocumented migrants. It seems that in situations in which the generally available services are not available, or are denied to a certain population group, the Court is willing to assess compliance with the rights set out in the (Revised) ESC.

3. OTHER HEALTH-RELATED RIGHTS

3.1. INTRODUCTION

As mentioned above, the right to health does not stand alone, but is reinforced and supported by several other rights. General Comment 14 affirms that:

> 'the right to health is closely related to and dependent upon the realisation of other human rights, as contained in the International Bill of Rights, including the rights to food, housing, work, education, human dignity, life, non-discrimination, equality, the prohibition against torture, privacy, access to information, and the freedoms of association, assembly and movement.'[62]

It goes well beyond the scope of this chapter to discuss all the rights elaborately. However, in order to outline the scope of the area of 'health and human rights', some of the rights will be discussed more briefly below. Where relevant, references will be made to other chapters in this book.

---

human rights framework to health', *Health and Human Rights*, Vol. 12, No 2 (2010), *inter alia*, p. 4, available at www.hhrjournal.org/index.php/hhr/article/view/78/163, accessed September 2011.

61 A well-known example concerns the decision of the South African Constitutional Court in *Minister of Health and Others v. Treatment Action Campaign and Others*, CCT 8/02 (decision July 5 2002), on the general availability of the drug *nevirapine*, which is used to prevent the spread of HIV from mother to child.

62 General Comment 14, paragraph 3.

3.2. THE RIGHT TO LIFE

The right to life is sometimes called the most important of all human rights. But there is also a danger in calling it the 'supreme' right, or in placing it at the top of a hierarchy. This could imply that the right to life should always prevail, while there may be occasions where a right to life is to be balanced against other rights or interests. An example concerns situations in which the right to life of a foetus is recognised as conflicting with the rights to health and privacy of the woman[63]

A core aspect of right to life is the *deprivation* of life, including the issue of the death penalty.[64] However, the scope of the right to life has expanded gradually, and is now embracing a broader set of issues, several of which have clear connections to health, and the sphere of medical care. Altogether, we can roughly identify three dimensions in the right to life: issues covering the mentioned *deprivation* of life, the *parameters* of life, and the *protection* of life.[65] It is especially these two last dimensions that are relevant for the protection of health.

With the *parameters of life*, we refer to decisions surrounding the beginning and the end of life. The beginning of life touches upon the issue of abortion – and whether the unborn has a right to life, as opposed to the concurring rights of the pregnant woman. Starting at the UN level, where this question remains largely unresolved, a development in this debate can be observed in the decision of *KL* v. *Peru*. In this decision, the Human Rights Committee (HRC), the treaty monitoring body of the ICCPR, ruled that the refusal of the medical authorities to carry out a therapeutic abortion constituted a violation of Article 2 (life), in conjunction with Articles 7, 17 (privacy) and 24 of the ICCPR, of the woman.[66] Furthermore, at the regional level, some differences can be observed when it comes to the status of the foetus: the American Convention on Human Rights (ACHR) protects the right to life 'from the moment of conception' (although the scope of this provision has been expanded in case law).[67] Contrary to the

63 See ECtHR 16 December 2010, *A., B. & C. t. Ireland* (GC), no. 25579/05 and ECtHR 26 May 2011, *R.R. v. Poland*, no. 27617/04.

64 See Articles 2 ECHR and 6 ICCPR.

65 See, also, Rhona K.M. Smith, *Textbook on International Human Rights*, OUP (2nd Ed.), 2005, Chapter 13.

66 Human Rights Committee, *KL v. Peru*, Communication No. 1153/2003, UN Doc. CCPR/C/85/D/1153/2003, 22 November 2005, available at http://reproductiverights.org/sites/crr.civicactions.net/files/documents/KL%20HRC%20final%20decision.pdf, accessed June 2011.

67 Article 4 ACHR. See the decision of the Inter-American Commission on Human Rights (IACHR) in *Christian B. White & Gary K. Potter v. United States* ('Case of Baby Boy'), Case 2.141, Resolution No. 23/81 (Merits), Inter-Am. C.H.R., OEA/Ser.L/V/II.54 Doc. 9 rev. 1 (1981) (Mar. 6, 1981), in which the Commission rejected the existence of a right to life from the moment of conception.

ACHR, the ECHR does not recognise the right to life from the moment of conception, but allows Contract States to do so. As is more elaborately discussed in Chapters 1 and 5, the ECtHR leaves Contracting States with a wide margin of appreciation, while abortions are, under certain circumstances, considered to be in conformity with the ECHR.[68] Lastly, in the African context, a clear provision is contained in the 'Protocol to the African Charter on Human and Peoples' Rights on the Rights of Women in Africa', better known as the 'Maputo Protocol'. Article 14 (2) (c) of this Protocol urges States Parties to authorise medical abortion 'in cases of sexual assault, rape, incest, and where the continued pregnancy endangers the mental and physical health of the mother or the life of the mother or the foetus.'[69]

Issues surrounding the end of life have also been addressed in the framework of the right to life. In Chapters 1 and 6, the well-known *Pretty* judgment is discussed, and the question of whether the right to life embraces a 'right to die'.[70] While the ECtHR has rejected this assumption, it seems that other rights, including the prohibition of torture and the right to private and family life may play a more significant role when it comes to respecting or fulfilling a person's wish to die.[71]

Thirdly, the right to life embraces positive obligations to take measures to *protect* life. This means, *inter alia*, that states must adopt criminal legislation to punish individuals who deprive others of their right to life, and must establish a police force and take other measures to maintain law and order.[72] But it may also embrace positive measures to offer protection against serious health and environmental problems, and to offer essential health services. The Human Rights Committee (HRC) gives a broad interpretation of the right to life, by claiming that it 'cannot properly be interpreted in a restrictive manner, and the protection of this right requires that States adopt positive measures.'[73] With respect to such positive measures, the HRC refers to measures to reduce infant mortality and to increase life expectancy, especially in adopting measures to eliminate malnutrition and epidemics.[74]

---

68 See, also, for a more elaborate discussion, Chapters 1 and 5.

69 Maputo Protocol, adopted on 11 July 2003, available at www.achpr.org/english/women/protocolwomen.pdf, accessed August 2011.

70 ECtHR 29 April 2002, *Pretty v. the UK*, no. 2346/02.

71 See, notably, ECtHR 20 January 2011, *Haas v. Switzerland*, no. 31322/07.

72 ECtHR 10 October 2000, *Akkoc v. Turkey*, Nos.n 22947 & 8/93 (in which the Court held that the right to life had been violated by the respondent state, as it had not taken sufficient steps to protect the applicant's (Kurdish) husband from being murdered).

73 HRC General Comment No. 06: The right to life, 30/04/1982 (sixteenth session, 1982), available at www.unhchr.ch.

74 HRC, General Comment 6, paragraph 5.

The ECtHR takes an approach comparable to the HRC. In *Cyprus* v. *Turkey*, the ECtHR recognised that 'an issue may arise under Article 2 of the Convention where it is shown that the authorities put an individual's life at risk through the denial of healthcare which they have made available to the population generally.'[75] As was also discussed in Chapter 1, the 'protection of life' also embraces the questions surrounding hunger strike, and the duty to investigate deaths. Furthermore, the protection of life may entail protection against environmental health threats, such as in the case of *Öneryildiz v. Turkey*, where a methane explosion at a rubbish tip caused the death of 39 slum dwellers.[76] Altogether, when it comes to the duty to protect life under the right to life, the right to life clearly has a health-related dimension, and in this regard, it connects and overlaps with the scope of the right to health.

3.3. THE RIGHT TO LIBERTY AND SECURITY OF THE PERSON

The right to liberty and security of the person is set out in, *inter alia*, Article 5 ECHR. This provision primarily stipulates the right to (physical) liberty, subject only to lawful arrest or detention under certain other circumstances, such as arrest on suspicion of a crime or imprisonment in fulfilment of a sentence. But as discussed in Chapters 1, 4 and 5, there are several ECtHR judgments concerning the deprivation of liberty of persons with a mental disability.[77]

In addition, the right to liberty and security of persons can be relevant in relation to matters relating to reproductive health, including the wish to have an abortion and the issues of forced sterilisation and female genital mutilation.[78] For example, the right to liberty may imply a right on the part of the woman to choose to have an abortion, and as such, it may support the right to privacy. While the ECtHR has not addressed the right to liberty and security in such a way, some domestic courts have based access to an abortion on the basis of this right.[79]

---

75 ECtHR 10 May 2001, *Cyprus v Turkey*, no. 25781/94, paragraph 219.

76 ECtHR 30 November 2004, *Öneryildiz v. Turkey* (GC), no. 48939/99.

77 *Inter alia*, ECtHR 24 October 1979, *Winterwerp v. the Netherlands,* no. 6301/73, paragraph 39.

78 See, also, Cook and Fathalla, 1996, p. 118.

79 Cook and Fathalla (1996, p. 118) refer to several decisions by Constitutional courts in Europe in which the right to liberty and security was applied to protect the rights to liberty and security of the mother. For a discussion of the French approach, in which the right to liberty plays a role, see Danielle Keats Morris, 'Planned Parenthood v. Kasey: From U.S. "Rights Talk" to Western "Responsibility Talk"', *Fordham International Law Journal*, Volume 6, Issue 3, 1992, pp. 2–40.

3.4. THE RIGHT TO PRIVACY AND FAMILY LIFE

Article 8 ECHR combines the right to respect for privacy with the right to family life. This provision has several health-related dimensions, which are discussed more elaborately in Chapters 1, 4, 5, and 6. It emerges that the rights to privacy and family life are connected to issues of personal autonomy, including access to medical data, the disclosure of confidential information, abortion, transsexualism, and end-of-life decisions.

Another dimension of the right to respect for privacy and family life concerns the protection against health risks and environmental harm in particular. In several decisions, the ECtHR has established a link between such health risks and the enjoyment of the right to privacy and family life.[80]

3.5. FREEDOM OF EXPRESSION AND THE RIGHT TO INFORMATION

Article 10 ECHR contains the freedom to receive and impart information. The ECtHR does not construe this provision as imposing on a state a positive obligation to disseminate information or to disclose information to the public.[81] As was discussed elaborately by Aart Hendriks in Chapter 1, this right contains a negative obligation to refrain from interfering with the right to freely disseminate information, for example, about the availability of abortion services.[82] While the ECtHR does not recognise a positive obligation on the part of governments to disseminate information on the basis of Article 10 ECHR, Article 8 ECHR offers some solace: the ECtHR has recognised that Article 8 ECHR entails a duty of healthcare providers to inform patients prior to treatment as part of the informed consent principle, reflecting the patient's right to personal autonomy. Another dimension of Article 8 ECHR concerns the confidentiality of medical files, and the physician's duty not to disclose medical data to others without the patient's consent (see Chapter 1). Mette Hartlev concludes that the guidance provided by the case law is rather general, and that in order to acquire a more detailed picture of the scope of a right to information, it is necessary to look into patients' rights legislation (see, for a more elaborate discussion, Chapter 4).

---

80 *Inter alia*, ECtHR 9 December 1994, *Lopez-Ostra v. Spain*, ECHR, Series A, number 303C, ECtHR 19 February 1998, *Anna Guerra et al v. Italy*, no. 14967/89, ECtHR 9 June 2005, *Fadeyeva v. Russia*, no. 55723/00, and ECtHR 19 October 2005, *Roche v. UK* (GC), no. 32555/96.

81 See, also, Dirk Voorhoof, *Sdružení Jihočeské Matky v. The Czech Republic*, available at http://merlin.obs.coe.int/iris/2006/9/article1.en.html, accessed September 2011.

82 ECtHR 29 October 1992, *Open Door & Dublin Well Woman v. Ireland*, no. 14234/88 & 14235/88.

The issue of access to information has also come up in a few cases concerning (environmental) health risks. In relation to the provision of environmental information, the ECtHR has stated that the freedom to receive and impart information cannot be 'construed as imposing on a State, (...) positive obligations to collect and disseminate information of its own motion.' Such an obligation is, nonetheless, (again) based on Article 8 ECHR.[83] In a more recent decision against the Czech Republic, the Court slightly expanded the scope of Article 10 ECHR. It recognised that the refusal of the Czech authorities to grant access to administrative documents regarding plans for a new nuclear power station is to be considered as an interference with the right to receive information, as granted under Article 10 ECHR. This did not, however, lead to a violation of Article 10 ECHR, because according to the Court, the Czech authorities had reasoned in a pertinent and sufficient manner the refusal to grant access to the requested documents.[84] Yet the implication of this decision is that restrictions of access to administrative documents now have to be assessed in light of the limitations clause in Article 10, paragraph 2 ECHR. According to Voorhoof, this decision 'opens new perspectives for citizens, journalists and NGOs for accessing administrative documents in matters of public interest.'[85]

3.6. THE RIGHT TO MARRY AND FOUND A FAMILY

The general approach of the ECtHR is that the right to found a family does not embrace a positive right to increase the size of the family.[86] In a decision of 2003, the Court found that 'the right to have grandchildren or the right to procreation is not covered by Article 12 or any other Article of the Convention.'[87]

Yet the right to found a family may offer (additional) protection in situations in which states are putting obstacles in the way of couples who wish to exercise their ability to procreate (see, also, Chapter 5).[88] An example concerns situations in which the authorities seek to submit women to forced sterilisation or abortion. For example, in the case of the ECtHR in *V.C. v. Slovakia*, the complainant

---

83 ECtHR 19 February 1998, *Anna Guerra et al v. Italy*, no. 14967/89 (where the Court decided that there was a violation of 8 ECHR). For other recent environmental cases, see, *inter alia*, ECtHR 30 November 2004, *Öneryildiz v. Turkey* (GC), no. 48939/99 (violation of Article 2 ECHR) and ECtHR 19 October 2005, *Roche v. UK* (GC), no. 32555/96 (violation of Article 8 ECHR).

84 ECtHR 10 July 2006, *Sdružení Jihočeské Matky v. The Czech Republic* (admiss. dec.), no. 19101/03.

85 See Voorhoof *supra*, note 81.

86 Pieter van Dijk *et al.*, *Theory and Practice of the European Convention on Human Rights*, Antwerp-Oxford: Intersentia, 2006 (4th ed.), p. 856.

87 *Margarita Šijakova e.a. v. Macedonia* (admissibility dec.), 6 March 2003, no. 67914/01.

88 Van Dijk *et al.*, 2006, pp. 853–856.

argued, *inter alia*, that her right to found a family had been breached on account of her sterilisation without her full and informed consent.[89] Furthermore, the right to found a family could potentially entail a positive obligation to provide relevant information and services on family planning and fertility, for example, to prevent a frequently occurring curable infection.[90]

3.7. THE RIGHTS TO BENEFIT FROM SCIENTIFIC PROGRESS

Contrary to the American and African frameworks,[91] the ECHR does not contain a right to enjoy the benefits of scientific progress. Nonetheless, several UN Treaties contain this right, as well as the Declaration of Helsinki of the World Medical Association (see Box 1), and as such, this norm influences the European (domestic) legal orders. The right to enjoy the benefits of scientific progress could require European governments and European institutions to give a high priority to medical research into the needs of vulnerable population groups, including women, children, and ethnic minorities.

3.8. ECONOMIC, SOCIAL AND CULTURAL RIGHTS, AND THE PROTECTION OF HEALTH

Other economic, social and cultural rights include the rights to housing, education, food and work. As will be addressed more elaborately in Chapter 7, there is growing awareness that the way in which people are raised, educated, live and work are decisive for people's health, or the so-called 'social determinants of health'. The other economic, social and cultural rights have the potential to enhance the improvement of people's social determinants of health.

The right to education is of particular importance for the promotion and protection of health. Article 13(1) ICESCR affirms that education shall 'enable all persons to participate effectively in society.' Research has consistently shown that people's health is determined, to a significant extent, by the level to which they are educated. Women's education, in particular, strongly influences

89 ECtHR, *V.C. v. Slovakia*, case no. 18968/07 (admissibility decision of 16 June 2009).

90 Cook and Fathalla give the example of a urinary tract infection, which is a serious cause of infertility in some parts of Africa. Cook and Fathalla, 1996, p. 119.

91 WMA Declaration of Helsinki, Ethical Principles for Medical Research Involving Human Subjects, Adopted by the 18th WMA General Assembly, Helsinki, Finland, June 1964 (last amended in 2008).

improved reproductive health, including infant survival and the healthy growth of children.[92]

4. CONCLUSIONS

A wide range of rights was presented in this Chapter which have the potential to protect and to promote health, and which are relevant in a healthcare setting. Based on the internationally guaranteed right to health, there is a legally binding right to healthcare services and a right ensuring the necessary conditions for health, including access to health-related information, access to safe drinking water, occupational health, and the protection of environmental health. It remains unclear what services are granted exactly on the basis of the right to health, and the question arises as to whether it can be a useful tool for priority-setting in healthcare. For these reasons, courts are reluctant to judge cases on the basis of this right. Nonetheless, in combination with the principle of non-discrimination, the right to health proves an effective tool for protecting the health needs of vulnerable population groups, including women, children, and (undocumented) migrants.

Several other health-related human rights were mentioned in this Chapter. On some occasions, such rights reinforce the right to health, for example, when it comes to the principle of non-discrimination, and in situations in which the right to life protects health. On other occasions, such rights have a distinct meaning for the protection of health, for example, where the right to privacy gives women the freedom to choose to have an abortion. Lastly, some rights have a specific meaning in healthcare settings, for example, the right to liberty and security, which sets limits to the involuntary placement in institutions of persons with mental disabilities.

---

92 Cook and Fathalla, 1996, referring to J.N. Hobcraft, 'Women's Education, Child Welfare and Child Survical: A Review of the Evidence', *Health Transition Review*, 3:150–175, 1993.

CHAPTER 4
PATIENTS' RIGHTS

Mette Hartlev

1. INTRODUCTION

Since the 1970s, patients' rights have attracted increasing political and legal attention. Before then it was not common for patients' relationships with healthcare services to be conceptualised in *'rights terms'*. Rather, such relationships were governed by the duties and discretion of healthcare professionals, and patients were supposed to 'follow doctors' orders'. Nowadays, patients' rights are commonly recognised, both nationally and internationally.

Despite the widespread recognition of patients' rights, there is no specific definition of what we mean by them. Generally speaking, patients' rights can be defined as the rights patients have when interacting with healthcare services and providers. Consequently, patients' rights can be understood as a cluster of rights that includes the right to become a patient, rights while receiving treatment, and rights after treatment.[1] As will be further discussed in Section 2, this definition is very broad. It covers a number of different rights, the content of which may differ according to the specific situation. Hence, there are differences between a patient who receives treatment for a conventional disorder, and situations in which patients have to deal with, for example, organ transplantation or infertility treatment. Likewise, some patients are more vulnerable than others, and may require special attention. Patients' rights therefore involve a number of complicated issues

The previous chapters have already revealed that human rights have an impact on the rights of patients, both more generally (Chapters 1 and 2), and with regard to the specific issue of access to health services (Chapter 3). In this chapter we will first look more closely at the definition and development of patients' rights, and see how they are related to human rights (paragraph 2). Patients' rights and human rights share a number of general legal principles of significance in interpreting and applying patients' rights. These principles,

---

1 See, e.g., A. Kjønstad, 'Twelve main principles in Norwegian health law', 33(3) *Retfærd* (2010), pp. 60–78.

together with the international patients' rights instrument, will be presented and explained (paragraph 3) before we embark on a more thorough analysis of basic patients' rights. As other chapters in the book deal with specific patients' rights (Chapter 3 – access to health services) and with patients' rights in specific situations or for vulnerable groups (Chapters 7–10), the focus of this chapter will be on patients right to self-determination, information, confidentiality, and access to justice and compensation (paragraphs 3–6 and 8). The rights of patients participating in medical research will also be addressed (paragraph 7).

2. DEFINITION AND DEVELOPMENT OF PATIENTS' RIGHTS

2.1. CONCEPT OF PATIENTS' RIGHTS

Even though patients' rights were not high on the agenda before the 1970s, it would be wrong to take this period of time as the point at which patients' rights began to be recognised. Patients did have rights before this, and, as we shall see later, indeed some patients' rights date far back in time. However, these rights were neither very visible nor comprehensive. Hence, since the 1970s older rights have been named and codified as patients' rights, and new and more comprehensive patients' rights have been recognised as a response to technological advances and other changes in society.

When discussing patients' rights, it is, first of all, necessary to consider what we understand as a 'patient'. Are we talking exclusively about persons who have been diagnosed with a disease, or do we also include those who suspect they are sick but have not yet been diagnosed, as well as healthy persons who are subject to preventive measures, such as screening programmes? Together with other concepts such as sickness and health, it is not easy to agree on a single definition of what constitutes 'a patient'. However, the World Health Organization (WHO) works with a definition of patients as 'user(s) of health care systems whether healthy or sick' – a definition that will also be used in this context.[2] This characterisation is very broad as it includes all persons – sick and healthy – who use healthcare services, whether or not on their own initiative. Because of the breadth of the patient concept, it is important to be aware of the actual diversity among patients of different genders, ages, social and cultural backgrounds, levels of education, beliefs, needs, and resources – differences which may call for special concern with regard to both the individual patient and special groups of patients.

---

2 WHO, A Declaration of the Promotions of Rights of Patients in Europe, Copenhagen 1994, part 7.

What kind of rights should thus be considered patients' rights? No distinct, uniform definition of patients' rights exists, but it is possible to get an idea about the delimitation of patients' rights from international patients' rights legislation and from text books and other academic writings in this particular field of law.[3] The WHO's regional European office was the first to initiate a more systematic approach to patients' rights. It instigated two separate studies on health law and patients' rights in Europe in the early 1980s, thereby providing very valuable knowledge about the legal situation in this area.[4] These studies also became instrumental when experts drafted 'The Principles of Patients Rights' for a consultation meeting in Amsterdam in 1994 hosted by the Dutch government, and under the auspices of the WHO's regional office for Europe. The outcome of this meeting was 'A Declaration of the Promotion of Patients Rights in Europe' (hereafter, the WHO Declaration), the first comprehensive, international legal instrument dealing with patients' rights. The Declaration provides a picture of the different rights attributed to patients, namely, the right to information (principle 2), to consent (principle 3), to confidentiality and privacy (principle 4), to care and treatment (principle 5), and to application (access to justice and compensation) (principle 6). The basic rights stipulated in the WHO Declaration have received general recognition in both international and national patients' rights legislation, and they have also served as a source of inspiration for academic lawyers in the field of health law.

As mentioned by way of introduction, the rights of patients can roughly be divided into three categories: First is the right to be treated as a patient. This includes the right to have access to care, and also rights with regard to the quality of such care, waiting times, *etc.* Secondly, there are the rights patients have while receiving treatment. This includes the right to self-determination, the right to information and the right to confidentiality. Finally, there are the rights patients have after treatment, including post-treatment information (including access to one's file and to have this information destroyed), access to justice (the right to complain) and the ability to be compensated for harm caused by the treatment.[5] This categorisation provides a useful point of departure for the discussion.

In discussing patients' rights, it is also common to make a distinction between *positive* and *negative* rights.[6] Whereas a positive right is a 'right to' something, a negative right is defined as a 'right from' something. Positive rights

---

3 L. Fallberg, 'Patients' Rights in the Nordic Countries', 7 *European Journal of Health Law*, pp. 123–143.

4 H.J.J. Leenen, G. Pinet and A.V. Prims, *Trends in Health Legislation in Europe*, Paris: Masson 1986, H.J.J. Leenen, J.K.M Gevers and G. Pinet, *Patients' Rights in Europe*, Netherlands: Kluwer 1993. See also H.J.J. Leenen, 'Patients' Rights', 1 *European Journal of Health Law* (1994), pp. 5–13.

5 Kjønstad, *supra*, note 1.

6 See, e.g., Fallberg, *supra*, note 3, and Leenen, *supra*, note 4. The distinction between positive and negative rights is also addressed in Chapters 1 and 3.

oblige somebody (e.g. governments) to fulfil the right, for example, to ensure sufficient and equal distribution of resources, such as access to healthcare. Negative rights impose a duty on governments to ensure that individuals are not subjected to unjustified infringement of their freedoms and other fundamental individual rights, for example, treatment that is against the patients' will. The distinction between positive rights and negative rights is closely related to the discussion of the relationship between social and economic rights *vis-à-vis* civil and political rights, which has been intensively debated in the human rights literature. However, even though the distinction between social and economic rights, on the one hand, and civil and political rights, on the other, is reflected and confirmed in human rights law, it seems to be the general perception among human rights scholars that these rights are indivisible and interdependent.[7] This is also confirmed by the concept of patients' rights, which includes both positive and negative rights, as well as rights which both include positive and negative aspects.

2.2. DEVELOPMENT OF PATIENTS' RIGHTS

If we look more closely at the list of patients' rights, we find both very old rights and quite new ones. The right to *confidentiality* is probably the oldest patient right, even though it was commonly considered the physician's prerogative to remain silent. It dates back to the writings of Hippocrates on medical ethics, in which it is stipulated that: 'Whatever, in connection with my professional practice or not, in connection with it, I see or hear, in the life of men, which ought not to be spoken of abroad, I will not divulge, as reckoning that all such should be kept secret.'[8] The Hippocratic Oath is framed as a *duty* that doctors must comply with, and this duty-oriented approach dominated the relationship between patients and healthcare professionals until recently.

Respect of patients' *autonomy and right to self-determination* is often associated with the Nuremberg code and the requirement of informed *consent* laid down in this text (see below). However, patients' right to self-determination was acknowledged long before World War II. Plato discusses the importance of obtaining consent from 'free men' (in contrast to slaves) in the *Laws*,[9] and the enlightenment brought the idea of personal freedom to the fore, thereby supporting the requirement to obtain consent for medical treatment. Even though it was recognised both in medical ethics and the history of ideas that it

7 I.E. Koch, 'The Justiciability of Indivisible Rights', 72 *Nordic Journal of International Law* (2003), pp. 3–39.

8 Here cited from the *Encyclopaedia Britannica*. Hippocrates is supposed to have lived from around 460 to 370 BC.

9 P. Dalla-Vorgia, J. Lascaratos, P. Skiadas and T. Garanis-Parpadatos, 'Is consent in medicine a concept only of modern times?', 27 *Journal of Medical Ethics* 2001, pp. 59–61.

was normally not legitimate to expose patients to compulsory treatment, there was, until recently, the perception that a patient's voluntary contact with a doctor or with healthcare services in itself implied sufficient consent to necessary treatment. To understand the full scope of the right to self-determination, it is thus necessary not only to look at the patient's right to consent, but also to include the right to information and the right to privacy.

The idea that patients are entitled to *information* – in contrast to the right to consent – is quite new, and was developed in close collaboration with the increasing importance attached to the right to self-determination under the Nuremberg Code. This Code was established in connection with the so-called Medicine Case, which formed part of the war crimes trials held in Nuremberg after World War II. The Medicine Case was concerned with the medical experiments performed by doctors on prisoners in concentration camps. These experiments exposed the prisoners to immense suffering, damage and death, and it was clear that the prisoners did not have any choice regarding whether or not to participate. However, when preparing the case, the prosecution was faced with a difficult legal challenge, because the doctors had not violated any laws in performing these experiments. Since no German or international law prohibited experiments on human beings, the Nuremberg Code was drafted during the case to establish the general legal principles that all doctors are supposed to comply with, whether they are stipulated in positive law or not. The Code stresses, as its first principle, the importance of obtaining *voluntary, informed consent* from the research subject.

Even though the Code reflected the general principles of medical ethics, the requirement to inform patients about the diagnosis and the risks associated with the treatment was not considered good medical practice in medical history. Previously, professional medical ethics required doctors to remain silent on the diagnosis – especially if the patient was suffering from a serious condition – and not to reveal the risks and side effects associated with the treatment to the patient. Consequently, it was considered not to be in the patient's best interest to receive complicated and sometimes disappointing information about their health and treatment options, and it was the 'doctor's privilege' to assess whether patients should be informed or not.[10] However, gradually this attitude changed. The Nuremberg Code paved the way for this change, but it did not represent a genuine breakthrough for the principle of informed consent, given that the code focuses on regulating medical experiments and not medical treatment in general. After the war crimes trials in Nuremberg, the informed consent requirement was largely ignored, but in the 1950s and 1960s a number of US court cases revitalised the discussion about patients' rights to information, and it is now generally acknowledged that in giving valid and proper consent to

10 J. Katz, *The Silent World of Doctor and Patient*, Johns Hopkins University Press: Baltimore 2001.

treatment, patients are entitled to information about their health condition, treatment opportunities and the possible advantages and side-effects of specific kinds of treatment.[11] Another dimension of the right to information is the patient's right to have access to their medical file. This right is also of more recent date and has been influenced by the development of data protection law.

Compared with the right to information, the right of *complaint* and to be *compensated* for medical malpractice is of longer standing. However, in practice patients often face difficulties in getting their complaints and compensation claims through the normal judicial system (health authorities and/or courts). Hence, this is an area in which many countries have taken initiatives to strengthen patients' rights by introducing patient ombudsmen or other specific complaints mechanisms, and some countries have also established special no-fault compensation schemes which provide patients with easier access to compensation in cases of medical malpractice.[12]

All in all, the development of patients' rights has been a long journey from the ancient writings in medical ethics of 400–300 BC, through the recognition of individual liberty advanced during the Enlightenment, passing further through the post-war reaction to the medical atrocities of World War II – especially the recognition of dignity and equal worth of all human beings – and finally to today, where new technologies and the development of welfare societies have added new dimensions to the concept of patients' rights. New rights have been recognised during the journey, most notably the right to information and more specific rights with regard to access to health, and the old rights have all been revised and supplemented over time to be adapted to developments in society. Along this journey, patients' rights have also changed in character, from being reflections of duties imposed on doctors, to being stipulated as the individual rights of patients. This transformation to a rights-based approach has been supported by the general recognition of human rights in most of the world, especially since the end of the 1980s.

Human rights have been a faithful travel partner in the last part of this journey, and, since the Nuremberg Code, health law and human rights law have developed in close collaboration as an interaction between national experts and scholars and initiatives taken by international organisations.[13] Legal developments at national levels have influenced the initiatives taken by the international community, which in turn have been a source of inspiration for

11 For more details, see R. Faden and T.L. Beauchamp, *A History and Theory of Informed Consent*, Oxford University Press: USA 1986.

12 This is the case in, for example, the Nordic countries and New Zealand.

13 J. Dute, 'The Leading Principles of the Convention of Human Rights and Biomedicine', in J.K.M. Gevers, E.H. Hondius and J.H. Hubben (eds.), *Health Law, Human Rights and the Biomedicine Convention: Essays in Honour of Henriette Roscam Abbing* Koninklijke Brill NV: Leuven 2005, pp. 3–12; and Mette Hartlev, 'Diversity and Harmonisation: Trends and Challenges in European Health Law', 17 *European Journal for Health Law* (2010), pp. 37–50.

further national developments.[14] The WHO was very instrumental in the development of the first comprehensive patients' rights instrument, and both the Council of Europe and UNESCO have been very active in this field of law during the last 20 years. These new patient-oriented human rights instruments have supplemented the general human rights instruments, which have also proved to be of importance for patients' rights (for more detail, see Chapter 1). The EU is also playing an increasingly important role in this area, a role that has been strengthened due to the Lisbon Treaty and the formal role of the EU Charter of Fundamental Rights (for more detail, see Chapter 2). Consequently, it is not possible to understand patients' rights properly without including a human rights perspective.

3. PATIENTS' RIGHTS IN INTERNATIONAL LAW: GENERAL PRINCIPLES AND LEGAL INSTRUMENTS

3.1. LEGAL INSTRUMENTS

A number of international legal instruments of importance for health and human rights have already been introduced in Chapter 1 (general human rights instruments) and Chapter 2 (EU law). In addition to these general legal instruments, there are a number of human rights instruments that deal more specifically with patients' rights issues, and thus serve to specify and contextualise the meaning of general human rights law in the fields of healthcare and biomedical research. Furthermore, there are also other international guidelines concerned with patients' rights, which have been drafted by various non-governmental organisations and which have been influential in the development of patients' rights. Accordingly, before we embark on more specific patients' rights issues in paragraphs 4–8, the most important of these rules will be identified and briefly presented.

In *human rights law* the principal patients' rights instruments – apart from provisions in the general human rights instruments – are the WHO Declaration;[15] the Biomedicine Convention, with its additional protocols;[16] the

14 Leenen, *supra*, note 4.

15 *Supra*, note 2.

16 Convention for the Protection of Human Rights and Dignity of the Human Being with regard to the Application of Biology and Medicine: Convention on Human Rights and Biomedicine, CETS 164, Oviedo 1997; Additional Protocol to the Convention on Human Rights and Biomedicine on the Prohibition of Cloning Human Beings, CETS 168, Paris 1998; Additional Protocol to the Convention on Human Rights and Biomedicine on Transplantation of Organs and Tissues of Human Origin, CETS 186, Strasbourg 2002; Additional Protocol to the Convention on Human Rights and Biomedicine concerning Biomedical Research, CETS 195,

CoE recommendations in the field of patients' rights and biotechnology;[17] and the three UNESCO Declarations on bioethics and genetics.[18] The Biomedicine Convention is of special importance. As mentioned in Chapter 1, the convention has a status as *lex specialis vis-à-vis* the ECHR. Hence, although the Convention itself does not entail strong enforcement mechanisms, the provisions and general principles of the Convention may be legally enforceable through the case law of the ECtHR.[19] Furthermore, the Convention has also served as a source of inspiration for the EU Charter on Fundamental Rights (especially Articles 1-3).[20]

In addition to the Biomedicine Convention, the CoE Data Protection Convention has also had an impact on patients' rights with regard to confidentiality and the self-determination of health information.[21] In *EU law* the most important instruments seen from a patients' rights perspective – apart from the provisions of the Treaty and of the Charter on Fundamental Rights – are Regulation 1408/71 EEC, the clinical trials Directives,[22] and the Directive on cross-border care.[23] The data protection Directive may also have an impact on patients' rights with regard to confidentiality and the self-determination of health information.[24]

A few other patients' rights texts deserve to be mentioned in this context, notably, the Helsinki Declaration issued by the World Medical Association.[25] Although this text does not have formal legal force, it has been a source of inspiration for many of the international patients' rights instruments. Another

---

Strasbourg 2005; and Additional Protocol to the Convention on Human Rights and Biomedicine concerning Genetic Testing for Health Purposes, CETS 203, Strasbourg 2008.

17 A complete list of recommendations issued in the field of biotechnology is available on the CoE website: www.coe.int/t/dg3/healthbioethic/texts_and_documents/default_en.asp#TaD_RecCM.

18 Universal Declaration on the Human Genome and Human Rights, Paris 1997; International Declaration on Human Genetic Data, Paris 2003; and Universal Declaration on Bioethics and Human Rights, Paris 2005.

19 See Chapter 1, section 5.

20 See Chapter 2.

21 Convention for the Protection of Individuals with regard to Automatic Processing of Personal Data, CETS 108, Strasbourg 1981. CoE has also issued a number of recommendations, some of which are concerned with the protection of health information; see www.coe.int/t/dghl/standardsetting/dataprotection/Legal_instruments_en.asp.

22 Directive 2001/20/EC on the approximation of the laws, regulations and administrative provisions of the Member States relating to the implementation of good clinical practice in the conduct of clinical trials on medicinal products for human use (the Clinical Trials Directive), and Directive 2005/28/EC, laying down principles and detailed guidelines for good clinical practice as regards investigational medicinal products for human use, as well as the requirements for authorisation of the manufacturing or importation of such products (the Good Clinical Practice Directive).

23 Directive 2011/24/EU on the application of patients' rights in cross-border health care.

24 Directive 95/46/EC on the protection of individuals with regard to the processing of personal data and on the free movement of such data.

25 World Medical Association, Declaration of Helsinki (last revised 2008).

document called the 'European Charter of Patients' Rights' has been developed by the Active Citizenship Network, a European network of citizens' organisations.[26]

3.2. GENERAL LEGAL PRINCIPLES

All legal disciplines have a number of general legal principles that encapsulate the basic values of this particular field of law. Such legal principles are often closely related to the general ethics of society and have a more robust and durable character than specific legal provisions.[27] General legal principles are important because they frame a legal field and serve as a source of interpretation of more specific rules.

Not surprisingly, the general legal principles operating in the area of health law are inspired by human rights law. Respect for patients' dignity, autonomy, integrity and confidentiality, together with the right to equal treatment and non-discrimination, are important legal principles that are detectable in both human rights and patients' rights law.[28] Since these principles serve as an important source for the interpretation of patients' rights instruments, it is essential to have a basic understanding of their substance and interrelationships.

Dignity is a core concept in health and human rights law. Respect for dignity is stipulated as a key concept in many of the important legal instruments.[29] The principle of dignity is influenced by the thinking of the German philosopher Immanuel Kant, and in particular, the distinction in Kantian thinking between *objects*, which have a *price* (because they are replaceable by an equivalent), and *persons*, who have *dignity* (intrinsic worth), and who are irreplaceable.[30] On the basis of this distinction, Kant argued that human beings should always be treated as aims in themselves, and never merely as a means (prohibition of the instrumentalisation of human beings). Although there are divergent positions in moral philosophy regarding the understanding of dignity, the way in which this concept is used in human rights and patients' rights law reflects the general idea of the intrinsic and equal worth of all human beings.[31]

---

26 European Charter of Patients' Rights, Active Citizenship Network, Brussels, 15 November 2002, available at www.activecitizenship.net/images/stories/media/EuropeanCharter/europeancharter_integrale_ing.pdf (retrieved 18 July 2011).

27 Kjønstad, *supra*, note 1.

28 Dute, *supra*, note 13.

29 See, e.g. Article 1 of the Biomedicine Convention, Article 2 of UNESCO Declaration on Bioethics and Human Rights, paragraph 1.2 of the WHO Declaration on Patients Rights, and Article 1 of the EU Charter on Fundamental Rights.

30 I. Kant, *Foundations of the Metaphysics of Morals*, London: Hutchinson University Library 1966, pp. 96–97.

31 A.B. Da Silva, 'Autonomy, Dignity and Integrity in Health Care Ethics: A Moral Philosophical Perspective', in H.S. Aasen, R. Halvorson, A.B. Da Silva and J.F. Bernt (eds.), *Human Rights,*

The principle of *integrity* is closely related to that of dignity. It generally expresses respect for the untouchability of the individual, both mentally and physically, and, as with dignity, the integrity of a person is considered intrinsic and unchangeable.[32] References to integrity are found in a number of health and human rights instruments, both as a general principle, and, more specifically, in provisions regarding respect for privacy and autonomy.[33]

Autonomy is also an essential concept in health and human rights law. As with the concepts of dignity and integrity, there are also different theoretical positions in moral philosophy with regard to the meaning of autonomy. However, it expresses profoundly the idea of freedom of the will and respect for individual freedom and the right to self-determination.[34] Accordingly, individuals should have the authority to make decisions regarding their personal affairs in order to live a life in accordance with their own preferences. From this idea flow a number of freedoms such as freedom of expression and thought, and the principle of autonomy is also expressed in many health and human rights instruments, both as a general principle, and, more specifically, as consent requirements with regard to medical interventions and the processing of personal information.[35]

The importance of respecting individuals' *privacy* has already been touched upon in the presentation of integrity and autonomy. However, although privacy is closely related to these principles, it cannot be reduced to other principles, but must be considered as a principle in its own right. Privacy is concerned with respect for the individual's private life, and requires both that privacy should be respected and protected, and that the individual should have a right to informational self-determination. *Privacy* and *confidentiality* are often used

---

Dignity and Autonomy in Health Care and Social Services: Nordic Perspectives, Antwerp-Oxford-Portland: Intersentia 2009, pp. 13–52; H.S. Aasen, 'Dignity and Human Rights in the Modern Welfare State', in H.S. Aasen, R. Halvorson, A.B. Da Silva and J.F. Bernt (eds.), *Human Rights, Dignity and Autonomy in Health Care and Social Services: Nordic Perspectives*, Antwerp-Oxford-Portland: Intersentia 2009, pp. 53–68; and M. Hartlev, 'Coercive Treatment and Human Dignity', in H.S. Aasen, R. Halvorson, A.B. Da Silva and J.F. Bernt (eds.), *Human Rights, Dignity and Autonomy in Health Care and Social Services: Nordic Perspectives*, Antwerp-Oxford-Portland: Intersentia 2009, pp. 129–144.

32 Da Silva, *supra*, note 31; K. E. Tranöy, 'The Roots of medical Ethics in a Shared Morality', in P. Allebeck and B. Jansson (eds.), *Ethics in Medicine: Individual Integrity Versus Demands of Society*, Karolinska Institute Nobel Conference Series, New York: Raven Press 1990, pp. 23–31; and E. Pellegrino, 'The Relationship of Autonomy and Integrity in Medical Ethics', in P. Allebeck and B. Jansson (eds.), *Ethics in Medicine: Individual Integrity Versus Demands of Society*, Karolinska Institute Nobel Conference Series, New York: Raven Press 1990, pp. 3–21.

33 See, e.g., Article 1 of the Biomedicine Convention, Article 8 of UNESCO Declaration on Bioethics and Human Rights, paragraph 1.3 of the WHO Declaration, and Article 3 of the EU Charter on Fundamental Rights.

34 Da Silva, *supra*, note 31.

35 See references to autonomy as a general principle in Article 1 of the Biomedicine Convention, Article 5 of UNESCO Declaration on Bioethics and Human Rights, paragraph 1.2 of the WHO Declaration, and Article 3 of the EU Charter on Fundamental Rights.

interchangeably, but the two concepts have slightly different meanings and also serve somewhat different purposes. This is expressed very clearly by Beauchamp and Childress:

> An infringement of a person's right to confidentiality occurs only if the person (or institution) to whom the information was disclosed in confidence fails to protect the information or deliberately discloses it to someone without first-party consent. By contrast, a person who without authorisation enters a hospital record room or computer data-bank violates rights of privacy rather than rights of confidentiality. Only the person (or institution) who receives information in a confidential relationship can be charged with violating rights of confidentiality.[36]

Accordingly, confidentiality has to do with a relationship and with the entrusting of personal and intimate details to healthcare providers. Privacy, in contrast, does not require the existence of a relationship. Patients' rights to privacy and confidentiality are very well-established legal principles and are set out in all patients' rights instruments.[37]

The principles of *equal treatment* and *non-discrimination* are very prominent in human rights law, and are also reflected in a number of patients' rights instruments.[38] They basically express the idea that individuals should be considered of equal worth and should be treated equally and without discrimination by healthcare services with regard to access to care, as well as in other respects. The principle of non-discrimination does not prescribe that patients should be treated 'the same', but, rather, with due respect to relevant differences, such as health status.

As will be clear, the general legal principles are partly overlapping and interconnected. Equal treatment is closely related to dignity and the perception of the equal worth of all human beings. Dignity, integrity and autonomy are also interwoven in complex ways. Individuals may exercise autonomy with regard to legitimate infringement of their integrity, e.g. when consenting to treatment that involves an intervention of their body, or when agreeing to the disclosure of health information to third parties. However, as we shall see in paragraph 4, the principle of dignity places a limit on the individual's exercise of self-determination.

---

36 T.L. Beauchamp and J.F. Childress, *Principles of Biomedical Ethics*, 5th edition, New York: Oxford University Press 2001, p. 304.

37 See references to privacy and confidentiality in Article 10 of the Biomedicine Convention, Article 9 of UNESCO Declaration on Bioethics and Human Rights, paragraph 1.4 and 4 of the WHO Declaration, and Articles 7–8 of the EU Charter on Fundamental Rights.

38 See references to equal treatment in Articles 1, 11 and 14 of the Biomedicine Convention, Articles 10–12 of UNESCO Declaration on Bioethics and Human Rights, paragraphs 5.1 and 6.2 of the WHO Declaration on Patients Rights, and Articles 20–26 of the EU Charter on Fundamental Rights.

4. RIGHT TO SELF-DETERMINATION

4.1. AUTONOMY, SELF-DETERMINATION AND CONSENT

As mentioned in paragraph 3, the general idea of autonomy is that individuals are entitled to live their lives in accordance with their own preferences. In other words, it is the individual herself – and not other persons – who is in a position to make decisions regarding important personal matters, and these decisions must be respected, including in situations in which other persons would have chosen differently.[39] Health related decisions touching upon issues of life and death are definitely issues that belong to the individual's personal sphere. It is therefore not surprising that autonomy plays an important role in patients' rights law. Respect for patient autonomy and the right to self-determination is often expressed in terms of *consent requirements*, and thus as recognition of a 'negative right' to self-determination. However, the right to self-determination also includes certain positive rights, such as the right to have access to treatment and to choose from among various types of treatment. The focus in this chapter will primarily be on consent requirements, as the positive variant of patients' right to self-determination – access to health services – is addressed in Chapter 3. However, a few issues relating to a positive right to self-determination need to be mentioned in this chapter as well.

To be able to exercise autonomy and give valid informed consent presupposes, first of all, that the individual has *decision-making capacity*, legally, as well as factually. Legal capacity presupposes the personal capacity to make a rational decision, and it requires a certain age that is laid down in national legal orders. Children below the stipulated age do not have decision-making capacity in a legal sense, and adults may also lack legal capacity if they are mentally incapacitated. Hence, a person without legal capacity is not autonomous, and thus, not in a position to exercise self-determination. The same goes for persons who normally have legal capacity but temporarily lack the ability to make a rational decision, for example, because they are unconscious. If a patient is not autonomous, he or she cannot provide valid consent to medical treatment, and it is thus necessary to consider another legal basis for the medical intervention (see, further, paragraph 6).

Another precondition for the exercise of self-determination is the ability to act *voluntarily*. Persons who are subjected to pressure or influence from other persons or institutions, or who are in a position where they have difficulties in making decisions in accordance with their own preferences, cannot give valid consent to treatment. Hence, the prisoners in the German concentration camps were not in a position to make a voluntary decision, and the same goes for

39 Da Silva, *supra*, note 31, and Hartlev, *supra*, note 31.

patients who are in detention.[40] There are also other situations which call for protective measures, for example, where it may be suspected that patients are under a certain pressure and not able to act voluntarily. With regard to organ donation, for example, in the Additional Protocol on Organ Donation it is stipulated that donors are not allowed to put their own health at serious risk.[41] Even though some donors may be prepared to take a considerable risk to save the life of a family member, this is not permitted.[42] The same reasoning is reflected in the rules regarding acceptable risks in the Additional Protocol on Biomedical Research.[43]

Finally, it is also required that the patient be properly *informed*. If information is concealed from the patient, it is difficult for the latter to make an informed decision. The information requirement will be addressed in paragraph 5.

Valid consent is normally a precondition for a medical intervention. However, as we shall see in paragraph 4.3, there are situations in which medical treatment is justified without the patients' consent, and situations may also occur where medical treatment is unjustified, despite the consent of the patient.

4.2. PATIENTS' RIGHT TO SELF-DETERMINATION IN HUMAN RIGHTS AND PATIENTS' RIGHTS LAW

The ECHR does not specifically mention a right to autonomy and self-determination, nor does it address the question of obtaining consent to treatment, but the ECtHR has stressed that a right to autonomy is protected by Article 8 ECHR (right to private and family life),[44] and in a number of cases the Court has also ruled that there has been a violation of Article 8.1, because the individual concerned had been subjected to a medical intervention *against his or her will*.[45] The importance of obtaining express *consent* was also addressed by the Court in *Glass* v. *UK*, in which it held that the British Government had not succeeded in establishing that free, expressed and informed consent was given.[46]

---

40 E.g. prisoners and involuntarily institutionalised psychiatric patients.

41 Article 11 of Additional Protocol to the Convention on Human Rights and Biomedicine on Transplantation of Organs and Tissues of Human Origin, CETS 186, Strasbourg 2002.

42 See paragraph 69 in the Explanatory Report to the Additional Protocol to the Convention on Human Rights and Biomedicine on Transplantation of Organs and Tissues of Human Origin, CETS 186, Strasbourg 2002.

43 Article 6 of the Additional Protocol to the Convention on Human Rights and Biomedicine concerning Biomedical Research, CETS 195, Strasbourg 2005.

44 ECtHR 29 April 2002, *Pretty v. the UK*, no. 2346/02 and ECtHR 10 April 2007, *Evans* v. *UK*, no. 6339/05, paragraph 71. In general, it is considered that an individual can only refrain from his or her human rights after voluntarily and unambigously consenting to it; see Chapter 1.

45 See, e.g., ECHR 16 June 2005, *Storck v. Germany*, no. 61603/00, paragraph 143; and ECtHR 2 September 2010 *Shopov v. Bulgaria*, no. 11373/04, paragraph 41.

46 ECtHR 9 March 2004, *Glass v. the UK*, no. 61827/00, paragraph 82.

In contrast to the ECHR, the EU Charter on Fundamental Rights specifically requires consent to medical interventions, and consent requirements are also very visible in international patients' rights law.[47] The visibility of consent requirement in more recent human rights and patients' rights instruments illustrates the growing recognition of autonomy in international law in the second part of the 20th century.

Article 5 of the Biomedicine Convention stipulates that: 'An intervention in the health field may only be carried out after the person concerned has given free and informed consent to it.' It follows, furthermore, that the '...person shall beforehand be given appropriate information as to the purpose and nature of the intervention as well as on its consequences and risks', and that consent may be withdrawn freely at any time. Similar expressions are found in other patients' rights instruments,[48] and this expresses the 'negative variant' of the right to self-determination, the right not to be subjected to an intervention.[49] According to the Explanatory Report, 'intervention' should be understood in a broad sense, covering '... all medical acts, in particular interventions performed for the purpose of preventive care, diagnosis, treatment or rehabilitation or in a research context.'[50] It is, furthermore, stipulated that consent may take various forms, implied or express, oral or written, depending on the nature of the intervention. Routine interventions will normally only require implied consent, whereas other more invasive interventions call for expressly articulated consent.[51] The Biomedicine Convention lays down more specific consent requirements with regard to medical research and organ transplantation (Articles 16 and 19), and the additional protocols to the Convention on organ transplantation, research and genetic testing also contain more specific rules regarding the quality of the patient's consent.[52] Furthermore, special issues regarding consent may occur in other areas, such as reproduction and end-of-life decisions (for more detail, see Chapters 5 and 6).

---

47 See Chapter 1 for further details regarding the right to consent in the ECHR and in case law from the ECtHR.

48 See, e.g., Article 6 of UNESCO Declaration on Bioethics and Human Rights, and Article 3 of the EU Charter on Fundamental Rights.

49 Positive and negative rights are introduced in paragraph 2.1. See, also, Chapter 1.

50 CoE, Explanatory Report to the Convention for the Protection of Human Rights and Dignity of the Human Being with regard to the Application of Biology and Medicine: Convention on Human Rights and Biomedicine, CETS 164, Oviedo 1997 (hereinafter Explanatory Report to the Biomedicine Convention), paragraph 34.

51 *Ibid*, paragraph 37.

52 Articles 12–13 of Additional Protocol to the Convention on Human Rights and Biomedicine on Transplantation of Organs and Tissues of Human Origin, CETS 186, Strasbourg 2002; Article 14 of Additional Protocol to the Convention on Human Rights and Biomedicine concerning Biomedical Research, CETS 195, Strasbourg 2005; and Articles 8–9 of Additional Protocol to the Convention on Human Rights and Biomedicine on Genetic Testing for Health Purposes, CETS 203, Strasbourg 2008.

4.3. RESTRICTION ON RIGHT TO SELF-DETERMINATION IN PATIENTS' RIGHTS LAW

Despite the importance attached to the autonomy of patients in international patients' rights law, it is recognised that patients' right to self-determination must be balanced with opposing interests, such as the interests and rights of other persons, and the vital interests of society. In some situations it is also necessary to take the best interest of the individual patient into consideration, including his or her dignity. Accordingly, there are limits to patients' autonomy and right to self-determination.

In general, most of the provisions in ECHR accept derogations from individual rights in certain situations. With regard to the right to self-determination, it is stipulated in ECHR Article 8.2 that the rights of the individual may be the limited according to law, provided the intervention is necessary for the protection of certain vital private and public interests. Similarly, Article 26 of the Biomedicine Convention acknowledges the necessity of balancing opposing interests, and that restrictions on the rights and protective provisions in the Convention is acceptable if they are: '... prescribed by law and are necessary in a democratic society in the interest of public safety, for the prevention of crime, for the protection of public health or for the protection of the rights and freedoms of others.'[53]

These exemptions are relevant to patients' rights to self-determination in a number of different – but partly overlapping – areas. First of all, there are situations in which the interests of public health and safety may necessitate a restriction of the patient's right to self-determination. Secondly, there are situations where, in exercising autonomy, the patient violates the rights of other persons. Thirdly, there are situations in which patients are acting contrary to what is considered to be in their own best interests. Finally, there are situations where the patient is exercising autonomy in a manner that violates fundamental human rights values, such as dignity.

It is generally recognised in both human rights and patients' rights law that the interests of *public health and safety* may justify restrictions to a patient's right to self-determination. This is especially relevant with regard to psychiatric patients who, due to mental illnesses, are considered to be a danger to other persons, or to public safety, as well as in situations in which patients are suffering from infectious diseases which, left untreated, could cause a serious epidemic. In such situations the first step will normally be detention of the patient, and coercive treatment will only be justified in situations where detention is not sufficient to avoid the danger. In any case, infringement of the individual's personal liberty and integrity must be prescribed by law and deemed to be

[53] According to Article 26.2 restrictions may not, however, affect the rights stipulated in Articles 11, 13–14, 16–17, and 19–21.

necessary for the protection of other persons or of public health and safety.[54] In a number of cases the ECtHR has addressed the infringement of personal liberty (ECHR Article 5) and the right to self-determination (ECHR Article 8) with regard to the detention and coercive treatment of *psychiatric patients*. In general, it is required that the mental disorder is of a character and degree making compulsory confinement absolutely necessary, and the continuation of compulsion must be justified by the persistence of the disorder. This issue is addressed comprehensively in Chapter 9.[55] Detention and coercive treatment in situations of *epidemic diseases* has not attracted the same attention from the convention bodies. However, the ECtHR laid down the basic criteria for the justification of detention in such cases in *Enhorn v. Sweden*, which concerned with the compulsory detention of a Mr Enhorn, who had been infected by the HIV virus.[56] As to the general criteria, the Court noted that:

> ... the essential criteria when assessing the "lawfulness" of the detention of a person "for the prevention of the spreading of infectious diseases" are whether the spreading of the infectious disease is dangerous to public health or safety, and whether detention of the person infected is the last resort in order to prevent the spreading of the disease, because less severe measures have been considered and found to be insufficient to safeguard the public interest.[57]

Having assessed the case, the Court reached the conclusion that the HIV virus was an infectious disease threatening public health, but it was not convinced that the detention of Mr. Enhorn was a last resort, because '... less severe measures had not been considered and found to be insufficient to safeguard the public interest.' Furthermore, it noted that the Swedish authorities failed to strike a fair balance between competing interests, because the detention amounted to 1½ years in total, which, in the Court's opinion, was not sufficiently balanced to the needs of society in preventing the spread of the HIV virus.[58] In addition to the treatment of psychiatric patients and epidemic diseases, the ECtHR has also

54 For justification of derogation from the CCPR in UN Commission on Human Rights, see the Siracusa Principles on the Limitation and Derogation Provisions in the international Covenant on Civil and Political Rights, 28 September 1984, E/CN.4/1985/4, www.unhcr.org/refworld/docid/4672bc122.html.

55 The landmark case is ECtHR 24 October 1979, *Winterverp v. The Netherlands*, no. 6301/73. For a detailed analysis of the use of detention and coercive treatment with regard to patients with mental impairments, see, in addition to Chapter 9, M. Wachenfeld, 'The Human Rights of the Mentally Ill in Europe: Under the European Convention on Human Rights', *Nordic Journal of International Law*, 1991, pp. 115–292; and M. Hartlev, *supra*, note 29. Council of Europe of Recommendation Rec. (2004) 10 of the Committee of Ministers to Member States concerning the protection of the human rights and dignity of persons with mental disorder, adopted 22 September 2004, also includes more detailed rules regarding detention and the use of coercive treatment in psychiatric care.

56 ECtHR 25 January 2005, *Enhorn v. Sweden*, no. 56529/00.

57 *Ibid.*, paragraph 41.

58 *Ibid.*, paragraph 55.

addressed the justiciability of medical interventions with a different purpose than medical treatment, such as forensic investigations (blood or saliva samples), injections and medical examinations (including virginity tests). Such interventions are accepted by the Court, provided it is convincingly justified on the facts of the particular case and that alternative and less intrusive methods of recovering evidence have been considered. The seriousness of the offence must be taken into consideration when assessing the legitimacy of the intervention, and if particularly intrusive procedures are used, strict scrutiny is required. Furthermore, the procedure must not entail any risk of lasting detriment to the person's health, and account must be taken of whether the person concerned experiences serious physical pain or suffering as a result of the forcible medical intervention. Finally, it must also be determined whether the forcible medical procedure was ordered and administered by medical doctors, and whether the person concerned was placed under constant medical supervision.[59]

The second situation in which restrictions to patients' right to self-determination may be justified is where the patient's decision regarding treatment *violates other persons' rights*. Some of these situations overlap with cases of public health and safety. Hence, patients who refuse to be treated for infectious diseases may be a threat to another person's right to health, as well as to public health. However, special situations may occur where it is exclusively a conflict between two persons' rights. This is especially relevant in cases concerning reproductive issues. In *Evans v. UK*, the ECtHR reached the conclusion that an applicant's right to dispose of frozen embryos in order to become a parent should be balanced against her former partner's decision not to have a genetically related child with her, and the Court found that her right to self-determination could not be accorded greater weight than the partner's right to self-determination.[60]

In some situations it may also be considered to *be in the patient's best interest* not to respect his or her decisions. This is a sensitive reason for derogating from the right to self-determination because a person's right to live a life in accordance with his or her own preferences – irrespective of what others believe – is an important justification for the principle of autonomy. Consequently, interventions in the right to self-determination, based on paternalistic considerations, are *de facto* in conflict with the essence of the autonomy principle. This was also recognised by the ECtHR in *Jehovah's Witnesses of Moscow v. Russia*, in which the Court clearly stated that:

> The ability to conduct one's life in a manner of one's own choosing includes the opportunity to pursue activities perceived to be of a physically harmful or dangerous

59 ECtHR 11 July 2006, *Jalloh v. Germany*, no. 54810/00, paragraph 69–74. See, also, ECtHR 7 October 2008, *Bogumil v. Portugal*, no. 35228/03, paragraph 77–79.

60 *Supra*, note 41. There is a more detailed discussion of the case in Chapter 6.

> nature for the individual concerned. In the sphere of medical assistance, even where the refusal to accept a particular treatment might lead to a fatal outcome, the imposition of medical treatment without the consent of a mentally competent adult patient would interfere with his or her right to physical integrity and impinge on the rights protected under Article 8 of the Convention.[61]

The Court further noted that:

> The freedom to accept or refuse specific medical treatment, or to select an alternative form of treatment, is vital to the principles of self-determination and personal autonomy. A competent adult patient is free to decide, for instance, whether or not to undergo surgery or treatment or, by the same token, to have a blood transfusion. However, for this freedom to be meaningful, patients must have the right to make choices that accord with their own views and values, regardless of how irrational, unwise or imprudent such choices may appear to others.[62]

Considering ECHR Article 8.2, it is interesting to observe that the interests of the individual concerned are not listed as a legitimate reason for an infringement of the right to private life and self-determination. Article 8.2 only covers the interests of other persons and of society. Article 26 of the Biomedicine Conventions takes exactly the same line as ECHR Article 8.2. However, Article 7 of the Biomedicine Convention specifically allows derogations from the right to self-determination with reference to the patient's best interest in cases of patients suffering from *mental disorders*. Article 7 stipulates that:

> Subject to protective conditions prescribed by law, including supervisory, control and appeal procedures, a person who has a mental disorder of a serious nature may be subjected, without his or her consent, to an intervention aimed at treating his or her mental disorder only where, without such treatment, serious harm is likely to result to his or her health.

The Explanatory Report acknowledges that this restriction is wider than the derogations legitimated by Article 26 of the Convention. The argument is not based on the assumption that the patient is not able to give valid consent – in this situation other rules apply. It is the risk to the health of the psychiatric patient that justifies the derogation. Article 7 is in accordance with the case law of the ECtHR, which, in a few cases has accepted the coercive treatment of detained patients with *mental disorders* with reference to 'therapeutic' or 'medical' necessity.[63] In a few other cases, too, the ECtHR has accepted use of coercive treatment in cases where detained persons have embarked on a life-

---

61 ECtHR 10 June 2010, *Jehovah's Witnesses of Moscow v. Russia*, no. 302/02, paragraph 135.
62 *Ibid.*, paragraph 136.
63 See ECtHR 24 September 1992, *Herczegfalvy v. Austria*, no. 10533/83.

threatening hunger strike.[64] In these cases, the Court was concerned with ECHR Article 2 and with the government's obligation to protect the life of detained persons. The insistence on the best interest of the patient could also be relevant in other cases. The Explanatory Report to the Biomedicine Convention (paragraph 38) states that a patient may not be entitled to withdraw consent to treatment during an operation if, according to professional standards and obligations, the doctor is obliged to complete the operation to avoid serious harm to the health of the patient. In addition to these examples, the ECtHR has also accepted medical interventions against a patient's will in other situations of medical necessity. In *Bogumil v Portugal*, the applicant had swallowed a packet of cocaine and tried to smuggle it into Portugal. He claimed not having consented to a medical intervention, to which he was subjected, to remove the packet from his stomach. This was initiated due to a risk of fatal intoxication, and the Court reached the conclusion that, irrespective of the lack of consent, the intervention was justified due to therapeutic necessity.[65]

Finally, the last examples of justified restrictions to patients' rights to self-determination refer to cases in which patients wish to exercise autonomy in a manner that is in contradiction to basic human rights. This could be the case in a variety of situations where patients wish to embark on treatment, which, from a human rights perspective, is considered problematic.[66] The Explanatory Report to the Biomedicine Convention draws attention to the risk associated with technological progress in the biomedical field, and stresses that: 'It is no longer the individual or society that may be at risk but the human species itself.'[67] The Biomedicine Convention deals with the risk to the human species, as such, in a few provisions, e.g. in Article 14 (non-selection of sex), and in Article 21 (prohibition of commercialisation of the human body). The Additional Protocol to the Convention on cloning also exemplifies the concern in this area in stressing in the preamble that: '... the instrumentalisation of human beings through the deliberate creation of genetically identical human beings is contrary

64 See *Herczegfalvy v. Austria*, 24 September 1992 (no violation), ECtHR 5 April 2005; *Nevmerzhitsky v Ukraine*, no. 54825/00 (violation), ECtHR 19 June 2007; and *Ciorap v. Moldova*, no. 120662/02 (violation).

65 ECtHR 7 October 2008, *Bogumil v. Portugal*, no. 35228/03, paragraphs 89–90.

66 It is a general rule in European human rights law that individuals cannot consent to treatment that is contrary to basic human rights, notably, the right to dignity (see Chapter 1). The ECtHR has addressed this issue in a few cases, which are not concerned with patients' rights, but which may, nevertheless, give the impression of a balancing of interests in such cases. See ECtHR 19 February 1997, *Laskey, Jaggard and Brown v. UK*, nos. 21627/93, 21826/93 and 21974/93 (sadomasochistic activities); and ECommissionHR 16 October 1996, *Wackenheim v. France*, no. 29961/96 (dwarf throwing). See, also, D. Beyleveld and R. Brownsword, *Human Dignity in Bioethics and Biolaw*, Oxford-New York: Oxford University Press 2001, in which they argue that the concept of dignity encompasses a right to respect for one's own dignity, as well as an obligation not to compromise one's dignity.

67 *Supra*, note 50, paragraph 14.

to human dignity.'[68] Other problematic interventions discussed in medical ethics include situations where patients ask for the amputation of a well-functioning arm or leg. The question of limiting the individual's right to self-determination in these situations is concerned with the risk that a more general lack of respect for human integrity and dignity may occur, if it is allowed for individuals to compromise their own dignity.

5. PATIENTS' RIGHT TO INFORMATION

5.1. PATIENTS' INTEREST IN INFORMATION

Patients' right to information is relevant in various ways. As already mentioned, it is, first of all, important for the exercise of self-determination, and to give valid, informed consent to medical interventions. However, patients may also have an interest in being given access to health information in other situations than those relating to specific medical decisions. Access to medical files may be important for various reasons, and it is also vital that patients have access to general information regarding the right to care and treatment possibilities.

5.2. RIGHT TO INFORMATION IN MEDICAL DECISION-MAKING

The importance of obtaining *informed* consent to medical treatment is stressed in all international patients' rights instruments.[69] The EU Charter on Fundamental Rights also mentions the importance of obtaining informed consent to treatment.[70] In contrast, the ECHR does not specifically address the right to information in connection with medical treatment, and ECHR Article 10 (freedom of information) is not considered to imply a general duty of providing information in connection with medical treatment.[71] However, a right to information may be deduced from ECHR Article 8, and in its case law, the ECtHR has stressed the importance of providing patients with information in order to ensure a sufficient basis for exercising the right to self-determination. Hence, in *Trocellier v. France*, the Court stated that the Contracting States are bound to: '... adopt the necessary regulatory measures to ensure that doctors

---

68 Additional Protocol to the Convention on Human Rights and Biomedicine on the Prohibition of Cloning Human Beings, CETS 168, Paris 1998.

69 The right to information is stressed in Article 5 of the Biomedicine Convention, Article 6 of UNESCO Declaration on Bioethics and Human Rights, and paragraph 2 of the WHO Declaration.

70 Article 3.2 of the EU Charter on Fundamental Rights.

71 See Chapter 1.

consider the foreseeable consequences of the planned medical procedure on their patients' physical integrity and to inform patients of these beforehand in such a way that they are able to give informed consent.'[72] Similarly, in *Testa v. Croatia*, it was stressed that the applicant (a prisoner) had not been provided with appropriate diagnostic treatment, and had been left without relevant information in respect of her illness, '...thus keeping her in dark about her health condition and depriving her of any control over it.'[73] The guidance provided by the case law is rather general. Hence, to acquire a more detailed picture of the scope of a right to information, it is necessary to look into patients' rights legislation.

Article 5 of the Biomedicine Convention stipulates that: a '... person shall beforehand be given appropriate information as to the purpose and nature of the intervention as well as on its consequences and risks.' According to the Explanatory Report, this is not an exhaustive list, and it specifies that the patient must be informed about the relevant facts, which include the purpose, nature and consequences of the intervention and the risks involved. With regard to risks and side effects, the patient must be informed of both the general risks associated with the treatment, and alternative methods, and of the risks relating to his or her specific situation. Article 5 of the Biomedicine Convention is supplemented by Article 10, according to which the patient is entitled to know any information gathered about his or her health, and the explanatory report specifies that this encompasses all information, including diagnosis, prognosis, and any other relevant facts.[74] The WHO Declaration (paragraph 2.2) similarly requires that:

> Patients have the right to be fully informed about their health status, including the medical facts about their condition; about the proposed medical procedures, together with the potential risks and benefits of each procedure; about alternatives to the proposed procedures, including the effect of non-treatment; and about the diagnosis, prognosis and progress of treatment.

Accordingly, the information provided to patients should concern the diagnosis and facts about their medical condition, the possible treatment measures (including alternatives to proposed procedures), the potential risks and benefits associated with the proposed medical procedures, and the potential effect of non-treatment. It is important to stress that the information requirements stipulated in these rules are not exhaustive, and that exactly how much information is needed to satisfy the informed consent requirement must always be assessed in each situation. Patients' requests for additional information must, of course, also be adequately answered.[75]

---

72 ECtHR 5 October 2006, *Trocellier v. France*, no. 75725/01.
73 ECtHR 12 July 2007, *Testa v. Croatia*, no. 20877/04, paragraph 52.
74 Explanatory Report to the Biomedicine Convention, *supra*, note 50, paragraph 66.
75 Explanatory Report to the Biomedicine Convention, *supra*, note 50, paragraph 35, and WHO Declaration, paragraph 2.5.

Having access to information is not only a right of the patient, but it is also a *duty* of the healthcare provider. Thus, irrespective of whether the patient asks for information or not, it is for the healthcare provider to ensure that the patient is sufficiently informed. Otherwise, the consent will not be valid.

However, the WHO Declaration and the Biomedicine Convention are both supportive of a doctor's right to withhold information from patients in special situations. According to paragraph 2.3 of the WHO Declaration, information may be withheld from patients in exceptional cases, when there is good reason to believe that this information would cause them serious harm, and with no expectation of obvious positive effects ('therapeutic exception'). In the same vein, Article 10.2 of the Biomedicine Convention allows health professionals to conceal information from patients in exceptional cases if it is considered to be in the patient's best interest.

It is vital that the patient understands the information, otherwise, the patient's consent to treatment is compromised. Both the WHO Declaration and the Biomedicine Convention stress the importance of communicating information in a language and manner that is adapted to the individual patient's capacity for understanding.[76]

5.3. RIGHT NOT TO KNOW

As the right to information is a component of patients' right to self-determination, it follows automatically that a patient's wish not to be informed should also be respected. Both the WHO Declaration and the Biomedicine Convention recognise patients' right 'not to know'.[77] This can be considered the non-paternalistic variant of the doctor's privilege, as it acknowledges that patients are in a position to decide themselves what is their best interest. The right not to know is of special importance with regard to genetic testing and genetic information, where it is recognised that the tested person may have good reasons for wishing not to know about, for example, the presence of a gene causing a serious disease for which there is currently no effective treatment.[78]

It is important to note that the right not to know typically applies to the conventional treatment setting, in which the treatment is deemed to have a therapeutic effect, or to serve diagnostic purposes. It is generally considered inappropriate to apply to situations in which the patient cannot expect a positive effect from the treatment, such as in the case of biomedical research and organ

76 Paragraph 2.4 of WHO Declaration and Explanatory Report to the Biomedicine Convention, *supra*, note 50, paragraph 36.

77 Article 10.2 of Biomedicine Convention and paragraph 2.5 of WHO Declaration.

78 Paragraph 134 in Explanatory Report to the Additional Protocol to the Convention on Human Rights and Biomedicine on Genetic Testing for Health Purposes, CETS 203, Strasbourg 2008.

donation. Here, providing information is considered indispensable to obtaining the consent of the patient.

5.4. ACCESS TO MEDICAL FILES

Individuals may have an interest in gaining access to their medical files, both in connection with medical treatments, and in other situations to obtain knowledge of their medical conditions, medical treatment, *etc.* Medical files may also contain information regarding birth, family relations, and other issues that are of importance to the individual's family life and the possibility of establishing an identity. These interests are recognised in human rights law, where access to personal information is considered part of the right to private and family life, and as such, is protected by ECHR Article 8 and Article 8.2 of the EU Charter on Fundamental Rights.[79] Included in the right to gain access is also a right to make photocopies of the files.[80]

International patients' rights law is also concerned with access to medical files, and the right to retrieve information is stipulated in both the Biomedicine Convention and the WHO Declaration.[81] However, as already mentioned in paragraph 5.3, it is also accepted in human rights and international patients' rights law that the right to information may be restricted, with reference to the patient's best interest. Furthermore, it is possible to withhold information from patients in situations where this is stipulated in law and is deemed necessary for the protection of the rights and freedoms of other persons, or in the interest of public health, public safety or the prevention of crime.

In contrast to the right to information described above in paragraph 5.3, the right to access personal and medical files does not impose a positive obligation on the Contracting States obliging them, on their own initiative, to provide comprehensive information to patients about the content of personal files. However, the EU Data Protection Directive requires that, in a number of situations, data subjects are informed about the processing of personal data, and this could impose a duty on healthcare providers to inform patients about the collection of medical data.[82]

5.5. GENERAL INFORMATION

Individualised information is naturally of immense importance to patients, but this may also be the case with regard to general health information about access

79 For further details and references to relevant case law, see Chapter 1.

80 ECtHR 28 April 2009, *K.H. and others v. Slovakia*, no. 32881/04, paragraphs 47–48.

81 See Article 10 of the Biomedicine Convention and paragraph 4.4 of the WHO Declaration.

82 Directive 95/46/EC on the protection of individuals with regard to the processing of personal data and on the free movement of such data, Articles 10–11.

to care and treatment possibilities, as well as information about health prevention and health risks. The right to health laid down in Article 12 of the ICESCR is interpreted as also including certain rights to information about health related matters and treatment possibilities. Hence, General Comment 14 notes that a state is required to meet '...its obligations in the dissemination of appropriate information relating to healthy lifestyles and nutrition, harmful traditional practices and the availability of services" and "to provide education and access to information concerning the main health problems in the community, including methods of preventing and controlling them.'[83] Similarly, the WHO Declaration (paragraph 2.1) prescribes that information about health services and how best to use them should be made available to the public so that everybody can benefit from them. Within the EU, the Directive on cross-border care is also concerned with the provision of adequate information to patients, and it prescribes (Articles 4.2 and 6.3) that it is the responsibility of the Member States to provide patients with information about treatment possibilities in cross-border care.[84] The ECHR does not oblige the Contracting States to issue general information about healthcare services, but ECHR Article 10 protects the right of healthcare providers or others to inform the public about treatment options.[85]

Turning to information about general health risks, case law from the ECtHR supports the existence of a general obligation to provide information to citizens in situations in which health hazards and risks have occurred, such as in cases of environmental disaster.[86] A similar obligation follows from Article 12 of ICESCR, which addresses the duty to provide information in cases of community health problems in general (e.g. epidemics).[87]

6. PATIENTS WHO ARE NOT COMPETENT TO GIVE CONSENT

There are groups of patients who are not competent to give informed consent to medical interventions. This includes children under a certain age, adults who are permanently mentally incapacitated, and adults who are temporarily unable to make rational decisions. Human rights law is particularly alert with regard to weak and vulnerable groups, and this is also reflected in international patients'

83 UN, CESCR, General Comment No. 14 (2000), *The right to the highest attainable standard of health (Article 12 of the International Covenant on Economic, Social and Cultural Rights)*, paragraph 37 and paragraph 43d.

84 Directive 2011/24/EU on the application of patients' rights in cross-border health care.

85 ECtHR 29 October 1992, *Open Door & Dublin Well Woman v. Ireland*, no. 14234/88 and no. 14235/88, paragraph 63. See, also, Chapter 5 (Reproductive health).

86 ECtHR 19 February 1998, *Guerra and others v. Italy*, no. 14967/89, paragraph 60.

87 *Supra*, note 83, paragraph 43.

rights law. There are two major concerns: to protect weak and vulnerable patients against mistreatment and exploitation, and to ensure that only those patients who are *de facto* incompetent and unable to exercise self-determination are categorised as such.

Article 6 of the Biomedicine Convention is concerned with the protection of persons not able to consent, and it emphasises, as a general rule, that interventions on persons not able to consent should be to his or her *direct benefit*. This reduces the risk of mistreatment and exploitation. However, as an exception the Convention still allows for interventions that have no direct benefit for such patients, that is, in certain situations of organ donation, and with regard to participation in medical research. In these specific situations, the benefits to other persons are considered to justify a medical intervention that only imposes minor risks on the patient.[88]

With regard to *children*, the Biomedicine Convention leaves it to the national legal order to determine when children have decision-making capacity (see Article 6.2). However, in this respect it is important to take the Convention on the Protection of the Right of the Child (CPR) into consideration, and notably, Article 12 of this Convention, which stresses that a child capable of forming his or her own views should have the right to express such views in all matters affecting him or her, and to have such views given due weight in accordance with his or her age and maturity. The age of legal capacity must therefore be determined in accordance with the CRC. When a child does not have the legal capacity to consent, the informed consent must, according to Article 6.2 of the Biomedicine Convention, be given by the child's representative (normally those with parental responsibility), or by a person or body authorised by law to give consent. In all cases the child's opinion must be taken into consideration 'as an increasingly determining factor in proportion to his or her age and degree of maturity.'[89]

Incapacitated adults are addressed in Article 6.3 of the Biomedicine Convention, and as the identification of such patients is not as straightforward as with regard to children, Article 6.3 lists the criteria which may be used to establish incapacity. These are mental disability, a disease, or a 'similar reasons'.[90] If an adult patient lacks decision-making capacity, informed consent must be provided by his or her representative, or by a person or body authorised

88 Articles 17 and 20 of the Biomedicine Convention. See, also, Article 14 of the Additional Protocol to the Convention on Human Rights and Biomedicine on Transplantation of Organs and Tissues of Human Origin, CETS 186, Strasbourg 2002, and Article 15 of Additional Protocol to the Convention on Human Rights and Biomedicine concerning Biomedical Research, CETS 195.

89 This is in accordance with CRC Article 12. See, also, the WHO Declaration, paragraph 3.5.

90 According to the Explanatory Report to Biomedicine Convention, the expression 'similar reasons' must be understood as accidents or states of coma, where, for example, the patient is unable to formulate his or her wishes or to communicate them: *supra*, note 50, paragraph 43.

by law. The patient must, as far as possible, take part in the decision-making process, and previously expressed wishes must be taken into consideration.[91]

The Biomedicine Convention does not distinguish between permanently incapacitated adults (e.g. patients suffering from Alzheimer's Disease) and *temporary incapacitation* (e.g. temporary unconsciousness), but the importance ascribed to the autonomy principle favours not relying on proxy consent in situations in which it is possible to delay the medical intervention until the patient has regained his or her decision-making capacity.

In situations where informed consent is given by a legal proxy, the same rules regarding informed consent apply, which means that the proxy must be provided with the same information as the patient, and that the decision of the proxy must be respected in the same way.[92] If the proxy refuses to consent to an intervention that is considered to be in the best interest of the incapacitated patient, according to paragraph 3.5 of the WHO Declaration the decision must be referred to a court or an arbitration mechanism.

Situations may occur where the patient needs immediate care for the benefit of his or her health, and where the patient or the proxy is not able to give timely consent. In such *emergency situations* the necessary medical interventions may be performed without informed consent.[93]

7. MEDICAL RESEARCH

Medical research is important if new knowledge of benefit to patients and society is to be developed. Consequently, medical research may support patients' rights to good quality care, and thereby serve to ensure and promote patients' rights.[94] At the same time, medical research gives rise to special human rights concerns with regard to the protection of persons participating in research. The dark side of medical science revealed during the Nuremberg trials and in other cases reminds us of the importance of taking account of the vulnerability of the patient *vis-à-vis* medical science. This concern is reflected in Article 7 of the ICCPR, according to which '... no one shall be subjected without his free consent to medical or scientific experimentation.' In contrast to the ICCPR, the ECHR does not explicitly address the question of medical research, but in its case law the ECtHR has established that participation in research is part of private life, and is thus protected by ECHR Article 8.[95]

91 Article 9 of the Biomedicine Convention and paragraph 3.7 of the WHO Declaration.

92 ECtHR 9 March 2004 *Glass* v. *UK*, no. 61827/00, paragraph 70.

93 Article 8 of the Biomedicine Convention, and paragraphs 3.3–3.4 of the WHO Declaration.

94 See, e.g., Article 2d and 2f of UNESCO Declaration, and paragraphs 95–96 of the Explanatory Report to the Biomedicine Convention, *supra*, note 50.

95 ECtHR 19 October 2005, *Roche v. the United Kingdom*, no. 32555/96, paragraph 155.

To acquire a more comprehensive and detailed impression of the legal standard applying in medical research, it is necessary to consult international patients' rights law. All international patients' rights instruments have special provisions concerned with the rights of research subjects. Article 2 of the Biomedicine Convention reflects the primacy of the human being and the weight attached to human dignity, in noting that: 'The interests and welfare of the human being shall prevail over the sole interest of society or science.'

The relationship between the patient and the healthcare professional in a research setting differs from the normal relationship in a treatment situation. Whereas in a treatment situation the healthcare professional is supposed to have the best interests of the patient as his or her primary concern, it is different with regard to research, where the primary aim is to obtain new, scientific knowledge. Consequently, there is a risk that the responsible healthcare professional will be biased towards the 'best interests' of the scientific process, and will not considered to be in the best interest of the patient, and thus, that the research subject will be reduced to a means for the advancement of science. To meet these concerns, international patients' rights laws prescribe a special authorisation requirement before medical research involving human beings can be initiated, and there are special, stricter rules with regard to informed consent and recruitment of research subjects.

In general, the legal framework for medical research is significantly influenced by the principle of *proportionality*.[96] Research on human beings may only be carried out if there is no alternative (e.g. animal research) of comparable effect (subsidiarity).[97] In cases where human participation is justified, the research must not involve risks and burdens to the research subject that are disproportionate to its potential benefits for the research subject herself or for other persons.[98] All research projects involving human research subjects must be assessed by an independent committee, which will make an assessment of the proportionality principle. However, the individual researcher is still responsible for applying the proportionality principle when recruiting research subjects and while performing the research.

In contrast to normal treatment, medical research normally involves more unknown risks and burdens for the patient. Furthermore, the research design often prescribes that some participants will receive a new drug or will be treated by a new method, whereas other participants will function as a control group.[99] The uncertainty concerning the benefits and risks involved in medical research

---

96 See S.Simonsen, *Acceptable risk in biomedical research. European perspectives*, International Library of Ethics, Law, and the New Medicine', Vol 50, Springer, 2012.

97 Article 5 of the Additional Protocol to the Convention on Human Rights and Biomedicine concerning Biomedical Research, CETS 195.

98 Article 16(ii) of the Biomedicine Convention and Article 6 of the Additional Protocol to the Convention on Human Rights and Biomedicine concerning Biomedical Research, CETS 195. See, along the same lines, Article 4 of the UNESCO Declaration.

99 In medical research it is normal to use the randomised clinical trial as a research design.

calls for special attention regarding informed consent, and international patients' rights law imposes stricter rules on informed consent than is the case in normal treatment. Generally, information must be more extensive, and a more explicit degree of consent is needed.[100]

Research on *weak and vulnerable* persons gives rise to special concern. *Persons who are not able to give informed consent* may only be included as research subjects if research of comparable efficiency cannot be performed on persons who have decision-making capacity. In contrast to research based on research subjects with decision-making capacity, it is also a condition that research participation is of *direct benefit* to the health of the individual (incapacitated) research subject. However, in exceptional cases it is possible to derogate from this condition, provided there is an aim to produce research results which will significantly improve the understanding of a particular condition or disease, and thereby produce research results which could be beneficial to the group to which the research subject belongs. In such situations it is a condition that the research only entails minimal risks and minimal burdens for the research subject, and research may never be carried out if the incapacitated person refuses to participate.[101] The EU Clinical Trials Directive imposes even stricter limits, as it is not accepted that the research involves any risks at all with regard to adults without decision-making capacity. *Persons deprived of liberty* are also in a very vulnerable situation, where the voluntariness of research participation could be questioned. Therefore, stricter rules are also laid down for this group in situations in which participation is not of direct benefit to the research subject. First of all, it is a condition that research of comparable effectiveness cannot be carried out on research subjects who are not deprived of liberty, and it is, furthermore, required that the research aims at producing results that could be beneficial to persons deprived of liberty, and that research participation only entails minimal risks and minimal burdens for the participant.[102]

8. PRIVACY AND CONFIDENTIALITY

8.1. CONFIDENTIAL RELATIONSHIPS AND INFORMATIONAL SELF-DETERMINATION.

Patients' contact with healthcare services will necessarily affect their private lives, as they will have to reveal information about their health status and expose their

100 Article 16 of the Additional Protocol to the Convention on Human Rights and Biomedicine concerning Biomedical Research, CETS 195.

101 Article 15 of the Additional Protocol to the Convention on Human Rights and Biomedicine concerning Biomedical Research, CETS 195.

102 Article 20 of the Additional Protocol to the Convention on Human Rights and Biomedicine concerning Biomedical Research, CETS 195.

bodies and thoughts to the healthcare professionals to obtain a diagnosis and to receive proper treatment. Information about an individual's health condition is very sensitive and belongs, clearly, to the private sphere. Medical ethics have, for many years, imposed a duty of confidentiality on doctors and other healthcare professionals, and the need to protect patients' right to privacy is recognised in human rights law, as well as in international patients' rights law.[103]

ECHR article 8 protects medical privacy, and the ECtHR has also, in several cases, emphasised that health information is very sensitive and at the heart of the protection offered by Article 8. In *Z. v. Finland* the Court stressed that: '... the protection of personal data, particularly medical data, is of fundamental importance to a person's enjoyment of his or her right to respect for private and family life as guaranteed by Article 8 of the Convention.'[104] The importance is not only attached to the privacy of the individual, but also to the protection of the confidential relationship between the patient and the healthcare provider.[105] This is acknowledged by the Court, which has also stressed that:

> It is crucial not only to respect the sense of privacy of a patient but also to preserve his or her confidence in the medical profession and in the health services in general. Without such protection, those in need of medical assistance may be deterred from revealing such information of a personal and intimate nature as may be necessary in order to receive appropriate treatment and, even, from seeking such assistance, thereby endangering their own health and, in the case of transmissible diseases, that of the community.[106]

Article 10 of the Biomedicine Convention is concerned with the protection of patients' right to privacy. However, neither this provision nor the Explanatory Report to the Biomedicine Convention provide more detailed guidance regarding the numerous situations in which patient's right to privacy is at stake in concurrence with other interests. In this area, data protection law and general human rights law seem to be more helpful.

Patients' right to privacy is also at issue with regard to the collection, storage, disclosure, alteration and erasure of health data. The case law of the ECtHR has primarily been concerned with the disclosure of medical data. However, it must be emphasised that the other forms of data processing – and especially the

---

103 See this chapter, section 3.2.

104 ECtHR 25 February 1997, *Z v. Finland*, no. 22009/93, paragraph 95. See, also, ECtHR, 27 August 1997, *M. S. v. Sweden*, no. 20837/92, paragraph 41.

105 For the distinction between privacy and confidentiality, see this chapter section 3.2.

106 ECtHR 25 February 1997, *Z v. Finland*, no. 22009/93, paragraph 95. The case concerned an individual affected by HIV, and the Court referred to CoE Recommendation no. R (89) 14 on 'The ethical issues of HIV infection in the health care and social settings', adopted by the Committee of Ministers of the Council of Europe on 24 October 1989, in particular, the general observations on confidentiality of medical data in paragraph 165 of the explanatory memorandum.

collection and storage of health data – are also important from a privacy perspective, and thus need justification.[107]

In general, data protection law puts the emphasis on the right to informational self-determination, and as a main rule it is necessary to obtain express consent to the processing of personal data.[108] However, the necessity to derogate from the consent requirement is also acknowledged under the conditions stipulated in ECHR Article 8.2, that is, if prescribed by law and deemed to be necessary in a democratic society to protect interests of, for example, public safety, the prevention of disorder or crime, the economic well-being of society, the protection of health or morals, or the protection of the rights and freedoms of others.

Third parties may wish to access medical data for different purposes, and it may be expedient to distinguish between situations where medical data are needed for the purpose of *medical treatment*, and situations where the processing of medical data serves *purposes which are not directly linked to the provision of medical care.*[109]

8.2. PROCESSING OF HEALTH DATA IN CONNECTION WITH MEDICAL TREATMENT

The collection and sharing of health data, laid down in a medical file, is mandatory to ensure the quality and continuity of medical treatment. Healthcare professionals need to have access to the patient's medical history, as well as to exchange information with other healthcare professionals involved in the actual treatment to be able to make a proper diagnosis and to provide good quality care.[110] Normally this will be in accordance with the patient's own will and interest, and it could be argued that when a patient gives informed consent to the proposed treatment, this also *implies consent* to the communication of information that is necessary to provide the patient with the proper treatment and care. This line of reasoning is reflected in the WHO Declaration, which requires consent as a point of departure (paragraph 4.1), but accepts (in paragraph 4.2) that: 'Consent may be presumed where disclosure is to other healthcare providers involved in that patient's treatment.' If we follow this line of

107 All sorts of processing are covered by the EU Directive 95/46/EC on the Protection of Individuals with regard to the Processing of Personal Data and by the CoE Convention for the Protection of Individuals with regard to Automatic Processing of Personal Data, CETS 108, Strasbourg 1981.

108 Consent requirements are stipulated in Articles 7.a and 8.2 of EU Directive 95/46/EC.

109 M. Hartlev, 'Striking the Right Balance: Patients Rights and Opposing Interests with regard to Health Information', 14 *European Journal of Health Law* 2007, pp. 165–176.

110 M. E. Sokalska, 'Medical Confidentiality: Quo Vadis?', 11(1) *European Journal of Health Law* 2004, pp. 35–43.

reasoning, this form of communication does not violate any right to privacy and confidentiality because the patient has given consent.

In data protection law it is also possible to detect another line of reasoning for the exchange of information without obtaining explicit consent. Article 8.3 of EU Directive 95/46/EC stipulates that the prohibition of the processing of sensitive data does not apply where personal data are required for medical diagnosis and the provision of care and treatment, provided these data are processed by '... a health care professional subject under national law or rules established by national competent bodies to the obligation of professional secrecy or by another person also subject to an equivalent obligation of secrecy.'[111] Accordingly, as long as health data are communicated to other healthcare professionals who are under a confidentiality obligation, the information stays within a *'circle of confidentiality'* and no infringement of privacy rights has occurred. This is in line with Council of Europe Recommendation R (97) 5 on the Protection of Medical Data, which, in principles 4.4 and 7.3, stipulates that data may be processed without explicit consent, if permitted by law, and provided it is necessary for preventive medical purposes or for diagnostic or therapeutic purposes with regard to the patient.[112] This indicates that, in principle, the disclosure of information to other healthcare professionals may be a violation of the patient's right to private life, as protected by ECHR Article 8, but that this right may be restricted in accordance with the conditions set out in ECHR Article 8.2.

In other words, the legal basis of communication among healthcare professionals may either be the presumed or implied consent of the patient, or may be based on a sufficiently clear legal basis in law. In the case of the latter, the other conditions laid down in ECHR Article 8.2 must also be fulfilled, which means that it must be necessary in a democratic society to ensure free communication among healthcare professionals in order to protect, for example, public security or public health, and it is, consequently, not sufficient that data be communicated to other healthcare professionals under a duty of confidentiality. This was stressed by the ECtHR in *I v. Finland*, in which the Court concluded that the patient's medical file had not been sufficiently protected against unauthorised disclosure to healthcare professionals who were not involved in the treatment of the patient. In this case, colleagues of an HIV infected nurse had accessed her medical file to acquire information about her health condition.[113]

---

111 See, also, recital 33 to Directive 95/46/EC, which stresses that derogation from the prohibition to process sensitive data is justified, particularly where the processing of data is being carried out for certain health related purposes, and by persons subject to a legal obligation of professional secrecy.

112 Council of Europe, Recommendation R (97) 5 on the protection of medical data.

113 ECtHR 17 July 2008, *I v. Finland*, no. 20511/03, paragraphs 38–49.

8.3. USE OF HEALTH DATA FOR PURPOSES OTHER THAN MEDICAL CARE

Data about an individual patient's health may also be important in *other settings than healthcare settings*. For example, the social services may require health information when assessing applications for sickness benefits or social pensions, insurance companies may have an interest in having access to health information in cases of insurance claims, the police can sometimes use medical information for forensic purposes, and others, such as employers and relatives, may also be interested in information about the health conditions of employees or their family members. Furthermore, health data may also be of interest for scientific and educational purposes.

In contrast to the situation described in the previous paragraph, there is no presumption in these situations that communication to third parties is in accordance with the patients will and best interests, and it is not, consequently, possible to rely on the implied consent of the patient. The legal basis for the processing of health information in these situations must therefore be considered separately.

EU Directive 95/46/EC Article 8.1 forbids – as a point of departure – the processing of sensitive data, but according to Article 8.2 such information may be processed with the individual's explicit consent, or if it is necessary for the establishment, exercise or defence of legal claims. The latter includes the processing of data for various legal purposes, including the settlement of insurance claims and claims relating to employment relations, forensic investigations and administrative purposes in general.[114] According to Article 8.2, sensitive data may also be processed if it is necessary to protect the vital interests of a person who is physically or legally incapable of giving her consent. This is relevant in cases of patients without decision-making capacities. All in all, it appears that the EU Directive ascribes equal importance to the patient's consent and to other legitimate reasons. In this respect, human rights law seems to attach more importance to the right to informational self-determination requiring that processing without the patient's consent needs special justification under ECHR Article 8.2. The balancing of competing interests may be illustrated by the ECtHR's ruling in *M.S. v. Sweden*.[115]

---

114 See, also, CoE Recommendation R (2002) 9 on the protection of personal data collected and processed for insurance purposes (18 September 2002) and CoE Recommendation R (89) 2 on the protection of personal data used for employment purposes (18 January 1989).

115 ECtHR 27 August 1997, *M.S. v. Sweden*, no. 20837/92. CoE has addressed the processing of personal data for social security purposes in Recommendation R (86) 1 on the protection of personal data for social security purposes (23 January 1986). It follows from principle 3.3 that sensitive information may only be obtained from others with the informed and express consent of the individual, or in accordance with other safeguards laid down by law.

> The case is concerned with a woman who had applied for compensation at the Social Insurance Office (hereinafter the SIO) due to a back injury she had experienced at work. The SIO had demanded and had been provided with information about her medical condition from the hospital clinic where she had received treatment for her back condition, as well as for other health problems. Her application was not successful as the SIO found that her back condition was caused by a chronic disorder and not by the work injury. The woman claimed a violation of her right to private life under ECHR article 8 because the clinic had provided more extensive information about her medical condition to the SIO than was justified by her application. The disclosed medical data included, for example, information about an abortion she had requested because of severe back pain. She also claimed that she should have been consulted prior to the disclosure of her medical data to the SIO. However, the Court found that the disclosure was justified under article 8.2 as the purpose was to enable the SIO to determine whether the conditions for granting compensation had been met, and this could be regarded as having pursued the aim of protecting the economic well-being of the country. Furthermore, the SIO also had a legitimate need to check information received from the patient herself to determine whether her claim was well-founded. In addition, the contested measure was subject to important limitations and accompanied by effective and adequate safeguards against abuse.

Other ECtHR cases have concerned the collection and retention of health data for forensic purposes[116] or for the settlement of other legal claims.[117] Consequently, irrespective of the emphasis put on privacy rights, both EU law and human rights law are sensitive to administrative interests in having access to health data to ensure law enforcement, to make proper administrative decisions, and to pursue legal claims.

The rights of other persons could also justify the dissemination of medical data, and this is especially relevant with regard to the patient's family members or partners. In cases of infectious diseases, it may be justified to inform other persons about the risk of having contracted a disease that may be fatal. The Explanatory Report to the Biomedicine Convention stipulates that, in the case of conditions transmissible to others, the prevention of the risk to the third party warrants his or her right taking precedence over the patient's right to privacy in accordance with Article 26 of the Biomedicine Convention.[118] The interests of family members may also justify restrictions to the right to privacy with regard to genetic information. The Additional Protocol on Genetic Testing does not provide clear guidance on the balancing of interests in situations where family members could benefit from obtaining knowledge of the risk of having a genetic

116 See, e.g., ECtHR 25 February 1997, *Z v. Finland*, no. 22009/93; and ECtHR 4 December 2008, *S and Marper v UK*, no. 30562/04 and 30566/04 (retention of DNA samples).

117 See, e.g., ECtHR 5 January 2006, *K.T. v. Norway*, no. 26664/03 (child custody); and ECtHR 10 October 2006, *L.L. v. France*, no. 7508/02 (divorce).

118 Explanatory Report to the Biomedicine Convention, *supra*, note 50, paragraph 70.

disorder, but leave it to the states to issue rules and regulations.[119] In some cases the ECtHR has ruled that the interests of other persons could justify the disclosure of medical information,[120] but the assessments of the Court have been thorough, and in other cases it has reached the opposite conclusion.[121]

All in all, patients' rights to privacy and confidentiality appear to be an area where the balancing of interests needs special consideration.

9. CONCLUDING REMARKS

This chapter was aimed at identifying and describing some of the most important patients' rights laid down in international patients' rights and human rights legislation. Historically, there has been a close connection between the development of human rights law and patients' rights law, and it is therefore not surprising that the important international patients' rights instruments have been developed by international (human rights) bodies (especially the Council of Europe, the WHO and UNESCO).[122] The European Union and EU Regulations are also playing an increasingly important role in this area. Thus, patients' rights is an area where the connection between health law and human rights law is very visible.

The rights-based approach promoted by the development of international patients' rights law has drastically changed the position of patients *vis-à-vis* healthcare services. Patients' rights have empowered patients and have made them the focus, instead of their assuming the role of passive and obedient subjects to doctors' orders. Recognition of patients' right to respect for dignity, integrity and autonomy, together with respect for privacy, confidentiality and non-discrimination, serve to ensure that patients are respected as persons, and not treated as mere means for medical sciences, or exposed to unacceptable intrusions by public authorities.

---

119 Explanatory Report to the Additional Protocol to the Convention on Human Rights and Biomedicine concerning Genetic Testing for Health Purposes, CETS 203, Strasbourg 2008, paragraph 140.

120 ECtHR 5 January 2006, *K.T. v. Norway*, no. 26664/03. In ECtHR 18 May 2004, *Plon (Société) v. France*, no. 58148/00, the Court's conclusion was based on an assessment of freedom of expression (ECHR Article 10) and the interest in protecting the privacy of deceased French President Mitterrand. In reaching the conclusion in favour of freedom of expression, the Court put emphasis on the fact that the medical condition of President Mitterrand had already been revealed, and on the passage of time since his the death (paragraph 53).

121 ECtHR 10 October 2006, *L.L. v. France*, no. 7508/02, paragraph 23.

122 See section 2.2 and further references, *supra*, note 13.

CHAPTER 5
REPRODUCTIVE HEALTH

Janne Rothmar Herrmann

1. INTRODUCTION

Because of the special biological functions performed by women in the reproductive process, particular healthcare needs and issues related to reproduction arise in relation to women. As such, women experiencing reproductive health issues can be seen as a group in need of special legal attention, first of all because of the special healthcare needs associated with reproduction, secondly because women's procreative role may lead to unequal access to healthcare treatment, and lastly, because women's reproductive autonomy has traditionally been subject to intense scrutiny by the state.

The most important legal landmark in addressing reproductive health was the development of the concept of reproductive rights[1] during The United Nations International Conference on Population and Development in Cairo in 1994, and the Fourth World Conference on Women in Beijing in 1995. The concept of reproductive rights is an interpretative framework to be applied to already-existing human rights. It focuses on *individual* rights and the reproductive needs of individuals, rather than on achieving demographic targets,[2] and thus relates to fundamental values such as equality, non-discrimination and justice. The concept emphasises a comprehensive approach to reproduction, integrating the various fragmented healthcare needs relating to the reproductive process, and puts women at the centre of the process, recognising, respecting and responding to the needs of women, and not only those of mothers.[3] Whereas health is

1 For a detailed overview of the development of this concept, see Laura Reichenbach & Mindy Jane Roseman (eds.), *Reproductive Health and Human Rights*, University of Pennsylvania Press, 2009.

2 Rebecca J. Cook, Bernard M. Dickens and Mahmoud F. Fathalla, *Reproductive Health and Human Rights – integrating medicine, ethics and law*, Oxford: Clarendon Press, 2003, p. 155.

3 Rebecca J. Cook, Bernard M. Dickens and Mahmoud F. Fathalla, *Reproductive Health and Human Rights – integrating medicine, ethics and law*, Oxford: Clarendon Press, 2003, pp. 11–13.

defined in the WHO Constitution as a 'state of complete physical, mental and social well-being', and thus more than the absence of disease or infirmity, the application of this definition to *reproductive health* would mean that 'reproductive health' covers more those aspects in relation to a person's reproductive system, its functions and processes. It also encompasses the achievement of a satisfactory and safe sex life, that the individual has a reproductive capacity, and the freedom to decide on when, how often, and with what intervals, procreation should happen. As such, the state of reproductive health also involves adequate education, information and counselling, as well as access to affordable family planning, further, that men and women are given a choice between various legal measures to control fertility, as well as being provided with adequate healthcare ensuring a safe medical environment for maternal health and child birth.[4]

The aim of this chapter is to provide an overview of the human rights and principles relevant to the notion of reproductive health, and to give an analysis of selected reproductive issues, including a detailed account of the relevant case law of the ECtHR.

2. WOMEN'S REPRODUCTIVE HEALTH AND HUMAN RIGHTS

2.1. INTRODUCTION

Biological differences between women and men may lead to differences in health status. The biological differences between the sexes afford women a special reproductive role that is linked to the female body. As such, the gender perspective is an important aspect to address. The fact that women's biological and social role in procreation can affect their options and possibilities of taking part in society is the perspective behind the UN Convention on the Elimination of All Forms of Discrimination of Women (CEDAW).[5] Among the international human rights treaties, the Convention takes an important place in bringing the female half of humanity into the focus of human rights concerns. The spirit of the Convention is rooted in the goals of the United Nations 'to reaffirm faith in fundamental human rights, in the dignity and worth of the human person, in the equal rights of men and women.'[6] Another important

4 Cairo Declaration, para. 7.2 (Programme of Action of the United Nations International Conference on Population and Development, 1994).

5 Convention on the Elimination of All Forms of Discrimination against Women, 1979.

6 Introduction to CEDAW, www.un.org/womenwatch/daw/cedaw/text/econvention.htm#intro, accessed May 1, 2011.

legal landmark in this respect was – as mentioned *supra* – the development of the concept of reproductive rights during The United Nations International Conference on Population and Development in Cairo in 1994, and the Fourth World Conference on Women in Beijing in 1995.

This chapter will introduce the interrelated rights and principles that form part of the reproductive rights framework, and will analyse various reproductive situations or choices relating to women's (and sometimes men's) reproductive capacities from a human rights perspective. These include the right to reproductive autonomy, including the right to (reproductive) healthcare services, the right to respect for private life and family life, and non-discrimination, which will be explored more in depth in the following. A comprehensive list of human rights and principles relevant to reproduction and reproductive health would further include the right to receive and impart information, the right to life, the right to liberty and security of person, the right to benefit from scientific progress, and the right to education. The relevance of (some of) the latter rights will be demonstrated in the analysis of selected ECtHR judgments, *supra*.

The topics selected to illustrate the theme of this chapter include family planning, abortion, and various issues related to fertility treatment.

2.2. REPRODUCTIVE AUTONOMY

Autonomy is a well-known principle in health law. It is one of the most basic liberty rights,[7] and is, as such, a fundamental right in both health law and medical ethics. The key role of this principle was expressed during the Nuremberg war crimes trials, which uncovered the horrors that had taken place in the Nazi concentration camps, as part of medical experiments.[8] The principle's function is, first and foremost, to ensure that human beings are not subjected to unwanted interventions, which is reflected in the legal requirements concerning information and consent in relation to medical treatment and biomedical research. The legal requirement to obtain the patient's consent minimises the risk of being subjected to harmful or unwanted interventions. As such, the principle ensures that the individual can freely chose her own preferences in life, and in relation to her own person and her own body, without

7 Henriette Sinding Aasen: 'Dignity and Human Rights in the Modern Welfare State' in Henriette Sinding Aasen, Rune Halvorsen & Antonio Barbosa da Silva (eds.), *Human Rights, Dignity and Autonomy in Health Care and Social Services: Nordic Perspectives*, Intersentia, 2009, pp. 64–66.

8 *Trials of war criminals before the Nuernberg Military Tribunals under Control Council Law* no. 10, Nuremberg October 1946 – April 1949, U.S. Government Printing Office, Washington, 1949–53, vol. 1 & 2: Case no. 1: Karl Brandt *et al.*, *The Medical Case.*

undue interference, coercion or control. To achieve this situation of free choice in relation to healthcare, she must, of course, be presented with all relevant information, including alternative options in a way that is tangible to her. The provision of this information enables her to exercise real autonomy. In relation to *procreative* autonomy, legal scholars such as Ronald Dworkin have argued that the freedom to make choices concerning reproduction is a vital aspect of human dignity, a principle that is a fundamental feature of all democratic societies.[9] Because of the role of women and the female body in procreation, the principle of reproductive autonomy becomes especially significant in a way that does not apply to men. Interventions into women's bodily autonomy that are not preceded by an informed consent infringe on their most basic human rights. If, for example, the woman's partner or husband prefers a pregnancy to be terminated or continued, contrary to her wishes, his autonomy may not be exercised without it involving an interference with *her* bodily *integrity*. As such, the rights of the woman carry more weight in the legal balancing between her rights and any competing rights of the man.[10]

The extent of the right to reproductive autonomy is, however, subject to theoretical dispute. Some view the right to reproductive autonomy as merely a negative right to be free from state interference in the reproductive sphere, while others regard it as a positive right to access medically assisted procreation.[11] Article 12 of the CEDAW Convention presents the most clearly worded protection of reproductive autonomy and choice. To what extent the right to reproductive choice exists in international human rights law is, however, an issue that divides the States Parties, depending on national perceptions, religious practices and culture. Some Parties to the CEDAW Convention are familiar with the democratic idea of equality between the sexes because of a non-democratic rule, others may formally recognise the equal worth and equal rights of women and men, but accept *de facto* discrimination because of tradition, religion and culture. As such, the road to achieving the full realisation of the reproductive rights enshrined in, e.g., the CEDAW Convention, is still long, but can be shortened by the monitoring committee who issue general recommendations on certain aspects of the Convention, as well as reports on each individual state in response to their country reports.

---

9 Ronald Dworkin, *Life's Dominion*, London: HarperCollins, 1993, pp. 166–167.

10 This balancing will be subject to further analysis infra in relation to the ECtHR case-law on abortion.

11 John A. Robertson, *Children of Choice: Freedom and New Reproductive Technologies*, Princeton: Princeton University Press, 1994, p. 23.

2.3. RIGHT TO RESPECT FOR PRIVACY AND FAMILY LIFE

Another key aspect of the concept of reproductive rights is the right to respect for private life and family life, which is protected in a variety of human rights documents, including ICCPR Article 23 and ECHR Articles 8 and 12. The right to respect for private life is a broad term encompassing, *inter alia*, aspects of an individual's physical and social identity, including the right to personal autonomy, personal development, and to establish and develop relationships with other human beings and the outside world, incorporating, in principle, the right to respect for both the decisions to become, and not to become, a parent. The extensive ECtHR case law invoking the right to respect for private life and family life in relation to reproductive issues will be presented more in depth *infra*, e.g. in relation to abortion and access to fertility treatment. However, included in the understanding of the concept of private life and family life would also be the right to control and to freely and responsibly decide on aspects of sexuality and sex life.[12] As such, the human rights law protection of reproductive autonomy and choice is also realised through the protection of the individual's right to privacy and family life.

2.4. THE PROHIBITION OF DISCRIMINATION

The final integral right of the overarching framework concept of reproductive rights is the requirement of non-discrimination, which means that the rights enshrined in, e.g., the ECHR must be secured 'without discrimination on any grounds such as sex, race, colour, language, religion, political or other opinion, national or social origin, association with a national minority, property, birth or other status' (cf. Article 14).

Furthermore, as sketched *supra*, it is also the explicit intention of the CEDAW Convention to address and eliminate discrimination of women, including those types of discrimination that relate to the female body, women's procreative role, and their reproductive healthcare needs. As such, the right to reproductive health services becomes a prerequisite, as it would be discriminatory (discrimination on the grounds of sex) to deny women medical services that only women need.

3. FAMILY PLANNING

The first topic to serve as an illustration of how health and human rights relate to the area of reproductive health is family planning. This topic includes both the

12 Beijing Declaration and Platform for Action 1995, para. 96.

access to contraceptive devices or medicines to prevent pregnancy, and the medical and surgical termination of a pregnancy.

3.1. ABORTION

3.1.1. The UN Conventions

In my view, the relevant UN human rights conventions can be said to reflect and encompass three different elements or approaches to the regulation of abortion: the right to abortion as part of the right to reproductive health, the right to abortion and other healthcare services only applicable to women as part of the non-discrimination concept, and the regulation of abortion as a legitimate area of regulatory concern for the state.

The Universal Declaration of Human Rights (1948) protects the right to life in Article 3: '*Everyone has the right to life, liberty and security of person.*' The right enshrined in the Declaration apply to everyone '*without distinction of any kind, such as...birth or other status*' (Article 2). Whether or not the right to life applies to the unborn foetus is one of the key legal issues in the abortion debate. Zampas[13] has argued that foetuses are excluded from the protection, given the use of the term 'born free' in Article 1: '*All human beings are born free and equal in dignity and rights. They are endowed with reason and conscience and should act towards one another in a spirit of brotherhood.*' A further argument in support of this interpretation is the fact that foetuses cannot be said to be endowed with neither 'reason' nor 'conscience',[14] and thus fall outside the scope of the Convention.

After the adoption of the Universal Declaration of Human Rights, the Human Rights Commission of the Economic and Social Council were given the task of drafting two covenants that would elaborate on the rights laid down in the Declaration, the International Covenant on Civil and Political Rights (ICCPR),[15] and the International Covenant on Economic, Social and Cultural Rights (ICESCR), both adopted in 1966. The ICCPR protects the right to life in Article 6 (1): '*Every human being has the inherent right to life. This right shall be protected by law. No one shall be arbitrarily deprived of his life.*' The question of whether or not this right included the human foetus was deliberately left open at the time of

13 Christina Zampas & Jamie M. Gher, 'Abortion as a Human Right – International and Regional Standards', 8 *Human Rights Law Review* pp. 249–294 (2008).

14 In liberal moral philosophy, the lack/presence of these characteristics determines the moral status of an entity, see, e.g., Peter Singer, *Rethinking Life & Death*, Oxford University Press, Oxford, 1994.

15 International Covenant on Economic, Social and Cultural Rights, 1966.

the drafting.[16] The Human Rights Committee, which publishes its interpretation of the Covenant in its *General Comments*, has never addressed the issue of whether or not the right to life is applicable to the foetus. The Human Rights Committee has, rather, focused its application of Article 6 on women's right to life in connection with terminations of pregnancy requiring states to ensure that women do not have to resort to clandestine, life-threatening abortions.[17]

The CEDAW Convention focuses special attention on women's health and well-being in Article 12, which requires States Parties to '*take all appropriate measures to eliminate discrimination against women in the field of health care in order to ensure, on a basis of equality of men and women, access to health care services, including those related to family planning.*' As stated in the preambular recitals, the CEDAW Convention is the only human rights convention explicitly addressing family planning, and its main purpose is to establish and ensure the protection of women's reproductive rights, by linking the female reproductive role to the objective of creating equality both between the sexes, and between different groups of women: '*the role of women in procreation should not be a basis for discrimination*' (cf. preambular recital 13).

In 1999 the CEDAW Committee adopted General Recommendation no. 24, which clarifies the states' obligations under Article 12 of the Convention, and consequently, the various factors that the states should account for in their reports to the Committee. The states must, *inter alia*, include an account of how policies and measures adopted in national healthcare systems address women's right to health, and in doing so, must choose a perspective which takes as its point of departure women's needs and interests. Due regard should be taken of biological factors, including the difference in reproductive healthcare needs and functions. Organisational factors should also address these differences, such as, e.g., ensuring the right to confidentiality, especially in potentially stigmatising situations, such as unwanted pregnancy. It is also emphasised that healthcare services should be provided in a way that respects the dignity of women. This norm could be seen to entail that criminalisation of healthcare services only needed by women is a hindrance to women's right to health, and as such, can be characterised as discrimination; as stated in General Recommendation no. 24, 'measures to eliminate discrimination against women are considered to be inappropriate if a healthcare system lacks services to prevent, detect and treat illnesses specific to women. It is discriminatory for a State party to refuse to legally provide for the performance of certain reproductive health services for women. For instance, if health service providers refuse to perform such services

16 UN Doc. A/3764, para. 112.

17 General Comment 28, CCPR/C/21/Rev.1/Add.10, para. 10; and the Human Rights Committee's decision in *KL v. Peru*, communication no. 1153/2003, adopted 24 October 2005.

based on conscientious objection, measures should be introduced to ensure that women are referred to alternative health providers.'[18] How authoritative the statements of the CEDAW committee are is subject to academic debate, however, in my view, they clarify the Convention text, and are of an equally binding nature to the ratifying states.

Finally, Article 16.1.e. of the CEDAW Convention stipulates that women should have the same right as men to choose freely and responsibly on the number and spacing of their children. As such, the States Parties are, to some extent, obliged to make abortion available to women. Whereas Article 12 must be understood as an obligation to make abortion available if a termination is necessary to protect the life or health of the woman, it is uncertain as to what extent Article 16.1.e implicates a right to autonomy-based abortion.

3.1.2. The European Convention on Human Rights

The European Court of Human Rights (ECtHR) and the former European Commission of Human Rights (which, prior to the reorganisation of the Court, functioned as a kind of first instance review body) have both had the opportunity to address the question of abortion. The cases brought before the Strasbourg court have dealt with the issue of whether or not women have a right to abortion under Article 8 of the European Convention on Human Rights, whether the foetus has a right to life under Article 2, and whether prospective fathers have any rights under Article 8 which limit women's reproductive choices.

The case law taken as a whole demonstrates a considerable reluctance in taking a stance on many of the issues, although some of the issues involved which require that rights must be prioritised in the balancing between the various involved actors, have been clearly established.

The structure of the following cases is thematic rather can chronological.

a. The Balancing of Interests between Woman and Foetus

The first theme that can be identified from the ECtHR is how the rights of the woman are balanced against the rights or interest of the foetus.

In 1980 the European Commission on Human Rights, in their second ever case on abortion, *X v. UK (Paton v. UK)*,[19] identified three possible views of the foetus' right to life, and laid down some basic principles in the balancing of interests

18 Para. 11.

19 ECmHR *X v. the United Kingdom*, application 8416/79, decision of 13 May 1980 on the admissibility of the application. The underlying national case was *Paton v. British Pregnancy*

between woman and foetus. In this case, a husband had unsuccessfully tried to get an injunction against his wife undergoing a termination. The case had been dismissed by the national court on the grounds that no rights stood to be violated by the proposed termination. Neither the foetus nor the husband held any rights under English law, and consequently, the woman terminated the pregnancy a few hours after the court hearing. Mr. Paton subsequently complained to the European Commission on Human Rights, claiming that the English Abortion Act violated the ECHR, by allowing abortion, by refusing to grant the foetus any rights, and by denying the father his rights over the foetus.

The Commission first of all noted that whether or not the foetus had a right to life under Article 2 was a question which had been left open in its first ever case on abortion, *Brüggemann & Scheuten v. Germany* (this case is discussed in more detail *infra*). However, it was clear that the limitations to the right to life included in Article 2 (i.e. the scope for the use of the death penalty and the use of force) referred to persons already born, and as such, were not applicable to the foetus. On the other hand, the wording of Article 2 does not exclude the foetus from being included in its scope. The Commission outlined three possible approaches. Firstly, the Article may be interpreted in a way that excludes the foetus completely. Another possible interpretation would be to understand Article 2 as including the foetus in its scope, but with *'certain implied limitations'*. Lastly, the protection laid down in Article 2 could be understood as awarding the foetus an absolute right to life. The latter option was dismissed by the Commission, as this would render abortion impossible, even in emergency cases, in which a termination of the pregnancy is necessary in order to save the woman's life. To place a higher value on the potential life of the unborn than that of the woman would be contrary to the ECHR's purpose. In reaching this conclusion, the Commission relied on the argument that all of the contracting states, except only one, allowed for abortion under such circumstances at the time of the drafting of the Convention. However, the foetus' life is intimately connected to, and cannot be viewed separately from, the woman's life. Thus, the Commission dismissed only one of three identified possible approaches, but did not take an explicit stand on the remaining two perspectives. However, the dismissal of the view that the foetus holds an absolute right to life implicates that national regulations *must* include a right to abortion when the woman's life is at stake, in order to respect Article 2 of the Convention.

In *Tysiac v. Poland*,[20] a pregnant woman risked losing her eyesight if she carried the pregnancy to term. Her general practitioner advised an abortion and referred

---

Advisory Service Trustees [1979] QB 276; [1978] 3 WLR 687; [1978] 2 All ER 987, and as such, the case is often referred to as *Paton v. UK*.

20 ECtHR *Tysiac v. Poland*, application no. 5410/03, judgment, 20 March 2007.

her to a gynaecologist. The gynaecologist, however, did not find that she met the criteria for a termination. Consequently, she gave birth to a child and subsequently became blind. The woman claimed that the state's failure to provide her with an abortion in this situation, where such a procedure was actually legal under national law, amounted to a violation of her right to respect for private life, as she was exposed to a considerable risk to her health. The Court agreed, and found that the state had a positive obligation to protect her right effectively. Thus, it was not sufficient that an abortion was *in concreto* legal – the state was also obliged to provide her with an *effective judicial remedy* which could have tested her right, especially so when she was referred to a specialist by her general practitioner who found that she met the criteria for having the pregnancy terminated, but the specialist declined.[21]

The issue of whether or not the foetus was afforded a right to life under Article 2 has, as illustrated, been left largely undecided in every case law document concerning the conflict of rights/interests between the woman and the foetus. However, in 2004 the perfect test case to decide this issue presented itself. Because of the facts of the case, the Court could, if it wished to do so, finally reconsider this difficult issue, and even in a context where the status of the foetus was detached from the sensitive and delicate balancing of rights *vis-à-vis* the pregnant woman. In *Vo v. France*,[22] the applicant, Thi-Nho Vo, was scheduled to undergo a routine medical examination during her sixth month of pregnancy. At the same time, another woman, Thi Thanh Van Vo, was scheduled to have her coil removed. The applicant, who did not speak French, answered when the doctor called for Mrs Vo. Because of the mistaken identity, and the fact that the doctor did not examine the applicant prior to attempting to remove the coil, the amniotic sac was pierced and as a result, a few days later, the woman had to have her pregnancy terminated on the grounds of the health of the foetus. Subsequently, the applicant had no legal remedies in relation to pressing criminal charges, as the foetus was not considered a person under French law. Despite this opportunity for the Court to interpret the scope of Article 2 in relation to the foetus, the Court, to many commentators' surprise,[23] in effect, refused to decide on this aspect, and found no violation of Article 2.

In conclusion, while *Paton v. UK* stipulated that national regulations must provide women with abortion when it is necessary to save the woman's life in

---

21 Paras. 74–85.

22 ECtHR application no. 53924/00, judgment of 8 July 2004.

23 See, for example, J.K. Mason's remark: '*Thus, in the end, what it had been hoped might be an "evolutive interpretation" of a "living instrument" petered out into a non-decision – the reader of the judgment is likely to feel, by analogy, that it had been a long journey to the pub with no beer*' in 'What's in a name? The vagaries of Vo v France', *Child and Family Law Quarterly*, 2005:17:1, pp. 97–112.

order to comply with the protection in ECHR Article 2, *Tysiac v. Poland* afforded equal protection to the woman's health, as part of her right to respect for private life under Article 8. Whereas the general issue of abortion had been a question of balancing the right to privacy against the state's legitimate interest in safeguarding public morality, the issue of therapeutic abortion also had to address the state's positive obligation to safeguard women's physical integrity.[24] Although the Court emphasised that it was not for the Court, in the present case, to assess whether or not the ECHR guaranteed a right to abortion, because Tysiac already had such a right under national law in the case of serious risk to her life or her health,[25] the judgment does, none the less, appear to be a first step towards a more dynamic interpretation of the Convention in relation to the sensitive issue of abortion. Notwithstanding that the Convention '*does not guarantee as such a right to any specific level of medical care*', the Court stressed that the concept of private life had been interpreted in the case law to encompass physical and mental integrity, and that states had a positive obligation to ensure that individuals were given an effective respect of their integrity. The view that a real and effective protection of women's integrity implicitly implicates access to therapeutic abortion may well be the first step towards the creation of greater legal certainty in relation to abortion in human rights law. As for the general question of the status of the foetus in relation to the Convention, and how such a status might affect and limit female reproductive autonomy, the Court avoided interpreting the scope of Article 2, even in a case such as *Vo*, where there was no clash of interests to be balanced between woman and foetus. This reluctance seems to be contrary to the style of the Court in general, which is characterised by a dynamic interpretation. As a whole, the relevant case law is illustrative of the sensitivity that is still associated with the abortion issue from a human rights perspective.

b. The Balancing of Interests between Woman and State

A second theme that can be identified in the ECtHR case law is the woman's right to make autonomous decisions regarding her own body, as part of the privacy concept, and how this right is balanced *vis-à-vis* the state's right to regulate the termination of pregnancy. The case law demonstrates that the state may have a legitimate interest in this issue, but also establishes certain boundaries and limitations.

In *Brüggemann & Scheuten v. Germany*,[26] the issue at stake was whether or not pregnancy and abortion pertained to the private sphere under Article 8 of the Convention.

---

24 Para. 107.

25 Para. 104.

26 ECmHR *Rose Marie Brüggemann & Adelheid Scheuten v. the Federal Republic of Germany*, application no. 6959/75, Report adopted by the Commission on 12 July 1977.

> In 1974 the German Federal Parliament had adopted a reform of the Criminal Code which gave wider access to abortion. However, the German Constitutional Court held that the amendment was unconstitutional and referred to the fact that the unborn life held a higher protection than the autonomy of the woman. Thus, the increased access to autonomy-based abortion could not enter into force. The introduction of an ethical and eugenic indication was, however, allowed on the grounds that it would be burdensome to demand that pregnancies were carried to term in such cases.

The applicants held that the Constitutional Court's judgment, and the modified amendment of the Criminal Code deprived them of the right to autonomy, and amounted to an interference with their right to respect for private life and family life. The Commission held that the right to respect for private life ensured the individual a sphere where she could develop her personality and freely establish relationships, including sexual ones, with others. However, '*the claim to respect for private life is automatically reduced to the extend that the individual himself brings his private life into contact with public life or into close connection with other protected interests...pregnancy cannot be said to pertain uniquely to the sphere of private life. Whenever a woman is pregnant her private life becomes closely connected with the developing foetus.*'[27]

The Commission also did not find it necessary to decide if the foetus could be considered a form of 'life' in the meaning of Article 2, or whether it could be regarded as '*an entity which under Art. 8 (2) could justify an interference "for the protection of others".*' On the contrary, it was emphasised that certain interests pertaining to pregnancy were protected legally, including the right to inheritance of the unborn, which was implemented in all ECHR states, and the regulation of abortion, which was also in place, in some way or another, in every single Contracting State. Such regulation reflected that pregnancy and abortion did not pertain solely to the private sphere of the woman, and consequently, regulation of the issue did not amount to an interference. Based on this line of reasoning, the Commission found that the German regulation did not infringe on the applicants' right to respect for private life. Although the increased access to autonomy-based abortion had been quashed by the Constitutional Court, there were still other legal options available allowing for terminations, and criminal sanctions had also been removed for certain types of abortions.[28]

In *Open Door v. Ireland*,[29] the issue to be decided was whether or not the right to freedom of information in Article 10 of the Convention included the right to

---

27 Paras. 55–56 and 59.

28 Para. 63, cf. 62.

29 ECtHR *Open Door and Dublin Well Woman v. Ireland*, application no. 14234/88; 14235/88, judgment, 29 October 1992.

receive and impart information about abortion. The applicants were councillors who complained of the prohibition on imparting information about the availability of abortions in other countries, and women of reproductive age who complained of the ban on receiving this information in the case of pregnancy. The Court, first of all, noted that it fell within the scope of the Court's competency to test the state's margin of appreciation, even when the issue at stake is a morally sensitive one regulated with reference to the national Constitution:

> *'The Court cannot agree that the State's discretion in the field of the protection of morals is unfettered and unreviewable ... It acknowledges that the national authorities enjoy a wide margin of appreciation in matters of morals, particularly in an area such as the present which touches on matters of belief concerning the nature of human life. As the Court has observed before, it is not possible to find in the legal and social orders of the Contracting States a uniform European conception of morals, and the State authorities are, in principle, in a better position than the international judge to give an opinion on the exact content of the requirements of morals as well as on the "necessity" of a "restriction" or "penalty" intended to meet them ... However this power of appreciation is not unlimited. It is for the Court, in this field also, to supervise whether a restriction is compatible with the Convention.'*[30]

The Court, in its assessment of the restriction of the applicants' right to freedom of information, first of all recalled that Article 10 applies to any kind of information or ideas, including those that are shocking, offensive, or which embarrass the state or certain population groups. This fact follows from concepts such as tolerance, and pluralism, which are the prerequisites of democracy. The restrictions to the freedom of information in the present case regarded services which could be obtained legally in the countries where they were provided, and which impacted immensely on the health and well-being of women. This fact called '*for careful scrutiny by the Convention institutions as to their conformity with the tenets of a democratic society.*' Relevant factors that the Court took into account in its assessment on proportionality were that the counselling was neutral, allowing the women to choose freely between continuing the pregnancy, or travelling abroad to have a termination, and most importantly, the health related perspectives involved. The Court emphasised that without the counselling, the women were left with information in advertisements and imported magazines and phone books. Thus, it was, in fact, possible to obtain information in Ireland about abortion from elsewhere, but in a way that did not involve qualified staff, and as such, offered a minimum level of protection of the women's health in comparison. Furthermore, the Court found that the submitted evidence suggested that the prohibition had created a risk that women were seeking terminations later on in their pregnancies because of the lack of

30 Para. 68.

counselling, and that subsequently, they did not seek out medical attention to follow up on any post-termination complications. On that basis, the Court found that the prohibition did violate Article 10 of the ECHR.

Whereas *Brüggemann & Scheuten v. Germany* established that pregnancy did not pertain solely to the private sphere of the pregnant woman, *Open Doors v. Ireland* established that the state's right to infringe on her privacy in relation to pregnancy and abortion is subject to limitations. The fact that the Irish women's health were at risk carried more weight in the balancing, and thus although the state's margin of appreciation is quite broad in matters that are sensitive and which relate to national moral convictions, the margin is not unreviewable. The Court has, however, never narrowed the margin of appreciation in relation to whether or not there is a right to abortion, even though many of the same arguments apply: If no right to autonomy-based abortion exists, women will subject themselves to clandestine procedures, not carried out by qualified doctors in a safe environment.

In *Tysiac v. Poland,* there had been, as mentioned *supra*, access to legal abortion on health grounds. However, the legislation had failed to take into account that differences of opinions might exist between the woman and the doctor, or indeed between doctors, and consequently, no judicial review system was in place to provide the woman with easy access to have her right tested and enforced. As such, the case did not go further than *Brüggemann & Scheuten* in relation to establishing whether women have a right to abortion based on human rights law. However, the key point in *Tysiac v. Poland* was that the state was obliged, under Article 8, to ensure an effective protection of women's physical integrity, and as such, it would seem to imply a right to therapeutic abortion when the woman's health is at risk.

c. The Balancing of Interests between Woman and Man

A third theme that can be identified from the ECtHR case law on abortion concerns the woman's right to control her own body in relation to the prospective father.

In *R.H. v. Norway,*[31] the applicant was a man whose partner had had her pregnancy terminated during the 14th week. He claimed that the lack of foetal protection in Norwegian law amounted to a violation of Article 2 of the ECHR. He referred to the fact that the abortion had not been necessary to protect the life or health of the mother, that he had expressly assumed the responsibility for the

[31] ECtHR *R.H. v. Norway*, application no. 17004/90, decision of 19 May 1992 on the admissibility of the application.

upbringing of, and care for, the child after birth, and that he had protested from the time that the woman had considered a termination. He also claimed, *inter alia*, a violation of Article 9, since he had not been allowed access to the remains of the aborted foetus, which he wanted to be buried in accordance with his religious beliefs.

The Commission found that '*having regard to … [the] Norwegian legislation, its requirements for the termination of pregnancy as well as the specific circumstances of the present case, the Commission does not find that the respondent State has gone beyond its discretion which the Commission considers it has in this sensitive area of abortion.*' Thus, the claim regarding both Articles 2 and 9 was dismissed by the Court. The applicant further claimed that Article 8 afforded the father a degree of rights over the foetus when the woman's life was not at risk. Also, a foetus at a gestational age of 14 weeks had to be considered part of his family. The Commission remarked that: '*it is true that Articles 8 and 9 of the Convention guarantee the right to respect for private and family life and freedom to manifest one's religion. However, the Commission finds that any interpretation of the potential father's right under these provisions in connection with an abortion which the mother intends to have performed on her, must first of all take into account her rights, she being the person primarily concerned by the pregnancy and its continuation or termination. The Commission therefore finds that any possible interference which might be assumed in the circumstances of the present case was justified as being necessary for the protection of the rights of another person.*'[32]

In *Boso v. Italy*,[33] the Court dismissed an application from a man whose wife had had an abortion. As in the previous case law, the Court refused to decide the degree of protection the foetus is afforded under Article 2, but simply noted that: '*even supposing that, in certain circumstances, the foetus might be considered to have rights protected by Article 2 of the Convention, the Court notes that in the instant case … it appears … that his wife's pregnancy was terminated in conformity with section 5 of Law no. 194 of 1978.*' The Italian Abortion Act permitted an autonomy-based right to abortion until the 12th week of pregnancy, and after that time, abortion could be permitted on medical or eugenic indication. This legislation did, in the Court's view, '*strike a fair balance between, on the one hand, the need to ensure protection of the foetus and, on the other, the woman's interests … the Court does not find that the respondent State has gone beyond its discretion in such a sensitive area.*' As for the father's inability to influence the decision, '*any interpretation of a potential father's rights under Article 8 of the Convention when the mother intends to have an abortion should*

32 Para. 4 of the section 'the law'.

33 ECtHR *Giampiero Boso v. Italy*, application no. 50490/99, decision as to the admissibility, 5 September 2002.

above all take into account her rights, as she is the person primarily concerned by the pregnancy and its continuation or termination ... Accordingly, any interference with the right protected under Article 8 which might be assumed in the circumstances of the case was justified as being necessary for the protection of the rights of another person'.[34]

Both in *Boso v. Italy* and *R.H v. Norway*, the original reasoning laid down in *Paton v. UK* was reaffirmed and elaborated on, thus illustrating that the man has no rights in relation to abortion. Not only does the woman's right to bodily autonomy outweigh any rights of the man, but he also holds no entitlement to the aborted foetal tissue.

3.2. CONTRACEPTION

States Parties' compliance with Article 12 of the CEDAW Convention is central to the health and well-being of women. Read in the light of General Recommendation no. 24/1999, it requires states to eliminate discrimination against women in their access to healthcare services, throughout the life cycle, particularly in the areas of family planning, pregnancy, confinement, and during the post-natal period.[35] The demand in the General Recommendation for easy and affordable access to contraception has (together with access to abortion) been one of the major controversies associated with the CEDAW Convention and the CEDAW Committee, as this is an area which is continuously raised by the Committee in response to the country reports submitted by the States Parties.

General recommendation no. 24 (1999) on women and health elaborates on the Committee's understanding of Article 12, and addresses measures to eliminate discrimination in order to realise the right of women to the highest attainable standard of health. These measures include not only the obligation to provide women with *access* to healthcare on the basis of equality between men and women, but also to impart relevant *information*, to provide *education*, and to secure respect for *confidentiality*, as it may deter women from seeking advice and treatment, and thereby adversely affect their health and well-being, if there is a lack of confidentiality, because women will be less willing, for that reason, to seek medical care for, e.g., contraception.[36]

Case law from the ECtHR shows that it falls within the state's prerogative in the interest of health, education, and as part of maintaining a democratic society, to

34 Para. 1 of the section 'the law'.
35 CEDAW General Recommendation no. 24/1999, para. 2.
36 Para. 12 (d).

making general sex education, including education concerning the use of contraceptive products, mandatory in the elementary school curriculum, even against the wishes of the parents.[37]

Furthermore, it could be argued that Member States to the European Social Charter should provide scientifically-based and non-discriminatory sex education to young people, that does not involve censoring, withholding, or intentionally misrepresenting information, such as on contraception: The monitoring European Committee of Social Rights recommended in Decision no. 45/2007 (*INTERIGHTS v. Croatia*)[38] that such education be provided throughout the entire period of schooling. It stated that sexual and reproductive health education should be aimed at developing the capacity of children and young people to understand their sexuality in its biological and cultural dimensions, with the aim of enabling them to make responsible decisions with regard to sexual and reproductive health behaviour (see, also, Chapter 1).

4. PROCREATIVE HEALTHCARE SERVICES

In the late 1960s, British scientist and later Nobel Laureate, Dr Robert Edwards, together with physician Patrick Steptoe, developed the *in vitro* fertilisation (IVF) procedure which in 1978 resulted in the birth of the world's first ever test tube baby, Louise Brown. New reproductive technologies have since made their way to clinical practice, and a wide range of assisted reproductive healthcare services are on offer in today's healthcare systems. Furthermore, medical advances in the field have also created various possibilities of not only assisting conception, but also of selecting the embryos to be implanted using pre-implantation genetic diagnosis, or even cloning. As a result, in today's healthcare systems, infertile men and women, as well as single or lesbian women, may be medically aided in becoming parents. But even among heterosexual couples, an increasing number of children are born as a result of assisted reproduction. The increasing age of first-time mothers and environmental factors influencing the human reproductive capacities are among the parameters that might explain this development.

As mentioned in the introduction to this chapter in relation to the Cairo Declaration and the development of the reproductive rights framework, reproductive health encompasses a person's reproductive system, its functions

---

37 See ECtHR *Kjeldsen, Busk Madsen & Pedersen v. Denmark*, application nos. 5095/71; 5920/72; 5926/72, judgment 7 December 1976.

38 No. 45/2007, International Centre for the Legal Protection of Human Rights (*INTERIGHTS v. Croatia*), available at www.coe.int/t/dghl/monitoring/socialcharter/Complaints/Complaints_en.asp (retrieved 23 May 2011).

and processes. It also includes a state of being in which the individual has a reproductive capacity and the freedom to decide on when, how often, and with what intervals, procreation should happen. However, the realisation of this state of reproductive health, when aided by medical technology, also raises a number of sensitive issues. The provision of fertility treatment, such as IVF treatment and treatments aimed at choosing a healthy embryo, will serve as the case studies *infra*.

4.1. FERTILITY TREATMENT

4.1.1. A privacy issue?

Reproduction is central to our personal identity, and as such, it forms part of the very core of the concept of private life within the meaning of Article 8 in the ECHR. In *Evans v. UK*,[39] a woman had, prior to undergoing treatment for cancer that included the surgical removal of her ovaries, had one cycle of fertility treatment. The resulting ova were fertilised with the sperm of her partner, and the embryos were then deposited in the freezer to be implanted once the applicant had recovered from cancer. By that time, however, she and her partner had separated, and he had subsequently formed a new family. The applicant wanted to be given the right to use the frozen embryos for implantation, as they represented her only means of becoming a parent. Her former partner had, however, refused to consent to the use of the embryos, and asked that they be destroyed in accordance with the national Human Fertilisation and Embryology Act. The European Court of Human Rights, in the first instance chamber, held that Article 8 was applicable, since the notion of 'private life' incorporated the right to respect for both the decisions to become, and not to become, a parent. The question which arose under Article 8 was whether there exists a positive obligation on the state to ensure that a woman who has embarked on treatment for the specific purpose of giving birth to a genetically related child should be permitted to proceed to implantation of the embryo, notwithstanding the withdrawal of consent by her former partner, the male gamete provider.

The national Act which was at issue in the case had been the culmination of an exceptionally detailed examination of the social, ethical and legal implications of developments in the field of human fertilisation and embryology.[40] Its policy was to ensure continuing consent from the commencement of treatment to the point of implantation in the woman. While the pressing nature of the applicant's

39 ECtHR *Evans v. UK*, application no. 6339/05, judgment of 10 April 2007.

40 It was preceded by the Warnock Report, Mary Warnock, *A Question of Life: Warnock Report on Human Fertilization and Embryology*, Wiley-Blackwell, 1985.

medical condition required that she and her partner reach a decision about the fertilisation of her eggs without as much time for reflection and advice as might ordinarily be desired, it was undisputed that it was explained to them both that either was free to withdraw consent at any time before the resulting embryos were implanted in the applicant's uterus. The Court held that strong policy considerations underlay the decision of the legislature to favour a clear or 'bright-line' rule, which would serve both to produce legal certainty and to maintain public confidence in the law in a sensitive field. Like the national courts, the Chamber did not find, therefore, that the absence of a power to override a genetic parent's withdrawal of consent, even in the exceptional circumstances of the applicant's case, was such as to upset the fair balance required by Article 8, or to exceed the wide margin of appreciation afforded to the state.[41] The Grand Chamber agreed with the Chamber that the right to become, or not to become, a parent, did indeed fall within the private life concept protected by Article 8, but emphasised that she was not in any way prevented from becoming a mother in a social, legal, or even physical sense, since there was no rule of domestic law or practice to stop her from adopting a child or even giving birth to a child originally created *in vitro* from donated gametes. The applicant's complaint was therefore, more precisely, that the consent provisions of the national Act prevented her from using the embryos she and her former partner had created together, and thus, given her particular circumstances, from ever having a child to whom she was genetically related. The Grand Chamber, however, also considered that this more limited issue, concerning the right to respect for the decision to become a parent in the genetic sense, also fell within the scope of Article 8.[42] The dilemma central to the *Evans* case was that it involved a conflict between the Article 8 rights of two private individuals: the applicant and her former partner. Moreover, each person's interest was entirely irreconcilable with the other's, since if the applicant was permitted to use the embryos, her former partner would be forced to become a father, whereas if his refusal or withdrawal of consent was upheld, the applicant would be denied the opportunity of becoming a genetic parent. The Grand Chamber, like the Chamber, accepted the Government's submission[43] that the case did not involve simply a conflict between individuals; the legislation in question also served a number of wider, public interests, in upholding the principle of the primacy of consent and promoting legal clarity and certainty. Given that there was no international or European consensus with regard to the regulation of IVF treatment, the use of embryos created by such treatment, or the point at which consent to the use of genetic material provided as part of IVF treatment might be withdrawn, and since the use of IVF treatment gave rise to sensitive moral and

41 Paras. 58–59 and 71.
42 Para. 72–74.
43 Para. 68.

ethical issues against a background of fast-moving medical and scientific developments, the margin of appreciation to be afforded to the respondent state had, therefore, in the view of the Court, to be a wide one.

In the subsequent case of *S.H. and others v. Austria*[44] (which will be discussed in more detail *infra*), the Court also considered the right of a couple to conceive a child and to make use of medically assisted procreation for that end to fall within the ambit of Article 8, as such a choice was clearly an expression of private and family life.[45]

In conclusion, the right to conceive a genetically related child and the use of fertility treatment to obtain that goal is considered to be a part of the scope of Article 8 of the ECHR. However, as the case law *supra* has demonstrated, this right is not of an absolute nature, and state interference may be legitimate. This is due to the fact that medically assisted reproduction is still considered an ethically sensitive practice, and that the interests of the other parent may play a role.

4.1.2. Access to treatment?

The denial of access to treatment would, as argued *supra*, in many cases qualify as an infringement of the individual's right to respect for private life and family life. Likewise, denial of access to treatment, e.g., on the grounds of sexuality, appears to be discrimination contrary to Article 14. However, the right to reproduce is not absolute, and so the individual's right must be balanced against any conflicting interests.[46] Access to fertility treatment services can be restricted on many grounds, and states do, in principle, have a wide margin of appreciation in regulating access to fertility treatment. The individual (human) right to access fertility treatment, the legitimate restrictions which a state may enforce, and the scope of the margin of appreciation afforded to the state in this matter have been addressed in two cases:

In *Dickson v. the United Kingdom*,[47] which concerned the refusal of facilities for artificial insemination to the applicants, a prisoner and his wife, who, given the first applicant's earliest release date and the second applicant's age, needed artificial insemination facilities in order to be able to have a child together, the Court found that Article 8 was applicable in that the artificial insemination facilities at issue concerned their private and family lives -notions which

44 ECtHR application no. 57813/00, judgment 1 April 2010.
45 Para. 60.
46 See, also, Elizabeth Wicks, *Human Rights and Healthcare*, Oxford: Hart Publishing, 2007, p. 165.
47 ECtHR application no. 44362/04, judgment of 4 December 2007.

incorporate the right to respect for their decision to become genetic parents. The government relied on three justifications for the policy to limit access to artificial insemination facilities: First of all, that losing the opportunity to beget children was an inevitable and necessary consequence of imprisonment. The Court's response was that whilst the inability to beget a child might be a consequence of imprisonment, it is not an inevitable one, it not being suggested that the grant of artificial insemination facilities would involve any security issues or impose any significant administrative or financial demands on the state.[48] Secondly, the government argued that public confidence in the prison system would be undermined if the punitive and deterrent elements of a sentence were circumvented by allowing prisoners guilty of certain serious offences to conceive children. The Court noted that there was 'no place under the Convention system, where tolerance and broadmindedness are the acknowledged hallmarks of democratic society, for automatic forfeiture of rights by prisoners based purely on what might offend public opinion.' However, the Court accepted that the maintaining of public confidence in the penal system had a role to play in the development of penal policy. However, the Court underlined that the evolution in European penal policy was increasingly moving towards emphasising the rehabilitative aim of imprisonment, particularly towards the end of a long prison sentence. Thirdly, the government asserted that the absence of a parent for a long period would have a negative impact on any child conceived and, consequently, on society as a whole. The Court accepted this policy view as legitimate, for the purposes of the second paragraph of Article 8, that the authorities, when developing and applying a policy, should concern themselves, as a matter of principle, with the welfare of any child. Moreover, the state had a positive obligation to ensure the effective protection of children. However, that could not go so far as to prevent parents who so wished from attempting to conceive a child, especially as the second applicant was at liberty, and could have taken care of any child conceived until such time as her husband was released.[49] In conclusion, the Court found that the policy, as structured, effectively excluded any real weighing of the competing individual and public interests, and prevented the required assessment of the proportionality of a restriction, in any individual case. Further, since the policy was not embodied in primary legislation, the various competing interests had never been weighed up, nor had the issues of proportionality ever been assessed by the British Parliament. Thus, the Court found that the absence of such an assessment fell outside any acceptable margin of appreciation, so that a fair balance was not struck between the competing public and private interests involved. There had, accordingly, been a violation of Article 8 of the Convention.

---

48 Para. 74.

49 Para. 76.

In *S.H. and others v. Austria*, the applicants were two married couples, of which one couple needed donated sperm, as well as medical help, with regard to fertilising the woman's eggs, as her fallopian tubes were blocked, and the other couple needed donated eggs. Both claimed to be in an analogous position to other couples who wished to avail themselves of medically assisted procreation techniques but who, because they suffered from different medical conditions than the applicants, did not need *donated gametes* for *in vitro* fertilisation. The applicants therefore were subject to a difference in treatment because as a consequence of the prohibition of heterologous artificial procreation techniques for *in vitro* fertilisation laid down by the applicable Austrian law, they were unable to access treatment and to procreate. The Court first of all noted that it had to consider the aim behind that difference in treatment and, if the aim was legitimate, to consider whether the different treatment was justified.[50] For the purposes of Article 14, a difference in treatment is discriminatory if it has no objective and reasonable justification, which means that it does not pursue a 'legitimate aim' or that there is no 'reasonable proportionality between the means employed and the aim sought to be realised'. Reiterating that the ECHR is a living instrument to be interpreted in light of present-day conditions and that the Contracting States enjoy a margin of appreciation in assessing whether, and to what extent, differences in otherwise similar situations justify a different treatment, the Court noted that in the field of medically assisted procreation there was no uniform approach to this question among the States Parties. Medically assisted procreation is regulated in detail in some countries, to a certain extent in others, and in some countries, not at all. Since the use of IVF treatment gives rise to sensitive moral and ethical issues against a background of fast-moving medical and scientific developments, and since the questions raised by the case touched on areas where there is no clear common ground amongst the Member States, the Court argued that the margin of appreciation to be afforded to the respondent state had to be wide.[51] The state's wide margin in principle extends both to its decision to intervene in the area, and, once having intervened, to the detailed rules it lays down in order to achieve a balance between the competing public and private interests. However, the differences in the approaches adopted by the Contracting States do not, as such, make any solution reached by a legislature acceptable. It is still for the Court to carefully examine the arguments discussed in the legislative process and to assess whether the arguments advanced by the government for justifying the difference in treatment at issue are relevant and sufficient. The Court started with the second couple, who, owing to the woman's medical condition, would only have their wish for a child, of which at least one of the applicants was the genetic parent, fulfilled if they were allowed to use *in vitro* fertilisation with the use of ova from

50 Para. 63.
51 Para. 69.

a donor. First of all, the Court stated that it had established in its case law that in order for an issue to arise under Article 14, there must be a difference in the treatment of persons in relatively similar situations. Such a difference in treatment is discriminatory if it has no objective and no reasonable justification; in other words, if it does not pursue a legitimate aim or if there is not a reasonable relationship of proportionality between the means employed and the aim sought to be realised. The Contracting State enjoys a margin of appreciation in assessing whether, and to what extent, differences in otherwise similar situations justify a different treatment. Thus, the Court had to examine whether the difference in treatment between the couple in question, and a couple which, to fulfil their wish for a child, may make use of artificial procreation techniques without resorting to ova donation, had an objective and reasonable justification, i.e. pursued a legitimate aim, or if there was a reasonable relationship of proportionality between the means employed and the aim sought to be realised.[52] The Court considered that:

> *'concerns based on moral considerations or on social acceptability are not in themselves sufficient reasons for a complete ban on a specific artificial procreation technique such as ova donation. Such reasons may be particularly weighty at the stage of deciding whether or not to allow artificial procreation in general, and the Court would emphasise that there is no obligation on a State to enact legislation of the kind and to allow artificial procreation. However, once the decision has been taken to allow artificial procreation and notwithstanding the wide margin of appreciation afforded to the Contracting States, the legal framework devised for this purpose must be shaped in a coherent manner which allows the different legitimate interests involved to be taken into account adequately and in accordance with the obligations deriving from the Convention ... The Court considers that the risks associated with new techniques in a sensitive field like medically assisted procreation must be taken seriously and that it is in the first place for the domestic legislator to assess these risks after carefully weighing the different public and private interests involved and the dangers which might be faced. However, a complete ban on the medical technique at issue would not be proportionate unless, after careful reflection, it was deemed to be the only means of effectively preventing serious repercussions. In the present case the Court is not persuaded that a complete ban was the only means at the disposal of the Austrian legislature. Given that the Artificial Procreation Act reserves this kind of intervention to specialised medical doctors, who have particular knowledge and experience in this field and are themselves bound by the ethical rules of their profession, and that the Act provides for further safeguards in order to minimise the risk, the Court finds that the prohibition of ova and sperm donation for in vitro fertilisation cannot be considered the only or the least intrusive means of achieving the aim pursued.'*[53]

52 Para. 72.

53 Paras. 74 and 76.

Based on a detailed and comprehensive analysis, the Court concluded that the Austrian government had not submitted a reasonable and objective justification for the difference in treatment between the couple in question, who were prevented by the prohibition of ova donation for artificial procreation under the Artificial Procreation Act from fulfilling their wish for a child, and a couple which may make use of artificial procreation techniques without resorting to ova donation. Accordingly, there had been a violation of Article 14 of the Convention, taken in conjunction with Article 8, as regards this couple.

As for the first couple, they could only fulfil their wish for a child, of which at least one of the applicants was the genetic parent, with the use of sperm from a donor and *in vitro* fertilisation. Therefore, the Court had to examine whether the difference in treatment between this couple who, to fulfil their wish for a child, could only resort to sperm donation for *in vitro* fertilisation, and a couple which lawfully may make use of sperm donation for *in vivo* fertilisation, had an objective and reasonable justification, i.e. pursued a legitimate aim, or if there was a reasonable relationship of proportionality between the means employed and the aim sought to be realised. The Court observed at the outset that:

> *'this artificial procreation technique combines two techniques which taken alone are allowed under the Artificial Procreation Act, namely in vitro fertilisation with the gametes of the couple on the one and sperm donation on the other hand. Thus, a prohibition of the combination of these lawful techniques requires, in the Court's view, particularly persuasive arguments by the Government. In justifying the prohibition of sperm donation the Government has submitted a further argument. The reasons given for justifying this difference in treatment between in vitro fertilisation and artificial insemination were that the latter technique had already been in use for a considerable time when the Artificial Procreation Act entered into force and, because it was easy to handle and did not necessarily require the assistance of a trained medical surgeon, compliance with a prohibition would have been impossible to monitor. It must be remembered that the Convention is designed to "guarantee not rights that are theoretical or illusory but rights that are practical and effective". The Court must therefore take into account the effectiveness of a given instance of interference when assessing whether there exists a reasonable relationship of proportionality between the means employed and the aim sought to be realised. Thus, the Court finds that it is legitimate to take also into account whether the interference envisaged by the State would be an effective means of pursuing a legitimate goal. Even if one were to accept this argument submitted by the Government as a question of mere efficiency it must be balanced against the interests of private individuals involved. In this respect the Court reiterates that where a particularly important facet of an individual's existence or identity is at stake, the margin allowed to the State will be restricted. In the Court's view the wish for a child is one such particularly important facet and, in the circumstances of the case, outweighs arguments of efficiency. Thus, the prohibition at issue lacked a reasonable relationship of proportionality between the means employed and the aim sought to be realised.'*

The Court therefore found that the difference in treatment between the couple who, to fulfil their wish for a child, could only resort to sperm donation for *in vitro* fertilisation, and a couple which lawfully may make use of sperm donation for in *vivo* fertilisation, had no objective and reasonable justification, and was disproportionate. Accordingly, there had been a violation of Article 14 of the Convention, taken in conjunction with Article 8, regarding this couple.[54]

In conclusion, fertility treatment techniques do, as a general rule, fall within the sensitive area of regulation in which states are given a wide margin of appreciation. However, the case law demonstrates that when this margin is used to restrict access to fertility treatment, and when the issue at hand is an important facet of our existence, such restrictions are subject to close scrutiny by the Court, especially in testing the restrictions in a discrimination perspective.

4.2. EMBRYO AND FOETUS SELECTION

Fertility technologies today also include techniques that allow parents to select particular embryos. Most commonly, parents use embryo selection because they want a healthy child. Diagnosing the embryos *in vitro* and selecting one that is healthy is seen by many as more preferable than letting the woman become pregnant and risking having to terminate the pregnancy following foetal diagnostics, such as the double or triple test, or an ultrasound scan during weeks 12 to 20 of a pregnancy. Sometimes the selection is based on sex, as hundreds of diseases are only carried on by men, and as such, selection on the basis of sex may be more efficient than testing each embryo for a particular disease present in the families of the couple.

Whether the potential right to reproduce also includes the right to have a healthy child is untested in human rights case law. However, it is clear from a human rights perspective that the pertinent issues to be addressed as a consequence of this technology have focused primarily on the selection practice and what this practice entails for our understanding of human dignity, equal worth and equality, and less so on the reproductive rights aspect. While the Oviedo Convention, perhaps surprisingly, does not provide any specific individual rights in relation to the medically assisted reproductive area, it does declare in Article 14 that medically assisted procreation techniques should not be used for the purpose of sex selection.[55] As such, the Convention mirrors the perspective that has dominated the human rights discourse regarding PGD.

---

54 Paras. 86–94.

55 See, for a more in-depth discussion, Brigit Toebes, 'Sex Selection under International Human Rights Law' in *Medical Law International* 2008, vol. 9, pp. 197–225.

However, in most cases where a couple is denied the use of PGD, it does not affect their right to reproduce *as such*. They may not get the child with the traits they wanted, but the option to have a child is still available to them.[56]

Another issue arises in relation to the selection of foetuses. The use of both non-invasive foetal diagnostic methods, such as the ultrasound scan, and invasive methods, such as amniocentesis, can reveal malformations and illnesses in the foetus prior to birth. The information generated by these examinations may (subject to the legality of abortion) assist the woman in making informed choices as to the continuation or termination of her pregnancy. *In R.R. v. Poland*,[57] the applicant, who was 18 weeks pregnant, had an ultrasound scan, following which her family doctor told her that he could not rule out the possibility that the foetus was malformed. She told him she wished to have an abortion if his suspicion proved true. She was married with two children at the time. Two further scans confirmed that her foetus was probably malformed, and it was recommended that she have an amniocentesis. The applicant then saw a specialist in clinical genetics who recommended that she ask for a formal referral from her family doctor to have the amniocentesis carried out in a public hospital, a request which her doctor refused.

She then travelled 150 kilometres to a university hospital in Kraków, to which she had been referred by her local hospital. The doctor she consulted criticised her for considering an abortion, and refused to authorise genetic tests. She was also informed that the hospital refused to carry out abortions, and that no abortions had been performed there for the last 150 years. She stayed in the hospital for three days and had another scan, with inconclusive results. She maintained that medical staff made degrading remarks about her and kept her in the hospital without explanation, only to conduct tests unrelated to her concerns. Her discharge record and medical certificate stated that the foetus had developmental abnormalities. A further scan confirmed that the foetus was malformed. She then had an amniocentesis in the 23rd week of pregnancy, reporting to the hospital as an emergency patient, without a valid doctor's referral (which she had tried and failed to obtain). She was told that she had to wait two weeks for the results. She then submitted a written request to her local hospital for an abortion under the Polish Family Planning Act, which stipulates that an abortion on the grounds of foetal abnormality can only be performed before the foetus is considered capable of independent life, normally thought to be in the 24th week of pregnancy. Within a week she returned to the hospital and

56 Elizabeth Wicks, *Human Rights and Healthcare*, Oxford: Hart Publishing, 2007, pp. 176–177.

57 ECtHR application no. 27617/04, judgment of 26 May, 2011. The references to the facts of the case are taken from the press release issued by the registrar (ECHR 020 2011) dated 26.05.2011, as the written judgment was not yet available at the time of writing this chapter.

was told that the consultant could not see her because he was ill. Two weeks after the amniocentesis had been carried out, she received the results of the genetic tests, which confirmed that her child had Turner Syndrome. She renewed her request for an abortion the same day. The doctors in the hospital refused the request because the legal time limit for abortion had passed. She eventually gave birth to a girl with Turner Syndrome. The applicant's husband left her after the baby was born.

The Court observed that the scan carried out in the 18th week of the applicant's pregnancy confirmed the likelihood that the foetus was affected with an unidentified malformation. Following that scan the applicant feared that the foetus was affected with a genetic disorder and, in the light of the results of subsequent scans, her fears could not be said to have been without foundation. She tried repeatedly (and failed) to obtain access to genetic tests which would have provided her with information confirming or dispelling her fears. For weeks she was made to believe that she would undergo the necessary tests. She was repeatedly sent to various doctors, clinics and hospitals far from her home, and was even hospitalised for several days for no clear clinical purpose. The Court found that 'the determination of whether the applicant should have had access to genetic tests, as recommended by doctors, was marred by procrastination, confusion and lack of proper counselling and information.'

Ultimately, she only obtained admission to the local hospital by means of subterfuge, where she finally had the tests conducted in the 23rd week of her pregnancy. It was not in dispute that it was possible only by means of genetic tests to establish whether the initial diagnosis was correct, and it had not been argued, let alone shown, that at the relevant time genetic tests were unavailable due to a lack of equipment, medical expertise or funding. Under the national Act, the state was obliged to ensure unimpeded access to prenatal information and testing, particularly where there was a possible genetic disorder or development problem. There were various unequivocal legal provisions in force at the relevant time that specified the state's obligations to pregnant women regarding their access to information about their health and that of the foetus. However, there was no indication that the legal obligations of the state and of the medical staff regarding the applicant's rights as a patient were taken into consideration by the people and institutions dealing with the applicant's requests to have access to genetic tests.

The Court noted that she was in a very vulnerable position.

> *'Like any other pregnant woman in her situation, she was deeply distressed about the possibility that her foetus could be malformed and it was therefore natural that she wanted to obtain as much information as possible in order to decide what to do. As a*

> *result of the procrastination of medical professionals, she had had to endure weeks of painful uncertainty concerning the health of the foetus, her own and her family's future and the prospect of raising a child suffering from an incurable illness. She suffered acute anguish through having to think about how she and her family would be able to ensure the child's welfare, happiness and appropriate long-term medical care. Her concerns were not properly acknowledged and addressed by the health professionals dealing with her case. Six weeks elapsed between the first relevant ultrasound scan and the results of the amniocentisis, too late for her to make an informed decision on whether to continue the pregnancy or to ask for a legal abortion, as the legal time limit had by then expired. Her suffering, both before the results of the tests became known and after that date, could be said to have been aggravated by the fact that she was legally entitled to the diagnostic services requested and that those services were at all times available.'*

It was, noted the Court, 'a matter of great regret that she was so shabbily treated by the doctors dealing with her case.' The Court consequently found that the applicant had been humiliated, and that this constituted a violation of Article 3 of the ECHR.

In relation to Article 8, the Court noted that while states had a broad margin of appreciation regarding the circumstances in which an abortion would be permitted, once that decision had been taken, there had to be a coherent legal framework in place to allow the different legitimate interests involved to be adequately taken into account in accordance with the Convention. The Court reiterated that the prohibition of the termination of pregnancies sought for reasons of health and/or well-being amounted to an interference with the applicant's right to respect for her private life. A pregnant woman should at least have a chance to be heard in person, and to have her views considered. The competent body or person should also issue written grounds for its decision. The Court noted that the national Act specified situations in which abortion was allowed. A doctor who terminated a pregnancy in breach of the conditions specified in that Act was guilty of a criminal offence, punishable by up to three years' imprisonment. The Court reiterated that the legal restrictions to abortion in Poland, taken together with the risk of their incurring criminal responsibility under the Criminal Code, could well have a 'chilling effect' on doctors when deciding whether the requirements of legal abortion had been met in an individual case. The Court considered that provisions regulating the availability of lawful abortion should be formulated in such a way as to alleviate that 'chilling effect'.

In the applicant's case, what was at stake was essentially timely access to a medical diagnostic service that would, in turn, make it possible to determine whether or not the conditions for lawful abortion had been met. In the context of pregnancy, the effective access to relevant information on the health of the mother and the foetus, where legislation allowed for abortion in certain situations, was directly relevant to the exercise of personal autonomy. The difficulties the applicant experienced seemed to have been caused, in part, by reluctance on the part of certain doctors involved to issue a referral, and also by a certain organisational and administrative confusion in Poland's health system. The Court stressed that as Polish domestic law allowed for abortion in cases of foetal malformation, there had to be an adequate legal and procedural framework to guarantee that relevant, full and reliable information on the foetus' health be made available to pregnant women. In the present case, however, there had been a six-week wait between the first relevant scan and the receipt of the amniocentesis results. It was important to note, too, that the Polish Supreme Court had criticised the conduct of the medical professionals who had been involved in her case, and the procrastination shown in deciding whether to give her a referral for genetic tests. As a result, she was unable to obtain a diagnosis of the foetus' condition, established with the requisite certainty, by genetic tests within the time-limit, for abortion to remain a lawful option for her. The Court did not agree with the Polish government that providing access to antenatal genetic tests was, in effect, providing access to abortion. Women sought access to such tests for many reasons. In addition, states were obliged 'to organise their health services to ensure that an effective exercise of the freedom of conscience of health professionals in a professional context did not prevent patients from obtaining access to services to which they were legally entitled.' The Court argued that it had not been demonstrated that Polish law contained any effective mechanisms which would have enabled the applicant to have access to the available diagnostic services and to take, in the light of their results, an informed decision as to whether or not to seek an abortion. The Court reiterated that effective implementation of the relevant part of the national Act would necessitate ensuring that pregnant women had access to diagnostic services which would show whether or not the foetus was damaged – services which were available. The Court also noted that legislation in many other European countries specified the conditions governing effective access to a lawful abortion, and established procedures to implement those laws. The Court concluded that the Polish authorities had failed to comply with their obligations to ensure the effective respect of the woman's private life, and that there had therefore been a violation of Article 8.

The case is in line with the Court's previous findings in *Tysiac v. Poland.* It is, however, an important landmark in the Court's case law that the denial of access to genetic testing and the degrading treatment to which she was subjected by the medical staff was also considered a violation of Article 3 of the Convention. These two Polish judgments also marked another watershed for the Court, which previously respected the margin of appreciation of more liberal Western European countries, in that it is now willing to limit the margin of appreciation of a more conservative state. As such, the way is slowly being paved for embracing modern day reproductive issues with the same dynamic and evolutive spirit that is characteristic of much of the Court's case law in other areas of life and law.

5. PREGNANCY, HEALTH AND AUTONOMY

5.1. MATERNAL AND FOETAL HEALTH

The relationship between the pregnant woman's lifestyle choices and the effects they have on foetal health and development is an area of rapidly growing medical knowledge. The fact that the woman's use of alcohol, tobacco, medicinal drugs and illicit drugs affects the foetus has been known to science for a long time, and is reflected in the offers and information given to pregnant women in many countries.[58]

Any foetal right to health is closely connected to any right women may have to a healthy pregnancy.[59] The Universal Declaration of Human Rights affirms, in Article 25, that '*Everyone has the right to a standard of living adequate for the health and well-being of* ***himself and of his family****, including food, clothing, housing and medical care and necessary social services, and the right to security in the event of unemployment, sickness, disability, widowhood, old age or other lack of livelihood in circumstances beyond his control ...* ***Motherhood*** *and childhood are entitled to special care and assistance ...*' The CEDAW Convention stipulates, in Article 12.2, that: '*States Parties shall ensure to women appropriate services in connection with pregnancy, confinement and the post-natal period, granting free services where necessary, as well as adequate nutrition during pregnancy and lactation.*' As such, the health of pregnant women is assigned special legal emphasis, and one might also argue that the foetus has a right to health derived from her rights. The fact that it is, however, first and foremost the pregnant woman who is the protected individual is reflected in Article 16.1 (e), the purpose of which is to give the woman reproductive autonomy and allow her to make reproductive choices without being subjected to discrimination.[60] As such, the protection of foetal health is secondary and relies on the woman's lifestyle choices and willingness to seek medical antenatal care. On the other hand, the foetus is also given a legal protection against health discrimination through the

58 Use of the said substances are a public health concern, and consequently, the WHO has also developed a tool to aid in the detection and treatment of such patients, see www.who.int/substance_abuse/activities/en/Draft_The_ASSIST_Guidelines.pdf (retrieved 24 May 2011).

59 See, also, Rebecca J. Cook, Bernard M. Dickens & Mahmoud F. Fathalla: *Reproductive Health and Human Rights*, Oxford, 2003, pp. 158–165.

60 The special duty to tend to the health and well-being of pregnant women seems, in General Recommendation 24/1999, to be based on the fact that pregnancy and childbirth is a unique feature of womanhood, and as such, raises particular concern in relation to discrimination (see paras. 1, 2. 6, 12a and 27 of the General Recommendation).

protection of the woman. As a result, the foetus is entitled to receive medical care through its relationship to the woman.

Article 12 of the CESCR acknowledges '*the right of everyone to the enjoyment of the highest attainable standard of physical and mental health.*' To fully realise this goal the state is also obliged to take steps for '*the reduction of the stillbirth-rate and of infant mortality and for the healthy development of the child*' (cf. Article 12.2 (a)). One could argue that pregnant women, as a result of this provision, are also entitled to access healthcare services specifically intended for the foetus.[61]

Adequate care and treatment relating to pregnancy and childbirth thus form part of the woman's fundamental human rights.

5.2. FORCED TREATMENT OF PREGNANT WOMEN

As outlined above, there is a correlation between the woman's lifestyle choices and foetal health, due to the fact that alcohol, medicinal products and illicit drugs all pass into the foetus' blood stream though the placenta. As such, there is a potential conflict of interests between the pregnant woman's autonomy and any right to health that the foetus might have.

In response to this conflict, some countries, e.g. Norway,[62] have chosen to make legal provisions for the forceful detention of pregnant women until birth. An assessment of such interventions into the woman's basic liberty rights in an international human rights law perspective must, in my view, first and foremost be made on the basis of the CEDAW Convention, which is the only international human rights law document addressing reproduction and women's rights in this area.

In its General Recommendation 19,[63] the CEDAW Committee underlines that coercive abortion poses a threat to women's physical and mental health. Whereas the term '*compulsory* abortion' is used in para. 22, para. 24 (m) talks of preventing '*coercion* in regard to fertility and reproduction.' Thus, the scope of its notion of coercion seems to be quite broad, both regarding the applicable reproductive area and the nature of the coercion, thus implying that coerced continuation of a pregnancy would also be within its scope. A pregnant substance abuser has, in my view, a different threshold in relation to what might

61 See, also, CESCR General Comment 14 UN doc. E7C.12/2000/4, paras. 18–19.
62 See, e.g., Karl Harald Søvig: Deprivation of liberty of pregnant women to protect the foetus, abstract from Nordic Welfare's conference available at www.nordicwelfare.org/filearchive/1/117902/ Sovig_Karl_Harald_abstract.pdf (retrieved 17 August 2011) and Karl Harald Søvig, 'Detention of pregnant women to protect the foetus', in E. Rynning and M. Hartlev (eds.), *Nordic Health Law in a European Context* (Liber/Brill, 2011) pp. 158–180.
63 Paras. 22 and 24(m).

be considered coercion, compared to other pregnant women. To be detained against one's wishes is a severe infringement of the personal right to liberty by any standards, although this is, in fact, acknowledged as a legitimate measure under the ECHR in relation to abuse, psychiatric care, *etc.* However, the detention of a *pregnant* woman, enforced with a view to safeguarding the foetus, might also have the effect of controlling her reproductive choices in a non-voluntary way. As such, the issue is not solely one of deprivation of liberty. Women's reproductive freedom is linked to both a health perspective and a non-discrimination perspective. Pregnant substance abusers are different from other pregnant women in that they may experience the detention as a coercive measure in relation to abortion, as a termination would also ensure the woman her freedom. As a result, although the detention is meant to improve the women's health, the unintended side effect can be a diminished respect for their reproductive autonomy, even though this group of women is a vulnerable group in need of special legal care in relation to securing their rights, and as such, are afforded special rights and legal emphasis in both the CEDAW Convention and the Convention on the Rights of the Child. As such, one might argue that coercive measures taken against pregnant women are legally problematic and incompatible with the reasoning and spirit of the CEDAW Convention.

6. CONCLUDING REMARKS

Reproduction is a function which gives rise to special healthcare needs. In this chapter it has been demonstrated how various human rights together form a coherent platform for acknowledging and effectively protecting this specific area of human health. These rights include the right to respect for private life and family life, the right to reproductive autonomy, as well as the right not to be discriminated against on the basis of gender and reproductive capabilities, and the right to have reproductive healthcare needs met.

The area of reproduction is a sensitive one, since it touches on matters such as the beginning of life. This sensitivity is not going to diminish, as progress in medical science and technology will probably continue to raise moral and ethical concerns. For this reason, the area of reproduction is constantly evolving, including in legal terms. Reproduction and the scope and extent of individual reproductive rights will likely continue to give rise to legal litigation in an international and regional human rights law setting. Human rights are especially well equipped to address these developments if they are applied as 'living instruments' in light of 'present-day conditions' in line with the interpretative frame applied by the ECtHR. On the other hand, reproductive rights have not been subjected to the same evolutive interpretation as many other subject matters by the ECtHR because of the lack of international or European consensus, and because of the inherent moral sensitivity.

CHAPTER 6

EUTHANASIA AND PHYSICIAN-ASSISTED SUICIDE FROM A HUMAN RIGHTS PERSPECTIVE

Jozef Dorscheidt

1. INTRODUCTION

One of the most controversial issues in healthcare is the admissibility of end-of-life decisions. This issue is known to generate large differences of opinion, often originating from several social, cultural, psychological, emotional or religious backgrounds. These different visions on this issue also affect the legal point of view. Although the law in a democratic society generally reflects the attitude of the majority towards social issues, it is sometimes difficult to grasp where society stands. The large variety in lines of moral argumentation in healthcare matters often refers to insecurity with regard to an adequate legal approach. To find such an approach in relation to the ending of life in medical care is a challenge.

The human rights perspective on this matter has its particular significance, as it usually marks a starting point for reflection on the legal permissibility of life-ending performances in medical care. This perspective is also guiding for further considerations regarding the same issue at the level of national law. Although the relevance of certain human rights to the legitimacy of these end-of-life decisions is hardly disputed, the validity of their interpretation is often subject of debate. To answer the fundamental questions in this debate in view of corresponding treaty provisions or decisions by authoritative courts is a noble cause. At the same time, this is problematic. Here, the lack of an ultimate, unambiguous authoritative source of interpretation is particularly tangible.

This chapter explores some of the issues raised by a human rights approach to end-of-life decisions in medical care. To that purpose, matters concerning death at request of a competent person are particularly highlighted. First, some terminological matters will be explained. Then, a review of related human rights is presented. After an overview of basic human rights aspects of current euthanasia legislation in the Netherlands and Belgium, and assisted suicide law in Switzerland, relevant jurisprudence of the European Court of Human Rights (ECtHR) will be discussed. With reference to the ECtHR's ruling in the case of *Pretty v. The United Kingdom*, a reflection on a human right to die will precede the closing remarks.

2. TERMINOLOGY

Before we turn to the human rights aspects of particular end-of-life actions in medicine, it is necessary to address some matters of terminology.

The phrase 'end-of-life decisions in medicine' is a collective noun for decisions in medical care that lead to the death of a patient. Differentiation and specification of the various decisions and acts, however, is important in view of their different legal connotations. Some acts in the context of end-of-life in healthcare are known by a specific phrase: euthanasia, physician-assisted suicide (PAS), withdrawal or withholding of treatment (non-treatment), or refusal of treatment. Administering pain relief or sedative medication in doses likely to shorten a patient's life has meaning in this regard as well. A special legal category is the deliberate ending of an incompetent patients' life. No matter how interesting the human rights issues concerning the latter category are, dealing with them in detail goes beyond the scope of this chapter. These issues deserve to be discussed separately.[1] The focus in this chapter is therefore on euthanasia and PAS.

The wording 'euthanasia' is often interpreted in an ambiguous fashion. In some countries the word covers a whole range of end-of-life matters, in others it is reserved for a particular constellation, and is consequently used in a narrow sense.

'Euthanasia' is often referred to as a situation in which a physician deliberately ends the life of a severely suffering patient.[2] This definition, however, is not entirely adequate, as it leaves out important nuances such as how death is realised, or whether this occurs in accordance with the wishes of the person

1 A general overview of some of these issues is provided in J. Griffiths, H. Weyers, M. Adams: *Euthanasia and the Law in Europe*, Oxford & Portland: Hart Publishing, 2008. With regard to neonates, see J.H.H.M. Dorscheidt: Assessment procedures regarding end-of-life decisions in neonatology in the Netherlands, 24 *Medicine and Law* (2005); 803–829; A.A.E. Verhagen, J.H.H.M. Dorscheidt, B. Engels, et al.: End-of-life decisions in severely ill newborns in the Dutch NICU, 163 *Archives of Pediatrics & Adolescent Medicine* (2009) 10; 895–901; J.H.H.M Dorscheidt, A.A.E. Verhagen, P.J.J. Sauer *et al.*: Parental involvement in end-of-life decisions in neonatology: legal considerations with regard to Dutch medical practice, 11 *Medical Law International* (2011) 1; 1–22.

2 See J. Griffiths, H. Weyers, M. Adams, *op. cit.*, pp. 2–3. See, also, D. Giesen: Dilemmas at life's end: a comparative legal perspective, in J. Keown (ed.): *Euthanasia Examined. Ethical, Clinical and Legal Perspectives*, Cambridge University Press, 1995, pp. 202–205.

concerned. For purposes of proper legal review, a strict definition is necessary. In a majority of countries 'euthanasia' is therefore defined as the deliberate ending of a person's life at his explicit request, by a third person – usually a physician. This purposeful life-ending act involves the administering of a (cocktail of) lethal drug(s), through an injection or infusion, as a result of which a competent person, who has asked to die, passes away in a course of minutes. Euthanasia differs from PAS, as the latter involves a less active part of the physician. Here, the physician merely provides appropriate medication, while the patient himself 'commits' the life-ending act by 'consuming' the thanatic drug(s). Whereas the penalization of euthanasia is connected to the executioner of the life-ending act, the legal inadmissibility of PAS is related to the supply of the medication to be used, or to otherwise helping or directing a person to fulfil his wish to die.

Euthanasia is often subdivided into various subdivisions: active *vs.* passive euthanasia, direct *vs.* indirect euthanasia, or even voluntary *vs.* involuntary euthanasia.[3] The usefulness of these distinctions, however, can be disputed. In the Netherlands, such subdivisions were abandoned in 1985, as they were considered to add little to the clarification of the concept. In fact, they were believed to obscure proper understanding of the normative aspects of life-ending behaviour, especially when it comes to matters of legal review. Some distinctions imply a type of euthanasia which is actually no differentiation of the original course of action, but is quite another concept of behaviour. The prefix 'active' in 'active euthanasia', for instance, is redundant, as euthanasia in the above-mentioned meaning presupposes an act by commission. Passive euthanasia is often referred to as 'death by requested omission'. However, a patient who rejects life-saving medical treatment and consequently departs this life does not die because of a life-ending act, but merely as a result of practicing his right to refuse treatment. This situation has no legal consequences for the attending physician, provided that the patient has reached his decision *compos mentis* and in full awareness of the consequences. Furthermore, the distinction between direct and indirect euthanasia seems to have lost its significance too, as the latter type refers to the situation where the involved person's death is realised as an unintended side effect of pain relief medication primarily administered to ease suffering. Direct euthanasia coincides with a life-ending conduct which instantly causes a requested death. This conduct, however, is not entirely similar to the course of action regarded as euthanasia, as this can also involve the instant removal of life-prolonging mechanical respiration. Lastly, since euthanasia encompasses the involved person's explicit, voluntary, and lasting, wish to die, the phrase 'voluntary euthanasia' is a pleonasm. Likewise, the wording 'involuntary euthanasia' contains a contradiction in terms, as the idea of a patient's

[3] See M. Groenhuijsen: Euthanasia and the criminal justice system. General report on the state of the arts in 14 jurisdictions, in M. Groenhuijsen, F. van Laanen (eds.), *Euthanasia in International and Comparative Perspective*, Nijmegen: Wolf Legal Publishers, 2006, pp. 3–26.

compulsory death is quite odd and seems valid only in relation to a court ordered death sentence.

To deliberately end the life of a person who did not explicitly request to die does not count as euthanasia, and is consequently not punishable as euthanasia. Such a life-ending act rather constitutes homicide or murder. Besides, such an act is sometimes denominated by a typical wording. The deliberate ending of a new-born child's life by a physician, for instance, is currently referred to as medical neonaticide. To indicate such an act as 'neonatal euthanasia' is obviously inadequate, and suggests, at least in my view, the use of careless language.

A legitimate non-treatment decision or abstinence policy is a medical decision based on admissible professional grounds, such as the inability to realise the treatment's goal and/or disproportionality between the ends and means of the treatment. Generally, a patient cannot force his physician to provide medical treatment that is considered medically futile and/or unethical.[4] If the grounds for a non-treatment decision are legally unsound, or even negligent, the physician in charge can be held accountable. In appropriate circumstances, this may lead to disciplinary or even criminal charges being brought against the physician.

Palliative care is referred to as care that improves the quality of life of patients and their families facing the problems associated with life-threatening illness, through the prevention and relief of suffering by the treatment of pain and other problems – physical, psychosocial and spiritual.[5] In this context, care providers sometimes apply palliative sedation (also known as terminal sedation), which primarily aims at lowering a patient's consciousness in the final phase of his life in order to reduce discomfort and awareness of illness related symptoms. Palliative sedation is part of the regular treatment catalogue, which means that it requires the patient's consent. Furthermore, it is a reversible treatment. Palliative sedation used with the intention of hastening a patient's death goes beyond the goals of palliative care, and thus does not comply with the standards of normal medical treatment.

---

4 However, this is not always the case. An English court rejected a medical team's advice to withdraw artificial ventilation from a 18-month-old baby, MB, and agreed with the infant's parents' wish to continue ventilation, which they considered to be in the best interest of their child. See *An NHS Trust v. MB & Anor* (2006) EWHC 507 (Fam). In the American case of Baby K a physician's order to withhold life-saving mechanical ventilation from an anencephalic infant was regarded inadmissible, as it violated the federal statutory prohibition of disability discrimination. See *In re Baby K*, 832 F. Supp. 1022, ED Va 1993; *In re Baby K*, 832 F. Supp. 1022, ED Va 1993 as well as US Supreme Court, 513 US 825 resp. 115 S. Ct. 91; 63 USLW 3258, October 3, 1994.

5 Definition by the World Health Organization (WHO). See: ww.who.int/cancer/palliative/definition/en/.

3. END-OF-LIFE DECISIONS AND HUMAN RIGHTS

To elucidate the significance of human rights law for the legal admissibility of acts ending a patient's life at his request, several fundamental rights must be examined. Crucial rights in this regard are the right to life, the right to be safeguarded from inhuman or degrading treatment, and the right to protection of one's private life. Furthermore, the content and purpose of treaty provisions expressing these rights must be considered. Legal practice even brings forth clues for legal recognition of a (moral) right to die or to respect for human dignity in the final phase of life.

A short overview of applicable treaty provisions and the meaning of the fundamental rights they contain is presented below.

3.1. END-OF-LIFE DECISIONS AND THE RIGHT TO LIFE

During the genesis of the Universal Declaration on Human Rights (UDHR), the drafters sought to confirm the protectability of all human life as a basic rule of law, in response to the atrocities committed by the Nazi regime and others before and during World War II.[6] Ultimately, this resulted in Article 3 UDHR, which states: *'Everyone has the right to life, liberty and security of person.'* The provision expresses three fundamental claims of the human individual: the claim to (the protection of) life, freedom and the inviolability of the human person.[7] Some authors have acknowledged that end-of-life decisions in medical care are covered by Article 3 UDHR.[8]

It was obvious that after the declaratory right to life in Article 3 UDHR a legally binding equivalent would be adopted in the International Covenant on Civil and Political Rights (ICCPR). In consequence, Article 6(1) ICCPR now states: *'Every human being has the inherent right to life. This right shall be protected by law. No one shall be arbitrarily deprived of his life.'* This wording expresses that the right to life is the most essential right in the entire human rights catalogue. This special status is widely denominated and emphasised by many scholars.[9]

---

6 J. Morsink, *The Universal Declaration of Human Rights. Origins, drafting & intent*, Philadelphia: University of Pennsylvania Press, 1999, pp. 39–41.

7 L.A. Rehof, Article 3, in G. Alfredsson, A. Eide (eds.), *The Universal Declaration of Human Rights. A Common Standard of Achievement*, The Hague: Martinus Nijhoff, 1999, pp. 89–101, particularly p. 89.

8 See L.A Rehof: Article 3, in G. Alfredsson, A. Eide (eds.), *op. cit.*, p. 94.

9 M.J. Bossuyt, *Guide to the 'Travaux Préparatoires' of the International Covenant on Civil and Political Rights*, Dordrecht: Kluwer, 1987, p. 115 (A/2929, ch. VI); Y. Dinstein: The right to life, physical integrity, and liberty, in L. Henkin (ed.), *The International Bill of Rights: The Covenant on Civil and Political Rights*, New York: Columbia University Press, 1981, pp. 114–137, here p. 114. See, also, The drafting history of Article 6 of the International Covenant on

The provision's wording does not refer to medical acts that end the life of patients. How such acts relate to Article 6(1) ICCPR is therefore unclear. Dinstein has observed that the protective effect of the right to life counts for everybody, including seriously ill people, neonates with severe abnormalities, senile men and women, people with mental disorders, *etc.* In the case of death at request of the involved person, Dinstein wonders how far such a death wish can legitimise what would otherwise be considered a violation of the right to life. At issue is, in particular, whether or not it is possible to waiver the right to life. Dinstein sees possibilities for legislation on euthanasia only if it provides guarantees for an authentic request to die, as well as the specific way in which the involved person can admissibly abandon his right to life. Actually, ending of life by, or authorised by, the State is a suspicious constellation.[10] Nowak agrees with Dinstein, and adds that a legal limitation of the penalisation of euthanasia, including a reflection on all involved interests and a minimisation of the risk of abuse, could well be within a State's competence to provide legal protection of the right to life according to its own views and beliefs. It may even be assumed that the State has no duty to protect the life and health of its citizens against their explicit will.[11]

According to Zdenkowski, much depends on the particular situation, whether or not life-ending performances are compatible with Article 6(1) ICCPR. Medical ending of life without a request of the involved person he regards as always being in conflict with this provision. After all, the protective effect of the right to life does not expire because someone suffers from certain disorders.[12] Yet, in cases where death results from legitimate and circumstantially appropriate pain relief medication, Zdenkowski believes there is no violation of Article 6(1) ICCPR. The same goes for cases in which the involved (competent) person refuses life-saving treatment. Even in the case of death as a result of the withdrawal of medical treatment (usually artificial nutrition and hydration) from a patient in a Persistent Vegetative State (PVS), a violation of Article 6(1) ICCPR is not likely. In this context, Dinstein refers to human dignity and states: '*... when life becomes an indignity endured without autonomy or awareness, death may be permitted to take its natural course.*'[13]

Civil and Political Rights – Note by the Editor, in B.G. Ramcharan (ed.), *The Right to Life in International Law*, Dordrecht: Martinus Nijhoff Publishers, 1985, p. 43.

10 Y. Dinstein, in L. Henkin (ed.), *op. cit.*, pp. 120–121.

11 M. Nowak, *UN Covenant on Civil and Political Rights. CCPR Commentary*, Kehl: Engel Publisher, 1993, pp. 124–125. See also M. Nowak, *UN Covenant on Civil and Political Rights. CCPR Commentary*, 2nd revised edition, Kehl: Engel Publisher, 2005, pp. 155–156.

12 G. Zdenkowski, 'The International Covenant on Civil and Political Rights and Euthanasia', 20 *University of New South Wales Law Journal* (1997) 1; 170–194.

13 Y. Dinstein, in L. Henkin (ed.), *op. cit.*, p. 121.

From a European perspective, the right to life laid down in Article 2 (1) of the European Convention on Human Rights and fundamental freedoms (ECHR) is of great significance. This provision states: *'Everyone's right to life shall be protected by law. Nobody shall be deprived of his life intentionally save in the execution of a court's sentence following his conviction of a crime for which this penalty is provided by law.'* Obviously, the provision's goal is not to protect human life, as such. Yet, it enjoins the State not only to refrain from the intentional and unlawful taking of life, but also to take all appropriate steps to safeguard the lives of everyone within its jurisdiction. For that, the State must put in place a legislative and administrative framework designed to provide effective deterrence against threats to the right to life. Furthermore, the State must ensure, by all means at its disposal, an adequate response – judicial or otherwise – so that this framework is properly implemented, and that any breaches of the right to life are repressed and punished.[14] A crucial measure in this regard is the statutory prohibition of the intentional deprivation of life. This prohibition applies to the State and to private parties as well.[15] If the State does not meet its obligations under the Convention, it can be held accountable by means of the supervisory mechanism laid down in the ECHR.[16]

Despite its fundamental character, the right to life is not absolute. Article 2(2) ECHR mentions three situations in which the deprivation of life is not regarded as inflicted in contravention with the prohibition mentioned in section 1. Furthermore, Article 15(2) ECHR mentions exceptions to the rule that no derogation from Article 2 shall be made. Moreover, several decisions by the former European Commission of Human Rights (ECmHR) and the ECtHR indicate that certain deliberate deprivations of life are not in conflict with the right to life.[17]

---

14 See the ECtHR's considerations in *Öneryildiz v. Turkey*, ECHR (GC) Judgment of 30 November 2004, Appl. no. 48939/99, par. 89 and 91.

15 Regarding the horizontal effect of Article 2 ECHR, see E.A. Alkema, 'The third-party applicability or 'Drittwirkung' of the European Convention on Human Rights', in F. Matscher, H. Petzold (eds.), *Protection of Human Rights: The European Dimension*, Köln-Berlin, etc.: Carl Heymanns Verlag, 1988, pp. 33–45 especially p. 37; A. Clapham, 'The 'Drittwirkung' of the Convention', in R.St.J. Macdonald, F. Matscher, H. Petzold (eds.), *The European System for the Protection of Human Rights*, Dordrecht-Boston-New York: Martinus Nijhoff Publishers 1993, pp. 163–206, particularly pp. 176–179.

16 P. van Dijk, G.J.H. van Hoof *et al.*, *Theory and Practice of the European Convention on Human Rights*, fourth edition, Antwerpen/Oxford: Intersentia, 2006, pp. 351–367; Jacobs, White & Ovey, *The European Convention on Human Rights*, fifth edition (R.C.A. White, C. Ovey), Oxford/New York: Oxford University Press, 2010, pp. 145–147 and 152–156.

17 For instance, it is the current view of the Strasbourg judges that the unborn child derives no legal protection from Article 2 ECHR. National legislation permitting abortion under specific circumstances, and in accordance with special requirements of due care, is not regarded as being incompatible with this provision. See J.H.H.M. Dorscheidt, 'Developments in Legal and Medical Practice Regarding the Unborn Child and the Need to Expand Prenatal Legal Protection', 17 *European Journal of Health Law* (2010) 5; 433–454.

During the drafting process of Article 2 ECHR, no attention was paid to the possible meaning of the provision in relation to end-of-life decisions in a medical setting.[18] This is no surprise, as the provision was conceived between 1949 and 1950, while the memory of the euthanasia programme in Nazi Germany was still fresh.[19] Besides, some years earlier, Nazi physicians[20] and Nazi lawyers[21] were convicted by Nuremburg War Crimes Tribunals for their part in the execution of this programme.

For many years the Strasbourg jurisprudence offered no specific clues as to this matter. In the last decade, however, cases came to light and confronted the Strasbourg Court with piercing legal questions, also in relation to Article 2.[22]

In *Nitecki v Poland*[23] the ECtHR acknowledged that acts of policy makers in healthcare can, in certain circumstances, be covered by Article 2. In earlier cases concerning alleged medical liability,[24] the ECtHR has considered that States Parties' obligations under Article 2 also involve that hospitals issue directives to protect the lives of patients, and States provide effective legal procedures to establish causes of death in healthcare and to determine the possible liability of healthcare personnel. Furthermore, the ECtHR has stated that Article 2 is at stake in cases where there is evidence to the fact that a State Party has endangered the life of a citizen by withholding healthcare that is considered accessible to the whole population.[25]

---

18 In fact, the issue was not addressed, according to A.H. Robertson (ed.), *Collected edition of the 'travaux préparatoires' of the European Convention on Human Rights*, 1975–1985, Council of Europe, Strasbourg, Vol. 3 and 4, The Hague: Martinus Nijhoff, 1976 and 1977. B.G. Ramcharan, 'The drafting history of Article 2 of the European Convention on Human Rights', in B.G. Ramcharan (ed.), *op. cit.* pp. 57–62 does not hint at this topic either.

19 A. Platen-Hallermund, *Die Tötung Geisteskranker in Deutschland*, Frankfurt am Main: Verlag der Frankfurter Hefte, 1948, pp. 43–58; A. Mitscherlich & F. Mielke (Hrsg.), *Medizin ohne Menschlichkeit. Dokumenten des Nürnberger Ärzteprozesses*, Frankfurt am Main: Fischer Taschenbuchverlag, 1978, pp. 210–212; M. Burleigh, *Death and Deliverance;* 'Euthanasia' in Germany 1900–1945, Cambridge University Press, 1994, pp. 93–129.

20 G. Steinbauer, *Die Euthanasie im Lichte des Nürnberger Ärzteprozesses*, Wien: Kapri & Co, 1947, pp. 13–24; P.J. Weindling, *Nazi Medicine and the Nuremberg Trials*, From Medical War Crimes to Informed Consent, Hampshire/New York: Palgrave MacMillan, 2004, pp. 250–256.

21 L. Gruchmann, *Justiz im Dritten Reich, 1933–1940. Anpassung und Unterwerfung in der Ära Gürnter*, Dritte verbesserte Auflage, München: Oldenbourg, 2001, pp. 497–534; H. Kramer, 'Gerichtstag halten über uns selbst. Das Verfahren Fritz Bauers zur Beteiligung der Justiz am Anstaltmord', in H. Loewy, B. Winter (Hg.), *NS-"Euthanasie" vor Gericht. Fritz Bauer und die Grenzen juristischer Bewältigung*, Frankfurt am Main/New York: Campus Verlag, 1996, pp. 81–131.

22 An overview of constitutional and Strasbourg jurisprudence on right to life issues in biomedicine is provided in B. Mathieu: *The Right to Life*, Council of Europe Publishing, 2006.

23 *Nitecki v. Poland*, ECHR 21 March 2002, Appl. no. 65653/01 (inadmissible).

24 See *Erikson v. Italy*, ECHR 26 October 1999, Appl. no. 37900/97 (inadmissible); *Calvelli & Ciglio v. Italy*, ECHR 17 January 2002, Appl. no. 32967/96, par. 49.

25 *Cyprus v. Turkey*, ECHR (GC) 10 May 2001 Appl. no. 25781/94, par. 219, EHRC 2001/41.

In *Glass v. The United Kingdom* a mother filed a complaint under Article 2 ECHR that the Portsmouth Hospitals NHS Trust and its (medical) employees had put her sick son's life at risk of premature termination by administering to him sedative and pain relief medication (Diamorphine), including an adult dose, without her consent and placing a Do-Not-Resuscitate (DNR) order in his medical files without her consent or knowledge. Hence, the boy's right to life was at issue. The ECtHR interpreted the mother's complaint under Article 2 primarily as a criticism of the physicians' clinical judgment. It noted that the medical assessments and decisions in this case were made in view of the boy's earlier state of health, his recent case history, and the physicians' perception of the boy's distress and pain and the need to alleviate his respiratory difficulties. While it cannot be excluded that the acts and omissions of healthcare professionals in certain circumstances may engage their positive responsibilities under Article 2, the ECtHR states that if a State Party has made adequate provisions to secure high professional standards for healthcare workers and to protect the lives of patients, matters of error of professional judgment (even if established) by health professionals in the treatment of a particular patient are not of themselves sufficient to call that State to account from the standpoint of its positive obligations under Article 2. Ultimately, the ECtHR found this complaint under Article 2 to be manifestly ill-founded, and therefore inadmissible.[26]

The decision in *Pretty v. The United Kingdom* was the ECtHR's first explicit ruling on the relationship between deliberate ending of life at request and provisions of the ECHR, among which Article 2. Paragraph 5 deals with this case, as well as with others.

3.2. END-OF-LIFE DECISIONS AND FREEDOM FROM INHUMAN OR DEGRADING TREATMENT

An intriguing question is whether the fundamental right to protection against inhuman or degrading treatment, as mentioned in Article 7 ICCPR and Article 3 ECHR, plays a role in establishing the legal admissibility of end-of-life decisions in medical care. The heart of the matter is: can the State be held accountable for an individual's suffering due to his or her state of health, or even a continuation of life-sustaining treatment?

In the literature, the opinion is found that euthanasia is not *per se* in conflict with Article 3 ECHR, as the value of the life to be protected should be weighed against other rights of the person concerned, particularly his right to be protected from inhuman and degrading treatment. In theory, the involved person himself is the only one entitled to make this estimation. Whether others

26 Decision on admissibility of 18 March 2003, Appl. no. 61827/00.

can make this decision for him in case he is incapable of doing so, is questionable in view of the right to life's ascribed inalienable character.[27] This characteristic implies that the exercise of this right is non-transferable to others, that respect for this right cannot be suspended, annulled or made void, and that the bearer of this right cannot waive it.[28] Because of this, a third person has no competence to exercise the right to life of another person on his behalf, even if this person is incompetent. Yet, medical practice shows that in some cases, such as regarding severely suffering neonates[29] or PVS patients,[30] it is inevitable that a medical professional will make substituted judgments which are considered in the best interest of the incompetent patient. Some have asserted that in exceptional cases withholding or withdrawing of life-sustaining measures may be justified, because to start or to continue such measures would amount to inhuman treatment.[31] Up to now, this argument, however understandable, has not (yet) been exposed as a legally sustainable view. The success of an appeal to Article 3 ECHR, for that matter, is even uncertain, in view of the wording of the provision and its case history. Even though concepts such as 'torture', 'inhuman treatment' and 'degrading treatment' refer to violations of human dignity, albeit at different levels,[32] it seems difficult to substantiate that a certain treatment comes down to

27 P. van Dijk, G.J.H. van Hoof *et al.*, *op. cit.*, pp. 391–392.

28 The concept of this inalienability has been explored by F. Przetacznik: The right to life a basic human right, *Revue des droits de l'homme/Human Rights Journal. Droit international et Droit compare: International and Comparative Law* IX 1976, pp. 589–590, who discusses whether the right to life is an inalienable or an indefeasible right. Taken as an inalienable right, the right to life cannot be alienated from its bearer, nor transported by him or given away. Neither can it be invalidated or waived, even at will. Przetacznik believes the right to life to be 'inalienable' because man cannot decide to dispose of its human nature. As an 'indefeasible right' the right to life cannot be annulled or cancelled, be taken away, or withheld from its bearer, without his permission. This, however, would imply that one could choose to dispose of the exercise of the right to life. See, further, J. Feinberg, *Rights, Justice and the Bounds of Liberty*, Essays in Social Philosophy, Princeton/New Jersey: Princeton University Press, 1980, pp. 221–251, who inquires two interpretations of alienating: waiving and relinquishing.

29 Research shows that in Dutch Neonatal Intensive Care Units parents sometimes explicitly ask the neonatologist to end their baby's hopeless and unbearable suffering; a request, which, in appropriate cases, is carried out by the attending physician. See J.H.H.M Dorscheidt, A.A.E. Verhagen, P.J.J. Sauer *et al.*, *op. cit.*, 12–16.

30 A legal analysis of the *Schiavo* case in the USA is provided in K.L. Cerminara, 'The Schiavo Maelstrom's Potential Impact on the Law of End-of-Life Decision Making', in K.W. Goodman (ed.), *The case of Terri Schiavo. Ethics, politics and death in the 21st century*, Oxford/New York: Oxford University Press, 2010, pp. 78–100. See, also, J. Dute, 'The Terri Schiavo Case in a Comparative Perspective', pp. 317–319 and other contributions to 12 *European Journal of Health Law* (2005) 4, a special issue on PVS.

31 H.J.J. Leenen: Artikel 2, in J.K.M. Gevers (ed.): *Het EVRM en de gezondheidszorg*, Nijmegen: Ars Aequi Libri, 1994, pp. 34–40.

32 Essential considerations as to the particular meaning of the wording of Article 3 ECHR are expressed in 12 *Yearbook of the European Convention of Human Rights (1969) The Greek Case*, pp. 80–83 and p. 186. See, also, A. Cassese, 'Prohibition of Torture and Inhuman or Degrading Treatment, or Punishment', in R.St.J. Macdonald, F. Matscher, H. Petzold (eds.), *op. cit.*, pp. 225–261, here p. 248.

deliberately causing a particular intensity of physical or mental harm to the person concerned. Another issue is whether it matters in what capacity the one who brings about this harm carries out his performance. Regardless of these elements to be considered, there have been indirect precedents, which could provide clues for our present context. In *Herczegfalvy v. Austria*, for instance, it was acknowledged that the application of medical treatment in certain circumstances (i.e. forced-feeding and medication of a detained psychiatric patient, who was also kept in isolation and tied up to a safety bed) can amount to a violation of Article 3 ECHR.[33] Be this as it may, it is clear that even if a start or a continuation of life-sustaining measures constitutes inhuman treatment under international human rights law, this does not guarantee that a physician who performs euthanasia or who assists to suicide remains unpunished. Moreover, it can never justify a deliberate ending of life without the involved person's request. In other words, can a violation of the right to life under Article 2 ECHR be excused to avoid a violation of Article 3 ECHR?

3.3. END-OF-LIFE DECISIONS AND THE RIGHT TO PRIVACY

Decisions regarding medical treatment also relate to the right to private life. Here, a particular question is to what extent this right determines the legal admissibility of end-of-life decisions. After all, the meaning of the right to privacy with regard to decisions to undergo or to refuse treatment is different from the importance of that right in relation to euthanasia, PAS, or even layperson assisted suicide.

The connection between informed consent for medical treatment and private life under Article 8 ECHR was recognised in *Glass v. The United Kingdom*.[34] In this case, the ECtHR held that the decision to impose medical treatment on a critically ill 12-year-old boy in defiance of his mother's objections interfered with the child's right to respect for private life, particularly his right to physical integrity. Such interference is generally admissible only if it occurs after free, expressed and informed consent. The Court observed that the boy's mother had clearly withdrawn her consent, while the physicians and their employer –

33 *Herczegfalvy v. Austria* (Appl. no. 105233/83), Judgment of 24 September 1992, Publ. ECHR, Series A, Vol. 244. It is remarkable that while the former ECmHR found a violation of Article 3, the ECtHR concluded later that no proof of such a violation could be established in this case.

34 While complaints under Articles 2, 6, 13 and 14 ECHR were considered to be manifestly ill-founded and therefore inadmissible, the ECtHR concluded that a complaint under Article 8 in this case raised serious issues of fact and law under the Convention, which needed to be examined. This complaint was therefore found to be admissible. See Decision on admissibility of Appl. no. 61827/00, 18 March 2003.

Portsmouth Hospitals National Health Service (NHS) – should have respected her change of mind, and should not have engaged in rather intensive attempts to overcome her opposition. As a result, the ECtHR concluded that the decision by the authorities to override the boy's mother's objection to the proposed treatment, in absence of a court authorisation, resulted in a breach of Article 8 ECHR.[35]

In *Jehovah's Witnesses of Moscow and Others v. Russia*, the ECtHR addressed the scope of Article 8, particularly in relation to the refusal of medical treatment. Here, the Strasbourg Court confirmed that the essence of the ECHR is respect for human dignity, and that the notions of self-determination and personal autonomy are important principles underlying the interpretation of the safeguards laid down in the Convention. It has considered, further, that the possibility of living one's life according to one's own choosing includes the opportunity to engage in activities causing physical harm or danger to oneself. With regard to medical assistance, the ECtHR acknowledged that imposing compulsory care on someone who refuses to accept a particular treatment is likely to interfere with this person's right to physical integrity, and to infringe upon his or her rights protected under Article 8 ECHR. The freedom to refuse medical treatment, even if its concerns potentially life-saving medical treatment, is therefore considered vital to the principles of self-determination and personal autonomy, as a competent adult patient must have the right to make choices according to his own view and values, regardless of how irrational, unwise or imprudent such choices may appear to others. The State must refrain from interfering with this individual freedom of choice in the sphere of healthcare, for such interference would only lessen and not enhance the value of life. Restrictions with this freedom are only justified in the case of a necessity to protect third parties, e.g., in the case of care to prevent the spread of contagious diseases. Moreover, the ECtHR accepted that establishing the authenticity of a patient's refusal of medical care in situations where health, and possibly life, is at stake constitutes a legitimate concern.[36]

It seems quite clear that the Strasbourg Court sympathises with the view that a person's authentic decision to end his life is part of his or her private life. However, how much space a States Party is obliged to provide in order for its citizens to exercise their terminal freedom remains under discussion. After all, the space for a specific manner of exercising one right can very well be limited by the State, due to its obligations under human rights law to protect another right. The debate regarding the recognition of a personal freedom to end one's life

---

35 *Glass v. The United Kingdom*, Judgment of 9 March 2004, Appl. no. 61827/00, (2004) 39 EHRR 341, par. 70, 82 and 83.

36 *Jehovah's Witnesses of Moscow and Others v. Russia*, Judgment of 10 June 2010, Appl. no. 302/02, EHRC 2010/89, par. 135–138.

seems, therefore, no longer focused on arguing for such a freedom, but, rather, on the justification of statutory limitations to this freedom. This implies that the protection of the right to private life is not infinite. For reasons that reflect a higher legal interest, the State may interfere with our private life, provided these interferences have good cause and a basis in law. Furthermore, restrictions to the right to privacy must be proportionate and reasonable in view of the justified goal(s) they pursue. In the end, statutory limitations to the exercise of one's freedom to end one's life may be legitimate in view of a State's responsibility under Article 8(2) ECHR. They may even be argued in view of the current Strasbourgian interpretation of the right to life under Article 2 ECHR, which is discussed in paragraph 5.

Whether euthanasia or PAS is covered by the protection of Article 8 ECHR in a way that failing to implement legislation which conditionally tolerates these life-ending acts – including safeguards from abuse of vulnerable persons – constitutes a violation of the right to privacy remains to be seen. For now, the Strasbourg jurisprudence shows no clear indications of such a view. Besides, an argument to that purpose, however tempting for its advocates, would also require a sustainable association with Article 2 ECHR. It is my estimation that countries with a constitutionally guaranteed respect for human dignity are particularly suited to compose such an argument.

4. NATIONAL LEGISLATION ON EUTHANASIA AND PAS

Three countries – the Netherlands, Belgium and Luxemburg[37] – have issued specific legislation on deliberate ending of life at request. The main question is whether this legislation, which conditionally tolerates a physician ending a patient's life at his explicit request, is compatible with human rights law.

This paragraph contains an overview of this legislation in the Netherlands and Belgium, and explores how this main question was addressed in the legislative history of the respective Acts of Parliament. In addition, this paragraph discusses the law on death at request and assisted suicide in Switzerland. Although this country has no specified regulations on euthanasia or PAS, its current life-ending practice relates, in a particular way, to human rights.

---

[37] As of March 2009, Luxemburg enacted an Act allowing euthanasia and medically assisted suicide for the terminally ill. Under the new Act a physician is exempted from criminal charges if he complies with a request for euthanasia or assisted suicide by an adult or a minor, diagnosed with an irreversible illness. The involved person's request to die must have been repeatedly expressed, while confirmation of this must be evident in documentation and statements of witnesses. Furthermore, the consent of two physicians and a panel of experts is required. For pragmatic reasons, however, a further analysis of this legislation in this chapter has been omitted.

4.1. THE NETHERLANDS

The Netherlands was the first country to adopt and consolidate[38] regulations dealing with the legal admissibility of end-of-life decisions in medicine. After a long and intense debate in society, and well-considered conclusions in ample jurisprudence, the Dutch legislature adopted the so-called[39] Euthanasia Act. Under this Act, which entered into force on 1 April 2002, the ending of life at request and assisted suicide remain criminal offences under Articles 293 and 294 of the Dutch Penal Code. Yet, if such an act is carried out by a physician in agreement with specific requirements of due care, and afterwards is reported to the judicial authorities, the physician involved will not be prosecuted. For, if these conditions are met, it is expected that the physician, in the case of criminal prosecution, can successfully invoke a special ground for impunity, introduced by the Euthanasia Act. Failing to report a case that should have been reported constitutes a criminal offence.

One of five Regional Euthanasia Review Committees, established by law,[40] will review a reported case against the requirements of due care laid down in the Euthanasia Act. According to these requirements the physician must:

a. be convinced that the patient's request is voluntary and well-considered;
b. be convinced that the patient's suffering is unbearable and that there is no prospect of improvement;
c. have informed the patient about his situation and further prognosis;
d. have discussed the situation with the patient and have come to the conclusion that there is no reasonable alternative;
e. have consulted at least one other physician with no connection to the case, who then must have seen the patient and has stated in writing that the

---

38 The Australian Euthanasia Laws Act 1997 amended the Northern Territory Self Government Act 1978 (as well as the Australian Capital Territory Self Government Act 1988 and the Norfolk Island Act 1979) to disallow the making of laws which permit, or have the effect of permitting (whether subject to conditions or not), the form of intentional killing of another called euthanasia (which includes mercy killing) or the assisting of a person to terminate his or her life. Through this federal Act, the earlier Rights of the Terminally Ill Act 1996, effective as of 1 July 1996, and providing the possibility to legalise euthanasia and physician assisted suicide in the Northern Territory, was invalidated. For an overview of developments, see M. Otlowski, *Voluntary Euthanasia and the Common Law*, Oxford/New York: Oxford University Press, 1997, pp. 339–361.

39 Officially, the Act is called: Act on the assessment of ending of life on request and assisted suicide. Act of 12 April 2001, *Staatsblad* (Governmental Gazette) 2001, 194.

40 Actually, these Committees were introduced in 1998. At that time, however, they functioned as an advisory board to the Public Prosecution regarding the physician's careful performance. In 2002 the Committees' competences were changed. Consequently, they take a prominent position in the settlement of cases of euthanasia and PAS.

attending physician has satisfied the criteria listed in a. to d. above; and finally,

f. have exercised due medical care and attention in terminating the patient's life or assisting in his suicide.

If the Committee concludes that the physician involved acted in accordance with these requirements, the case is settled. In consequence, the Public Prosecutor will not be informed about the case. If the due care requirements are not met, the case will be reported to the Public Prosecutor's office. The Board of Procurators-General, the highest body of the Dutch Public Prosecution, ultimately decides whether or not the physician will be prosecuted.

Apart from this, the Euthanasia Act also contains provisions governing requests for ending of life or assisted suicide in respect of minors. In essence, such requests may be taken into consideration if the minor is competent and aged 12 years or older. Additionally, the minor's parents must agree with their child's wish. If the minor is aged 16 or older, his parents are merely to be involved in the decision-making process. Furthermore, the Euthanasia Act recognises the validity of written living wills. Although the physician is allowed to grant both oral and written requests for euthanasia or PAS, he is never obliged to do so. As a result, the Euthanasia Act creates no right to euthanasia or PAS.

In its annual report of 2010, the Regional Euthanasia Review Committees jointly stated that just like in the six previous years, the number of cases of death at request in 2010 had increased from 2636, in 2009, to 3136; an increase of 19%. The reasons for this growth in numbers remain unclear and are, therefore, made subject of the current second evaluation of the Euthanasia Act.[41] Of all 3136 reported cases the Committees came to a conclusion in 2667 cases. In 9 of these cases, it was found that the physician involved did not meet all due care requirements..[42] Since the Euthanasia Act came into force in 2002, some 50 cases were considered to be in conflict with the due care criteria. The main reasons for this were doubts as to meeting the norm of unbearable suffering (b) and insufficient consultation (e). In several cases the physician involved was consequently summoned to the Public Prosecutor's Office in view of a personal dialogue. In others, the case was still dismissed. Until now, none of the physicians who officially did not meet the due care requirements have been prosecuted.[43]

41 The results of this evaluation are expected at the end of 2012.

42 Regional Euthanasia Review Committees, *Annual Report 2010*, The Hague, August 2011. See also www.euthanasiecommissie.nl.

43 A. Muizelaar, *Wet toetsing levensbeëindiging op verzoek en hulp bij zelfdoding. Wie bewaakt de grenzen?* Master Thesis, Groningen, 2010 (unpublished).

A central question during the drafting of the Euthanasia Act was whether or not the Act is compatible with Article 2(1) ECHR. To answer this question the Dutch government returned, in part, to the Report of the State Commission on Euthanasia of 1985. In this report, the conclusion that an Act of Parliament that conditionally permits euthanasia and PAS is not necessarily in conflict with this treaty provision[44] was regarded as a widely accepted viewpoint in the Netherlands, because of the developments in Dutch jurisprudence.[45] During discussion in Parliament, the involved Ministers also concluded that the new Act was not incompatible with the duty under Article 2(1) ECHR to protect the right to life by law, as the particular nature of this intentional ending of life was not considered to be in conflict with the provision. Moreover, it was assumed that the right to life laid down in Article 2(1) ECHR is not an inalienable right. According to the Dutch government, rights are inalienable only if a person never has a respectable interest in the possibility of waiving that right.[46] A person who requests explicitly and consciously to end his life expresses an interest in renouncing the protection of his right to life. Legislation that allows a person to weigh his interests in this regard must be considered to be in accordance with the ECHR provision. The denial of a person's liberty to waive the protection of the right to life would mean that the exercise of this right can result in a limitation of the freedom of self-determination.[47] Therefore, the Dutch government assumes that Article 2 does not include the obligation for States Parties to protect a person's right to life against his explicit and conscious will. Moreover, through upholding the penalisation of euthanasia and PAS under the Penal Code, the Euthanasia Act sufficiently secures the protectability of human life. Besides, to investigate whether or not a physician's conduct in an individual case amounts to a criminal offence is still possible because of the standard set by the special ground for impunity.[48]

Legislation that allows a physician in specific circumstances to deliberately end the life of an incompetent patient is generally regarded to be in conflict with Article 2 ECHR.[49] To end a patient's life without his explicit request amounts to a unpermitted intentional deprivation of life, and is incompatible with the

44 *Rapport van de Staatscommissie Euthanasie,* Deel 1: Advies. Staatsuitgeverij 's-Gravenhage 1985, pp. 36–39.

45 H.J.J. Leenen, 'Artikel 2', in J.K.M. Gevers (ed.), *op. cit.* pp. 34–35; J. Remmelink, 'The legal position on euthanasia in the Netherlands in the light of article 2 of the ECHR', in P. Mahoney, *et al.* (eds.), *Protecting Human Rights: The European Perspective, Studies in Memory of Rolv Ryssdal*, Köln: Carl Heymanns Verlag, 2000, pp. 1157–1171.

46 Plenary Notes II 2000–2001, nr. 27, p. 2247; Parliamentary Papers I 2000–2001, 26691, nr. 137a, pp. 15–17.

47 Parliamentary Papers II 1999–2000, 26691, nr. 6, p. 114.

48 Among others, Parliamentary Papers II 1999–2000, 26691, nr. 6, pp. 9–10 and 26; Parliamentary Papers II 2000–2001, 26691, nr. 41, pp. 1–2; Plenary Notes II 2000–2001, nr. 25, p. 2035–2037; Parliamentary Papers I 2000–2001, 26691, nr. 137b, p. 39–41.

49 Parliamentary Papers II 1997–1998, 26000, nr. 3, p. 5.

positive obligations of States Parties under Article 2.[50] This viewpoint enjoys widespread support from Dutch health law experts.[51]

In the summer of 2001 the ICCPR Committee expressed concerns regarding the expected Dutch euthanasia legislation.[52] In its Concluding Observations/ Comments[53] following the third periodical Report of the Kingdom of the Netherlands to the Committee,[54] special concerns were raised as to the maintenance of the new legislation. Although aware that this new legislation aims to provide legal certainty and clarity on an issue that has already been developing in medical practice for many years, and is not going to abolish the penalisation of euthanasia or PAS, the Committee asserted: '... *where a State party seeks to relax legal protection with respect to an act deliberately intended to put an end to human life, the Committee believes that the Covenant obliges it to apply the most rigorous scrutiny to determine whether the State party's obligations to ensure the right to life are being complied with (Articles 2 and 6 of the Covenant).*' Despite the statutory due care requirements for impunity of the physician who ends life at request, the Committee was not entirely satisfied '... *lest such a system may fail to detect and prevent situations where undue pressure could lead to these criteria being circumvented.*' There was fear of a routine based and less attentive application of these due care requirements in a way unforeseen. Moreover, the Committee was worried about the effectiveness and validity of the review procedure, as well as the special regime concerning minors.

In its reply, the Dutch government said it was convinced that the Committee had no doubts as to the compatibility of the Euthanasia Act with Articles 2 and 6 ICCPR.[55] The Committee's primary concerns were, yet, directed to the new Act's practical level of protection. In this regard, the Netherlands had already

---

50 H.J.J. Leenen, 'Levensbeëindiging bij ernstig gehandicapte pasgeborenen. Van neonatologie naar neothanatologie?' 43 *Medisch Contact* (1988) 36; 1050–1052; H.J.J. Leenen, 'Mag een zorgvuldig handelende arts het leven beëindigen zonder verzoek?' 2 *Tijdschrift voor Geneeskunde en Ethiek* (1992) 2; 47–48; H.J.J. Leenen: Artikel 2, in J.K.M. Gevers (ed.), *op. cit.*, pp. 35–39; H.J.J. Leenen, 'Levensbeëindiging zonder verzoek', 56 *Medisch Contact* (2001) 20; 775–777.

51 H.D.C Roscam Abbing, 'Medisch handelen bij het begin van leven; enkele juridische kanttekeningen', 132 *Nederlands Tijdschrift voor Geneeskunde* (1988) 33; 1540–1544; J.H. Hubben, 'Levensbeëindiging van ernstige gehandicapte pasgeborenen en ernstig demente bejaarden: waar ligt de grens?' 16 *Tijdschrift voor Gezondheidsrecht* (1993); 207–213; J. Legemaate, E.J.C. de Jong, 'Medische beslissingen rond het levenseinde van wilsonbekwame patiënten: juridische aspecten', in J. Legemaate, R.J.M. Dillmann (eds.): *Levensbeëindigend handelen door een arts: tussen norm en praktijk*, Houten/Diegem: Bohn Stafleu Van Loghum, 1998, p. 159.

52 S. Joseph, J. Schultz & M. Castan, *The International Covenant on Civil and Political Rights. Cases, Materials, and Commentary*, Second edition, Oxford/New York: Oxford University Press, 2004, pp. 191–192.

53 Concluding Observations of the Human Right Committee: Netherlands. 72nd Session, 20/07/01, CCPR/CO/72/NET.

54 CCPR/C/NET/99/3 and CCPR/C/NET/99/3/Add.1.

55 Parliamentary Papers II 2000–2001, 26691 and 22588, nr. 42.

initiated a system of close evaluation of the instruments of enforcement under the Act. As regards euthanasia or PAS in minors, the Dutch government proclaims a high level of due care and legal protection. The annual report of the Regional Euthanasia Review Committees actually pays special attention to cases of death at request of a minor. In medical practice, however, such cases are rare, and there is no reason to assume any irregularities in this area.[56]

A short remark is to be made here regarding a separate matter. The Committee was also gravely concerned about reports that new-born disabled infants had had their lives ended by medical personnel. The Committee urged the Netherlands to scrupulously investigate any such allegations of violations of the right to life under Article 6 ICCPR, which fall outside the law on euthanasia, and expected to be informed on the number of such cases and on the results of court proceedings arising out of them. Similar concerns were expressed by the UN Children's Rights Committee. In response, the Dutch government merely reported that a special expert review committee on end-of-life decisions regarding neonates and late termination of pregnancy was established in 2007. To date (early 2012), only one case of medical neonaticide has been reported to this committee.[57]

4.2. BELGIUM

In several respects the Belgian Euthanasia Act,[58] which was also adopted in 2002, is remarkable.[59] Unlike in the Netherlands, the Belgian legislative process was not substantiated by developments in national jurisprudence. The legal debate on the matter was therefore unable to take advantage of substantial jurisprudence.[60] Furthermore, the Belgian Medical Order chose to play no significant role in the legislative process. This seems rather odd given the importance of the medical perspective to the content of the Euthanasia Act, especially if we consider that most Belgian physicians did not really believe in legislation on this subject. Moreover, this Act does not explicitly cover PAS, but

---

56 Letter of 15 May 2003, BUZA 030180, non-dossier file 2002–2003, Parliamentary Paper II, Doc.id. NDS9111. Letter to Parliament concerning interlocutory report ICCPR – Annex I.

57 Dutch Central Committee on Late Termination of Pregnancy and Ending of Life of Newborn Infants: *Combined Annual Report 2009/2010*, The Hague, 2011, pp. 21–23 (case no. LP2009001).

58 Act of 28 May 2002 regarding Euthanasia, published in the Belgian Governmental Gazette of 22 June 2002, valid as of 23 September 2002. The Act is reproduced (in English) in 10 *European Journal of Health Law* (2003) 3; 329–335.

59 An overview of developments offers M. Adams, 'Het rechtsvormingsproces inzake euthanasie in België', *Res Publica* XLIV, 2002/4, pp. 599–625.

60 Actually, the first criminal case in Belgium against two physicians who administered lethal barbiturates to a patient at his request occurred at the beginning of the 21st century.

merely affects euthanasia, even though, ethically and legally, euthanasia and PAS differ only marginally.[61] Some observers, however, assume that the Act does not apply to PAS because of political reasons. Interestingly, the Federal Control and Evaluation Commission Euthanasia (FCECE), established by the Euthanasia Act, and charged with reviewing reported cases, as well as evaluating the general practice of euthanasia in Belgium, stated in 2004 that PAS falls within the definition of euthanasia, at least as far as during its execution the statutory terms and conditions are met.[62]

The Belgian Euthanasia Act covers two situations of euthanasia. The first relates to a current request, the second to an advance directive. With regard to the first situation, Article 3 states that a physician who performs euthanasia in agreement with the terms and procedures of the Euthanasia Act commits no crime, provided the patient who requested to die, is

1. aged 18 years or older, or a minor emancipated by the decision of a judge; and
2. in a medically hopeless situation of persistent and unbearable physical or mental suffering, which cannot be alleviated, and which results from a serious and incurable disorder, caused by an accident or disease.

The patient's request must be voluntary, well-considered, and must have been expressed repeatedly without external pressure. Furthermore, the request must be put in writing and must be documented in the patient's medical file.

Article 4 states that a physician who performs euthanasia on the basis of a patient's written directive, drawn up in view of a future incompetency, commits no criminal offence if he ascertains that the patient

1. suffers from a serious and incurable disorder, caused by an accident or disease;
2. is no longer conscious; and
3. is in an irreversible condition according to current medical-scientific understanding.

Apart from special due care requirements such as adequate information to the patient, consulting another physician, the nursing staff and relatives, or ensuring the proper use of appropriate pharmaceutical drugs, the Euthanasia Act also contains a special system of control. Under this system, a physician who has performed euthanasia must report the case to the above-mentioned FCECE, by using a special registration form. Even though failing to report a case in itself constitutes no crime, it is clear that to meet this obligation is an implicit part of

61 H. Nys, 'Physician Assisted Suicide in Belgian Law', 12 *European Journal of Health Law* (2005) 1; 39–42.
62 See J. Griffiths, H. Weyers, M. Adams, *op. cit.*, pp. 306–311.

the terms and procedures relevant for impunity. The FCECE reviews the content of the completed form and decides whether or not the requirements of careful practice have been met. If the Commission concludes the physician has not complied with these requirements, the case files are sent to the Public Prosecutor, to whom it is up to decide independently whether or not the physician will be prosecuted.

Finally, it is confirmed in the Euthanasia Act that it creates no right to euthanasia, and that no person can be forced to cooperate in performing euthanasia. Additionally, the Act states that death resulting from euthanasia, in accordance with the law, counts as a natural death with regard to the execution of (insurance) contracts concluded by the deceased person.[63]

During the genesis of the Euthanasia Act, the question of whether the Act is compatible with the fundamental right to life, as laid down in Article 2 ECHR, was thoroughly discussed. The Belgian Council of State specifically addressed[64] the issue and considered that the State's obligation to protect this right provides no basis for an unconditional protection of life in all circumstances, even against a person's free will. The scope of every single right should always be determined in relation to the characteristics of a particular situation. In this regard, it was argued that the State's obligation to protect this fundamental right must be weighed against a person's freedom of autonomy, in particular, his right to be safeguarded from inhuman or degrading treatment, and his right to protection of his private life. Statutory regulations that prohibit someone from helping another person to end his life are obviously compatible with the State's obligation to protect the right to life. Yet, at issue is whether the latter obligation is violated if a state, through legislation, seeks to make less stringent such a prohibition in circumstances which the person concerned considers to be no longer dignified. The question is whether implementing such legislation can be at the discretion of the national legislature. According to the Belgian Council of State, such legislation is not contrary to a State Party's obligation to protect everyone's right to life by law, provided that cases that are not covered by the particular circumstances mentioned in the proposed Act are (or remain) punishable under national criminal law.

At this point, the Belgian euthanasia regulations produce a notable consideration. Euthanasia and medically assisted suicide have never been recognised as distinct crimes under Belgian criminal law; a fact which tends to complicate the legal aftermath of these life-ending acts, especially in cases where they have been performed contrary to the requirements of the law. Some

63 A comment on the Belgian Euthanasia Act is provided in H. Nys, E. Deckers, *Nieuwe wetgeving inzake euthanasie*, Mechelen: Kluwer, 2003; J. Griffiths, H. Weyers, M. Adams, *op. cit.*, pp. 306–329; W. de Bondt, Th. Vansweevelt, 'Euthanasia in Belgium', in M. Groenhuijsen, F. van Laanen (eds.), *op. cit.*, pp. 27–54.

64 Advice of the Council of State, *Parliamentary Proceedings*, Senaat 2000–2001, no. 2–244/21.

commentators believe that offences such as murder, manslaughter, or even poisoning, would apply,[65] but these crimes lack the element of the patient's request. Besides, an 'illegal' euthanasia may constitute murder – as a majority of Belgian scholars postulates – particularly if it occurred without the patient's request. It is unlikely that murder applies if the requested life-ending act was merely performed without the required consultations, or while using inappropriate pharmaceutical drugs. While the Euthanasia Act exclusively aims to ensure that requests for euthanasia are granted only in specified circumstances, it fails to provide a proper penal regime for cases that do not meet the statutory requirements. Because it is unclear – probably due to the absence of relevant jurisprudence – which criminal offence under the Belgian Penal Code – if any at all – is committed in the case of 'illegal' euthanasia, there is room for doubt as to whether this Euthanasia Act is compatible with the right to life under European human rights law. All things considered, the Belgian State is also obliged under Article 2 ECHR to provide legal protection of the right to life in cases of 'illegal' euthanasia.

To date, the FCECE has produced four reports[66] on (the amount of) the registration documents reviewed by the Committee and evaluations and clarifications as regards the application of the Euthanasia Act. The reports also cover suggestions that may lead to alterations of Euthanasia policy in Belgium. In 2008 and 2009, some 63 cases of euthanasia were reported each month. In the previous report (2006–2007), the FCECE referred to an average number of 38 cases each month. In 2008 and 2009, there were 36 cases of euthanasia resulting from an advanced directive. To date (early 2012), there have been no cases which did not meet the due care requirements.[67] Consequently, no case has been referred to the Public Prosecutor.

4.3. SWITZERLAND

Switzerland has attracted worldwide attention because of the public activities of domestic organisations such as Dignitas[68] and EXIT.[69] These Right-to-Die societies play an important role in providing appropriate assistance to persons

65 See, for instance, M. Locher-Lin, J.C. Oudijk, 'Belgien', in A. Eser, H.-G. Koch (eds.), *Materialien zur Sterbehilfe. Eine internationale Dokumentation*, Freiburg im Breisgau, 1991, pp. 252–280, particularly pp. 252–253.

66 The last report is: Federale Controle- en Evaluatiecommissie Euthanasie. Vierde verslag aan de wetgevende kamers, 2008–2009, Brussel. See www.health.fgov.be/euthanasie.

67 In literature the Belgian practice of euthanasia was scrutinised by P. Lewis, 'Euthanasia in Belgium Five years After Legislation', 16 *European Journal of Health Law* (2009) 2; 125–138.

68 See www.dignitas.ch.

69 See www.exit.ch.

who wish to commit suicide. This 'Dying Aid' (*Sterbehilfe*) is not limited to Swiss residents only.

The legal framework applicable to the current life-ending practice in Switzerland involves Articles 114 and 115 of the Swiss Penal Code.[70] Article 114 states that everyone, who, for honourable reasons – which is compassion – ends the life of another person at his serious and explicit request, is punishable (with up to 3 years' imprisonment or a fine). Article 115 contains a provision on assisted suicide. It declares that everyone, who, for selfish reasons, aids or abets another person in committing suicide is punishable (with up to 5 years imprisonment). Principally, Swiss criminal law does not penalise suicide and attempted suicide. As a consequence, he who takes part in these acts, meaning he who instigates or supports them, will remain unpunished as well. Yet, everyone who tempts or helps to commit suicide commits a crime under Article 115. However, according to Article 64 of the Swiss Penal Code, the sentence for this can be moderated in cases where the offence occurred for 'honourable reasons' or 'under severe pressure'.[71]

Cases of assisted suicide are considered to be an 'exceptional death', and must be reported to, and investigated by, the judicial authorities. A person's death resulting from his genuine refusal to undergo potentially life-saving treatment falls outside the scope of Articles 114 and 115. Failing to provide such treatment contrary to a legal duty to give this treatment is likely to be punishable as death by omission under Article 111 of the Swiss Penal Code.

Switzerland has no specific regulations on euthanasia and PAS, although there have been several attempts (Cavalli Initiative, Vallender Initiative) to modify Article 114 and to decriminalise death at request. The current legal framework in a way resembles the Dutch framework prior to the Euthanasia Act. Similar to its Dutch counterpart before April 2002 (the old Article 293 PC), Article 114 does not mention the physician, nor refers to some privileged position of this professional in this regard. The same goes for Article 115 (the old Article 294 PC in the Netherlands). Actually, it follows from the latter provision that everyone – including laypeople (e.g. friends, relatives) – who assist to suicide for unselfish reasons can be exempt from committing this criminal offence. Furthermore, unlike in the Netherlands, only a few cases ended up before a Swiss criminal

---

70 For an overall view, see G. Bosshard: Switzerland, in J. Griffiths, H. Weyers, M. Adams, *op. cit.*, pp. 463–481. As regards the ethical aspects, see A. Bondolfi, 'Switzerland – Defending assisted death', in *Ethical Eye: Euthanasia, Vol. II. National and European perspectives*, Council of Europe Publishing, 2004, pp. 85–94.

71 F. Riklin, 'Die strafrechtliche Regelung der Sterbehilfe. Zum Stand der Reformdiskussion in der Schweiz', in A. Holderegger (ed.), *Das medizinisch assistierte Sterben. Zur Sterbehilfe aus medizinischer, ethischer, juristischer und theologischer Sicht*, Freiburg i. Br.: Universitätsverlag, 1998, pp. 328–350.

court.[72] This is regrettable, as case law would contribute to clarifying interpretational matters, such as what constitutes 'compassion', which motivation for assisted suicide other than material gain counts as 'selfish', or which performance equates to 'aids' or 'abets'. Moreover, it remains unclear whether or not the admissibility of providing a requested 'Dying Aid' is linked to any medical precondition. In the Netherlands, for instance, the Supreme Court ruled in 2002[73] that PAS is not permitted if the person concerned suffers from a societal condition (e.g. loneliness), as the physician is not qualified to verify whether suffering from an non-medical condition constitutes 'hopeless and unbearable suffering' in the sense adopted in consistent Dutch jurisprudence. This case has opened a debate in the Netherlands as to whether assisted suicide by definition must involve a physician, or if there is room for involvement of non-medical assistants to suicide as well. The latter viewpoint is accepted in assisted suicide practice in Switzerland. For that matter, the involvement of a Right-to-Die society is of importance.

A person who wants to commit suicide can contact such an organisation. During an intake procedure, the concerned person's medical condition(s), the corresponding (poor) prognosis, the hopeless and unbearable suffering, *etc.* are assessed. After admittance, this person must contact a physician and ask him to prescribe a lethal dose of sodium pentobarbital. If provided, the drugs are handed over to the Right-to-Die society, which then keeps charge of them. At the time of the suicide, the representative of the society provides essential guidance and support concerning the effective use of the lethal medication to ensure that the terminal objective is realised. Assisted suicide practice shows that the physician who prescribed the lethal dose of barbiturate is often not present during the suicide.[74]

The role of the physician in assisted suicide is basically to examine the authenticity of the request to die, to assess the medical circumstance(s) that have caused the desire to depart this life, and to prescribe the lethal dose of sodium pentobarbital. In this regard, the ethical guidelines of the Swiss Academy of Medical Sciences are an important point of reference.[75] These guidelines deal,

---

72 Literature often refers to the historic case against Prof. Haemmerli in 1976, who was accused of having withheld nourishment from 27 dying patients. At the time, this case gave rise to several political initiatives to issue precise regulations to legalise Dying Aid. See G. Heine, 'Schweiz', in A. Eser, H.-G. Koch (eds.), *op. cit.*, pp. 593–649, particularly pp. 593–595. G. Bosshard, 'Switzerland', in J. Griffiths, H. Weyers, M. Adams, *op. cit.*, pp. 468 refers to some 'rare cases of serial offences' and (p. 473) a few court rulings limiting a physician's involvement in assisted suicide.

73 Supreme Court 24 December 2002 (Brongersma case), LJN AE8772.

74 G. Bosshard, 'Switzerland,' in J. Griffiths, H. Weyers, M. Adams, *op. cit.*, pp. 474–475. See also notes 68 and 69.

75 Schweizerische Akademie der Medizinischen Wissenschaften, *Betreuung von Patientinnen und Patienten am Lebensende,* Medizinisch-ethische Richtlinien der SAMW, November 2004. See www.samw.ch.

among other things, with establishing a person's competency, decision-making regarding a continuation or withdrawal of treatment, and palliative care. They also express that the physician willing to assist in suicide must examine whether:

- the concerned person's health state justifies the belief that he will die soon;
- alternatives were considered and even used where appropriate; and
- the person concerned is capable of requesting to die, and the request is voluntary, well-considered, and consistently articulated. These latter requirements must be reviewed by an independent third person who does not need to be a physician.

The Swiss regime does not involve an independent body like the Dutch Regional Euthanasia Review Committees or the Belgian FCECE to review cases of death at request or assisted suicide once they have occurred. Is this surprising? On the one hand, the significant role of the Right-to-Die societies suggests that the strict assessment of a case occurs before the decision to provide the requested life-ending assistance. The justification of such assistance is therefore established in advance, rather than in retrospect. Yet, does this not imply that there is a limited timeframe for the validity of this assessment? On the other hand, the absence of an adequate review procedure afterwards may lead to an inaccurate view on the actual fulfilment of due care requirements in this Right-to-Die practice. While Swiss prosecution authorities do not seem to be aware of 'illegal' cases, since these have not been presented to them, and because of a tendency among Swiss prosecutors to prosecute only extreme (pharmaceutical) performances,[76] the question is how effective the maintenance of Swiss law on assisted suicide actually is in preventing abuse.

The main difference between the Dutch and the Belgian system, on the one hand, and the Swiss, on the other, is, as was already mentioned, that the Swiss model explicitly allows others than physicians to assist in suicide.[77] In this regard, it has been asserted that the Swiss model interprets assisted suicide as a human rights issue rather than a healthcare issue.[78] An interesting observation, one might say. While Article 7 of the Swiss Constitution ('Human dignity must be respected and protected') qualifies human dignity as a legal concept, and thus enables its legal application, it is no surprise that recognition of the fundamental right to decide on the circumstances and the moment of one's death underlies Swiss law on assisted suicide.

---

76 G. Bosshard, 'Switzerland', in J. Griffiths, H. Weyers, M. Adams, *op. cit.*, p. 468.

77 See, explicitly, Schweizerische Akademie der Medizinischen Wissenschaften 2004, *op. cit.*, p. 6.

78 G. Bosshard, 'Switzerland', in J. Griffiths, H. Weyers, M. Adams, *op. cit.*, pp. 463 and 473. Bosshard refers, in particular, to the decision by the Federal Supreme Court of Switzerland, Entscheid 2A.4812006, 2006.

5. STRASBOURG JURISPRUDENCE ON END-OF-LIFE DECISIONS

This paragraph provides an overview of the most relevant judgments by the ECtHR concerning end-of-life matters at request of the person concerned. While discussing significant aspects of these cases, the meaning of Articles 2 and 8 ECHR stands at the centre of consideration.

5.1. *PRETTY V. UNITED KINGDOM*

Dianne Pretty suffered from Motor Neurone Disease (MND), a progressive neurodegenerative disorder of the motoric cells of the central nervous system. This disease leads to a weakened muscular system, affecting the muscles in the arms and legs, but of the respiratory organs as well. In time, an MND patient will experience severe breathing difficulties, eventually resulting in death by suffocation. Progressive MND, at least at that particular time, was untreatable.

To prevent serious deterioration Pretty wanted to end her life in a humane and dignified way. Due to her bad physical condition she was unable to end her life herself. In consequence, she wanted her husband to end her suffering. Yet, assisted suicide is a criminal offence in the United Kingdom. Pretty therefore asked the Director of Public Prosecutions to declare that her husband would not be prosecuted if he helped her to die. The request was denied. An appeal to the Divisional Court, and later to the House of Lords, did not succeed either. Finally, she presented her case to the ECtHR. In Strasbourg she argued that the refusal of the British judicial authorities to grant her husband immunity from prosecution constituted a violation of Articles 2, 3, 8, and 14 ECHR.[79]

Regarding Article 2 Pretty asserted that the British authorities' reluctant attitude obstructed the way she wanted to execute her right to life. In her view, allowing one to end one's life is no infringement of Article 2 ECHR, for if it were, countries where suicide is considered no crime under national penal law would be acting contrary to the ECHR provision. According to Pretty, Article 2 ECHR not only protects the right to life, but also entails the right to choose whether or not to continue living. Moreover, the prohibition of intentional deprivation of life concerns the State and third parties, but not the bearer of the right to life. Pretty was convinced that Article 2 ECHR includes the right to die in order to prevent unbearable suffering and indignity.[80]

The ECtHR ruled that the right to life in Article 2 ECHR involves no negative dimension and covers no issues that touch upon a person's quality of life or what

[79] *Pretty v. United Kingdom* 29 April 2002, Appl. no. 2346/02, (2002) 35 EHRR 1.

[80] (2002) 35 EHRR 1, par. 35.

he freely chooses to do with his life. With regard to Pretty's interpretation of Article 2, the ECtHR concluded:

> *'Article 2 cannot, without distortion of language,*[81] *be interpreted as conferring the diametrically opposite right, namely a right to die; nor can it create a right to self-determination in the sense of conferring on an individual the entitlement to choose death rather than life. The Court accordingly finds that no right to die, whether at the hands of a third person or with the assistance of a public authority, can be derived from Article 2 of the Convention. It is confirmed in this view by the recent Recommendation 1418 (1999) of the Parliamentary Assembly of the Council of Europe.'*[82]

Pretty's reference to existing viewpoints in legal systems outside of the United Kingdom was considered irrelevant. Although in some countries assisted suicide is not punishable in certain circumstances, Article 2 ECHR holds no obligation for the United Kingdom to accept a similar criminal regime regarding such conduct. It is considered to fall under a State Party's *'margin of appreciation'* to deal with such an act in a way corresponding with accepted understanding of national criminal law with proper notice of the State's responsibilities under the ECHR. In this particular case, the ECtHR found it unnecessary to investigate whether or not a State Party's protection of the right to life by national law is adequate. Consequently, the ECtHR concluded there was no violation of Article 2 in this case.[83]

Pretty further asserted that her suffering constitutes degrading treatment within the meaning of Article 3 ECHR. Although she admitted that the State bears no direct responsibility for this treatment, she argued that the State not only must refrain from such treatment, but has a duty to protect its civilians against it as well. As a consequence, the United Kingdom would be obliged to take measures in this case to protect Pretty against further suffering.

The ECtHR concluded that there was no violation of Article 3. The UK authorities' refusal to grant Pretty's husband immunity from prosecution is, according to the Strasbourg Court, not equal to inhuman or degrading treatment for which the State bears responsibility if it fails to protect Pretty against the suffering she must face. Besides, 'treatment' in the usual sense of the word is out of the question here. Although the ECtHR understands Pretty's view that without the possibility of suicide she would be left with the prospect of unbearable suffering, the Court is unwilling to commit the United Kingdom to

---

81 By using the wording *'without distortion of language'* the European Court seems to express that its view on Article 2 ECHR marks the limits of the treaty provision's textual interpretation in this particular context.

82 (2002) 35 EHRR 1, par. 39 and 40. See, also, Recommendation 1418 (1999). *Protection of the human rights and dignity of the terminally ill and the dying.* Text adopted by the Assembly on 25 June 1999 (24th Sitting). Official Gazette of the Council of Europe – June 1999.

83 (2002) 35 EHRR 1, par. 42.

sanction actions which end life. No such positive obligation for a State can be derived from Article 3 ECHR, no more than a duty for the British State to declare that Pretty's husband will not be prosecuted if he assisted his wife in ending her life.[84]

Pretty also appealed to her right to self-determination, as in Article 8(1) ECHR, and contended that this right includes the right to dispose of one's own body according to one's personal views. This, she argued, involves the right to choose the moment and the place of one's death. Pretty asserted that the refusal to grant her husband the requested immunity, as well as the British ban on assisted suicide, constitute violations of her right to privacy; that is to say, her freedom to make choices to prevent that her life will end in an undignified and burdensome way.

However, Pretty's appeal to Article 8(1) ECHR was dismissed by the Strasbourg Court as well. The Court did not want to exclude that this situation is an infringement of Pretty's private life. In fact, the ECtHR considered that the very essence of the Convention is respect for human dignity and human freedom, and that it is under Article 8 that notions of the quality of life take on significance.[85] Yet, it was upheld that the right to privacy laid down in Article 8 is not absolute. In consequence, States Parties are permitted to impose certain limitations to the exercise of this right. In this regard, it must be examined whether a statutory limitation is a necessary infringement of the right to privacy and whether it aims to serve a higher purpose of law. In the ECtHR's view, the United Kingdom is permitted to establish regulations of criminal law applying to behaviour which endangers people's lives or safety. The greater the danger, the more the idea of personal autonomy must be considered inferior to the interest of public health or public safety. Regardless of the variety of circumstances in which terminally ill people may find themselves, their vulnerability as a group is found to be a justifiable reason for the current penalisation of assisted suicide. This, reasonably, constitutes a legitimate goal of this particular regime under the law. Here, the Strasbourg Court recognised that, while choosing to implement such a regime, a State Party deserves a margin in order to weigh up the involved interests. Additionally, the ECtHR observed that there is no doubt about the risk of abuse, although assisted suicide regulations may contain procedural safeguards. In conclusion, the ECtHR found that the English penalisation of assisted suicide serves a legitimate purpose and constitutes a necessary infringement of the right to privacy under Article 8(2) ECHR.[86]

On 11 May 2002, about two weeks after the Strasbourg ruling, Dianne Pretty died in a hospice near her home.

---

84 (2002) 35 EHRR 1, par. 54–56.

85 (2002) 35 EHRR 1, par. 65.

86 (2002) 35 EHRR 1, par. 76–78.

5.2. *HAAS V. SWITZERLAND*

In view of the earlier deliberations on Swiss law on assisted suicide the case concerning Swiss resident Ernst G. Haas deserves special attention.

Haas suffered, for about 20 years, from a severe bipolar affective disorder. As a result of this condition, he felt that he could no longer live in a dignified manner. After two suicide attempts, Haas decided to obtain sodium pentobarbital, which would enable him to end his life safely and with dignity. Since the substance is only available on prescription, he approached several psychiatrists to obtain it, but without success. Later, he approached various federal and cantonal authorities (Federal Departments of Justice and Public Health and the Department of Health of the Canton of Zurich), seeking permission to obtain sodium pentobarbital from a pharmacy without a prescription. In his petitions, Haas argued that under Article 8 ECHR, the State has a positive duty to facilitate suicide to be committed without the risk of failure and without pain. The authorities rejected his application and his appeal against this decision was declined by the Federal Department of the Interior and the Zurich Administrative Court. Haas finally appealed to the Federal Court, but did not succeed in his action. Among other things, the Court found that a distinction had to be made between the right to decide on one's own death – which was not at issue – and the right to commit suicide assisted by the State or a third party.

Before the Strasbourg judges Haas argued, relying on Article 8, that his right to end his life in a safe and dignified manner had been violated by Switzerland, due to the conditions that had to be met – and which he did not – to obtain sodium pentobarbital. The complaint was found admissible and the ECtHR handed down its judgment at the beginning of 2011.[87]

As in the *Pretty* case, the Court acknowledged that the right of a competent individual to decide how and when to end his life is one aspect of the right to respect for private life. However, in the ECtHR's view, the case of Haas concerned a different matter. While in the *Pretty* case the ECtHR ruled on whether the English penalisation of assisted suicide served a legitimate purpose and constituted a necessary infringement of the right to privacy under Article 8(2) ECHR, the *Haas* case concerned whether or not under Article 8 the State has the positive obligation to enable Haas to obtain, without a prescription, a substance enabling him to end his life without pain and without risk of failure. After noting that there is no consensus among the Member States of the Council of Europe as

87 Case *Haas c. Suisse*, Arrêt, 20 January 2011, Appl. no. 31322/07. The decision has only been published in French. For an English review of the case, see S.H.E. Harmon, N. Sethi, 'Preserving Life and Facilitating Death: What Role for Government after Haas v. Switzerland?', 18 *European Journal of Health Law* (2011)4; 355–364.

to the right of an individual to choose how and when to end his life, the ECtHR argued that the vast majority of Member States still tends to place more weight on the protection of an individual's life (Article 2) than on the right to end one's life (Article 8). Hence, the Court confirmed that States have a wide margin of discretion in this respect.

Against the background of the existing risk of abuse inherent in a system that facilitates assisted suicide, the Court agreed with the Swiss government's argument that the restriction on access to sodium pentobarbital aimed to protect health and public safety and to prevent crime. It also shared the Swiss Federal Court's view that the right to life obliged States to establish a procedure to ensure that a decision to end one's life reflects the involved person's free will. The ECtHR considered that the need for a prescription, issued on the basis of a full psychiatric report, constitutes a means of fulfilling that requirement. This regime, the Court asserted, is proportionate and justified, and also sustainable under Article 8(2) ECHR, while at the same time leaving room for choices concerning death.

Whether Haas had had effective access to a medical report allowing him to obtain the desired substance remained unsolved. Although Haas stated that he had no appropriate access to medical experts, which caused him to fail to meet the legal requirements to obtain sodium pentobarbital (some 170 psychiatrists he wrote to declined to help him), the Court was ultimately not convinced that Haas had been unable to find a psychiatrist willing to assist him. In view of all considerations, with regard to the margin of appreciation enjoyed by national authorities on this issue, the ECtHR concluded there had been no violation of Article 8.

5.3. *KOCH V. GERMANY*

A case showing similarities to *Haas v. Switzerland* emerged in Germany. Here, in 2002, Bettina Koch, a lawyer, became almost completely paralysed (total sensorimotor quadriplegia, C2) after falling at her doorstep. As a consequence, she was in need of artificial ventilation and constant care from a nursing staff. Without any prospect of recovery, she ultimately wished to end her undignified life by committing suicide. At the end of 2004, she applied to the Federal Institute for Drugs and Medical Devices in Germany for authorisation to obtain a lethal dose of sodium pentobarbital, enabling her to commit suicide at home. The Federal Institute refused to grant her the authorisation, for her wish to commit suicide was in conflict with the German Narcotics Act, which aims to secure the necessary medical care of the population. Ulrich Koch and his wife appealed against the decision, but the appeal was turned down. Finally, they left for Switzerland, where, on 12 February 2005, Bettina Koch committed suicide with assistance of Dignitas.

In June 2011 the ECtHR declared widower Koch's application admissible.[88] He complained that the refusal to grant his wife authorisation to obtain a lethal dose of medication infringed her rights under Article 8 ECHR, in particular, her right to a dignified death, as well as his own right to respect for private and family life, as he was forced to travel to Switzerland to enable his wife to commit suicide. Furthermore, Koch complained that the German courts violated his rights under Article 13 ECHR, by not allowing him to challenge the refusal of the Federal Institute to grant his wife the requested authorisation.

The ECtHR's ruling in this case is eagerly awaited, as Koch links the violation of his wife's right to a dignified death to Article 8 ECHR. It seems, however, that to actually have a right to a dignified death is something else than arguing that to exercise such a right falls within the scope of one's legally protected private life. In its decision confirming the earlier refusal to grant the requested authorisation, the Federal Institute expressed doubts as to whether an individual's right, approved by the State, to commit suicide could be derived from Article 8 ECHR. In any event, Article 8 could not be interpreted as imposing an obligation on the State to facilitate the act of suicide with narcotic drugs by granting authorisation to acquire the fatal dose of medication. Furthermore, a right to commit suicide would be inconsistent with the higher-ranking principle enshrined in Article 2, section 2 of the German Constitution, which contains the comprehensive obligation of the State to protect life, *inter alia* by refusing to grant authorisation to obtain a lethal dose of a drug for the purpose of committing suicide.

6. A HUMAN RIGHT TO DIE?

What is striking is the European Court's conclusion, expressed in the *Pretty* decision, that the right to life – at least the one laid down in Article 2(1) ECHR – does not involve the diametrically opposite right, a right to die, nor does it provide an individual entitlement to choose death rather than life. Consequently, the Court has ruled that no right to die at the hand of a third person or someone acting on public authority can be derived from this treaty provision. What is interesting, though, is that in the literature a right to die (with dignity) has

88 *Koch v. Germany* (Appl. no. 497/09) Admissibility Decision of 10 June 2011. Hearing on 23 November 2010 (no. 497/09).

regularly been advocated,[89] albeit mainly in a moral sense.[90] However, in countries such as Germany, Ireland, Greece, Spain, Sweden, Switzerland and Canada, where human dignity is an accepted constitutional notion, the argument even has a special weight.[91] An appropriate question therefore is: were the Strasbourg judges right to dismiss Pretty's acclaimed right to die?

It is beyond dispute that Pretty's position was all but enviable. Striking, though, was the fact that no physician was involved in the realisation of her intended death; from a human rights perspective, a rather crucial element in this case, one might add. In very few countries the legal authorities would have been willing to grant Pretty's request for immunity from prosecution of her non-medically trained husband, even before the life-ending act was performed. The Dutch authorities, for instance, probably would have dismissed her request too, as the Dutch Euthanasia Act – similar to the Belgian and Luxemburg[92] ones – explicitly links the impunity of death on request to the medical background of the offender. Yet, if Pretty had opted for the assisted suicide in Switzerland, there was a chance she would have achieved the realisation of her final wish.

However much one might sympathise with the idea of a right to die (and I believe there are some convincing arguments for doing so), the poor quality of Pretty's plea to respect this right undermined her prospects of persuading the Strasbourg judges. Another argumentative approach probably would have increased her chances of a ruling in her favour. In my opinion, it is clear that the refusal to grant the requested immunity can hardly be considered a violation of Article 2 ECHR. This follows already from the invoked right's nature. An argument for recognising the right to one's own death as a variation of the right to life presumes an understanding of a State Party's specific obligations in respect of the legal protection of the right to life. The question is: how is a State Party to give shape to these obligations when it would also recognise the legal right to die? After all, these obligations would not cease to exist if Article 2 included this right. Obviously, it means that a State Party would be permitted to

---

89 See A. Meisel, K.L. Cerminara, *The Right to Die: The Law of End-of-Life Decision making*, third edition, New York: Aspen Publ., 2004, par. 1.01, par. 2-01 – 2.03 and 2.06. Both authors derive the right to one's own death, on the basis of extensive American jurisprudence in this area, from an individual's right to refuse treatment. The latter right is subsequently based on recognition of the right to personal autonomy. Burkart argues that the right to one's own death even includes the right to be killed. See M. Burkart, *Das Recht, in Würde zu sterben – Ein Menschenrecht. Eine verfassungsrechtliche Studie zur Frage der menschwürdigen Grenze zwischen Leben und Tod*, Zürich: Schultes Polygraphischer Verlag, 1983, pp. 90–92.

90 National "Pro-choice" associations usually argue such a position. A well-known example of this in the USA is D. Humphry, A. Wicket, *A Right to Die, Understanding euthanasia*, New York/Sydney: Harper Collins, 1986, pp. 241–293.

91 A timeless work in this matter is P. Tiedemann, *Menschenwürde als Rechtsbegriff.* Eine philosophische Klärung, Berliner Wissenschafts-Verlag, 2010. Regarding the meaning of the legal concept of human dignity in end-of-life issues in healthcare, see pp. 423–435.

92 See note 37.

deviate from some of these obligations under strict conditions. Recognition, even protection of the right to die, could then require that the national legislature codifies the specific circumstances inextricably linked to lifting the legal protection of a person's right to life, in consequence of which a third person who assists in dying would commit no crime. Strictly speaking, however, it is doubtful whether Pretty's assumed right to die was violated by the refusal to grant the requested immunity from prosecution of her husband. Under English law, the refusal would merely have led to (a reasonable expectation of) criminal charges against Pretty's husband. All things considered, Pretty actually claimed the right to an assisted death without legal consequences for the non-medical assistant, rather than the right to die. Therefore, it is questionable why her husband's willingness to let Pretty exercise her right to die would provide a foundation for his impunity. Lastly, Pretty failed to pay attention to the fact that her husband was no physician, not even in an attempt to tone down the need to comply with this premise – which is, nonetheless, the current procedure in the countries to which Pretty referred.

Crucial is the Strasbourg Court's view that Article 2 ECHR cannot (textually) be interpreted as a negotiable right diametrically opposite to the right to life. The rationale behind this strict maintenance of Article 2 ECHR with regard to a chosen death does not seem to come merely from the need to oppose the risk of abuse of authority in respect of vulnerable persons. In a sense, the ECtHR's conclusion also points at a kind of human rights based imperative as to the way terminally ill or dying persons should deal with their most fundamental right. A person who grants a third person's request to die does not just seem to act imputably because he might end this person's life for unsound reasons, he also cooperates in fulfilling a wish which is considered reprehensible from a human rights perspective. This impression is enforced by the ECtHR's view that, on the basis of Article 2, no person has a legitimate claim to die by a third person[93] or someone acting on public authority. Through its reading of Article 2 the ECtHR indeed made a distinction between a human rights based permissibility of a specific, personally preferred exercise of the right to life on the one hand, and the legal assessment of termination of life by a third person, either a layperson or a physician, on the other hand. The Court's interpretation of Article 2 actually imposes limits to the individual's freedom to exercise the right to life to his own liking, which also restricts the impunity of every behaviour regarded as falling under Article 8(1) ECHR. Pretty's claim that her right to life includes a right to die exceeded this boundary. Correct, but rather awkward is that Pretty was yet free to refuse any life-sustaining measures; in the opinion of the ECtHR,

93 Besides, it is unclear whether the wording 'third person' also includes a physician. All in all, the ECtHR's ruling does not explicitly exclude this possibility.

probably a more appropriate way to reluctantly exercise one's right to life.[94] Moreover, nobody contested her freedom to be killed by her husband. This summarises the basic legal issue in the *Pretty* case: was the United Kingdom obliged to allow Dianne Pretty's husband, with impunity, to help his wife to die in order to respect her acclaimed negative variation of her right to life?[95] Arguably, this was not an appropriate starting point for a successful plea for recognition of a human right to die.

Still, an unanswered question is whether Pretty would have been more successful had she linked her plea for recognition of her right to die to Article 8 ECHR. To me, it would seem rather inconsistent if the ECtHR refuses to recognise a right to die under Article 2 ECHR due to substantial objections, but acknowledges such a right under Article 8. The latter would inevitably have an impact on the obligations of States Parties under Article 2. To outline these obligations is a challenge indeed.

In my view, to recognise one's personal freedom to decide when and how your life will end does not involve an enforceable legal duty to others – the State as well as private parties – to facilitate one's ultimate exercise of that freedom. However, in order to provide room for well-considered and careful life-ending aid in exceptional cases, the State should adopt strict and clear legislation which offers a solution to those without prospect, yet obstructs those who are not concerned.

7. FINAL REMARKS

The aim of this chapter was to go into the meaning of a human rights approach for the legal admissibility of end-of-life matters in medical care, especially those concerning death at request of the person concerned. Even though the relevance of such an approach is hardly disputed, its specific benefit for national contemplations on this matter is not always clear. In part, this originates from the rather vague wording of treaty provisions, the difficulty of interpreting them in accordance with current notions in a society, and maybe even from a lack of visionary attitude in Strasbourg and at the UN level.

---

94 Benatar has argued that in order to conclude that particular end-of-life decisions are not contrary to the right to life, recognition of a right to die is not necessary. See D. Benatar, 'Assisted Suicide, Voluntary Euthanasia and the Right to Life', in J. Yorke (ed.): *The Right to life and the Value of Life, Orientations in Law, Politics and Ethics*, Farnham/Burlington: Ashgate, 2010, pp. 291–310.

95 Formally, a terminally ill or dying person's wish to die, as such, is no legal justification to grant such a wish, nor is this sufficient for impunity of the person who complies with this request. See Recommendation 1418 (1999). *Protection of the human rights and dignity of the terminally ill and the dying.* Text adopted by the Assembly on 25 June 1999 (24th Sitting). Official Gazette of the Council of Europe – June 1999.

There is a strange dichotomy to this human rights approach. As I stated before, this approach is often a starting point for reflection on the permissibility of end-of-life decisions. At the same time, the rulings of the ECtHR have a far-reaching effect on the legal space States are willing to provide to people who believe that to depart from this life is a final relief. In a way, it takes courage to issue specific legislation on this matter, as it will surely attract criticism. It remains to be seen whether the regulations in the Netherlands, Belgium and Luxemburg will stand firm if they are challenged in Strasbourg. While in *Haas v. Switzerland* the Swiss regime on assisted suicide was not overthrown, the case of *Koch v Germany* is expected to provide definite clues on the relationship between a right to die and Article 8 ECHR. At the time it is, rather, the absence of adequate regulations within many European jurisdictions providing for a strictly conditioned tolerance regarding life-ending autonomy that seems to generate feelings of discontent.

PART III

VULNERABLE GROUPS, HEALTH INEQUALITIES, AND THE SOCIAL DETERMINANTS OF HEALTH

CHAPTER 7

HEALTH INEQUALITIES AND THE SOCIAL DETERMINANTS OF HEALTH

Brigit TOEBES, Aart HENDRIKS and Karien STRONKS*

1. INTRODUCTION

There is a vast amount of research indicating that there are wide health inequalities between and within countries, including European countries. An extensive study by Mackenbach *et al.* focusing on 22 European countries demonstrates that in all countries under scrutiny the rates of death and poorer self-assessment of health are substantially higher in groups of lower socioeconomic status.[1] Responding to these widening inequalities, the World Health Organization (WHO) established the Commission on the Social Determinants of Health (CSDH, 2005) to provide advice on how to reduce them.[2] The CSDH's final report was published in August 2008. In this report it was asserted that one needs to go beyond the contemporary concentration on the immediate causes of diseases and focus instead on the 'causes of the causes': the fundamental structures of social hierarchy and socially determined conditions that determine how people live, work, are raised and educated, which subsequently determine people's state of health.[3] The CSDH concluded that

* This chapter is based on a more elaborate paper that we prepared for the WHO on the links between health inequalities, the social determinants of health and human rights (2011).

1 Johan P. Mackenbach *et al*, 'Socioeconomic Inequalities in Health in 22 European Countries', *The New England Journal of Medicine*', June 5, 2008; 358: 2468–81. The authors of this study added that the magnitude of the inequalities was much larger in some countries than in others: small in some southern European countries, and very large in most countries in the eastern and Baltic regions.

2 See, also, www.who.int/social_determinants/en/, accessed October 2011.

3 World Health Organization/Commission on the Social Determinants of Health (chaired by Sir Michael Marmot), *Closing the gap in a generation*, Health equity through action on the social determinants of health, WHO 2008, p. 42, available at www.who.int/social_determinants/thecommission/finalreport/en/index.html, accessed October 2011. See, also, 'The Marmot Review' which assesses health inequalities in England post 2010, available at www.marmotreview.org/AssetLibrary/pdfs/Reports/FairSocietyHealthyLives.pdf, accessed October 2011.

health inequities arise because of the unequal distribution of power, income, goods, and services, and because of the circumstances in which people live, including their access to healthcare, education, their conditions of work and leisure, their homes, and communities.[4] Based on these findings, the CSDH, in its report, firmly concluded that such health inequities are a matter of social justice:

> 'Reducing health inequities is, for the Commission on Social Determinants of Health [...], an ethical imperative. Social injustice is killing people on a grand scale.' (p. 10)

In its report, the CSDPH made three overarching recommendations for all actors to reduce health inequities: 1) to improve daily living conditions; 2) to tackle the inequitable distribution of power, money, and resources; and 3) to measure and understand the problem and assess the impact of action. Within these areas of action the Commission made further recommendations in twelve areas (see Box 1):

Box 1. The CDSH objectives (WHO 2008)

1) 'improve daily living conditions'	1) early childhood development and education 2) healthy places – the living environment 3) fair employment and decent work 4) social protection across the life course 5) universal healthcare
2) 'tackle the inequitable distribution of power, money, and resources'	6) health equity in all policies 7) fair financing 8) market responsibility 9) gender equity 10) political empowerment 11) good global governance
3) 'measure and understand the problem and assess the impact of action'	12) knowledge, monitoring, and skills

As mentioned above, the CSDH has argued that such health inequalities are matters of social injustice. This raises the question of whether these are also human rights issues. One year before this report came out the CSDH's Secretariat

4 World Health Organization/Commission on the Social Determinants of Health (chaired by Sir Michael Marmot), *Closing the gap in a generation*, Health equity through action on the social determinants of health, WHO 2008. See, also, 'Fair Society, Healthy Lives' (the 'Marmot Review'), which assesses health inequalities in England post 2010, available at www.marmotreview.org/AssetLibrary/pdfs/Reports/FairSocietyHealthyLives.pdf, accessed October 2011.

recommended that the CSCH adopt an international human rights framework within which to advance towards health equity through action on the social determinants of health. The framework document explained:

> 'Human rights offer more than a conceptual armature connecting health, social conditions and broad governance principles, however. Rights concepts and standards provide an instrument for turning diffuse social demand into focused legal and political claims, as well as a set of criteria by which to evaluate the performance of political authorities in promoting people's wellbeing and creating conditions for equitable enjoyment of the fruits of development.'[5]

In this chapter we take as a starting point that the social determinants are matters of human rights. We will look at how the human rights framework can be used to achieve the CSDP objectives. For this, we will establish the normative links between the CSDP's findings and the human rights framework (Sections 2–4). Subsequently, in Section 5, we will focus on the question of how states can be held accountable for human rights violations – in terms of not fulfilling their obligations – in connection with the social determinants of health. For an outline of the human rights framework, reference is made to Chapter 3 of this book.

2. THE HUMAN RIGHTS FRAMEWORK

As was explained in Chapter 3, an important landmark for the definition of the right to health was the adoption of General Comment No. 14 of the UN Committee on Economic, Social and Cultural Rights, which outlines the framework of the 'right to the highest attainable standard of health' in Article 12 ICESCR. This document accurately describes the meaning and implications of the right to health. It is, therefore, worthwhile to take this document as a starting point of a human rights analysis in relation to the social determinants of health. Although the document is not legally binding, it is an authoritative source that gives a comprehensive explanation of the meaning and implications of the right to health in Article 12 ICESCR.[6] As was also explained in Chapter 3, General Comment No. 14 takes a broad approach to the definition of health as a human right. In paragraph 4, it recognises that the broad scope of the right to health:

5 CSDH, (secretariat, Orielle Solar and Alec Irwin), *A Conceptual Framework for Action on the Social Determinants of Health*, draft April 2007, available at www.who.int/social_determinants/resources/csdh_framework_action_05_07.pdf, accessed October 2011.

6 UN Committee on Economic, Social and Cultural Rights (CESCR), General Comment No. 14 on the Right to the Highest Attainable Standard of Health, UN Doc. E/C.12/2000/4, 11 August 2000, available at www.un.org/en/rights/, accessed October 2011.

> '(...) "the highest attainable standard of physical and mental health" is not confined to the right to health care. On the contrary, the drafting history and the express wording of article 12.2 acknowledge that the right to health embraces a wide range of socio-economic factors that promote conditions in which people can lead a healthy life, and extends to the underlying determinants of health, such as food and nutrition, housing, access to safe and potable water and adequate sanitation, safe and healthy working conditions, and a healthy environment.'

This understanding of the right to health, which builds on the WHO's broad definition of health, as laid down in its Constitution (1946), explicitly recognises that 'underlying determinants of health' are as important for people's health as access to healthcare services. This broad approach to a right to health is very much in line with the current findings about the 'social determinants of health', i.e. that socioeconomic conditions are often decisive for people's health. As was also discussed in Chapter 3, the right to health in the European Social Charter (ESC) is interpreted in a similar broad fashion. In an explanatory document the Secretariat of the ESC states that Article 11 covers numerous issues relating to public health, such as food safety, protection of the environment, vaccination programmes and alcoholism (Secretariat to the ESC), an approach which is also reflected by the case law of the European Committee of Social Rights.[7]

Furthermore, it was explained in Chapter 3 that the right to health does not stand alone, but is reinforced and supported by several other rights. General Comment No. 14 affirms in paragraph 3 that:

> 'the right to health is closely related to and dependent upon the realisation of other human rights, as contained in the International Bill of Rights, including the rights to food, housing, work, education, human dignity, life, non-discrimination, equality, the prohibition against torture, privacy, access to information, and the freedoms of association, assembly and movement.'

These and other rights and freedoms address integral components of the right to health. Some of the most prominent rights linked to health are the rights to life, an adequate standard of living, information and participation, social security, food, housing, property, education, and employment (see, also, the box in Chapter 3). Such rights imply legal obligations to ensure access to, *inter alia*, housing, a safe and clean living environment, education and social protection. In conjunction with the right to health, these rights have the potential to address poor housing conditions, the lack of access to proper education and the state of

---

7 Secretariat of the ESC, *The right to health and the European Social Charter*, March 2009, available at www.coe.int/T/DGHL/Monitoring/SocialCharter/Theme%20factsheets/FactsheetHealth_en.pdf, accessed November 2011. The document indicates that it is not binding on the European Committee of Social Rights.

people's neighbourhoods and their workplaces. For example, Braveman emphasises the connections between the rights to a standard of living and education on the one hand, and health, on the other.[8] Access to general schooling appears to be a crucial social determinant of health. Braveman argues, in line with Amartya Sen's 'capabilities' approach, that education can be seen as an essential capability or factor for achieving one's health potential.[9] Article 13(1) ICESCR affirms that education shall 'enable all persons to participate effectively in society'.

3. HUMAN RIGHTS AND THE SOCIAL DETERMINANTS OF HEALTH

A key question is whether this broad underpinning of the right to health, in conjunction with the other related rights, has the potential to offer a framework for addressing the social determinants of health inequalities. Hunt asserts that there are multiple, dense connections between social determinants and human rights.[10] He states that:

> 'There is considerable congruity between the Commission's mandate and the "underlying determinants of health" dimension of the right to health, as well as other interconnected human rights such as adequate housing, food and water. In other words, national and international human rights law informs and reinforces the Commission's mandate.'[11]

What we need to find out more precisely is whether the mentioned 'underlying determinants of health' under the right to health, in conjunction with the other related rights, are congruent with the 'social determinants of health', as outlined in the CSDH report. As such, we can ascertain the added value of the human rights approach when addressing the social determinants of health. Below, a number of core notions from General Comment No. 14 are discussed, so as to explore how we can use these as tools to address the social determinants of health.

---

8 Paula Braveman, 'Social conditions, health equity, and human rights', *Health and Human Rights*, Vol 12, No 2 (2010), available at www.hhrjournal.org/index.php/hhr/article/view/367/563, p. 8.

9 Braveman, 2010, p. 8.

10 Paul Hunt, 'Missed opportunities: Human rights and the Commission on Social Determinants of Health', *Global Health Promotion* 16/1 Supp (2009), p. 36.

11 Paul Hunt, UN Special Rapporteur on the right of everyone to the enjoyment of the highest attainable standard of physical and mental health, *The right of everyone to the enjoyment of the highest attainable standard of physical and mental health*, UN Doc. A/60/348, 12 September 2005, paragraph 7, available at www.essex.ac.uk/human_rights_centre/research/rth/docs/GA2005.pdf, accessed February 2012.

3.1. AVAILABILITY, ACCESSIBILITY, ACCEPTABILITY, QUALITY, ACCOUNTABILITY AND PARTICIPATION: 'AAAQ-AP'

As was also discussed in Chapter 3, paragraph 12 of General Comment No. 14 enumerates a set of principles that relate to the provision of health-related services. Similar principles can be found in the General Comments on the right to food, housing, and education, also adopted by the UN Committee on Economic, Social and Cultural Rights.[12] This set of principles underlying the right to health is widely referred to as 'AAAQ' – availability, accessibility, acceptability and quality. Accessibility has four overlapping dimensions: *non-discrimination, physical accessibility, economic accessibility,* and *information accessibility.*

While at first sight this set of principles seems very much directed to health*care* settings, we may presume that the 'AAAQ', or a set of similar principles, relates very much to all the determinants of health, and that all services relating to the determinants of health should meet such conditions. Firstly, General Comment No. 14 explicitly states that these principles also address the determinants of health (paragraph 12). This means, for example, that health-related information will have to be provided on the basis of the principle of non-discrimination, while occupational health facilities must be accessible and affordable to everyone. A second reason to presume that these principles relate to all the determinants of health is that these principles are common to many of the other General Comments.[13] For example, education has to be 'available, accessible, acceptable and adaptable.'[14]

In addition to the above-mentioned principles, it is increasingly recognised that the principles of 'accountability' and 'participation' are important conditions for realising the right to health. Accountability means holding all responsible actors accountable for human rights violations. Accountability for human rights is not only about judicial accountability or 'naming and shaming'. In a comprehensive report, Potts describes accountability for the right to health as 'the process that requires government to show, explain and justify how it has discharged its obligations regarding the right to the highest attainable standard of health.'[15]

---

12 The text of these documents can be found on www2.ohchr.org/english/bodies/cescr/comments.htm, accessed November 2011.

13 Respectively, UN General Comments Nos. 4, 12, 13, and 15, see www2.ohchr.org/english/bodies/cescr/comments.htm, accessed October 2011.

14 General Comment 13 on the right to education, paragraph 6.

15 Helen Potts, *Participation and the Right to the Highest Attainable Standard of Health*, and *Accountability and the Right to the Highest Attainable Standard of Health*, University of Essex Human Rights Centre/Open Society Institute, 2008, available at www.essex.ac.uk/human_rights_centre/research/rth/projects.aspx, accessed October 2011, p. 13.

Potts distinguishes between five forms of accountability: judicial (judicial review, constitutional redress, public interest litigation), quasi-judicial (national human rights institutions, regional and international human rights treaty bodies), administrative (e.g. human rights impact assessments), political (e.g. parliamentary bodies), and social accountability (NGOs, the media). As such, accountability can be a broad process involving various stakeholders in the health sector and beyond. As is stressed by Yamin, legal accountability or litigation is very much intertwined with the other, more political strategies.[16] This means, for example, that court cases are increasingly used to generate political change. Altogether, it is important to trace (judicial and non-judicial) cases in which human rights law is successfully employed to address the social determinants of health.

The principle of *participation*, secondly, is essential for giving the population as a whole, as well as vulnerable population groups, a voice in addressing their specific health vulnerabilities. Potts gives various interesting examples of how the public can have a say in important decisions in the health decision-making process: regional and national conferences, permanent or time bound forums, local health committees or teams, focus groups and individual interviews, citizens' jury's/planning cells, public meetings, budgetary oversight, and local committee selections.[17] Potts stresses that an important purpose of participation in the context of the right to health is to recognise and respect difference and diversity within the population, and to ensure inclusiveness in the development of health policy.[18] This is also important in the context of health inequalities: a participatory decision-making process can bring the different health inequalities and the underlying causes to the table.

3.2. VULNERABLE GROUPS AND NON-DISCRIMINATION

General Comment No. 14 pays specific attention to the position of vulnerable groups. It emphasises, in paragraph 19, that states have a special obligation to provide those who do not have sufficient means with the necessary health insurance and healthcare facilities, and to prevent any discrimination on internationally prohibited grounds in the provision of healthcare and health services. It mentions the following vulnerable groups: women, children and adolescents, older persons, persons with disabilities, and indigenous peoples. It is perhaps somewhat limiting that only some vulnerable groups are mentioned, but by placing emphasis on the need to enhance access to health services for

---

16 Yamin, 'Beyond compassion: The central role of accountability in applying a human rights framework to health', *Health and Human Rights*, Vol. 12, No. 2 (2010), available at www.hhrjournal.org/index.php/hhr/article/view/78/163, accessed October 2011, p. 2.

17 Potts, 2010, p. 20.

18 Potts, 2010, p. 20.

disadvantaged individuals, the General Comment clearly opens the door to addressing health inequalities.

There are, of course, other human rights treaties that pay attention to specific vulnerable groups, such as CEDAW (women), CRC, (children), CRPD (people with disabilities), and MWC (migrant workers). These treaties spell out concrete state obligations in the areas of health, education, social security and employment that fall under the social determinants of health. The emphasis on vulnerable groups is a strength of human rights law, especially when it comes to accountability for human rights violations. However, addressing the needs of vulnerable population groups does not fully cover the broad range of problems that arise under the social determinants of health. Inequalities in health are not confined to poor health among the most deprived. The 'Marmot Review' refers to this notion as 'proportionate universalism':

> 'Focusing solely on the most disadvantaged will not reduce health inequalities sufficiently. To reduce the steepness of the social gradient in health, actions must be universal, but with a scale and intensity that is proportionate to the level of disadvantage. We call this proportionate universalism.'[19]

In other words, while social determinants affect the poorest the most, they also affect everyone in society. As such, when addressing the social determinants of health we must not solely focus on specific 'vulnerable groups', but must also address the population at large.

3.3. DEFINITION OF LEGAL STATE OBLIGATIONS

Another important concept that is elaborated upon in General Comment No. 14 concerns the distinction between three types of state obligations, as was also discussed in Chapter 3. General Comment 14 explains that the right to health, like all human rights, imposes three types or levels of obligations on States Parties: the obligations 'to respect', 'to protect', and 'to fulfil'. This is a useful tool for identifying the legal obligations of states in relation to a right to health.

The obligation to respect is a negative state obligation and requires states to refrain from interfering directly or indirectly with the enjoyment of the right to health. When it comes to the underlying determinants of health, this implies a duty on the part of governments to refrain from denying or limiting equal access to all health-related services, as well as abstaining from enforcing discriminatory practices as a state policy in this regard (General Comment No. 14, paragraph 34).

19 Marmot Review, 2008, pp. 17 and 42.

The obligations to protect and to fulfil are positive state obligations, requiring states to provide certain basic social conditions. This includes measures that prevent third parties from interfering with Article 12 ICESCR guarantees (protect), and to adopt appropriate legislative, administrative, budgetary, judicial, promotional and other measures with a view to the full realisation of the right to health (fulfil). The obligation to protect is important when tackling the role of private industry in relation to the social determinants: there is a clear role for governments to regulate private industry so as to ensure that they do not market unhealthy products (see also below). In turn, the obligation to fulfil is about ensuring access to not only access to health services, but also to the underlying determinants of health. Reading the right to health in conjunction with the other economic and social rights, it means an obligation to ensure access to early childhood services and conditions including education, housing, employment, and a clean environment.

3.4. PROGRESSIVE REALISATION AND CORE OBLIGATIONS

The right to health, like all human rights, is subject to resource availability, meaning that rich countries can do more than poor ones. The right to health is therefore subject to 'progressive realisation', meaning that governments are required to progressively work towards its realisation (Article 2-1 ICESCR). States are to take steps 'to the maximum of their available resources'. Progressive realisation also means that retrogressive measures are not justified.[20] In all cases, a distinction should be made between 'inability' to realise – e.g. due to a natural disaster or financial constraints – and 'unwillingness'. The latter is particularly problematic from a human rights perspective.

To ensure that there is a basic or minimum level of service provision, below which no government should fall, General Comment No. 14 outlines, in paragraphs 43–44, a number of 'core obligations' which states have to meet under all circumstances. For the definition of these core obligations, General Comment No. 14 draws on the Programme of Action of the International Conference on Population and Development (UNDP 1994), and the Primary Health Care Strategy, as set out in the Alma-Ata Declaration (WHO 1978). Among the core obligations are a number of services that address the so-called 'underlying determinants of health': minimum essential food, basic shelter,

[20] The European Committee of Social Rights has dealt with the matter of retrogressive measures on several occasions. In a decision against Italy about the housing conditions of the Roma, it used the term 'aggravated violation' to refer to a situation in which the human rights violation had worsened (European Committee of Social Rights, *Centre on Housing Rights and Evictions (COHRE) v. Italy*, Complaint No. 58/2009, decision on the merits of 6 July 2010, paragraph 76).

housing and sanitation, child healthcare, and education and access to information concerning the main health problems. This means that irrespective of a state's available resources, based on the right to health, it has to guarantee minimum essential food, basic shelter and education concerning the main health problems. This approach affirms the importance of such conditions for health, in addition to health*care*, and strengthens the notion that states can be held accountable for guaranteeing such conditions under the right to health.

3.5. INDICATORS AND BENCHMARKS

A possible way to monitor the right to health is through the use of indicators and benchmarks. Indicators are tools to indicate the situation at a particular point in time, or, for example, the maternal mortality rate. Benchmarks are self-set goals or targets to be achieved at some future date, e.g. the reduction of the maternal mortality rate by half by 2020.[21] In order to give full expression to the human rights perspective in such an assessment, it is important that these indicators be disaggregated by sex, urban/rural, and/or socioeconomic or ethnic group, or any other category that may reveal meaningful inequalities. These indicators could then function as the key indicators on the basis of which national benchmarks could be further developed. In this process it is important to guarantee respect for the privacy of individuals, while the results of such measurements should not lead to the stigmatisation and discrimination of vulnerable population groups.

In a report of 2008, the Officer of the High Commissioner for Human Rights of the United Nations distinguished between structural, process and outcome indicators for each human right.[22] It is encouraging to note that the report contained a large proportion of the indicators for the right to health focus on the underlying determinants for health: child health and nutrition, breastfeeding, access to safe drinking water and sanitation, populations living near hazardous conditions, road safety, abuse of substances, occupational deaths, injuries, and diseases. A number of social conditions that are important in Europe, including the lifestyle-related issues were, however, not mentioned: alcohol abuse, the prevalence of smoking, food consumption and obesity, and unhealthy lifestyles more generally. In addition, these indicators do not recognise the existence of the mentioned 'causes of the causes' of health, such as the structure of society,

21 Judith Asher, *The Right to Health: A Resource Manual for NGOs*, 2004, available at http://shr.aaas.org/pubs/rt_health/rt_health_manual.pdf, p. 89, accessed October 2011.

22 Office of the United Nations High Commissioner for Human Rights (OHCHR), *Report on Indicators for Promoting and Monitoring the Implementation of Human Rights*, UN Doc. HRI/MC/2008/3, 6 June 2008, available at www2.ohchr.org/english/issues/indicators/docs/HRI.MC.2008.3_en.pdf, accessed October 2011.

income inequality, and social and cultural norms and values. The indicators developed for the right to food clearly reflect the same broad, yet globally oriented, approach.

Altogether, the human rights framework lacks a European-specific set of indicators that is sufficiently geared towards addressing the social determinants of health. Some inspiration for this can be drawn from Fukuda-Parr, who distinguishes between indicators for low and middle-income countries on the one hand, and indicators for high-income countries in relation to a set of economic and social rights, on the other.[23] Furthermore, we may draw from the 'Marmot Review', which analysed health inequalities in England. This report presented 12 health indicators:

1) death rates from cancer and heart disease;
2) teenage conception rate;
3) road accident casualty rates in disadvantaged communities;
4) numbers of primary care professionals;
5) uptake of flu vaccinations;
6) smoking among manual occupation groups and among pregnant women;
7) educational attainment;
8) consumption of fruit and vegetables;
9) proportion of the population living in non-decent housing;
10) physical education and school sport;
11) children in poverty; and
12) homeless families living in temporary accommodation.[24]

The human rights framework could consider using a similar set of indicators to monitor compliance with the state's duty to ensure adequate 'social determinants of health' in Europe. It should, of course, be taken into account here that there are also considerable variations between the European nations.

3.6. OBLIGATIONS OF NON-STATE ACTORS

States, as the actors that have ratified the human rights treaties, bear primary responsibility for international human rights law. As was mentioned above, they have so-called duties to 'protect' right holders against the acts of private industry. In addition to this, it is increasingly argued that non-state actors bear a certain

23 Sakiko Fukuda-Parr, 'Measuring the Progressive Realization of Human Rights Obligations: An Index of Economic and Social Rights Fulfillment', *University of Connecticut Department of Economics Working Paper Series*. Working Paper 2008–22, August 2008, at p. 10, available at http://digitalcommons.uconn.edu/cgi/viewcontent.cgi?article=1361&context=econ_wpapers&sei- redir=1&referer, accessed October 2011.

24 Marmot Review, 2010, p. 85.

derived or indirect responsibility under human rights law.[25] To underline this responsibility, reference is often made to the preamble of the Universal Declaration of Human Rights (UDHR), which refers to the human rights responsibilities of 'every individual and every organ of society'. As such, while states bear primary responsibility for the realisation of the right to health, the fulfilment of the right to health requires a multi-stakeholder approach, where all actors, including governments, international organisations, professional associations, civil society organisations, and the business sector, each play their role. This is also confirmed in General Comment No. 14 in paragraph 42:

> 'While only States are parties to the Covenant and thus ultimately accountable for compliance with it, all members of society – individuals, including health professionals, families, local communities, intergovernmental and non-governmental organizations, as well as the private business sector – have responsibilities regarding the realization of the right to health (...).'

This is an important starting point for the further definition of obligations, be they legal or moral in character, of non-state actors in relation to the social determinants of health. The business sector plays a particularly important role when it comes to the production and marketing of (un)healthy products, for example, the sale of cigarettes. Generally, all non-state actors should be aware of the fact that people can be vulnerable when it comes to protecting their health, and that some (especially children) are not always able to protect themselves.

4. LINKING THE RIGHTS FRAMEWORK WITH THE CSDH GOALS ON THE SOCIAL DETERMINANTS

Above, the framework of the right to health and the other related rights was analysed and an attempt was made to discuss how this framework could be used as a tool for holding governments and other actors to account for addressing the social determinants of health. Based on these links, we can reinforce the claims under the CSDH with reference to the mentioned human rights norms. For example, we can affirm the state's duty to offer social protection with reference to the legal rights under Article 9 ICESCR (right to social security) and the other mentioned norms. More research is needed to more precisely link the legal state obligations to the CSDH goals, and to find out whether they are fully covered by the legal obligations.[26] It will emerge that many goals are fully covered by the legal obligations (e.g. primary and secondary education and quality healthcare services), yet that some other aspects are not fully covered (e.g. cross-government

25 *Inter alia*, Nicola Jägers, *Corporate human rights obligations; in search of accountability?*, Intersentia: Antwerp-Oxford-New York, 2002.

26 For a more precise overview see Toebes, Hendriks and Stonks, 2011 (see note 1).

action on the social determinants, and investments in generating and sharing evidence on social determinants).

Altogether, the current human rights framework offers a legal basis for addressing several of the 'causes of the causes', such as education and working conditions. However, it does not fully recognise that health is also determined by societal structures, and the way we are raised, educated, work, and relate to one another. In a similar vein, Chapman argues that the human rights approach insufficiently considers the role of determinants as factors that determine the health status and outcomes of individuals and communities.[27] Greater attention needs to be paid by the human rights community to how people's living conditions shape their health.[28] As such, while the 'underlying determinants of health' cover many of the issues that are mentioned in the CSDH report, some further sophistication of the 'underlying determinants' is needed to equip this framework fully for this task. The human rights framework needs to be inspired and fortified by the public health and epidemiological frameworks, which give evidence of a more thorough understanding of what causes health, for example, when it comes to the development of indicators. These areas are more refined because they base their findings on empirical research, while taking into account cumulative effects and interrelationships between different categories of determinants. Altogether, a process of cross-fertilisation between the areas of human rights and public health/epidemiology is needed to equip the human rights framework for addressing the social determinants of health, and to help health and social policy makers and planners to use human rights law as a tool to address the social determinants of health inequalities.

5. TOWARDS ACCOUNTABILITY FOR THE SOCIAL DETERMINANTS OF HEALTH

Having established the normative links between human rights and the social determinants of health, we need to address the question how human rights law can be used to hold states and other actors accountable for failing to ensure the social determinants of health.[29] Above, it was explained that 'accountability' for human rights violations is a key component of the human rights framework. It was also asserted that judicial or quasi-judicial procedures are not the only

27 Chapman (2010) 'The social determinants of health, health equity, and human rights', *Health and Human Rights*, Vol. 12, No 2 (2010), p. 4, available at www.hhrjournal.org/index.php/hhr/article/view/366/560, accessed October 2011.

28 Chapman, 2010, p. 4.

29 See, also, Alicia Ely Yamin, 'Beyond compassion: The central role of accountability in applying a human rights framework to health', *Health and Human Rights*, Vol. 12, No. 2 (2010), available at www.hhrjournal.org/index.php/hhr/article/view/78/163, accessed November 2011.

means for generating accountability for human rights violations. As is also argued by Potts, accountability can be a broad process, also involving administrative (e.g. human rights impact assessments), political (parliamentary debates) and social (NGOs) actions to generate attention for a failure to improve the social determinants of health.[30]

By looking at existing examples of cases in which the social determinants of health inequalities were addressed in terms of human rights, we can learn how we can successfully generate accountability for these matters. For this, we can look at the practices of judicial and quasi-judicial bodies at national and international levels, but also at the activities of national ombudsmen, parliamentary bodies, and civil society. It should be noted here that particularly in Europe, such examples are scarce. This may partly be due to a lack of knowledge about the social determinants of health, and about how these affect health, and how they can be framed in terms of human rights. More generally, domestic courts tend to be reluctant to invoke economic, social and cultural rights. Also, in the political arena 'human rights' are not always warmly received.

However, some promising examples are worth mentioning. In Chapters 1 and 3, the case law of the European Committee of Social Rights was discussed. The decisions of this Committee address several aspects of the social determinants of health, including social exclusion, lack of access to housing and social assistance, and environmental pollution.[31] Furthermore, there are some examples of national court cases that implicitly address the social determinants of health, which may give further inspiration for addressing such matters.[32] The social determinants have, to some extent, also been addressed by national ombudsmen and civil society organisations.[33]

---

30 Helen Potts, *Accountability and the Right to the Highest Attainable Standard of Health*, University of Essex Human Rights Centre/Open Society Institute, 2008, available at www.essex.ac.uk/human_rights_centre/research/rth/projects.aspx, accessed October 2011.

31 For an overview of the complaints and decisions, see www.coe.int/t/dghl/monitoring/socialcharter/Complaints/Complaints_en.asp, accessed October 2011.

32 See, for example, the court cases against Birmingham City Council (UK), addressing, *inter alia*, social care for disabled workers, *inter alia*, www.guardian.co.uk/society/2011/may/19/birmingham-council-cut-disabled-care-unlawful; and the court cases initiated by Fischer advocaten, Haarlem, the Netherlands, www.fischeradvocaten.nl, accessed November 2011.

33 See, for example, the report of the National Ombudsman in Slovenia, which addressed, *inter alia*, regional differences in education, at www.varuh-rs.si/publikacije-gradiva-izjave/govori-referati-in-clanki/novice/detajl/do-poorer-achievements-of-pupils-from-individual-regions-constitute-a-violation-of-human-rights/?L=6&cHash=bf120bcefb, accessed November 2011; and the initiative of Open Society Institute (OSI)/ 'I can live' coalition, addressing employment rights and rights of treatment for drug users, in Open Society Institute Public Health Program, Research Law and Health Initiative, *Evaluating the Impact of Integrating Legal Support and Health Care: A Call for Action*, February 2008.

CHAPTER 8
CHILDREN AND THE RIGHT TO HEALTH PROTECTION

Henriette Sinding Aasen

1. INTRODUCTION

> 'Health in childhood determines health throughout life and into the next generation. Despite overall improvements, children's health in the European Region shows large differences according to age, gender, geographical location and socioeconomic position, both within and between countries. Social inequalities are increasing in all countries, particularly in the eastern half of the Region'.[1]

Good health is a basic resource for all individuals in their everyday lives,[2] and a condition for social and economic development. Health is protected as a fundamental human right in several international human rights conventions, and is indispensable to the enjoyment of other human rights. In Europe, the European Social Charter plays an increasingly important role for the protection of social rights, including protection of health and the provision of medical and social assistance, as well as welfare services. The Charter of Fundamental Rights of the European Union, which is now legally binding for the Member States, is also becoming important in the field of social rights and health, also with regard to children. In this chapter, children's right to health is particularly addressed from a public health angle, i.e. as a collective mainstreaming obligation with regard to health protection.[3] The human rights perspective in this context implies particular concern for children as a vulnerable group, and for human dignity, equality and non-discrimination – all key elements of the human right to health. However, the existing health disparities among children indicate that children from poor families are far more vulnerable than children from more

---

1 WHO Regional Office for Europe, *The European Health Report 2005. Public health action for healthier children and populations*, Copenhagen 2005, p. 46.

2 Ottawa Charter for Health Promotion, WHO 1986.

3 T.K. Hervey, The 'Right to Health' in European Union Law, in Hervey and Kenner (eds.) *Economic and Social Rights under the EU Charter of Fundamental Rights. A Legal Perspective*, Oxford: Hart Publishing 2003, pp. 193–223, at pp. 196–197, 202–203.

affluent families, and thus focus on various socioeconomic health determinants becomes central. An overall summary of the public health challenges and health disparities relating to children across the European region forms the background for the discussion of how to use the human rights framework in order to understand, apply and implement the right to health of children in different social and environmental contexts.

2. LEGAL SOURCES AND STARTING POINTS

In this chapter, European human rights instruments, institutions and practices concerning the right to health of children are the focus. Both instruments from the Council of Europe and the European Union will be examined. As for Council of Europe instruments, the Convention for the Protection of Human Rights and Fundamental Freedoms (ECHR 1950), the Convention on Human Rights and Biomedicine (Biomedicine Convention 1997), and the revised European Social Charter (ESC 1996), are relevant, in particular, the ESC. At the EU level, the Charter of Fundamental Rights of the European Union (the EU Charter 2000),[4] and the Consolidated Version of the Treaty on the Functioning of the European Union (TFEU 2008) are the most significant instruments when it comes to the protection and promotion of the right to health. All the instruments (except the ECHR, which deals with civil and political rights) demonstrate a broad concept of human rights, and that individual and public health and social concerns are becoming increasingly important matters in European Regulations. The public health perspective – addressing social factors and underlying determinants of health – is gradually becoming more visible in the legal instruments and sources.

Although the European instruments are the main focus, international UN instruments will also be considered, i.e. provisions in the UN Convention on Economic, Social and Cultural Rights (ICESCR 1966), and in the Convention on the Rights of the Child (CRC 1989). These instruments have clearly influenced regional and national instruments and institutions all over the world, also in Europe. All governments in the world (except Somalia and the United States), including all Member States of the Council of Europe, have ratified the CRC, and all EU Member States and most Members of the Council of Europe have ratified the ICESCR.[5] Article 24 EU Charter, protecting, *inter alia*, the right of the child to protection and care, has a very similar formulation of the best interest of the child principle in Article 3 CRC. The European Committee of Social Rights

4 The Charter became legally binding when the EU Lisbon Reform Treaty entered into force in 2009 (see Chapter 2).

5 J. Hunt, Fair and Just Working Conditions, in Hervey and Kenner (eds.) *Economic and Social Rights under the EU Charter of Fundamental Rights. A Legal Perspective*, Oxford: Hart Publishing 2003, pp. 45–67, at p. 50.

considers itself bound by the CRC, as it is interpreted by the monitoring body, and, in particular, by the internationally recognised requirement of applying the best interests of the child principle.[6] Clearly, the international conventions form an important background and provide a relevant framework for the understanding of European regulations and practices, both at the institutional and national levels. Since the ECHR does not *per se* include the right to health or the rights of children, the ICESCR and CRC are of particular significance when it comes to children and health.

In the following, the European instruments will be the starting point of the analysis, but will be supplemented with international human rights instruments and sources, as is considered appropriate.

3. PUBLIC HEALTH ISSUES RELATING TO CHILDREN

Many factors shape the health of populations and children: genetic and biological factors, individual lifestyles, living conditions, environmental factors, and access to healthcare services. The main threat to children's life and health in Europe – and globally – is poverty. Rates of disease and health determinants are closely linked to socioeconomic factors, such as poor neonatal health (e.g. due to malnutrition), insufficient access to healthcare services, unhealthy or unsafe environments and living conditions, unhealthy behaviours (e.g. early smoking, drinking or drug taking), and poor diet.[7] In fact, socioeconomic factors underlie the major health determinants in both adults and children.[8] The multifactorial nature of health requires policymakers to take a broad view of all the factors that may affect health determinants and outcomes. Since each period of child and youth development poses particular health challenges and vulnerabilities, and each stage of development prepares the way for the next, health policies should be tailored to the protection of particular vulnerabilities related to biological, developmental, individual and socioeconomic determinants of health.[9] Thus, children and adolescents have particular needs relating to health, healthcare, and health related policies that are determined by their age and development, and which are also clearly related to the particular socioeconomic factors that impact upon their living conditions.

---

6 European Committee on Social Rights, *Defence for Children International v the Netherlands*, Decision of 20 October 2009, para. 29.

7 WHO Regional Office for Europe, *The European Health Report 2005. Public health action for healthier children and populations*, Copenhagen 2005, pp. IX-X, 51.

8 *Ibid.*, pp. 4, 66.

9 *Ibid.*, pp. 3–4 and 47.

In the following, the term 'children' covers individuals up to the age of 18, cf. Article 1 CRC. The term 'adolescents' is used when discussing issues of particular relevance for young people between 13–18 years of age, e.g., with regard to sexuality and pregnancy. Children are vulnerable not only because of their physical and mental constitutions, but also due to their strong dependency upon other people, as well as their physical and social environments. For example, children born into poor families are far more likely to be affected by health problems than children from more affluent families. In particular, children's health is closely related to the health and living conditions of their mother.[10] Children of parents without residence status are in a particularly vulnerable situation, and their legal rights are often disputed and contested.[11]

The European health report of 2005 summarised the major public health issues facing the European region, and in particular, children. It had a special focus on children's health, considering that health status in childhood determines health throughout life and into the next generation. According to the report, the period between birth and 5–6 years of age is critical. Bad health or harmful lifestyles in childhood can lead to health problems throughout life, and thereby creating long-term individual, social and financial burdens.[12]

The European strategy for child and adolescent health and development (2008) identifies numerous threats to health and well-being of children in Europe: malnutrition, perinatal problems and infectious diseases, as well as obesity, sexually transmitted diseases, and psychosocial and mental health disorders. In addition, polluted environments and health-compromising behaviours and lifestyles among young people, are risk factors.[13] With regard to environmental challenges, it is estimated that environmental factors account for over 30% of diseases in children under 5 years of age.[14] Furthermore, one in every five children suffers from a chronic respiratory condition or allergy, and a quarter of all European schoolchildren are overweight or obese.[15] These general challenges indicate that strategies at the individual level are not sufficient; rather, systematic national efforts at the societal level (public health initiatives) are urgently required, especially with regard to disadvantaged or at-risk groups[16] (see next section).

10 *Ibid.*, pp. 46–47, 66.

11 C. Øien and S. Sønsterudbråten, 'No way in, no way out? A study of living conditions of irregular migrants in Norway', *Fafo-report* 2011: 03, p. 61.

12 WHO Regional Office for Europe, *The European Health Report 2005. Public health action for healthier children and populations*, Copenhagen 2005, p. IX.

13 WHO Regional Office for Europe, *European strategy for child and adolescent health and development. From resolution to action*, Copenhagen, 2008, p. 4.

14 WHO Regional Office for Europe, *Protecting children's health in a changing environment.* Copenhagen 2010, p. 3.

15 *Ibid.*, p. 24.

16 WHO Regional Office for Europe, *European strategy for child and adolescent health and development. From resolution to action*, Copenhagen, 2008, p. 10.

From the human rights perspective, vulnerabilities, dependencies and special challenges relating to children and adolescents must be taken into consideration when health policies for this group are planned, designed and implemented. Of particular importance when considering the growing health inequalities across Europe is that children are independent holders of human rights, and that they should not suffer unnecessarily due to socioeconomic and environmental factors beyond their control.

4. HEALTH INEQUALITIES AFFECTING CHILDREN

In general, children in Europe have better health and development opportunities than ever before. Public health efforts during the last decades have succeeded in improving the overall health status of people, and infant and child mortality rates in some European countries are among the lowest in the world. However, despite the overall improvements, there are striking inequalities in health status and access to health services across Europe, and the differences in infant and child mortality rates are ten-fold. Inequalities are also growing within countries, and women, children and disadvantaged and marginalised groups are facing particular risks.[17] Children from socially disadvantaged groups get sicker and die sooner than children from the more privileged groups.[18]

The European health report 2005 stated that the European region displays glaring contrasts when it comes to health. Its richest and most developed countries are among the healthiest on the planet in terms of 'longevity, late onset of disease and disability and increased attention to the ability to function and the quality of life'[19], but on the other hand, Europe has also poor countries that are still struggling with severe health challenges among younger groups. According to the report, these countries carry a double burden of disease: 'they lack the advanced means of controlling the traditional burden of infectious diseases and injuries, while already carrying a large modern burden of non-communicable diseases.'[20] All countries, even the most affluent, have vast and growing inequalities in health status between rich and poor segments of the population. Thus, reducing these inequalities is a key challenge for every country.[21] These general observations are essential in order to understand the health situation for children in Europe.

---

17 WHO Regional Office for Europe, *European strategy for child and adolescent health and development. From resolution to action*, Copenhagen, 2008, p. 4.

18 WHO Regional Office for Europe, *The European Health Report 2005. Public health action for healthier children and populations*, Copenhagen 2005, p. 46.

19 *Ibid.*, p. 2.

20 *Ibid.*

21 *Ibid.*

The inequalities in the health status of children in Europe reflect the widening east-west gap also seen in adults. In addition, children's health status shows large differences according to age, gender, geographical location and socioeconomic status, both within and between countries. The overall improvements hide increasing social inequalities, which are increasing in all countries, but particularly in the eastern half of Europe. Even in the 15 more affluent countries, about 30–50% of all deaths and health problems that occur in children are estimated to be associated with the low socioeconomic status of their parents.[22] Countries, societies, communities, families and children with the fewest resources are mostly affected, and even in more affluent countries, the poorer members of society carry a disproportionate share of the disease burden.[23]

Most countries have made substantial progress in reducing mortality and morbidity from acute conditions. While Eastern European countries have higher morbidity and mortality from respiratory and infectious diseases, as well as injuries and poisoning, children's disease patterns in Western European countries include more non-communicable diseases, such as asthma and allergies, diabetes, obesity and neuropsychiatric disorders.[24]

Health inequities, in terms of unfair and avoidable differences in health status between children within and between countries, as well as inequalities in exposure to environmental risks, may indicate violations of children's right to health protection. In the following, the right to health of children in the European context will be explored, addressing, in particular, the challenges of health inequalities within and across the region.

5. STATE OBLIGATIONS TO PROVIDE EQUITABLE ACCESS TO HEALTHCARE FOR CHILDREN

5.1. THE BIOMEDICINE CONVENTION

The Biomedicine Convention is a legally binding framework convention consisting of principles, rights and standards that apply to the field of biology and medicine.[25] The preamble makes references to the Universal Declaration of Human Rights (UDHR), ICESCR, ICCPR and the CRC. The overall goal is to protect human dignity and to guarantee everyone, without discrimination, 'respect for their integrity and other rights and fundamental freedoms' (Article

22 *Ibid.*, p. 48.
23 *Ibid.*, pp. IX, 48 and 51.
24 *Ibid.*, pp. IX-X, 51.
25 See Chapter 1 for a general account of this Convention.

1). Article 3 formulates general state obligations with regard to the distribution of healthcare services:

> 'Parties, taking into account **health needs** and available resources, shall take **appropriate measures** with a view to providing, within their jurisdiction, **equitable access to health care of appropriate quality**' (emphasis added).

The provision contains two main obligations: providing equitable access to healthcare, and providing healthcare of appropriate quality. Both these dimensions, highly relevant when it comes to children, must be seen in light of the obligation to take into account 'health needs'. The term 'healthcare' includes services offering diagnostic, preventive, therapeutic and rehabilitative interventions, designed to maintain or improve a person's state of health or to alleviate suffering. This wording implies that the provision does not – in contrast to Article 12 ICESCR and Article 24 CRC – include socioeconomic factors and underlying health determinants.

Healthcare must be of a 'fitting standard' in light of scientific progress, and be subject to a continuous quality assessment.[26] With regard to children, this must be viewed also in relation to children's particular vulnerabilities and needs. Article 24 CRC, protecting the right of the child to 'the enjoyment of the highest attainable standard of health and to facilities for the treatment of illness and rehabilitation of health' (paragraph 1), directs states to diminish infant and child mortality and to ensure access to essential health services for children, as well as pre and post-natal care for mothers. Primary and preventive healthcare, including adequate nutrition, as well as accessible and appropriate information, education and guidance of parents and children, are emphasised in Article 24. These obligations should be kept in mind also with regard to the 'fitting standard' required by Article 3 Biomedicine Convention.

The Biomedicine Convention's requirement of appropriate measures and a 'fitting standard' may very well be understood in light of the requirement of acceptable services of good quality, as developed particularly by the UN Committee on Economic, Social and Cultural Rights (CESCR) with regard to Article 12 ICESCR, implying that all health services must be sensitive to gender and lifecycle requirements, and must be designed to improve the health status of those concerned.[27] Particular needs of children and adolescents must clearly be taken into account, and healthcare and health policies must address the needs of different groups of children depending on age, sex, social class, environmental challenges, *etc.*

---

26 Council of Europe, 1996. Explanatory Report to the Biomedicine Convention, paras. 24 and 25.

27 General Comment No. 14, para. 12 c.

The Explanatory Report to the Biomedicine Convention specifies that Article 3 does not create an individual right to healthcare, but rather prompts the state 'to adopt the requisite measures as part of its social policy in order to ensure equitable access to health care.'[28] Such measures may take many different forms 'and a wide variety of methods may be employed to this end'.[29] Thus, Article 3 expresses a 'mainstreaming' principle of state policies with regard to healthcare. In the Explanatory Report to the Convention, it is stated that the requirement of equitable access is not identical with absolute equality, but implies 'effectively obtaining a satisfactory degree of care.'[30] With regard to children and adolescents, states must provide children from various social groups with appropriate information, advice and healthcare services at a decent level. Keeping in mind General Comment No. 14, services must be not only available and accessible to children, but must also be acceptable and of good scientific and medical quality (paragraph 12). Services must be designed to meet the particular needs of young individuals of different cultural and social backgrounds (acceptability), and must meet all professional and ethical standards (quality).

5.2. THE CHARTER OF FUNDAMENTAL RIGHTS OF THE EUROPEAN UNION

Recently, the European Union (EU) has adopted interesting instruments with regard to healthcare. The Article 35 Charter of Fundamental Rights (ECFR)[31] states:

> '**Everyone** has the right of access to **preventive health care** and the right to benefit from **medical treatment** under the conditions established by national laws and practices. A high level of human health protection shall be ensured in the definition and implementation of all Union policies and activities' (emphasis added).[32]

While the first sentence of Article 35 of the Charter is formulated as an individual entitlement right (in contrast to the Biomedicine Convention) to preventive as well as curative healthcare, the second sentence expresses a 'mainstreaming' obligation. The provision is based on Article 11 ESC, and the former Article 152 EC Treaty,[33] both focusing on human health protection[34] (see Section 6, below, and Chapter 2).

28 Explanatory Report, para. 25.
29 *Ibid.*
30 *Ibid.*
31 This provision is based on Article 152 of the former EC Treaty, and on Article 11 of the European Social Charter (Draft Charter of Fundamental Rights of the European Union, CHARTE 4473/00, p. 32.
32 See Chapter 1 for more details on Article 35 ECFR.
33 Article 152 is replaced by Article 168 of the Treaty of the functioning of the European Union.
34 Draft Charter of Fundamental Rights of the European Union, CHARTE 4473/00, p. 32.

The general principle of non-discrimination in Article 21 of the Charter provides that any discrimination based on any ground such as sex, race, ethnic or social origin, *etc.*, and 'age', shall be prohibited. Thus, everyone shall be guaranteed the enjoyment of the right to healthcare, and Union policies and activities must ensure a high level of health protection for all segments of society, including children.[35] It is unclear to what extent this requirement also includes persons enjoying temporary protection, or persons without a legal status, or if a minimum standard applies within the EU Regulation.[36] However, from the international human rights perspective, a minimum standard must be secured for everyone within state jurisdiction.[37] Thus, if the EU ratifies the ICESCR or the CRC, the exclusion of undocumented migrant children from a minimum standard of health protection is not acceptable. Even though the EU has not ratified these conventions, it could be argued that compliance with the international human rights framework on health protection should be followed, since most Member States have ratified these conventions.

5.3. SPECIAL FOCUS ON CHILDREN AND ACCESSIBILITY OF HEALTHCARE SERVICES AND INFORMATION

The Committee on Economic, Social and Cultural Rights (CESCR), in General Comment No. 14, has developed the right to health (Article 12 ICESCR) in a way that is also relevant to the understanding of the European instruments concerning equitable access to healthcare. The Committee has stated that the right to health (also containing underlying health determinants such as clean water, hygiene, proper housing and nutrition, *etc.*) contains four basic elements: availability, accessibility, acceptability and quality.[38] In order to realise the right to health protection for children and adolescents, existence (availability) and accessibility of child and youth-friendly services is crucial.[39] In the context of social inequity among children, both within countries and across Europe, the requirement of *accessibility* to healthcare services and health determinants for everyone seems to be of particular importance.

Accessibility to health facilities, goods and services has four overlapping dimensions: Non-discrimination, physical accessibility for everyone, economic accessibility (affordable), and access to information.

35 The non-discrimination principle is to be applied in compliance with, *inter alia*, Article 14 of the ECHR (Draft Charter of Fundamental Rights of the European Union, CHARTE 4473/00, p. 23).

36 T.K. Hervey, The 'Right to Health' in European Union Law, see note 3, pp. 217–222.

37 Committee on Economic, Social and Cultural Rights, General Comment No. 14, para. 34.

38 See General Comment No. 14, para. 12. See, also, Committee on the Rights of the Child, General Comment No. 4 (2003), para. 41.

39 General Comment No. 14, para. 23.

Non-discrimination implies that health facilities, goods and services must be accessible to all, 'especially the most vulnerable or marginalized sections of the population, in law and in fact.'[40] It means that children cannot – intentionally or unintentionally – be excluded or ignored when it comes to healthcare services. Children are vulnerable *per se*, and must, therefore, be given particular attention in order to avoid discriminatory practices in which their needs are ignored or neglected. CESCR stresses that most strategies and programmes designed to eliminate health-related discrimination can, in fact, be pursued with minimum resource implications through the adoption, modification or abrogation of legislation or the dissemination of information. Furthermore, recalling General Comment No. 3, the Committee has stated that 'even in times of severe resource constraints, the vulnerable members of society must be protected by the adoption of relatively low-cost targeted programmes.'[41] This means that health protection for children, in particular, those who are at special risk of health damage, must always be prioritised, even when resources are scarce. States have a special obligation to provide health information, advice and services to families and children who do not have sufficient means to get such information and services on their own, e.g., due to a lack of income, health insurance (see below, about affordability), social networks and capacity. Furthermore, inappropriate health resource allocation, or a systematic lack of educational and research investments, can lead to *de facto* discrimination of children as a group. For example, health investments should not disproportionately favour expensive curative health services that are relevant or accessible only to a small, privileged group (e.g. middle-aged men).[42] More research on health issues of relevance to children seems to be urgently needed for the future, in order to combat some of the current health challenges for this group. Preventive and curative healthcare services addressing health problems of children (allergies, respiratory problems, obesity, unhealthy and risky behaviours, alcohol and drug abuse, *etc.*)[43] need to be addressed in public health and other health related political strategies and measures (e.g. environmental and social policies) in order to combat such threats to children's health. These are among the state obligations that may be drawn from Article 12 ICESCR (cf. Article 2 on the state obligation), and more indirectly, from Article 3 Biomedicine Convention and Article 35 EU Charter.

Physical accessibility means that health services must be within safe physical reach for everyone, including children and other vulnerable or marginalised groups, also in rural areas. Healthcare services located in school buildings are common in many countries, which would normally make healthcare services

40 *Ibid.*, para. 12 b.
41 *Ibid.*, para. 18.
42 *Ibid.*, paras. 18 and 19.
43 See sections 3 and 4, above.

physically accessible to those children who attend school. Children below school age, or who, due to disability or long-term illness, do not attend ordinary schools depend on parents or other adults in charge to take them to healthcare services. For these children, particular attention and follow-up of parents or caretakers is important in order to secure adequate healthcare services and the prevention of health-related problems. In order to secure physical accessibility for most children, it should be a goal to locate health centres in every little community, and to spread information about these centres and the services they provide to all children and their parents. In addition, particular (and non-stigmatising) strategies to reach the most vulnerable or at-risk children are needed, e.g. with regard to health checks, preventive measures, follow-up and advice concerning diet, unhealthy behaviours, contraception, *etc.*

Services must be **affordable** for all (economic accessibility), including for disadvantaged groups, whether these are privately or publicly provided. This is of particular relevance for children in poor families, who should be provided with appropriate healthcare, even if their parents or families lack the means to pay for services. The CESCR points out that equity demands that 'poorer households should not be disproportionately burdened with health expenses as compared to richer households.'[44] For children, who may not have money to pay for services even if their parents are affluent, health services should be free of charge in order to secure all children adequate preventive measures, treatment and rehabilitation.

Finally, accessibility includes the right to seek, receive and impart **information** and ideas on health issues, although with respect for confidentiality and privacy. This means that children – in particular, children from socially disadvantaged groups – must be given adequate and understandable information and advice about relevant health issues and services, preventive measures (including contraception), unhealthy behaviours and relationships, risk factors relating to alcohol, smoking, drugs, sexual practices, HIV/AIDS, early pregnancies, *etc.* Article 24 CRC (paragraph 2 e) stresses that States Parties shall take appropriate measures to ensure that 'all segments of society, in particular parents and children are informed, have access to education and are supported in the use of basic knowledge of child health and nutrition, the advantages of breast-feeding, hygiene and environmental sanitation and the prevention of accidents.' In order to act adequately on the information essential for their health, children also need to develop necessary self-care skills and other skills (e.g. on how to prepare nutritious meals, interpersonal communication, decision-making, coping with stress and conflict, *etc.*).[45] Thus, teaching children and adolescents basic health

44 General Comment No. 14, para. 12 b.
45 Committee on the Rights of the Child, General Comment No. 4 (2003), paras. 27–31.

skills seem to be important in both a public health and human rights perspective (see, also, Article 11 ESC, below, in Section 6.1.2).

The above-mentioned services, advice and information must be provided by health professionals who respect children's right to confidentiality and privacy in order to ensure that children are provided with real access, without fear of being punished by parents or other grown-ups.[46] This raises sometimes difficult questions regarding the relationship between, and balancing of, principles of parental responsibility, the best interest of the child, children's right to participation, professional responsibilities, *etc.*[47] However, possible conflicting principles and interests should be solved in a way that secure children and adolescents *de facto* access to adequate and timely healthcare services, guidance and information.

As observed by human rights scholar Brigit Toebes, 'a state may violate the right to health if it structurally fails to offer adequate health services to certain segments of society.'[48] She recalls that several international treaty-monitoring bodies have repeatedly urged states to ensure that vulnerable groups in the population have sufficient access to adequate healthcare services.[49] This obligation also follows from the Biomedicine Convention and the EU Charter, implying that the needs of children must be of special concern in the development, interpretation and implementation of European and national health and social policies, plans and regulations.

6. HEALTH PROTECTION AND PROMOTION

6.1. THE EUROPEAN SOCIAL CHARTER (ESC)

6.1.1. Overview

The ESC, either the 1961 or the 1996 version, has been (in May 2011) ratified by 43 out of 47 Member States of the Council of Europe. Most of these countries

46 *Ibid.*, paras. 11, 33.

47 H.S. Aasen, 'Barns rett til selvbestemmelse og medbestemmelse i beslutninger om helsehjelp' [Children's right to self-determination and participation in health care decisions]; *Tidsskrift for familierett, arverett og barnevernrettslige spørsmål [Journal of family law, inheritance law and child welfare law]*, No. 1, 2008, pp. 4–28.

48 B. Toebes, 'The Right to Health', in Eide, Krause and Rosas (eds.) *Economic, Social and Cultural Rights*, second revised edition, Dordrecht: Martinus Nijhoff Publishers 2001, pp. 169–191, at p. 181.

49 *Ibid.*

have ratified the 1996 revised version of the Charter.[50] The ESC, which complements the ECHR in the field of economic and social rights, is the most comprehensive treaty at the European level for the human rights of children. It guarantees a wide range of rights relating to housing, health, education, employment, social protection, non-discrimination, *etc.*, and establishes a supervisory mechanism based on collective complaints and state reports.[51] According to the European Committee of Social rights, the ESC, partly due to its comprehensive approach, is the most significant treaty at the European level for children's human rights.[52] Unfortunately, the ESC is still not widely recognised, and its content is not very well-known.[53] However, in order for the ESC to gain influence, and thereby to strengthen the rights of children, it is necessary to apply it in all legal discourses where its provisions are relevant. The Charter protects the rights of children in two ways: through its general provisions, e.g. provisions on housing and social protection of families, and through specific provisions for children.

6.1.2. General provisions

The ESC contains several provisions of relevance for the protection and promotion of children's health. Article 11 declares that States Parties, with a view to ensuring the effective exercise of 'the right to *protection of health*', undertake, either directly or in cooperation with public or private organisations, to take appropriate measures designed, *inter alia*, '*to remove as far as possible the causes of ill-health*', 'to provide *advisory and educational facilities* for the *promotion of health* ...', and to 'prevent as far as possible epidemic, endemic and other diseases, as well as accidents' (emphasis added). This provision has a much broader scope than Article 3 Biomedicine Convention and Article 35 EU Charter, as it is not limited to healthcare services.

Although the European Committee on Social Rights has not yet defined the minimum standard for a healthy and safe growing environment for children and young persons, Article 11, together with other ESC provisions, provides a comprehensive regulative framework at the European level. Article 11 concerns health protection, including requirements on food, drinking water, breathing air, construction standards, dangerous substances, radiation, *etc.* In addition, a nationwide healthcare system that includes a system of maternity and childcare, screening programmes for common health risks, and adequate vaccination programmes, must be available and accessible to all. Article 24 CRC, which is

50 www.coe.int/t/dghl/monitoring/socialcharter/Presentation/Overview_en.asp, checked at 22 September 2011.

51 For more information about the ESC, see Chapter 1.

52 *DCI v. the Netherlands*, Decision of 20 October 2009, para. 26.

53 M. Mikkola, *Social Human Rights of Europe*, Karelactio 2010, p. 3.

the most comprehensive provision at the international level, contains important supplementing requirements, and emphasises the development of primary healthcare (paragraph 2 b and c). The provision of adequate nutritious food and clean drinking water, and taking into consideration the dangers and risks of environmental pollution, are highlighted (paragraph 2 c).

Emergency services must be immediately accessible to all children, and also to those living in childcare institutions, without any unreasonable waiting time.[54] Health promotion includes diet, sleep, hygiene, health education, the prevention of contagious diseases and unhealthy behaviour (see above). With reference to case law from the European Committee on Social Rights, Mikkola asserts that health education is sufficient only if it is part of the school curricula and continued throughout basic education, and must include sex education and guidance on the prevention of sexually transmitted diseases, alcohol abuse, smoking and drug use. States must take special measures to prevent drug and alcohol abuse among young persons, and they may not allow the sale of cigarettes to persons below the legal age.[55]

The recent *International Federation of Human Rights (FIDH) v Greece*[56] case concerned the effects of massive environmental pollution on the health of persons living near the Asopos river, and in proximity to the industrial zone of Inofyta, located 50 km north of Athens. The complainant organisation alleged that the state das not taken adequate measures to eliminate or reduce these dangerous effects and to ensure the right to health protection, in violation of Article 11 (right to health) of the Social Charter. The Committee has not yet (September 2011) made a decision on the merits of the case. However, the case itself illustrates the importance of environmental concerns for health protection.[57]

Article 12 covers the right to social security, and Article 13 on the right to social and medical assistance obligates States Parties to ensure '*any person* who is without adequate resources and who is unable to secure such resources either by his own efforts or from other sources … be granted *adequate assistance*, and in case of sickness, *the care necessitated by his condition*' (paragraph 1, emphasis added). Noteworthy is that medical assistance in this paragraph does not refer to medical care or healthcare (cf. Article 11, above), but to financial aid to persons who cannot afford to purchase medical services or medicines, or to free healthcare.[58]

---

54 Mikkola, *Social Human Rights of Europe*, p. 485.
55 *Ibid.*, pp. 485–486.
56 Case No. 72/2011.
57 See, also, *Marangopoulos Foundation for Human Rights v Greece* (Collective complaint No. 30/2005), a similar case that has led to a violation of 11 ESC.
58 D. Harris and J. Darcy, *The European Social Charter*, New York: Transnational Publishers 2001, p. 167.

According to Article 14, States Parties undertake 'to promote or provide services which, by using methods of social work, would contribute to the welfare and development of both individuals and groups in the community' (paragraph 1).

Article 31 covers the right to housing, obligating states to promote 'access to housing of an adequate standard', to prevent and reduce homelessness, and to make the price of housing accessible to those without adequate resources. The European Committee of Social Rights (monitoring body) has stated that adequate housing under Article 31§1 means 'a dwelling which is safe from a sanitary and health point of view, i.e. it must possess all basic amenities, such as water, heating, waste disposal, sanitation facilities and electricity and must also be structurally secure, not overcrowded and with secure tenure supported by the law.'[59] These requirements are also essential with regard to the right to health, addressing very important determinants of health, not at least for children from poor households.

6.1.3. Child-specific provisions

The ESC protects rights of children from birth (and before) up to the age of 18 with regard to, *inter alia*, prenatal and maternal health protection; health protection of children; the special protection of children from violence, abuse and exploitation; education; the prohibition of child labour; the regulation of working conditions for children aged between 15–18; and the rights of migrant children. Of particular interest is the broadly formulated Article 17:

> 'With a view to ensuring the effective exercise of the right of *children* and young persons to grow up in an environment which encourages the *full development of their personality* and of their *physical and mental capacities*, the Parties undertake, either directly or in co-operation with public or private organisations, to take all appropriate and necessary measures designed ... to ensure that children and young persons, taking account of the rights and duties of their parents, *have the care, the assistance, the education and the training they need*, in particular by providing for the establishment or maintenance of *institutions and services* sufficient and adequate for this purpose' (paragraph 1a, emphasis added). In addition, states undertake 'to protect children and young persons against *negligence*, violence or exploitation', and 'provide *protection and special aid from the state* for children and young persons temporarily or definitively *deprived of their family's support*' (paragraph 1 b and c, emphasis added).

Clearly, this provision, together with other provisions, provides a broad approach to children's health and well-being, and represents a potent instrument in order

59 European Committee of Social Rights, Decision of 20 October 2009, para. 43.

to improve the health and social situations of children within states and across Europe.

The ESC also provides protection for illegally residing children. In the *International Federation of Human Rights Leagues (FIDH) v France* case,[60] the European Committee found a violation on Article 17 of the revised Charter concerning medical care and assistance to unaccompanied children with illegal status. The medical assistance to these children in France was limited to situations involving an immediate threat to life. Furthermore, children of illegal immigrants were only admitted to the medical assistance scheme after a certain time. For these reasons, the Committee considered that the situation was not in conformity with Article 17.[61] The Committee said that legislation or a practice that denies entitlement to medical assistance to foreign nationals, within the territory of a State Party, even if they are there illegally, is contrary to the Charter (paragraph 32). A similar decision was made in *Defence for Children International (DCI) v the Netherlands*,[62] in which the Committee found a violation under Article 31§2 on the ground that shelter was not provided to children unlawfully present in the Netherlands for as long as they were in its jurisdiction. The Committee also found a violation of Article 17§1c of the Revised Charter on the same ground (paragraph 71).

6.2. EU REGULATION

6.2.1. The Charter of Fundamental Rights

Chapter IV of the Charter of Fundamental Rights includes general provisions on solidarity rights, social security, social assistance and environmental protection, which are all important for the protection and promotion of children's health. As mentioned above (Section 5.2), Article 35 (second sentence) states that a 'high level of human health protection shall be ensured in the definition and implementation of all Union policies and activities.' This expresses a 'mainstreaming' obligation, which is based on the Article 11 ESC and the former Article 152 EC Treaty,[63] both focusing on human health protection.[64]

In addition, the rights of children *per se* are put in focus. The Charter of Fundamental Rights, Article 24, states:

60 Complaint No. 14/2003, Decision of 8 September 2004.

61 See paragraphs 33–37.

62 Complaint No. 4772008, Decision of 20 October 2009.

63 Article 152 is replaced by Article 168 of the Treaty of the functioning of the European Union (see Section 6.2.2, below).

64 Draft Charter of Fundamental Rights of the European Union, CHARTE 4473/00, p. 32.

'1. Children shall have the right to such **protection and care** as is necessary for their **well-being.** They may **express their views freely.** Such views shall be taken into consideration on matters which concern them in accordance with their age and maturity.
2. In all actions relating to children, whether taken by public authorities or private institutions, **the child's best interests** must be a primary consideration.'

The terms 'protection and care' and 'well-being' include not only medical services, but also a wide range of measures and services in order to protect children's health in a broad sense. In the explanatory comment to Article 24 in the draft Charter, it is stated that the provision is based on the CRC, particularly Articles 3, 9, 12 and 13.[65] Thus, the principle of the best interests of the child, and the right to freedom to express his or her views and to participate in decisions affecting the child, are central. In addition, CRC, Article 24 on the right of the child to the highest attainable standard of health,[66] is relevant to the understanding of state accountability, as well as for Union obligations with regard to such 'protection and care as is necessary for [children's] well-being.'

6.2.2. The Treaty on the Functioning of the European Union

The general Union policy is to strengthen public health initiatives, including health protection. According to the Treaty on the Functioning of the European Union (TFEU), Article 168, section 7, the European Union shall respect the responsibilities of the Member States for the definition of their health policy and for the organisation and delivery of health services and medical care. However, Article 168.1 authorises the EU to complement state efforts concerning health, in terms of a mainstreaming the principle of health protection at a high level, including research, information, education, and monitoring. This provision is relevant also for health policies directed towards children. According to the European Health Report (2005), improving the health of children will bring the greatest cumulative public health effects at the population level.[67] The report states: 'To be most successful, public health interventions need to address all the direct and indirect influences on children's health, and take action on many fronts and in many sectors.'[68] Implementation strategies are most successful when they are based on comprehensive national planning that involves children themselves, utilises the contributions of families and communities, schools, the mass media, the health system and government, and uses tools as policies, legislation and regulations.[69]

65 Draft Charter of Fundamental Rights of the European Union, Brussels, 11 October 2000 (CHARTE 4473/00) p. 25.
66 See the brief account of CRC, Article 24, in Section 5.1, above.
67 The European Health Report 2005, p. 2.
68 *Ibid.*, p. 80.
69 *Ibid.*

7. IMPLEMENTATION OF THE RIGHT TO HEALTH FOR CHILDREN: CHALLENGES AND STRATEGIES

The right to health, as with all human rights, must be implemented nationally by national and local institutions. International human rights bodies and other organisations can only monitor and supervise national implementation. The World Health Organization (WHO) is a central actor in global and regional health issues, and has also developed a strategy for the European region, addressing, in particular, the health of children and adolescents. The European strategy was adopted by the WHO Regional Committee in September 2005, and identifies seven priority areas of great relevance to child health: mothers and neonates, nutrition, communicable diseases, injuries and violence, physical environment, adolescent health, psychosocial development, and mental health.[70] The WHO European strategy for child and adolescent health and development is a natural starting point when discussing how the right to health protection for children should be approached and realised in Europe. The strategy is based on a wide range of data about children's and adolescent's health and health behaviours in Europe, and provides a framework that complements national efforts and allows countries and regions to develop their own policies and programmes according to their particular challenges, a range of policy options based on best evidence, an external impetus to encourage countries and regions to set their own targets and indicators, and a driver for action. Since social factors account for most of the health challenges and disparities among children in Europe, public health action must, in order to have effect, also address the root causes of morbidity and mortality. In many areas, the medical solution is simple and well-known, but fails to reach those in most need.[71] As observed above (see Section 4), the increasing health disparities among children indicate that children from poor families are far more vulnerable than children from more affluent families, and thus focus on socioeconomic health determinants becomes essential in order to improve their health status.

Four principles form the basis of this strategy: A **life-course approach** (from prenatal life to adolescence); recognition of the need for **equity** (giving particular attention to the most disadvantaged); **intersectoral action** (broad public health approach, addressing the fundamental determinants of health); and **participation** (involvement of young people in their own health and health

---

70 WHO Regional Office for Europe, *European strategy for child and adolescent health and development. From resolution to action*, Copenhagen, 2008, p. 4.

71 WHO Regional Office for Europe, *The European Health Report 2005. Public health action for healthier children and populations*, Copenhagen 2005, pp. 46–47.

related policies and services).[72] This comprehensive and intersectoral strategy seems to be in line with the human rights requirements of available, accessible and acceptable services of good quality, as well as access to health determinants (see Section 5.3, above) and also the broad approach found in the ESC (see Section 6.1). In addition, the requirement of participation of those concerned is observed (see Toebes in Chapter 3). The strategy is accompanied by a four-part toolkit consisting of assistance to countries in: 1) assessing existing policies and strategies, 2) identifying necessary data and information, 3) helping to get started on actions, and 4) enabling to incorporate gender analysis into child and adolescent programmes and to identify effective gender-based interventions.[73] This strategy seems to integrate another important aspect of the human rights framework, namely, the requirement of state accountability with regard to respecting, protecting and fulfilling the right to health for children.

Recognition of the need for *equity* (giving particular attention to the most disadvantaged) is also a human rights requirement, which means that particular attention must be given to the most vulnerable and marginalised groups of children, i.e. those from poor families and/or children whose parents belong to socially marginalised groups (ethnic minorities, asylum seekers, migrants, disabled persons, persons with alcohol or drug problems, *etc.*). In addition, particular conditions may be systematically awarded a lower priority n the healthcare system. In Norway, it has been reported that many municipalities have not developed appropriate treatment for children and adolescents with psychiatric conditions, and that children of parents with drug and alcohol problems are lagging behind in the healthcare system, especially if the parents have a foreign background. Children who have a mental disability in combination with a psychiatric condition are also lacking adequate services.[74] The Committee on the Rights of the Child has pointed out that homeless adolescents are vulnerable to violence, abuse and sexual exploitation, self-destructive behaviour, substance abuse, and mental disorders, and that these issues must be addressed in educational and social policies.[75] In addition, young mothers are typically in need of social protection in terms of follow-up to ensure access to services, obstetric care, counselling, and eventually safe abortion services (where abortion is not against the law).[76]

The regional WHO office has supported countries in implementing the strategy with regard to situation analysis in countries, workshops and seminars, and the

72 WHO Regional Office for Europe, *European strategy for child and adolescent health and development. From resolution to action*, Copenhagen, 2008, pp. 5–9.

73 *Ibid.*, p. 6.

74 Norwegian Health Inspection, Tilsynsmelding (yearly report) 2007.

75 General Comment No. 4, 2003 Adolescent health and development in the context of the Convention on the Rights of the Child, para. 36.

76 *Ibid.*, para. 31.

development of case studies identifying progress, challenges and successes. Lessons from the case studies show that political commitment, backed by action and resource allocation, are of paramount importance in making progress. Identifying and meeting the needs of at-risk groups is necessary in order to increase equity, and to pay systematic attention to gender differences in the area of child and adolescent health. Intersectoral collaboration has been identified as a major strength, and it is suggested that ministries of health should have an important leadership role. Direct youth participation in the health sector is not widely practiced and needs to be implemented, and it is suggested that NGOs and other organisations with extensive experience involving young people play a leading role.[77]

One major cause for concern is the continuing growth of inequalities in exposure to environmental risks. A study launched by the WHO has revealed that the social distribution of environmental exposures and related deaths and disease shows very significant inequalities both between and within countries.[78] Following the *Children's Environment and Health Action Plan for Europe* (CEHAPE),[79] countries need to increase the focus on children, to include scientific experts in the legislative process, to develop child injury prevention plans, to involve government agencies from the beginning of all intervention and development plans, to harmonise EU and national legislation, to use existing infrastructure for collaboration, to assess the comparative cost-effectiveness of synergy with a policy on climate change, to increasingly use and report to existing systems, and to collect better data on the regional priority goals.[80] In the *Parma Youth Declaration*,[81] youth participation, education, the protection of children's health through the CEHAPE priority goals (safe water and sanitation, protection from injuries, adequate physical activity, clean outdoor and indoor air, a chemical and biological risk free environment), and climate change, are essential concerns in order to secure the health and lives of future generations.

8. CONCLUSION: HUMAN RIGHTS NOT A MATTER OF CHOICE BUT OF LEGAL REQUIREMENT

The WHO Regional Office for Europe stated in its report on health and environment that: '(F)rom an ethical point of view, the people affected by inequalities, who are the most vulnerable in the current economic crisis, must be

77 *Ibid.*, p. 10.

78 WHO Regional Office for Europe, *Protecting children's health in a changing environment. Report from the Fifth ministerial Conference on Environment and Health.* Copenhagen, 2010, p. 3.

79 Adopted by the WHO Fourth Ministerial Conference on Environment and Health.

80 WHO Regional Office for Europe, *Protecting children's health in a changing environment. Report from the Fifth Ministerial Conference on Environment and Health.* Copenhagen, 2010, p. 16.

81 Adopted at the Fifth Ministerial Conference on Environment and Health, 2010.

considered.'[82] However, an important point is that not only ethics, or a suitable policy of good practice, but also human rights, demand not only consideration, but also *actions* to address such inequalities.[83] It is a matter of legal requirement, and not only a matter of political choice, to implement adequate strategies for the realisation of children's right to health protection, in line with human rights obligations and in response to the particular challenges in each country. As Paul Hunt convincingly argued, contemporary human rights are 'a powerful ally in the struggle against harmful social determinants.'[84] Indeed, the comprehensive approach to health, which is particularly visible in the European Social Charter, should be utilised to reach its full potential to the benefit of children's health and well-being in all European countries. The human rights perspective offers a legal dimension that contributes to the notions of responsibility, accountability and efficiency in the protection and promotion of children's right to health. Recommendations by the CESCR, in particular, General Comment No. 14, should be kept in mind. Services must be not only available and accessible to children, but also acceptable and of good scientific and medical quality (paragraph 12). Services must be designed to meet the particular needs of young individuals of different cultural and social backgrounds (acceptability), and must meet all professional and ethical standards (quality). It is essential to identify and give particular attention to marginalised and vulnerable groups in various countries and contexts in order to fulfil the human right to health for all children on a basis of equity.

---

82 WHO Regional Office for Europe, *Protecting children's health in a changing environment.* Copenhagen, 2010, p. 16.

83 Paul Hunt, Missed opportunities: human rights and the Commission on Social Determinants of Health, *Global Health Promotion* 2009, http://ped.sagepub.com, pp. 35–41, at p. 39.

84 *Ibid.*, p. 40.

CHAPTER 9

THE RIGHTS OF PERSONS WITH DISABILITIES IN THE CONTEXT OF HEALTHCARE

Oddný Mjöll Arnardóttir

1. INTRODUCTION

Persons with disabilities are faced with a wide array of human rights challenges in the context of healthcare. Disability, however, also intersects with other identity markers, and the human rights challenges experienced by women, children, the elderly, ethnic minorities and migrants may be even more complex and pronounced if the person at hand also has a disability.[1] It should also be kept in mind that persons with disabilities are not a homogenous group, and that the various sub-groups are each confronted with their own unique set of issues. Access to care for HIV positive persons, pre-natal screening for Down's Syndrome, and conditions and practices in psychiatric wards are all examples of issues that touch upon disability, healthcare and human rights with implications for particular sub-groups of disabled people. It is, of course, impossible to deal with all the issues that may arise in a short chapter like the present one. The following discussion will therefore necessarily have to be focused on selected issues that highlight key elements of the human rights challenges that disabled people may meet in the healthcare setting. The issues dealt with will be non-discrimination and accessibility, on one hand, and mental disability and autonomy, on the other. Autonomy is discussed in the context of mental disability, specifically because this group is particularly vulnerable to human rights violations. At the same time, readers are reminded that respect for disabled people's autonomy is, like non-discrimination and accessibility, a cross-cutting theme that has a general relevance in healthcare.

---

1 For example, one British study showed that individuals from minority groups were more likely to be compulsorily admitted into psychiatric wards than white patients, S.P. Singh and T. Burns, 'Race and mental health: there is more to race than racism', *British Medical Journal* 2006 pp. 648–651.

While the European context and legal sources, as defined in Chapters 1 (The Council of Europe) and 2 (The European Union) *supra*, remains the focus of this chapter, bringing the new UN Convention on the Rights of Persons with Disabilities (CRPD) into the discussion is unavoidable.[2] Firstly, this is necessary as it is the first human rights convention that the EU itself has become a party to. In the internal hierarchy of the EU legal order, international agreements binding on the EU rank second after the EU's primary law (Treaties) but before EU secondary law (Directives, Regulations).[3] It seems clear, therefore, that the CRPD will have a significant effect on the interpretation of secondary EU law. Secondly, as the CRPD is the first and only disability-specific human rights convention, it expresses an international consensus on the content of the human rights of persons with disabilities to a degree of specificity unparalleled by any other source of law. It is, therefore, highly likely to have an effect on the interpretation of other human rights norms, as they apply to persons with disabilities. This can, in fact, already be discerned in the case law under the European Convention on Human Rights (ECHR),[4] and is likely to apply similarly in the context of the European Charter of Fundamental Rights (ECFR) in future.

2. DISABILITY AND HEALTH

Defining disability is a highly complex endeavour. Historically, it can be said that there existed two competing approaches to understanding and defining disability – a medical understanding and a social understanding of disability. The World Health Organization (WHO) explains the conceptual difference in the following terms:

> The *medical model* views disability as a feature of the person, directly caused by disease, trauma or other health condition, which requires medical care provided in the form of individual treatment by professionals. Disability, on this model, calls for medical or other treatment or intervention, to 'correct' the problem with the individual.

---

2 Convention on the Rights of Persons with Disabilities, 13 December 2006, A/Res/61/106.

3 A. Rosas and L. Armati, *EU Constitutional Law: An Introduction*, Oxford: Hart Publishing 2010, p. 42.

4 ECtHR 30 April 2009, *Glor v. Switzerland*, no. 13444/04 (www.echr.coe.int), para. 53; and ECtHR 20 May 2010, *Alajos Kiss v. Hungary*, no. 38832/06 (www.echr.coe.int), para. 44. See, also, D. Björgvinsson, 'The Protection of the Rights of Persons with Disabilities in the Case Law of the European Court of Human Rights' in O.M. Arnardóttir and G. Quinn (eds.), *The UN Convention on the Rights of Persons with Disabilities – European and Scandinavian Perspectives*, Leiden: Martinus Nijhoff Publishers 2009, pp. 160–161.

> The *social model* of disability, on the other hand, sees disability as a socially created problem and not at all an attribute of an individual. On the social model, disability demands a political response, since the problem is created by an unaccommodating physical environment brought about by attitudes and other features of the social environment.
>
> On their own, neither model is adequate, although both are partially valid.[5]

The International Classification of Functioning, Disability and Health (ICF), which was adopted in 2001,[6] changed the WHO's previous focus on the medical model of disability. The ICF now forwards a '*biopsychosocial*' model of disability, which synthesises the medical and social models of disability without reducing the complex phenomenon of disability into either component. On this understanding:

> ... disability and functioning are viewed as outcomes of interactions between ***health conditions*** (diseases, disorders and injuries) and ***contextual factors.*** Among contextual factors are external ***environmental factors*** (for example, social attitudes, architectural characteristics, legal and social structures, as well as climate, terrain and so forth); and internal ***personal factors***, which include gender, age, coping styles, social background, education, profession, past and current experience, overall behaviour pattern, character and other factors that influence how disability is experienced by the individual.[7]

In a similar vein, Article 1 CRPD stipulates that '[p]ersons with disabilities include those who have long-term physical, mental, intellectual or sensory impairments which in interaction with various barriers may hinder their full and effective participation in society on an equal basis with others.' Disability, therefore, is not simply a synonym of 'illness', 'sickness' or 'health condition'. Instead, the concept indicates that disability is the result of the interaction between a person's health status or impairment and the context she finds herself in.[8] At the same time, a long-term health status or impairment is a necessary conceptual element, as passing or short-term ailments would not meet the criteria for constituting disability. This is clear from the wording of Article 1 CRPD, and has, in fact, also been confirmed by the European Court of Justice

---

5 World Health Organization, *Towards a Common Language for Functioning, Disability and Health*, WHO/EIP/GPE/CAS/01.3, Geneva 2002, pp. 8–9.

6 World Health Organization, *International Classification of Functioning, Disability and Health (ICF)*, Geneva 2001.

7 *Towards a Common Language for Functioning, Disability and Health*, see note 5, p. 10.

8 See, generally, R. Traustadóttir, 'Disability Studies, The Social Model and Legal Developments', in O.M. Arnardóttir and G. Quinn (eds.), *The UN Convention on the Rights of Persons with Disabilities – European and Scandinavian Perspectives*, Leiden: Martinus Nijhoff Publishers 2009, pp. 3–16.

(ECJ) in the context of Directive 2000/78/EC establishing a general framework for equal treatment in employment and occupation.[9]

The United Nations has referred to persons with disabilities as 'the world's largest minority'.[10] A recent World Report on Disability was prepared jointly by the World Bank and the WHO.[11] It explored evidence of the barriers that disabled people meet, identified needs, and provided examples of best practices in terms of improving the lives of disabled people in the socioeconomic sphere, including in the field of health and rehabilitation. In this way, it was, *inter alia*, intended to support the implementation of the CRPD. Based on this report, it is now estimated that around 15% of the world's population, or over a billion people, have some kind of a disability. Of these, between 110 and 190 million people are estimated to be severely disabled, and to experience significant problems with functioning.[12] According to the World Report, statistical evidence also shows 'a pronounced increase in the prevalence of chronic conditions in the general population',[13] and the world's population is also ageing at 'unprecedented rates.'[14] These trends together provide for an estimate that the prevalence of disability is generally on the increase. The UN Development Programme (UNDP) has estimated that 80 per cent of the world's disabled population lives in developing countries, and according to the UN Educational, Scientific and Cultural Organisation (UNESCO), an estimated 90 per cent of the children within this group do not attend school. While the figures on education may not be as alarming in the developed world, the Organisation for Economic Co-Operation and Development (OECD) has reported that the less educated groups within their Member States have a considerably higher proportion of persons with disabilities among them than the better educated groups, or 19% as compared to 11%.[15] When looking towards the elderly specifically, one study showed that among the oldest European men (aged 80+),

---

9 Directive 2000/78, OJ [2000] L303/16. ECJ, Case C-13/05 *Sonia Chacón Navas* [2006] ECR I-6467 (www.eur-lex.europa.eu). According to the Court: '(...) the concept of 'disability' must be understood as referring to a limitation which results in particular from physical, mental or psychological impairments and which hinders the participation of the person concerned in professional life' (cf. para. 43). The Court also stated that 'There is nothing in Directive 2000/78 to suggest that workers are protected by the prohibition of discrimination on grounds of disability as soon as they develop any type of sickness' (cf. para. 46).

10 United Nations Web Services Section, Department of Public Information, 2006, *Some Facts about Persons with Disabilities*, available at www.un.org/disabilities/convention/facts.shtml, accessed June 2011.

11 World Health Organization and World Bank, *World Report on Disability*, World Health Organization 2011, available at http://whqlibdoc.who.int/publications/2011/9789240685215_eng.pdf, accessed June 2011.

12 World Health Organization, *World Report on Disability Factsheet: main messages and recommendations*, available at www.who.int/disabilities/world_report/2011/factsheet.pdf, accessed June 2011.

13 *World Report on Disability*, 2011, see note 11, p. 32.

14 *Ibid.*, p. 35.

15 *Some Facts about Persons with Disabilities*, 2006, see note 10.

the prevalence of disability is 58.8% among the less educated, while it is 40.2% among the better educated.[16] In a similar vein, the International Labour Organization (ILO) reports that unemployment among persons with disabilities is significantly higher than for other groups.[17] It is, therefore, perhaps not surprising that the link between disability and poverty has also been documented in many studies.[18]

According to the WHO, the most common disabilities are associated with chronic health conditions, infectious diseases, malnutrition, mental illnesses and injuries.[19] Even if some disabled people are, in fact, healthy despite their disabilities (e.g. persons with intellectual and sensory impairments), it is clear that the socially disadvantaged position of disabled people as a group also has wide-reaching implications in terms of the social determinants of health.[20]

3. NON-DISCRIMINATION AND ACCESSIBILITY

Article 1 of the Universal Declaration of Human Rights (UDHR) proclaims that '[a]ll human beings are born free and equal in dignity and rights.' Further, Article 2 stipulates that everyone is entitled to all the rights and freedoms set forth in the Declaration, without distinction of any kind. The opening of the UDHR highlights the central role of the idea of equality in human rights discourses. In fact, the principle of equality is reflected in some form or another in all the major international human rights instruments. Claims to non-discrimination and respect for human dignity form the simplest, yet most fundamental, human rights claims of persons with disabilities. This is expressed in Article 1 of the CRPD, which stipulates that the purpose of the convention is to 'promote, protect and ensure the full and equal enjoyment of all human rights and fundamental freedoms by all persons with disabilities, and to promote respect for their inherent dignity.'

16 World Health Organization, Commission on Social Determinants of Health Final Report, *Closing the Gap in a Generation: health equity through action on the social determinants of health,* 2008, available at http://whqlibdoc.who.int/publications/2008/9789241563703_eng.pdf, accessed June 2011, p. 30.

17 *Some Facts about Persons with Disabilities,* 2006, see note 10.

18 J. Braithwaite and D. Mont, *Disability and Poverty: A Survey of World Bank Poverty Assessments and Implications,* The World Bank, SP Discussion Paper No. 0805, February 2008, available at http://siteresources.worldbank.org/DISABILITY/Resources/280658-1172608138489/WBPovertyAssessments.pdf, accessed June 2011.

19 World Health Organization, *Concept Note World Report on Disability and Rehabilitation,* available at www.who.int/disabilities/publications/dar_world_report_concept_note.pdf, accessed June 2011.

20 *Closing the Gap in a Generation: health equity through action on the social determinants of health,* see note 16. In fact, disability is an issue that cuts across the various themes addressed in the report, both with regards to the improvement of daily living conditions (Chapters 5, 6, 7, 8 and 9), and with regard to tackling the inequitable distribution of power and resources (Chapter 14).

The right to non-discrimination can either be formulated as a cross-cutting but accessory right that relates only to the equal enjoyment of other human rights (cf. Article 14 ECHR and Article 2 ICCPR), or as an independent right that also applies in all fields of life (cf. Protocol 12 to the ECHR, Article 26 ICCPR and Article 5 CRPD). Protocol 12 to the ECHR was adopted in 2000, but has only been ratified by 18 (mostly Central and Eastern European) Member States of the Council of Europe. For many Europeans, therefore, the right to non-discrimination in health-related matters only becomes effective to the extent that health rights have been interpreted as coming under the scope of protection ('ambit') of Articles 2, 3, 5 and 8 of the ECHR (cf. Chapter 1, *supra*). Non-discrimination based on disability is also dealt with in EU law to a certain extent. Article 21 of the ECFR contains a non-discrimination clause that bans discrimination on any ground, and Article 26 deals with the 'right of persons with disabilities to benefit from measures designed to ensure their independence, social and occupational integration and participation in the life of the community.' According to Article 10 TFEU, the EU shall also aim to combat discrimination based on the discrimination grounds of sex, racial or ethnic origin, religion or belief, disability, age or sexual orientation. Directive 2000/78/EC establishing a general framework for equal treatment in employment and occupation includes the discrimination ground of disability, but the scope of protection is confined to the labour market. This is in contrast to the wider scope of Directive 2000/43/EC implementing the principle of equal treatment between persons irrespective of racial or ethnic origin,[21] which extends the protection against racial discrimination to the field of social protection, including social security and healthcare (cf. its Article 3(1)(e)). Disabled Europeans who meet discriminatory barriers in the healthcare setting will not, therefore, find particularly effective protection against discrimination in the non-discrimination Directives unless Directive 2000/78 is changed.[22] However, according to Article 51 ECFR, the Charter is directed to the EU and the Member States when implementing EU law. To the extent that the EU has competencies and has legislated on issues involving health law (cf. Chapter 2, *supra*), this legislation and its implementation shall respect the principle of non-discrimination based on disability, as stipulated in Articles 21 and 26 ECFR. In conclusion, is seems clear that the non-discrimination obligation under Article 14 ECHR, Article 1 of protocol 12 to the ECHR, and Article 21 ECFR, can potentially apply to various health and healthcare related situations for persons with disabilities.

---

21 Directive 2000/43, OJ [2000] L180/22.

22 Proposal for a Council Directive on Implementing the Principle of Equal Treatment Between Person Irrespective of Religion or Belief, Disability, Age or Sexual Orientation, COM (2008) 426.

The analytical approach of the European Court of Human Rights in non-discrimination cases is well established, and includes that first it must find that different treatment has occurred, and then it will test whether it has an objective and reasonable justification which can be found if the treatment in question pursues a legitimate aim and satisfies the Court's proportionality test.[23] The width of the margin of appreciation and the corresponding strictness of review by the Court, however, varies. The discrimination ground in question is a key factor in that respect, as different treatment based on certain discrimination grounds can only be justified by 'very weighty reasons.'[24] The Court has established more or less clearly that the 'suspect' discrimination grounds calling for very weighty reasons include sex, ethnic origin/race, birth in or outside marriage, nationality, religion and sexual orientation. In 2009, it also added disability to this list of 'suspect' discrimination grounds by explicitly stating that the state's margin of appreciation is 'greatly reduced'[25] in cases involving discrimination on the grounds of disability. This indicates the importance that is by now attached in human rights law to the inclusion and equal treatment of persons with disabilities in society. The advent of the CRPD, with its clear emphasis on inclusion and non-discrimination, undoubtedly had a significant effect on this development.

The equal treatment of similar situations is not, however, the only facet of the prohibition of discrimination. The European Court of Human Rights has made clear that the right to non-discrimination is also violated 'when states without an objective and reasonable justification fail to treat differently persons whose situations are significantly different.'[26] This second aspect of the principle of equality calls for changes, accommodations or differences in approach when these are called for by the specific situation of certain groups of people, and are needed to ensure their participation in society on an equal footing with others. Two simple examples illustrate this. It is a fact of life that not everyone can use staircases or hear the spoken word. This disadvantage should be accommodated for by providing, e.g., lifts or other means of accessibility or interpretation in sign language in the context of healthcare. Only by way of such accommodation can non-discrimination truly prevail. This second facet of the prohibition of discrimination is also commonly referred to as 'reasonable accommodation'. The CRPD makes particularly clear the understanding that the concept of non-discrimination includes an obligation of reasonable accommodation in the context of disability. Its Article 5(3) stipulates that '[i]n order to promote equality and eliminate discrimination, States Parties shall take all appropriate steps to ensure that reasonable accommodation is provided.' Similarly, Article 2(4)

---

23 ECtHR 28 October 1987, *Inze v. Austria*, no. 8695/79 (www.echr.coe.int), para. 41.

24 *Ibid.*

25 *Glor v. Switzerland*, see note 4, para. 84 ('fortement réduite').

26 ECtHR 6 April 2000, *Thlimmenos v. Greece*, no. 34369/97 (www.echr.coe.int), para. 44.

defines the concept of discrimination as including 'all forms of discrimination, including denial of reasonable accommodation.' In the context of EU law, Article 5 of Directive 2000/78 also requires reasonable accommodation for disabled persons '[i]n order to guarantee compliance with the principle of equal treatment.' Although the protective scope of this Directive is limited to the labour market, and it is therefore not directly relevant to our present study, it confirms the importance of including reasonable accommodation in the right to non-discrimination in the context of disability.

The question of accessibility of facilities and services is closely related to the non-discrimination obligation. Disabled people meet various barriers to accessing health services on an equal basis with others. These barriers may, for example, lie in the lack of physical accessibility of buildings in which healthcare is provided, the lack of availability of appropriate transportation to get there, or the inaccessibility of information due to its format or the means of communication used.[27] Sometimes the barriers may lie beneath the surface, and originate in stereotypical views of disabled people and the attitudes of healthcare providers, which may lead to a lesser quality of care. For example, persons with disabilities are four times as likely to report being treated badly, and three times as likely to report being denied care, than non-disabled persons.[28]

Under the CRPD, Article 9 stipulates an independent right to accessibility and provides that states shall 'take appropriate measures to ensure to persons with disabilities access, on an equal basis with others, to the physical environment, to transportation, to information and communications, including information and communications technologies and systems, and to other facilities and services open or provided to the public, both in urban and in rural areas.' In this context, the facilities highlighted include schools, housing, medical facilities and workplaces (cf. Article 9(1)(a)). The right to accessibility in connection with healthcare is reinforced even further by the right to health. The right to health for persons with disabilities is provided for in Article 25 CRPD, as well as in Article 12 CESCR. As was also discussed in Chapter 3, *supra,* the right to health under Article 12 CESCR is considered to contain four interrelated and essential elements. These are the *availability* of functioning public health and healthcare facilities, goods and services, the *accessibility* of these to everyone without discrimination, the *acceptability* of these in light of ethical and cultural considerations, and the requirement of *quality* in terms of facilities, goods and services being scientifically and medically appropriate. Accessibility in this context has a fourfold meaning. Firstly, it refers to the general non-discrimination obligation; secondly, to physical accessibility, including health

---

27 A. Lawson, 'The United Nations Convention on the Rights of Persons With Disabilities: New Era or False Dawn?', 34 *Syracuse Journal of International Law and Commerce,* (2007), pp. 563619, at p. 567.

28 World Health Organization, *Disability and Health, Fact sheet no. 352, June 2011,* available at www.who.int/mediacentre/factsheets/fs352/en/index.html, accessed June 2011.

services within safe physical reach and access to buildings; thirdly, it refers to economic accessibility, including affordable health services for socially disadvantaged groups; and finally, it refers to information accessibility, including the right to seek, receive and impart information and ideas on health-related matters.[29] In conclusion, it can therefore be said that the requirement that the healthcare system must be accessible to persons with disabilities does not only draw on the normative force of the ban against discrimination, but also on the independent right to accessibility under the CRPD and the right to health under the ICCPR. Together these provide the normative key to unlocking many of the discriminatory barriers that disabled people may encounter in the healthcare setting.

4. MENTAL DISABILITY AND AUTONOMY

Persons with mental disabilities form a particular sub-group that is especially vulnerable to various human rights violations.[30] This is not, however, a completely homogenous group. It comprises both persons diagnosed with all kinds of mental illness, such as depression, bipolar disorder, schizophrenia, and anxiety disorders; people affected by intellectual impairments which include, e.g., learning disabilities and autism; and conditions related to age, such as dementia and Alzheimer's disease.[31] The human rights issues faced by this group relate, first and foremost, to institutionalisation and medical treatment, as well as issues regarding legal capacity. The issues raised in the context of healthcare include (but are not limited to) compulsory admission to psychiatric institutions or institutions for persons with intellectual impairments, over-crowded and/or out-dated facilities, the use of physical restraints, the over-use of sedative medication, violence, compulsory medical treatment, the over-controlling of the activities of admitted persons, and other forms of lack of respect for their privacy and autonomy.[32] In this context, the WHO has, in fact, emphasised that '[l]arge institutions, which are often associated with human rights violations, should be replaced by community care facilities, backed by

---

29 Committee on Economic, Social and Cultural Rights, *General Comment no. 14 - The Right to the Highest Attainable Standard of Health*, E/C.12/2000/4, para. 12.

30 For a good discussion of all these issues in the context of the European Court of Human Rights, see P. Bartlett, O. Lewis and O. Thorold, *Mental Disability and the European Convention on Human Rights*, Leiden: Martinus Nijhoff Publishers 2007.

31 *Ibid.*, 1.

32 ECtHR 27 March 2008, *Shtukaturov v. Russia*, no. 44009/05, para. 25. Also, Bartlett, Lewis and Thorold, 2007, see note 30, pp. 75–76; and J. Fiala and O. Lewis, 'Human rights aspects of deaths of institutionalized people with disabilities in Europe', in L. Clements and J. Reid (eds.), *Disabled People and the Right to Life*, London: Routledge 2008, pp. 127–147, at pp. 129–130.

general hospital psychiatric beds and home care support.'[33] Lack of respect for personal autonomy is an underlying theme in all these situations. The following analysis will discuss European standards with regard to admissions to institutions and medical treatment of persons with mental disabilities.

4.1. PLACEMENT IN INSTITUTIONS

The ECFR, Article 6, stipulates that everyone has the right to liberty and security of person. The CRPD does the same but, somewhat curiously, does not provide detailed guidelines on the conditions under which the involuntary placement of persons with mental disabilities in healthcare institutions might be considered legitimate, and when it might be considered illegitimate. Instead, its Article 14(2) simply stipulates that 'if persons with disabilities are deprived of their liberty through any process, they are, on an equal basis with others, entitled to guarantees in accordance with international human rights law and shall be treated in compliance with the objectives and principles of the present Convention, including by provision of reasonable accommodation.' Apart from stipulating in Article 14(1) that the existence of a disability *per se* should never suffice to justify a deprivation of liberty, these issues are therefore left to be regulated by other human rights conventions.

Looking at the Council of Europe, the most detailed regulation of the issue of placement in institutions is provided by Recommendation Rec(2004)10, on the protection of the human rights and dignity of persons with mental disorder.[34] While this recommendation only has the status of 'soft-law' and is not legally binding upon the Member States, it reflects European consensus on best practices in the field. It places a special emphasis on regulating involuntary placement and involuntary treatment of persons with mental disabilities, and stipulates detailed criteria for involuntary placement in psychiatric facilities in Article 17:

1. A person may be subject to involuntary placement only if all the following conditions are met:
   i. the person has a mental disorder;
   ii. the person's condition represents a significant risk of serious harm to his or her health or to other persons;
   iii. the placement includes a therapeutic purpose;

---

33 World Health Organization information sheet, *Promoting the Rights of People with Mental Disabilties,* available at www.who.int/mental_health/policy/legislation/1_PromotingHRofPWMD_Infosheet.pdf, accessed June 2011.

34 Recommendation No. Rec(2004)10 of the Committee of Ministers to member states concerning the protection of the human rights and dignity of persons with mental disorder, adopted 22 September 2004, available at www.coe.int/t/dg3/healthbioethic/texts_and_documents/Rec(2004)10_e.pdf, accessed June 2011.

iv. no less restrictive means of providing appropriate care are available;
v. the opinion of the person concerned has been taken into consideration.

2. The law may provide that exceptionally a person may be subject to involuntary placement, in accordance with the provisions of this chapter, for the minimum period necessary in order to determine whether he or she has a mental disorder that represents a significant risk of serious harm to his or her health or to others if:
   i. his or her behaviour is strongly suggestive of such a disorder;
   ii. his or her condition appears to represent such a risk;
   iii. there is no appropriate, less restrictive means of making this determination; and
   iv. the opinion of the person concerned has been taken into consideration.

More importantly, perhaps, the legally binding and justiciable Article 5 ECHR regulates the deprivation of liberty in the form of involuntary placements in psychiatric institutions. By now there exists considerable jurisprudence from the European Court of Human Rights on the relevant issues. Under Article 5 ECHR everyone has the right to liberty and security of person, and no one shall be deprived of their liberty. At the same time, Article 5(1)(a) to 5(1)(e) allow for certain types of deprivations of liberty, including, in Article 5(1)(e), the lawful detention of persons of 'unsound mind'. When approaching Article 5, it is important to bear in mind that any deprivation of liberty legitimised by this provision is an exception to the main principle of the right to liberty. The stipulations in Article 5(1)(a) to Article 5(1)(e) are, therefore, interpreted narrowly. The Court will carefully scrutinise whether a deprivation of liberty falls under any of these narrowly construed exceptions, both as regards the substantive guarantees against abuse contained therein, and their formal and procedural aspects.[35]

A preliminary question that arises is the issue of what actually constitutes a deprivation of liberty in the meaning of Article 5. The concept of a deprivation of liberty under Article 5 entails both an objective element and a subjective element. The objective element refers to a restriction on liberty of a kind exceeding that of a simple restriction on the freedom of movement. In *Guzzardi v. Italy,* the Court set out the relevant test for assessing the concrete situation at hand. Under this test 'account must be taken of a whole range of criteria such as the type, duration, effects and manner of implementation of the measure in question.'[36] While confinement to a particular 'closed' or 'locked' facility would be the clearest example of a deprivation of liberty, the Court also made clear that '[t]he difference between deprivation of and restriction upon liberty is nonetheless merely one of degree or intensity, and not one of nature or

35 See, e.g., ECtHR 13 January 2011, *Haidn v. Germany,* no. 6587/04 (www.echr.coe.int), paras. 81–97.

36 ECtHR 6 november 1980, *Guzzardi v. Italy,* no. 7367/76 (www.echr.coe.int), para. 92.

substance.'[37] The objective element of a deprivation of liberty can, therefore, either consist of 'confinement in a particular restricted space for a not negligible length of time'[38] or wide-reaching control and restrictions on movement continuously applied to persons placed in 'open' wards or institutions.[39] The subjective element of the concept of a deprivation of liberty additionally requires that the person in question has not validly consented to his or her confinement.[40]

If a deprivation of liberty occurs the Court has set out four key substantive guarantees for it to be 'lawful' under Article 5(1)(e). These guarantees against abuse can be derived from the *Winterwerp v. the Netherlands* and *Ashingdane v. the United Kingdom* judgments, and have been consequently applied and further elaborated in subsequent case law. Firstly, except in emergency cases, the presence of unsound mind must be reliably shown. More precisely, this means that a 'true mental disorder' must be established before a competent national authority on the basis of 'objective medical expertise.'[41] A medical indication for detention is therefore strictly needed, but the form and procedure for obtaining the required medical opinion may vary according to circumstances. If there is no emergency a *prior* consultation is necessary, or at least, if the person does not agree to a consultation, a prior assessment by a medical expert of his or her case file.[42] The assessment must, in all cases, focus on 'the actual state of mental health of the person concerned and not solely on past events.'[43] Therefore, a medical report will not be sufficient if it has not been recently prepared. In emergency situations, however, when the person in question has, for example, been arrested for violent behaviour, or presents a danger to other people, it may be acceptable to obtain a medical opinion after the arrest or detention.[44] Such emergency measures are, however, only justified 'for a short duration',[45] after which the usual guarantees must be met independently. Recommendation Rec

---

37 *Ibid.*, para. 93.

38 ECtHR 16 June 2005, *Storck v. Germany*, no. 61603/00 (www.echr.coe.int), para. 74.

39 In ECtHR 28 May 1985, *Ashingdane v the United Kingdom*, no. 8225/78 (www.echr.coe.int), the applicant was also considered detained during periods when he was in an open ward with the possibility of unescorted leave outside the hospital grounds (cf. paras 24 and 42). In ECtHR 5 October 2004, *H.L. v. the United Kingdom*, no 45508/99, the applicant 'was under continuous supervision and control and was not free to leave' (cf. para. 91). This included restricted contact with the outside world and the acknowledgment of the responsible medical officer that she would have prevented him from leaving had he tried.

40 *Storck v. Germany*, see note 38, para. 74. In a case involving a 12-year-old minor, however, the ECtHR established that '[i]t must be possible for a child like the applicant to be admitted to hospital at the request of the holder of parental rights, a case which clearly is not covered by paragraph 1 of Article 5...', see *Nielsen v. Denmark*, no. 10929/84 (www.echr.coe.int), para. 72.

41 ECtHR 24 October 1979, *Winterwerp v. the Netherlands*, no. 6301/73 (www.echr.coe.int), para. 39.

42 ECtHR 5 October 2000, *Varbanov v. Bulgaria*, no. 31365/96, (www.echr.coe.int), para. 47.

43 *Ibid.*

44 ECtHR 5 November 1981, *X v. the United Kingdom*, no. 7215/75 (www.echr.coe.int), paras. 44–45.

45 *Ibid.*, para. 46.

(2004) 10 also provides that the doctor preparing the medical report, or the court or other competent body making the decision, should inform any representative of the person concerned and consult those close to him or her, unless the person concerned objects, or it is impracticable or inappropriate to perform such a consultation. This applies to all involuntary placements, including emergency situations (cf. Articles 20(5), 20(6) and 21(2)).

The second substantive condition under Article 5(1)(e) ECHR requires that the person's condition 'must be of a kind or degree warranting compulsory confinement.'[46] Under this test, compulsory confinement can either be warranted by the person's need for clinical treatment or the fact that he or she poses a threat to him or herself or to other people, irrespective of whether the condition is amenable to medical treatment or not.[47] According to Article 17 of Recommendation Rec(2004)10, any such placement should, nevertheless, also have a therapeutic purpose, which may be prevention, diagnosis, control or cure of the disorder, and rehabilitation. Also, in light of the fact that a deprivation of liberty is a very serious interference with human rights, the European Court of Human Rights has emphasised the principle of proportionality in this context. Therefore, a deprivation of liberty 'is only justified where other, less severe measures have been considered and found to be insufficient to safeguard the individual or public interest which might require that the person concerned be detained.'[48] The Court has, accordingly, emphasised that compulsory admission to an institution must have been 'necessary in the circumstances'.[49] This coincides with the principle of least restriction stipulated in Article 8 of Recommendation Rec(2004)10, which provides that 'persons with mental disorder should have the right to be cared for in the least restrictive environment available and with the least restrictive or intrusive treatment available, taking into account their health needs and the need to protect the safety of others.'

---

46 *Winterwerp v. the Netherlands*, see note 41, para. 47.

47 ECtHR 20 February 2003, *Hutchison Reid v. The United Kingdom*, no. 50272/99 (www.echr.coe.int), para. 52.

48 ECtHR 4 April 2000, *Witold Litwa v. Poland*, no. 26629/95, (www.echr.coe.int), para. 78. The case concerned the detention of 'alcoholics' under Article 5(1)(e), as opposed to persons of 'unsound mind'. The same principles, nevertheless, apply. The applicant was accused of causing a row in a post office, and was detained as an alcoholic under Article 5(1)(e). He was kept for 6 ½ hours at a specific sobering-up centre. The Court found this disproportionate to the circumstances, as the police could just as well have taken less severe measures in the situation, such as taking him to a public healthcare establishment, or to his home (cf. para. 79).

49 ECtHR 20 April 2010, *C.B. v. Romania*, no. 21207/03 (www.echr.coe.int), para. 48 ('*indispensable au vu des circonstances*'). Here, the applicant was detained for 14 days in a maximum security ward at a psychiatric hospital where doctors actually found no obvious signs of any psychological disorder. His detention had not been based on the prior opinion of a psychiatrist, but simply on a public prosecutor's doubts as to his mental health, and on a medical certificate produced by a general practitioner who had never seen or examined the applicant. The Court emphasised the disproportionate nature of the measures applied to the applicant, and found a violation (cf. paras. 50–51).

The third condition of lawfulness deals with the length of confinement, and requires the persistence of the mental disorder to justify its continuation.[50] When interpreting this requirement under Article 5 ECHR, it is also helpful to look at the more detailed guidelines in Recommendation Rec(2004)10, which provide, in Article 24(1), that involuntary placement should be terminated if any of the criteria for the lawfulness of the measure are no longer met. Article 24(4) further stipulates that the duration of involuntary placement should be minimised by the provision of appropriate aftercare services.

Finally, the fourth substantive condition of lawfulness under Article 5 ECHR requires that the place and conditions of detention must be appropriate to the condition of the detainee. This means that if a person is to be detained on the ground that he/she is of 'unsound mind', the detention must take place in a therapeutic environment, i.e. in a 'hospital, clinic or other appropriate institution.'[51] At the same time, the Court has made clear that Article 5(1)(e) does not, in principle, deal with what is suitable in terms of treatment or conditions during placement.[52] On these questions, Articles 8 and 3 ECHR come into play instead, and will be discussed from the perspective of medical treatment in Section 4.2, *infra*.

As regards the formal and procedural guarantees under Article 5(1)(e) ECHR, the first requirement is that any deprivation of liberty shall be 'lawful' in the formal sense and 'in accordance with a procedure prescribed by law.' In light of the seriousness of any interference with people's liberty, the Court places a great emphasis on the principle of legal certainty, as expressed by these overlapping terms. They require, firstly, that the substantive and procedural rules of domestic law are strictly complied with.[53] Secondly, they require that the domestic law in question is of sufficient quality. As to the quality of the domestic law, the Court will carefully monitor that the domestic law in question is accessible, that it defines the conditions for deprivation of liberty in clear terms, and that the law is sufficiently precise to allow the person, if need be with appropriate advice, to foresee to a reasonable degree the consequences of his or her action.[54] Domestic law must, finally, provide fair and proper procedures to prevent any arbitrariness in how decisions are made in this area.[55] This seems to

50 *Winterwerp v. the Netherlands*, see note 41.

51 *Ashingdane v. the United Kingdom*, see note 39, para. 44. See, also, ECtHR 30 July 1998, *Aerts v. the Netherlands*, no. 25357/94 (www.echr.coe.int), para. 46; and for a recent example of the application of this condition, see *Haidn v. Germany*, see note 35, para. 94.

52 *Ashingdane v. the United Kingdom*, *ibid.*

53 In ECtHR 3 October 2006, *Gajcsi v. Hungary*, no. 24503/03 (www.echr.coe.int), for example, the domestic legislation in question required a patient's dangerousness as a condition for compulsory hospitalisation and treatment. As the domestic court's decisions in the case did not assess the applicant's alleged or potential 'dangerous conduct' the Court concluded that the prolongation of the applicant's compulsory treatment was not prescribed by law under Article 5(1) (cf. para. 21).

54 ECtHR 9 January 2001, *Kawka v. Poland*, no. 25874/94 (www.echr.coe.int), para. 49.

55 *H.L. v. the United Kingdom*, see note 39, para. 115.

require fixed procedural rules dealing with issues such as the grounds of admission, the time limits for compulsory placement, the continuing assessment of the disorder warranting detention and legitimising its continuation, and the appointment of a legal representative of patients in such procedures.[56] When interpreting Article 5 ECHR on the procedural guarantees required, it is again helpful to look at Recommendation Rec(2004)10. Under Article 20(1) of the Recommendation, the decision on involuntary placement should be taken by a court, or other competent body, which should take the opinion of the person concerned into account, and should hear the case in accordance with a procedure under which he or she is seen and consulted. Article 20(3), further, provides that the decision on involuntary placement should be documented and should state the maximum period beyond which it should be subject to review. Finally, and independently of the express review period required under Article 20(3), the Recommendation provides, in Articles 22 and 25, that the person subject to involuntary placement should have an independent right of review at reasonable intervals and a right to appeal, and should be duly informed of those rights.

4.2. TREATMENT

4.2.1. General principles

Article 17 CRPD provides the general principle that '[e]very person with disabilities has a right to respect for his or her physical and mental integrity on an equal basis with others.' Article 25(d) CRPD also stipulates that the same quality of care should be provided to persons with disabilities as others, including on the basis of free and informed consent. Similarly, Article 3 ECFR provides that in the fields of medicine and biology, the right to respect for physical and mental integrity requires the free and informed consent of the person concerned, according to procedures laid down by law. These are very important stipulations, and perhaps particularly so in the context of the treatment of mental health patients. Psychiatric treatments have, indeed, been referred to as extraordinarily personal in that they relate to 'altering the self.'[57] It is therefore of utmost importance that human rights standards regarding medical interventions are strictly applied in the context of psychiatric treatment.

Under the ECHR, Article 8 on the right to private life is the primary source of protection of personal autonomy in the context of medical interventions. The European Court of Human Rights has made clear that the protective scope of Article 8 ECHR includes the physical and psychological integrity of the

[56] *Ibid.*, para. 120.

[57] Bartlett, Lewis and Thorold, 2007, see note 30, p. 112.

person,[58] including a right to personal autonomy,[59] which obviously encompasses all interventions and decision-making in the health field. The Court has also made clear that any administration of medication is an interference with physical integrity, and that 'even a minor interference with the physical integrity of an individual must be regarded as an interference with the right to respect for private life under Article 8 if it is carried out against the individual's will.'[60] If the individual in question is a minor, or is completely unable to express his or her will, the will of his or her formal legal proxy must be respected in the same way.[61]

The requirement of informed consent is the primary medium for respecting a person's autonomy in relation to healthcare. Medical treatment that is based on informed consent would therefore not raise any serious issues under Article 8 ECHR. Article 8, however, does not provide the details on what is required by 'informed consent', and would, in this respect, be interpreted in light of the Biomedicine Convention. According to Article 5(1) of the Biomedicine Convention, interventions in the health field may only be carried out after the person concerned has given free and informed consent to it. As regards the question of whether 'free and informed' consent must also always be 'express', the explanatory report to the Biomedicine Convention clarifies that this is not always so. Consent may be implied in the context of routine medical acts, whereas express consent is rather required in cases involving invasive treatments.[62] In this context, the extraordinarily personal character of psychiatric treatments should be borne in mind, and lead to the conclusion that such interventions should as a general rule be regarded as invasive treatments requiring express consent. The Biomedicine Convention further stipulates that appropriate information shall be given to the patient on the purpose and nature of the intervention, as well as on its consequences and risks, and that consent may be freely withdrawn at any time (cf. Article 5(2) and 5(3)). Its Article 8, however, states that in emergencies any medically necessary interventions may be carried out without consent if they are for the immediate benefit of the individual concerned, and under Article 9, any previously expressed wishes should be taken into account when the patient is not in a state to express his or her wishes. Articles 6 and 7, however, contain specific rules on the protection of persons not able to consent, and on the compulsory treatment of persons with mental disorders. These provide exceptions to the general rule of informed consent in Article 5, and will be dealt with specifically in Sections 4.2.2 and 4.2.3.

---

58 ECtHR 29 April 2002, *Pretty v. UK*, no. 2346/02 (www.echr.coe.int), para. 61.

59 ECtHR 10 April 2007, *Evans* v. *UK*, no. 6339/05 (www.echr.coe.int), para. 71.

60 *Storck* v. *Germany*, see note 38, para. 143.

61 ECtHR 9 March 2004 *Glass* v. *UK*, no. 61827/00 (www.echr.coe.int), para. 70.

62 Biomedicine Convention, Explanatory Report, available at http://conventions.coe.int/treaty/en/Reports/Html/164.htm, accessed June 2011, para. 37. See, also, *Glass v. UK*, *ibid.*, para. 82.

4.2.2. Compulsory medical treatment

As established in the *Storck v. Germany* judgment, even minor interferences with physical integrity will be regarded as an interference with Article 8 if they are carried out against the patient's will. All compulsory interventions, therefore, raise serious issues under Article 8(1) ECHR. However, even if interference is found to have occurred, this does not necessarily lead to a finding of a violation of Article 8. Instead, it must be assessed whether this interference is, then, a justifiable limitation to the right to private life under Article 8(2), which provides that such limitations must be in accordance with the law, and necessary in a democratic society in the interests of the legitimate aims of, e.g., public security, for the protection of health, or for the protection of the rights and freedoms of others. In *Storck*, for example, the applicant had reached the age of majority and had not been placed under guardianship. Between 1977 and 1979 she was nevertheless involuntarily placed in a locked ward at a private psychiatric clinic and treated there for schizophrenia at the request of her father and against her own will. This was clearly an interference with her right to respect for private life under Article 8(1). It therefore had to be justified under Article 8(2). As the applicable German law on the detention of mental patients for the purpose of medical treatment necessitated a court order if the person concerned did not consent or was unable to consent, this led to the conclusion that the treatment of the applicant was not 'in accordance with the law' in the meaning of Article 8(2). Therefore, a violation was found. Even if all the correct procedures had been followed, the applicant's compulsory treatment would also have had to be 'necessary in a democratic society' and proportionate to the legitimate aims pursued under Article 8(2). As an expert report had concluded in 1994 that the applicant had, in fact, never suffered from schizophrenia, and that her behaviour had instead been caused by conflicts with her family, it can be concluded that there would still have been a violation of Article 8 on the basis of a violation of the principle of proportionality in this case.

In contrast to the protective scope of Article 8, which encompasses even minor interventions, Article 3 ECHR protects against torture, inhuman and degrading treatment, which means that the treatment complained of must attain a certain minimum level of severity. This must be assessed in each individual case with reference to 'the nature and context of the treatment, the manner and method of its execution, its duration, its physical or mental effects and, in some cases, the sex, age and state of health of the victim.'[63] Article 3 is therefore implicated in the more serious cases that involve the use of force or physical restraint. In *Herczegfalvy* v. *Austria*, for example, the patient was diagnosed with paranoia querulans, and was compulsorily detained under Article 5(1)(c), as he was considered dangerous and not criminally responsible for his acts. He

---

63 ECtHR 26 October 2000, *Kudla v. Poland*, no. 30210/96 (www.echr.coe.int), para. 91.

violently resisted both feeding and medication that were forcefully administered to him nevertheless. He was also at times kept in isolation and attached to a security bed with handcuffs. The minimum level of severity of Article 3 was reached in this situation and the case fell to be examined thereunder, instead of under Article 8. The Court emphasised that 'the position of inferiority and powerlessness which is typical of patients confined in psychiatric hospitals calls for increased vigilance in reviewing whether the Convention has been complied with.'[64] At the same time, however, the Court stated that a measure which is a therapeutic necessity cannot, as a matter of principle, be regarded as inhuman or degrading, and that it is 'for the medical authorities to decide, on the basis of the recognised rules of medical science, on the therapeutic methods to be used, if necessary by force, to preserve the physical and mental health of patients who are entirely incapable of deciding for themselves (...)'[65] The review of the Court was therefore limited to assessing whether it was convincingly shown that a medical necessity existed in the case at hand. When assessing medical necessity, however, the Court generally does not re-evaluate that which is supported by expert medical evidence before it.[66] Therefore, in *Herczegfalvy*, while noting that it found the treatment of the applicant worrying, it came to the conclusion that '(...) the evidence before the Court is not sufficient to disprove the Government's argument that, according to the psychiatric principles generally accepted at the time, medical necessity justified the treatment in issue.'[67] It therefore found no violation of Article 3. However, if arguable allegations of mistreatment reaching the minimum level of severity under Article 3 have not been sufficiently investigated at the domestic level, the Court may find a violation of the procedural element of Article 3, which requires a thorough and effective investigation into such allegations.[68]

While the key elements of the protection against compulsory medical interventions can be discerned from the ECHR case law discussed *supra*, they also stand to be supplemented by the more detailed provisions of the Biomedicine Convention and the Council of Europe Recommendation Rec(2004)10, on the protection of the human rights and dignity of persons with mental disorder. Article 7 of the Biomedicine Convention stipulates:

---

64 ECtHR 24 September 1992, *Herczegfalvy* v. *Austria*, no. 10533/83 (www.echr.coe.int), para. 82.

65 *Ibid.*

66 See, e.g., Y. Arai-Takahashi, *The Margin of Appreciation Doctrine and the Principle of Proportionality in the Jurisprudence of the ECHR*, Antwerpen: Intersentia 2001, p. 209.

67 *Herczegfalvy* v. *Austria*, see note 63, para. 83. Compare with ECtHR 11 July 2006, *Jalloh* v. *Germany*, no. 54810/00 (www.echr.coe.int). Here, the case concerned the forceful extraction of criminal evidence from a detainee's body. Emetics were forcefully administered orally, while the detainee was held down by four police officers, instead of waiting for the evidence to pass naturally. This was considered to be inhuman and degrading treatment in violation of Article 3 (cf. paras. 82–83).

68 ECtHR 14 December 2006, *Filip v. Romania*, no. 41124/02 (www.echr.coe.int), paras. 46–51.

> Subject to protective conditions prescribed by law, including supervisory, control and appeal procedures, a person who has a mental disorder of a serious nature may be subjected, with or without his or her consent, to an intervention aimed at treating his or her mental disorder only where, without such treatment, serious harm is likely to result to his or her health.

As expressly stated, Article 7 only legitimises the compulsory treatment of the mental disorder itself, but not of other medical problems.[69] It also requires that any compulsory treatment must be authorised by law and that this law must provide for supervisory, control and appeals procedures, such as those provided by a judicial process.[70] Further, Article 7 only permits compulsory treatment of a mental disorder if the patient's own health would otherwise be seriously endangered. Compulsory treatment of persons with mental disorders for the purpose of protecting other interests, therefore, does not fall under Article 7. Instead, this falls under the general limitation clause in Article 26 of the Biomedicine Convention, which is equivalent to the limitation clause in Article 8(2) ECHR. Both provide that the right to respect for privacy, including personal autonomy in the context of medical treatment, can be limited if such limitations are in accordance with the law, and necessary in a democratic society in the interest of public safety, the prevention of crime, for the protection of public health, or for the protection of the rights and freedoms (e.g. security) of others.

Council of Europe Recommendation Rec (2004) 10 adds even more detail to the appropriate substantive guarantees against abuse in the context of involuntary treatment for mental disorders. According to its Article 20(4), any involuntary treatment must be based on an examination by a doctor, and must in be accordance with valid and reliable professional standards. Articles 18 and 19 further provide that before compulsory treatment is resorted to, it must be established that no less intrusive means of providing appropriate care are available. It must also be ensured that such treatment takes place in an appropriate environment, and that the opinion of the person concerned is taken into consideration. The compulsory treatment itself should be proportionate to the patient's health and aim to enable treatment acceptable to him or her as soon as possible. Any such treatment also has to be documented and administered in accordance with a treatment plan prepared in consultation with the patient, or his or her representative. The possible duration of involuntary treatment is also circumscribed in Article 24, which provides that it should be discontinued if any of the substantive criteria are no longer met. Further, in emergency situations, Article 21 stipulates that involuntary treatment should only be allowed for a short period of time, after which all the usual substantive guarantees against abuse and the relevant procedural guarantees must be met.

---

69 Biomedicine Convention, Explanatory Report, see note 62, paras. 52–53.

70 *Ibid.*, para. 55.

As regards the appropriate procedural guarantees in cases of involuntary treatment, Article 20(2) of Recommendation Rec(2004)10 provides that the decision should be taken by a court or other competent body, which should take the opinion of the person concerned into account and should hear the case in accordance with a procedure under which he or she is seen and consulted. However, if the person is also under a compulsory placement in an institution, it is not considered necessary that a court or other competent body takes decision on compulsory treatment, as the Recommendation provides that '...the decision to subject that person to involuntary treatment may be taken by a doctor having the requisite competence and experience, after examination of the person concerned and taking into account his or her opinion.' In all other respects, the Recommendation subjects compulsory treatment to the same procedural guarantees as those that apply to involuntary placement in institutions. These include the documentation of decisions that must state the maximum period beyond which they should be reviewed (Article 20(3)), access to reviews and appeals concerning the lawfulness of involuntary treatment (Article 25), and the right to information about that access (Article 22).

4.2.3. The protection of persons not able to consent

Specific rules apply to minors and persons not able to consent to medical treatment due to mental disability, a disease or similar reasons. As opposed to the rules on involuntary treatment, these are not only relevant when the mental disorder itself is being treated, but also regarding other medical interventions. The Biomedicine Convention, Article 6, provides that in such situations, and instead of informed consent from the patient, the authorisation of parents, a legal representative, or any person or body provided for by law (proxy), should be sought. Article 6 provides:

1. Subject to Articles 17 and 20 below, an intervention may only be carried out on a person who does not have the capacity to consent, for his or her direct benefit.
2. Where, according to law, a minor does not have the capacity to consent to an intervention, the intervention may only be carried out with the authorisation of his or her representative or an authority or a person or body provided for by law.
   The opinion of the minor shall be taken into consideration as an increasingly determining factor in proportion to his or her age and degree of maturity.
3. Where, according to law, an adult does not have the capacity to consent to an intervention because of a mental disability, a disease or for similar reasons, the intervention may only be carried out with the authorisation of his or her representative or an authority or a person or body provided for by law.
   The individual concerned shall as far as possible take part in the authorisation procedure.

4. The representative, the authority, the person or the body mentioned in paragraphs 2 and 3 above shall be given, under the same conditions, the information referred to in Article 5.
5. The authorisation referred to in paragraphs 2 and 3 above may be withdrawn at any time in the best interests of the person concerned.

In the context of adults with mental disability, the key issue here is the question of when a person is actually incapable of providing consent. The explanatory report to the Biomedicine Convention explains that this must be understood in the context of a given intervention.[71] There is, in fact, considerable scope for abuse and disregard of the autonomy of persons with disabilities if the formal status of being declared legally incompetent or the formal status of having been medically diagnosed with a certain condition automatically lead to the fact that a person is classified as unable to consent to interventions in the health field. Such an overly formal and medicalised approach carries with it the danger that the legal system misjudges the mental capacity of persons with mental illness or intellectual disabilities. In fact, the presence of a mental illness or intellectual disability does not necessarily impact on all decision-making abilities. One study, for example, showed that around 50% of those diagnosed with schizophrenia did not have decreased decision-making capacities in relation to treatment decisions.[72] Like Bartlett, Lewis and Thorold have put it: 'It is simply wrong to assume that people with mental disorder are necessarily unable to make decisions: most can.'[73]

According to the explanatory report to the Biomedicine Convention, the question of when a person has the capacity to consent to medical interventions is not regulated by the Convention, but refers back to domestic legal systems. In some legal systems such capacity is verified for each intervention, whereas in other legal systems it relies on the institution of legal incapacitation where a person is declared legally incapable for making all or certain kinds of decisions in their lives. The explanatory report, however, emphasises that '[i]f adults have been declared incapable but at a certain time do not suffer from a reduced mental capacity (for example because their illness improves favourably), they must, according to Article 5, themselves consent.'[74] This means that domestic legal systems must require an adult patient's personal consent to an intervention if the facts of the case at the time of the intervention reveal that he or she does not suffer decreased decision-making ability with regard to the treatment options in question. This applies, irrespective of whether the patient has been formally

71 *Ibid.*, para. 42.

72 T. Grisso and P. Appelbaum, 'The MacArthur Treatment Competence Study III: Ability of Patients to Consent to Psychiatric and Medical Treatments', 19(2) *Law and Human Behaviour* (1995), pp. 149–174, at p. 169.

73 Bartlett, Lewis and Thorold, 2007, see note 30, p. 4.

74 Biomedicine Convention, Explanatory Report, see note 62, para. 43.

deprived of legal capacity, or not. This approach is clearly supported by the principle of respect for the dignity, autonomy and independence of persons with disabilities stipulated in Article 3(a) CRPD. It is also in concordance with Article 12(3) CRPD, which stipulates that states 'shall take appropriate measures to provide access by persons with disabilities to the support they may require in exercising their legal capacity.' Article 12(3), indeed, provides for a *supported* instead of a *substituted* decision-making model for persons with disabilities. Such a model requires the maximum preservation of decision-making capacity and autonomy for persons with disabilities, and includes a flexible approach that can be tailored to diverse situations. The decision-making model stipulated under Article 12(3) should obviously also be brought to bear on the interpretation of Article 25(d) CRPD, requiring support, flexibility and maximum preservation of decision-making capacity in the context of free and informed consent to medical treatment.[75] It should, further, be pointed out that the same flexible approach is also forwarded in Council of Europe Recommendation Rec (1999) 4 on the legal protection of incapable adults.[76]

All the sources on the protection of persons with diminished decision-making capacity referred to *supra* also influence the interpretation of the ECHR. In *Shtukaturov v Russia,* for example, the ECtHR referred to Recommendation Rec(1999)4, and interpreted Article 8 ECHR as requiring 'tailor-made responses'[77] to the kind or degree of mental disorder in question when it comes to legal incapacitation orders. By analogy, the same interpretation would appear appropriate under Article 8 in the context of consent for medical interventions.[78]

If, despite the cautious and flexible approach to decision-making capacity discussed *supra*, a person is found incapable of providing consent, Article 6 of the Biomedicine Convention on decision-making by proxy applies. However, if the patient nevertheless objects to placement in a psychiatric facility, or to treatment, Council of Europe Recommendation Rec(2004)10 provides yet another layer of protection. This additional layer of protection applies even when there is a legal proxy, and his or her will is clear. If the patient him or herself still objects to the placement or treatment concerned, Article 16 of the Recommendation provides that its Articles 17–25 on compulsory placement and

---

75 For a discussion of Article 12(3) CRPD, see *Study on challenges and good practices in the implementation of the UN Convention on the Rights of Persons with Disabilities – Final Report*, Brussels October 2010, available at www.study-uncrpd.eu/en/documents/show/&tid=51, accessed June 2011, pp. 91–93.

76 Recommendation No. R(99)4 of the Committee of Ministers to the Member States on principles concerning the legal protection of incapable adults, adopted 23 February 1999, available at www.coe.int/t/dg3/healthbioethic/texts_and_documents/Rec(99)4E.pdf, accessed June 2011. See particularly its principles 2 and 3.

77 *Shtukaturov v. Russia,* see note 32, paras. 94–95.

78 In the *Shtukaturov* judgment, however, the applicant's complaints regarding compulsory medical treatment were unsubstantiated, as he did not provide any evidence as to which medical treatment he received, or on how it affected him, *ibid.*, para. 128.

compulsory treatment apply, and provide both substantive and procedural guarantees against abuse (cf. Section 4.2.2, *supra*).

5. CONCLUDING REMARKS

According to Article 3 CRPD, the themes of dignity, autonomy and equality of persons with disabilities form the underlying principles of the Convention. These are, in fact, particularly important in the context of healthcare, which deals with fundamental issues of life and death and the human condition. The health rights of persons with disabilities must, therefore, always be understood and interpreted in light of these principles. Whereas these principles apply across the board for all groups of disabled persons, the vulnerability and history of human rights abuses also calls for a particular vigilance as regards mental health patients.

The increasing prevalence of chronic diseases, the growth and ageing of the world's population, and advances in medical science that enable the preservation and prolonging of life all contribute to a trend towards an increase in the world's disabled population.[79] It is, therefore, appropriate that the CRPD expresses a significantly increased emphasis on disability rights. The publication of the World Report on Disability further highlights how disability is a unique issue that must be addressed specifically in the context of healthcare. Together, these developments are bound to have an effect on how health law will evolve. As a concluding remark, it is asserted that an increased awareness of disability rights will be called for in future.

79 *World Report on Disability*, 2011, see note 11, pp. 32–35; and *Concept Note World Report on Disability and Rehabilitation*, see note 19.

CHAPTER 10

THE RIGHT TO HEALTH PROTECTION FOR THE ELDERLY: KEY ELEMENTS AND STATE OBLIGATIONS

Henriette SINDING AASEN

> 'We commit ourselves to providing older persons with universal and equal access to health care and services, including physical and mental health services, and we recognize that the growing needs of an ageing population require additional policies, in particular care and treatment, the promotion of healthy lifestyles and supportive environments'.[1]

1. INTRODUCTION

The number of people aged 60 and over is growing faster than any other age group. Between 1950 and 2005, people's chances of surviving to old age improved substantially in all world regions, including Europe. Currently, on a global scale, three quarters of those born can expect to reach the age of 60 (only 55% in Africa, 85% in Europe, and 91% in North America). Those who survive to age 60 can also expect to live longer than before, and women longer than men.[2] In Europe, it is estimated that between 1998 and 2025, the proportion of persons classified as older will increase from 20 to 28 per cent.[3] On average, life expectancy within the European Union (EU) is projected to increase from about 76 years in 2005, to nearly 82 in 2050.[4] Increased survival, however, does not automatically mean that all the added years will be lived in good health. Rather,

1 UN, Report of the Second World Assembly on Ageing, Madrid, 8–12 April 2002, Annex I, Political Declaration, extract from Article 14.

2 UN Department of Economic and Social Affairs, Office of the High Commissioner for Human Rights, Current Status of the social situation, well-being, participation in development and rights of older persons worldwide, draft report of August 2010, p. 36.

3 UN Report of the Second World Assembly on Ageing, Madrid, 8–12 April 2002, Annex 2: Madrid International Plan of Action on Ageing, para. 2.

4 E. Rynning with further references, 'The Ageing Population of Europe – Implications for Health Systems and Patients'Rights', in *European Journal of Health law* 15, 2008, pp. 297–306, at p. 298.

the expected number of healthy years is always lower than the life expectancy. As people age, health problems increase, disability and illness rise significantly, and the need for healthcare services increases, especially in very old age (80 years and above), which will be the fastest growing group in the years to come.[5]

This is sometimes called the health paradox: 'Instead of decreasing our overall healthcare needs, an improved standard of health may in fact generate increased healthcare needs.'[6]

The global demographic change towards an ageing population will affect all aspects of individual and social life, including healthcare systems. In most countries worldwide today, although with great regional and national variations, older persons do not have sufficient access to appropriate health care services, and training in geriatric medicine is lagging behind the demand. Even in a rich country like Norway, it has been documented that there is a lack of care for older patients.[7]

There is a growing need for long-term care services, and a significant level of abuse and neglect of older persons has been reported, across all economic and social strata.[8]

Patients with dementia are increasing, in particular, in high-income countries, due to the fact that more individuals reach the age of 80. It is estimated that the number of people living with Alzheimer's disease and other forms of dementia will double every 20 years, in particular in low and middle-income countries.[9]

Due to reduced mental capacity and communication abilities, these persons are particularly vulnerable to inadequate treatment, care and follow-up.

In recent years, the issue of human rights for the elderly has been addressed more frequently all over the world. Accordingly, the notions of 'active ageing' and 'a society for all ages'[10] are in frequent use in global as well as regional and

---

5 The European Health Report, 2009, pp. 13, 54. UN Department of Economic and Social Affairs, Office of the High Commissioner for Human Rights, Current Status of the social situation, well-being, participation in development and rights of older persons worldwide, draft report of August 2010, p. 41, Rynning with further references, *ibid.*

6 Rynning, *ibid.* See, also, WHO Europe, The European Health Report 2009. Health and Health Systems, p. 54.

7 R. Førde *et al.*, 'Får eldreomsorgen nok ressurser?' [Sufficient resources to the care for the elderly?] *Tidsskrift for Den norske legeforening* No. 15, 10 August 2006, www. tidsskriftet.no.

8 UN Department of Economic and Social Affairs, Office of the High Commissioner for Human Rights, Current Status of the social situation, well-being, participation in development and rights of older persons worldwide, draft report of August 2010, p. 66.

9 *Ibid.*, pp. 38–39, 41.

10 A society for all ages was the theme of the 1999 International Year of Older Persons, and reiterated at the Second World Assembly on Ageing in Madrid, in the Political Declaration (see, in particular, Article 3) and in the Madrid International Plan of Action on Ageing, para. 11.

national legal and policy frameworks. International organisations such as the UN, the WHO and the EU have condemned all forms of discrimination based on age ('ageism'), and governments are committed to eliminating age discrimination and to providing older persons with equal access to healthcare services. But still, older men and women are identified as a group at particular risk of human rights violations, and requiring specific measures of protection.[11]

Particular risks to old persons in institutions with mental disabilities, e.g., due to dementia, are various forms of autonomy and privacy violations relating to medical treatment and care.[12]

In this chapter, the right to health protection for the elderly is conceptualised within international and European human rights regulation, which includes access to appropriate healthcare services, as well as other health-related strategies. The chapter starts out with an overview of the legal sources and starting points (2), other important instruments (3), an overview of important health concerns relating to old age and so-called 'ageism' (4), a brief discussion of the right to protection from maltreatment and serious neglect derived from Article 3 of the European Convention for the Protection of Human Rights and Fundamental Freedoms (ECHR 1950) (5), and then a discussion of state obligations relating to the right to health protection for the elderly, including equitable access to healthcare of appropriate quality in Article 3 of the Convention on Human Rights and Biomedicine (Biomedicine Convention 1997) and relevant provisions on health protection in the revised European Social Charter (ESC 1996) and the Charter of Fundamental Rights of the European Union (EU Charter 2000) (6). The chapter ends with some final remarks (7).

The terminology used to describe older persons varies considerably, even in international instruments and documents ('elderly', 'seniors', 'older persons', 'the ageing', 'the aged', *etc.*). Also, the age at which a person becomes 'elderly' or 'old' varies. Harris and Darcy point out that an obvious definition of older persons would be the age at which a person becomes eligible for an old-age pension and other 'senior citizen' benefits. However, this age varies among different countries, and may also differ between men and women.[13]

In the European Union, the term 'older persons' or 'the elderly' refer to persons older than 65 years of age, while in UN statistical service and documents, the same term covers persons aged 60 and above.[14]

In this chapter, the term 'older persons', or 'the elderly', will be used interchangeably to refer to persons who are older than 60 years of age, since UN

11 UN Department of Economic and Social Affairs, Office of the High Commissioner for Human Rights, Current Status of the social situation, well-being, participation in development and rights of older persons worldwide, draft report of August 2010, pp. 61, 64.
12 See Chapter 9 in this volume.
13 The European Social Charter, p. 251.
14 General Comment No. 6, para. 9.

documents are also used to describe the health conditions of the elderly in Europe.

2. LEGAL SOURCES AND STARTING POINTS

Unlike the regulation of the right to health in Article 12 of International Covenant on Economic, Social and Cultural Rights (ICESCR 1966), which covers the main aspects of the right to health, the European Regulation is more fragmented (see Chapter 3 of this volume). Different instruments address different aspects of the right to health protection, access to healthcare, and other forms of health protection respectively. Both the Council of Europe and the European Union have produced important legal instruments in the field of health protection in Europe, also with regard to older persons. As for Council of Europe instruments, Article 3 ECHR will be discussed briefly, while Article 3 of the Biomedicine Convention and relevant provisions in the revised ESC will be given more attention. At the EU level, Article 35 EU Charter[15] is the most significant instrument. All the instruments (except the ECHR, which deals with civil and political rights[16]) demonstrate a broad concept of human rights (including social rights), and that individual and public health as well as social concerns relating to health protection are becoming increasingly important matters at the European level of law and government.

Although European instruments and sources are the main focus in this chapter, including the Explanatory Report to the Biomedicine Convention (Explanatory Report 1996)[17] and decisions by the European Court of Human Rights (ECtHR), regulation at the UN level forms an important background and context for the understanding of the European Regulation. Most important is Article 12 ICESCR, paragraph 1, on the 'right of everyone to the enjoyment of the highest attainable standard of physical and mental health',[18] and the specification, *inter alia*, in Article 12, paragraph 2, sub-paragraph d that States parties should take steps in order to create 'conditions which would assure to all medical service and medical attention in the event of sickness.' General Comment No. 14 (General Comment 14 2000) on the right to health, written by the Committee on Economic, Social and Cultural Rights (CESCR), is a significant source for the understanding of the right to health protection, internationally as well as regionally. Strictly speaking, General Comment No. 14 is not legally binding.

15 The Charter became legally binding when the EU Lisbon Reform Treaty entered into force in 2009 (see Chapter 2).

16 However, many of the provisions assume positive obligations to prevent violations, e.g., in terms of care for patients (see Section 5, below concerning Article 3 ECHR).

17 Council of Europe.

18 This is the general provision at the international level concerning the right to health.

However, it is considered as an authoritative document for the understanding of the right to health, referred to by all authorities and scholars in the field, and thus it will be referred to when considered appropriate. The three levels of state responsibility for human rights – respect, protect and fulfil[19] – will be integrated in the legal analysis as far as they give input to the understanding of state obligations in this context (see, also, Chapter 3).

In General Comment No. 14, the CESCR gives specific guidelines on how to understand and interpret the state obligations following from Article 12 ICESCR, i.e. the duty of making healthcare and underlying health determinants available, accessible, acceptable, and of good quality.[20]

All EU Member States and most Members of the Council of Europe have ratified the ICESCR, and thus Article 12 and General Comment 14 provide common references concerning the right to health protection. Another relevant instrument at the international level is the Convention on the Rights of Persons with Disabilities (CRPD), which contains significant provisions for elderly persons with health related disabilities, and to which the EU is a party. However, due to limited space, this Convention will not be discussed here, but is commented upon elsewhere in the volume (Chapter 9).

3. OTHER IMPORTANT INSTRUMENTS

In addition to the above-mentioned instruments, several soft law instruments form an important political-legal framework for the global, regional and national efforts to protect and promote the health and well-being of older persons. The opening sentence of the UN Declaration of the rights of the elderly (1991) states that the goal is '[t]o add life to the years that have been added to life',[21] signifying that the quality of life for older persons should be ensured. The Declaration formulates five interrelated principles in order to achieve this goal: independence, participation, care, self-fulfilment and dignity. The principle of care is the most relevant in relation to access to adequate healthcare and other services, while the other principles can only be achieved if the health and well-being of older persons are protected on a broad scale. The UN principles for older persons are

19 This tripartite understanding of state obligations was first presented by Asbjørn Eide at a seminar for the UN University in 1981 (A. Eide, 'State obligations revisited' in W.B. Eide and U. Kracht, *Food and Human Rights in Development*, vol. II, Antwerpen: Intersentia 2007, pp. 137–161. On p. 118 he comments on the relationship between his threefold typology and the American philosopher Henry Shue's comparable categorisation (*Basic Rights: Subsistence, Affluence and U.S. Foreign Policy*, Princeton University Press 1980).

20 The 'AAAQ' in paragraph 12 of General Comment No. 14, see, also, Chapter 3 in this book.

21 Adopted at the UN General Assembly on 16 December 1991 (Resolution No. 46/91).

reaffirmed in the Madrid Political Declaration and International Plan of Action on Ageing (MIPAA),[22] Article 3 in the Political Declaration.[23]

Article 14 of this Declaration puts sets out the commitment of 'providing older persons with universal and equal access to healthcare and services, including physical and mental health services.' Furthermore, it is recognised that 'the growing needs of an ageing population require additional policies, in particular care and treatment, the promotion of healthy lifestyles and supportive environments.'[24]

The MIPAA, which, in general, seeks to mainstream ageing into all global, regional and national economic and social policy fields, recommends actions in several priority areas, including health.[25]

Six overall health issues are pointed out: health promotion and well-being throughout life, universal and equal access to healthcare services, older persons and HIV/AIDS, the training of care providers and health professionals, mental health needs of older persons, and older persons and disabilities. Several objectives with related actions complement and concretise these issues, and some of them will be mentioned in the discussion of state obligations below.

At the European level, the UN Economic Commission for Europe (UNECE), embarked on a parallel regional strategy with the work on MIPAA. Five months after the World Assembly on Ageing in Madrid, the UNECE Ministerial Conference on Ageing took place in Berlin, resulting in a Ministerial Declaration and the Regional Implementation Strategy (RIS) for the MIPAA,[26] which includes a catalogue of ten main commitments (with several sub-commitments) in the field of ageing. Commitment 4 is to adjust social protection systems in response to demographic changes and their social and economic consequences, while Commitment 7 is to strive to ensure quality of life at all ages and to maintain independent living including health and well-being. Of interest concerning the implementation of the right to health protection for the elderly at the national level is the MIPAA Guiding Framework and Toolkit for Practitioners and Policy Makers, written by the UN Department of Economic and Social Affairs, Division for Social Policy and Development.[27]

I consider the aforementioned soft law instruments, which are, formally speaking, non-binding, as important documents when it comes to the national implementation of the right to health protection for older persons. Although these instruments are not legally binding, they are important documents that

22 Adopted at the UN World Assembly on Ageing, Madrid 8–12 April, 2002.

23 The Political Declaration constitutes Annex I of the resolution, while the Madrid International Plan of Action on Ageing is Annex II.

24 Article 14 of the Political Declaration.

25 Priority direction II: Advancing health and well-being into old age (pp. 22–32).

26 Berlin, 11–13 September 2002.

27 Document prepared by R. Lane and F. Serour, dated 07/03/2008.

provide necessary strategies and guidelines for mainstreaming public policies that need to be developed in order to realise the right to health protection for the elderly in Europe. This point is observed by CESCR, General Comment 6 on the economic, social and cultural rights of older persons, which points out that States Parties, in order to comply with Article 12 ICESCR, paragraph 1, should take into account the Vienna International Plan of Action on Ageing (1982),[28] which was the UN plan of action on ageing at that time (before the Madrid International Plan of Action on Ageing/MIPAA[29]).

4. HEALTH CONCERNS AND 'AGEISM'

Social inequality in health is widespread and rising in the European region,[30] affecting, in particular, poor people in need of costly healthcare and services, in particular, in countries with less developed welfare systems. As already mentioned, health problems and impairment tend to increase with age, as does the need for healthcare services. Among older people, non-communicable diseases such as cardiovascular disease, strokes and cancer account for most deaths and most of the disease burden. In 2004, non-communicable diseases caused 86 per cent of deaths at ages 60 or above (ranging from 77% of deaths in low-income countries, to 91% in high-income countries). The burden of non-communicable diseases is higher in low and middle-income countries than in high-income countries, especially for heart disease and stroke.

The leading causes of disability among older persons worldwide in high-income and lower-income countries include many of the same conditions, with hearing loss, vision problems, arthritis, heart and lung diseases, and Alzheimer's disease and other forms of dementia being among the ten most common in both groups of countries. Hearing loss ranks highest in both high-income and low and middle-income countries. Alzheimer's disease and other forms of dementia rank higher in high-income countries, while unintentional injuries are among the top ten causes of disability in the older population in low and middle-income countries.[31]

28 General Comment 6, Thirteenth session 1995, para. 34.
29 http://social.un.org/index/Ageing/Resources/MadridInternationalPlanofActiononAgeing.aspx.
30 WHO Europe: The European Health Report 2009. Health and health systems, p. 45. See also Chapters 7 and 8 in this volume.
31 United Nations, Department of Economic and Social Affairs, Office of the High Commissioner for Human Rights, Current Status of the social situation, well-being, participation in development and rights of older persons worldwide, draft report of August 2010, pp. 36–39.

Studies in both developed and developing countries show that women's advantage in life expectancy is accompanied by a greater burden of chronic disease and impairment in old age.[32]

Rising levels of obesity, increased tobacco and alcohol consumption in some groups, the emergence of new infectious diseases, including HIV/AIDS, and the resurgence of old ones (malaria and tuberculosis), combined with economic or political crisis have contributed to increased mortality in some countries. Many countries in Eastern Europe and the former USSR have experienced rising adult mortality since the 1970s, especially among men. Life expectancy also declined after the early 1990's in those countries hardest hit by HIV/AIDS.[33]

National studies show that a significant proportion of older persons suffer from depression, loneliness and anxiety, most often in connection with major life changes (e.g. the death of a spouse, the occurrence of cancer, stroke, diabetes, dementia, *etc.*). It is estimated that around 1–3% of people over 65 years of age are severely depressed, while 10–15% suffer from milder forms of depression. Depression is linked to the rise in suicide rates with advancing age, which is seen in many countries, especially among men. Despite the fact that depression often improves with treatment, the condition is often overlooked among the old due to a lack of knowledge among caregivers and health professionals.[34]

Another serious health issue with particular relevance to the elderly is neglect, abuse and violence, either in domestic or residential care, carried out by caregivers, staff, visiting family members, friends, or other residents. Stress related to caregiving can lead to neglect, abuse, and even violence. A German survey of nursing home staff showed that 79% of the staff acknowledged having abused or neglected a resident at least once during the prior two months, and 66 per cent witnessed comparable actions by other staff, with neglect and psychological abuse the most common forms. Institutional abuse is associated with poorly trained and/or overworked staff, and when care standards are low and inadequately monitored.[35]

Poor nutrition and malnutrition occur in 15 to 50 per cent of the elderly population, but the symptoms of malnutrition (weight loss, disorientation, lightheadedness, lethargy and loss of appetite) can easily be mistaken for illness or disease.[36]

---

32 UN Department of Economic and Social Affairs, Office of the High Commissioner for Human Rights, Current Status of the social situation, well-being, participation in development and rights of older persons worldwide, draft report of August 2010, p. 38.

33 *Ibid.*, p. 40.

34 *Ibid.*, p. 40–41.

35 *Ibid.*, p. 49.

36 www.sparkpeople.com/resource /nutrition_articles.asp?id=869, accessed 2 September 2011.

Age discrimination is reported in both developing and developed countries. In the more developed countries, age-based inequalities in clinical treatment are partly linked to a lack of gerontological or geriatric training. According to a research review from 18 developed countries, many physicians have preconceptions and negative attitudes towards older people, which sometimes lead to rationing of care on the basis of age rather than on an objective clinical assessment of the patient's likelihood of benefiting from treatment.[37]

Even in cases of solid evidence that older persons would benefit from treatment, they may be referred for diagnosis and treatment at a lower rate than younger persons with similar symptoms (e.g. with regard to cardiac testing, interventions and rehabilitation). Older women with breast cancer tend to receive different treatment than younger women, and eligible older persons are less likely to receive kidney transplants or to be referred for joint-replacement surgery than younger patients. A survey in the UK in 2009 found that more than 50 per cent of doctors who cared for older persons believed that the National Health Service was 'institutionally ageist'. 66 per cent claimed that older persons were less likely to have their symptoms examined, and 72 per cent believed that older persons were less likely to be referred to surgery or chemotherapy.[38]

In Norway, a study from 2006 showed that 75 per cent of the nurses, and 54 per cent of physicians, agreed with the statement that healthcare to older persons is not of equivalent quality as healthcare to younger persons. Among doctors in nursing homes, as many as 70 per cent agreed with this statement. More nurses than doctors thought that older patients are more often placed further down the priority scale today compared to ten years ago (1996).[39]

5. MALTREATMENT AND SERIOUS NEGLECT: APPLICATION OF ARTICLE 3 ECHR

A significant level of abuse and neglect of older persons has been reported.[40]

As noted in Chapter 1 of this volume, not only physical abuse, but depriving a person of necessary treatment and care may also constitute a violation of

37 UN Department of Economic and Social Affairs, Office of the High Commissioner for Human Rights, Current Status of the social situation, well-being, participation in development and rights of older persons worldwide, draft report of August 2010, pp. 44–45, with reference to Safiliou-Rothschild (2010).

38 *Ibid.*, p. 45, with reference to Lloyd-Sherlock (2010).

39 R. Førde *et al.*, 'Får eldreomsorgen nok ressurser?' [Sufficient resources to the care for the elderly?] *Tidsskrift for Den norske legeforening* No. 15, 10 August 2006, www.tidsskriftet.no.

40 See Section 1 above, with reference to UN Department of Economic and Social Affairs, Office of the High Commissioner for Human Rights, Current Status of the social situation, well-being, participation in development and rights of older persons worldwide, draft report of August 2010, p. 66.

Article 3 ECHR, which prohibits torture and inhuman or degrading treatment or punishment. A similar provision is to be found in Article 4 EU Charter. The lack of care must amount to a certain level of severity before these provisions are applicable, especially the alternative on torture.[41]

In *Price v. UK* (2001),[42] a severely disabled woman with numerous health problems was sent to prison for seven days. The European Court of Human Rights (ECtHR) found that she had been subjected to degrading treatment, taking her special situation into consideration and considering, *inter alia*, the significant neglect she suffered (i.e. dangerously low temperature, unable to keep clean, risk of developing bed sores).

Serious neglect, e.g. in terms of lack of emergency treatment or basic care, severe malnutrition and dehydration must, in my opinion, fall within the scope of Article 3 ECHR ('inhumane or degrading treatment'). As Mikkola points out, 'the provision is open for further development as a fundamental safeguard for survival, at least in the meaning of subsistence, emergency treatment, necessary care and housing of human dignity.'[43]

Furthermore, based on the case law of the ECtHR, Article 2 ECHR implies a state obligation to protect an individual's life, including a positive duty to provide effective measures in the context of any activity in which the right to life may be at stake.[44]

Health institutions and nursing homes must be organised and run in a manner that provides the necessary protection of the inmates lives, e.g. with regard to appropriate life-saving treatment, the prevention of life-threatening accidents and injuries, *etc*. The state is responsible for effective measures in order to protect the lives of older persons and to avoid or detect abuse or neglect amounting to a violation of Article 3 ECHR.[45]

The measures, in terms of healthcare and support, must meet certain quality requirements, and must also be provided in time and safely, so that human lives and health are not seriously jeopardised. The legal requirements following from Articles 3 and 2 ECHR are of a rather basic nature, but are still important for elderly patients at risk of suffering from a serious lack of adequate medical attention, healthcare and supervision (see Chapter 1).

---

41 Jacobs and White, *The European Convention on Human Rights*, Oxford: Oxford University press 2006, fourth ed., pp. 74–75, with reference to *Ireland v United Kingdom* (1978).

42 Application no. 33394/96.

43 M. Mikkola, *Social Human Rights of Europe*, Porvoo: Karelactio 2010, pp. 529–530.

44 *Öneryildiz v. Turkey* (2004, Application no. 48939/99).

45 J. Aall, *Rettsstat og menneskerettigheter* (second ed.), Bergen: Fagbokforlaget 2004, pp. 152–153.

6. RIGHT TO HEALTH PROTECTION FOR OLDER PERSONS: STATE OBLIGATIONS

6.1. OVERVIEW

The term 'health protection', or 'protection of health', which is used in both the European Social Charter/ESC and the EU Charter, includes a broad range of measures: healthcare services, public information, social and economic measures aimed at poverty reduction, health education, strategies for improved nutrition, physical activity, healthy behaviours, non-smoking initiatives, *etc.* Thus, this term is in accordance with the broad notion of the right to health in Article 12 ICESCR, which covers not only access to healthcare services, but also access to underlying health determinants, such as safe water and environment, adequate nutrition and housing, education, advice and information, *etc.* As a legal term, I think 'right to health protection' is a more accurate than the term 'right to health', as the right embraces not a right to be healthy but a right to certain state activities to secure the health of individuals.

In the following, while the focus will mainly be on the state obligation to secure equitable access to appropriate healthcare for older persons, to some extent it will also cover other relevant aspects of the right to health protection. In Section 6.2, Article 3 Biomedicine Convention is analysed in light of guidelines in the Explanatory Report to the Convention, the AAAQ recommendations in General Comment 14, and the soft law instruments mentioned in Section 3, above. In Sections 6.3 and 6.4, several provisions on health protection in the ESC and the EU Charter are discussed.

6.2. THE BIOMEDICINE CONVENTION AND EQUITABLE ACCESS TO APPROPRIATE HEALTHCARE

6.2.1. *Starting points*

The overall goal of this Convention is to protect human dignity and to guarantee everyone, without discrimination, 'respect for their integrity and other rights and fundamental freedoms' (Article 1). In the preamble, particular references are made to central human rights instruments. Article 3 formulates the general state obligation concerning the distribution of healthcare services:

> 'Parties, taking into account health needs and available resources, shall take appropriate measures with a view to providing, within their jurisdiction, equitable access to health care of appropriate quality' (emphasis added).

This provision is not too different from the right to access to healthcare in international human rights law, i.e. the ICESCR Article 12, as interpreted by the CESCR. In General Comment No. 14, the Committee has developed the right to health in a way that is clearly relevant to the understanding of the duty to ensure equitable access to healthcare of appropriate quality in Article 3 Biomedicine Convention. The Committee states that the right to health contains four basic elements: availability, accessibility, acceptability and quality,[46] which are all relevant with regard to the interpretation of Article 3 Biomedicine Convention, and therefore will be referred to in the following analysis.

6.2.2. *'Equitable access'*

The Biomedicine Convention Article 3 contains two main obligations: to provide equitable access to healthcare, and to provide healthcare of appropriate quality. Both these obligations must be seen in light of the duty to take into account 'health needs'. The term 'healthcare' includes services offering diagnostic, preventive, therapeutic and rehabilitative interventions, designed to maintain or improve a person's state of health or to alleviate suffering.[47]

The formulation of Article 3 in the Convention ('equitable access to health care'), and the wording in the Explanatory Report to the Biomedicine Convention, imply that the provision has a more limited scope than Article 12 ICESCR, which also includes access to underlying health determinants, such as clean water, adequate nutrition, sanitation, housing, *etc.*[48]

However, as I will argue below, in order to secure equitable access to healthcare, socioeconomic determinants relating to such access must be taken into account (see the following discussion).

Concerning 'equitable access', the Explanatory Report to the Biomedicine Convention specifies that this means 'first and foremost the absence of unjustified discrimination',[49] cf. the duty to respect the right to health in terms of refraining from all acts that negatively impact, directly or indirectly, upon this right.[50]

Furthermore, the Explanatory Report states that the requirement of equitable access is not identical to absolute equality. Rather, the state is under the duty of 'effectively obtaining a satisfactory degree of care'.[51]

---

46 See General Comment 14, para. 12.

47 Council of Europe, Explanatory Report to the Biomedicine Convention of 17 December 1996, para. 24.

48 M. Ssenyonjo, *Economic, Social and Cultural Rights in International Law*, chapter 8 on the right to health in Article 12 ICESCR (with further references), pp. 327–331.

49 Explanatory Report., para. 25.

50 M. Ssenyonjo, *Economic, Social and Cultural Rights in International Law*, p. 336.

51 Council of Europe, Explanatory Report to the Biomedicine Convention, para. 25.

This formulation indicates that an important aspect of the provision is to ensure satisfactory – although not equal – care for all groups, and thus, the requirement of 'equitable access' must include a requirement of reasonable accommodation for different needs.[52]

In *Thlimmenos v. Greece*, in which the European Court of Human Rights (ECtHR) analysed Article 14 ECHR on discrimination, the Court stated that discrimination occurs not only when states treat differently persons in analogous situations without providing an objective and reasonable justification, but also when the state 'without an objective and reasonable justification fails to treat differently persons whose situations are significantly different.'[53]

Despite the fact that Article 14 ECHR has no independent application outside rights and freedoms safeguarded by other substantive provisions of the Convention (which does not cover the right to health), the general understanding of what constitutes discrimination has relevance to the understanding of what is 'equitable' in Article 3 Biomedicine Convention: if healthcare policies are designed without taking into account the particular needs of elderly persons, these do not provide equitable access to healthcare, and they violate the goal of the Convention, which is, *inter alia,* to protect the dignity and rights of everyone without discrimination (see Article 1).

Also, healthcare services that are designed without taking into account the particular needs of different groups will hardly be 'appropriate' (see below, Section 6.1.3), which is also a requirement in Article 3 Biomedicine Convention. Thus, appropriate healthcare services must be designed and provided with consideration for the particular needs of all groups in society, including the elderly. As for older persons in particular, the lack of ability to request essential services, e.g., due to dementia, or the lack of physical capacity to visit health facilities, must be taken into account in order to secure equitable access to appropriate healthcare services.

In addition, and this concerns socioeconomic determinants of health, in order to secure equity, states must take differences in social status and resources into account, and must ensure access to services for everyone, irrespective of wealth economy, level of education, social situation, *etc.* The requirement of reasonable accommodation to avoid discrimination is particularly important for older persons with little financial and social resources, limited physical mobility, *etc.*

These observations are in harmony with the understanding of the accessibility criteria at the UN level. According to the CESCR, the accessibility of health

---

52 See Arnardottir in Chapter 9, with reference to CRPD, Article 2.4.

53 Judgment of 6 April 2000 (Application no. 34369/97), para. 44.

facilities, goods and services has four overlapping dimensions: non-discrimination, physical accessibility for everyone, economic accessibility (affordability), and access to information.[54]

In the following, Article 3 Biomedicine Convention is interpreted in light of these four dimensions/requirements elaborated in General Comment No. 14, and also in light of other sources that support the same line of argument.

Non-discrimination implies, *inter alia*, that health facilities, goods and services must be accessible to all, 'especially the most vulnerable or marginalized sections of the population, in law and in fact.'[55]

As observed by human rights scholar Brigit Toebes, 'a state may violate the right to health if it structurally fails to offer adequate health services to certain segments of society.'[56]

The current change of population structure and disease patterns due to a growing number of older persons could affect the ethics of healthcare delivery and prioritisation policies. As this could strengthen existing discriminatory practices in the field of healthcare, or lead to new ones, healthcare authorities must clarify the legal obligations of healthcare providers, to make sure that appropriate and sufficient services for older persons are provided.

An important dimension of accessibility is physical accessibility, which means that health services must be within safe physical reach for everyone, including older persons, both in cities and in rural areas. This is essential for older persons, who may have problems with walking and access public transportation, and who therefore need services in their homes in order to access them. Special attention should be paid to older persons living in rural or remote areas, who often have difficulties accessing healthcare and social services.[57]

Services must be affordable for all (economic accessibility), including for disadvantaged groups, whether these are privately or publicly provided. Financial barriers often make it impossible for poor families to obtain needed medical care, especially in low-income countries with a lack of public healthcare systems and services. But even in developed countries, healthcare may not be affordable for all. The Survey of Health, Ageing and Retirement in Europe has reported that the poorest spend a higher share of their income on health costs, and that out-of-pocket expenses were highest for the oldest, the less healthy, and for women. Even when exemptions from fees are guaranteed by the government,

54 General Comment No. 14, para. 12.
55 CESCR, General Comment No. 14, para. 12 b.
56 B. Toebes, 'The Right to Health', in Eide, Krause and Rosas (eds.), *Economic, Social and Cultural Rights*, 2nd revised edition, Dordrecht: Martinus Nijhoff Publishers 2001, pp. 169–191, at p. 181.
57 RIS, para. 70.

if this is not well-publicised, older persons might be unaware that they can request an exemption, which in turn may lead to greatly reduced access.[58]

The CESCR has pointed out that equity demands that 'poorer households should not be disproportionately burdened with health expenses as compared to richer households.'[59]

The European strategy document for the implementation of the MIPAA states that targeted efforts should be undertaken to decrease gender, age, race and income-related inequalities in access to health and social services.[60]

Finally, accessibility includes the right to seek, receive and impart information and ideas on health issues, although with respect for confidentiality and privacy. This means that older persons, in particular, from disadvantaged groups, must be given adequate and understandable information about relevant health services, preventive measures and available financial support.[61]

It follows from the Explanatory Report to the Biomedicine Convention that Article 3 does not create an individual right to healthcare, but rather, prompts the state 'to adopt the requisite measures as part of its social policy in order to ensure equitable access to healthcare.'[62]

Failure to do so would be a violation of the duty to protect the right to equitable access to healthcare. Such measures may take many different forms 'and a wide variety of methods may be employed to this end.'[63]

In this sense, Article 3 expresses a 'mainstreaming' principle of state policies with regard to healthcare, which must be adjusted to the needs of older persons, as well as to other vulnerable groups. Mainstreaming is a methodology to ensure that age-related issues and older persons are brought into the 'mainstream' of the policymaking process, rather than simply being 'added on' at the end. It is a strategy for making older persons' concerns and experiences an integral part of the design, implementation, monitoring and evaluation of policies and programmes.[64]

In the MIPAA, issue 2 on universal and equal access to healthcare services, several recommendations are made as to how to fulfil the right to health for

58 UN Department of Economic and Social Affairs, Office of the High Commissioner for Human Rights, Current Status of the social situation, well-being, participation in development and rights of older persons worldwide, draft report of August 2010, p. 43.

59 General Comment No. 14, para. 12 b.

60 RIS, Para. 70.

61 This is also recommended at the European level; see the RIS document (para. 64). It is also stressed that older persons need to be made aware of the range of social and health services available in their country (para. 67).

62 Explanatory Report, para. 25.

63 *Ibid.*

64 MIPAA Guiding Framework and Toolkit for Practitioners and Policy Makers, p. 12 (with reference to ECOSOC conclusions 1997/2).

older persons. They include taking measures to ensure equal distribution of health and rehabilitation resources to older persons and, in particular, to increase access to these resources for older persons who are poor, including affordable access to medications and other therapeutic measures. With regard to affordability, the reduction or elimination of user fees, provisions of insurance schemes, and other financial support measures are mentioned.[65]

Furthermore, the education and empowerment of older persons in the effective use and selection of health and rehabilitation services are recommended, as well as other strategies to reduce various barriers to access.[66]

These requirements come in addition to the AAAQ requirements (see Toebes, in Chapter 3 concerning a broader set of human rights requirements, including participation and accountability).

6.2.3. 'Appropriate healthcare'

As regards the quality requirement in the Biomedicine Convention Article 3 ('appropriate', which is also related to accessibility), healthcare must be of a 'fitting standard' in light of scientific progress, and must be subject to a continuous quality assessment.[67]

This is similar to the requirement of quality as pointed out in General Comment No. 14. The fitting standard must be determined according to the particular health needs of various groups, including elderly persons, which refers also to the requirement of acceptability. General Comment No. 14 on the right to health should also be kept in mind here. The CESCR has, in General Comment No. 14, paragraph 12 c, stated that all health services, in order to be acceptable, must be sensitive to gender and lifecycle requirements, and must be designed to improve the health status of those concerned. Thus, in order to protect the right to health for older persons, the particular needs of older persons must be taken into account and addressed by national as well as municipal authorities in their health plans, policies, and practical measures.

In the MIPAA, issue 2 on universal and equal access to healthcare services, several recommendations are made, including 'a continuum of care' ranging from health promotion and disease prevention to the provision of primary healthcare, acute treatment, rehabilitation, community care for chronic health problems, physical and mental rehabilitation for older persons, and palliative care for older persons suffering from painful or incurable illnesses or diseases. It is stated that effective care for older persons needs to 'integrate physical, mental, social and environmental factors.'[68]

---

65 Para. 74, a and b.
66 Para. 74, d-g.
67 Explanatory Report, para. 24.
68 MIPAA, para. 69.

An important objective is the development and strengthening of primary healthcare services to meet the needs of older persons and to promote their inclusion in the process. Actions to this end include, *inter alia*, taking measures to provide universal and equal access to primary healthcare, and establishing community health programmes for older persons, supporting local communities in providing health support services to older persons, and training primary healthcare workers and social workers in basic gerontology and geriatrics.[69]

Another objective is to develop a continuum of healthcare to meet the needs of older persons. Complementing actions include, *inter alia*, developing regulatory mechanisms at appropriate levels to set suitable standards of healthcare and rehabilitation of older persons, implementing community development strategies that determine a systematic needs assessment baseline for the planning, executing and evaluating locally based health programmes, improving the coordination of primary healthcare, long-term care and social services, and other community services, and developing specialised gerontological services and improving the coordination of their activities with primary healthcare and social services.[70]

As for dementia, which is a prevalent disease in old age, especially Alzheimer's, strategies to cope with such conditions, including diagnosis, medication, psychosocial factors, cognitive training programmes, training for caring family members and caring staff, and specific structures of inpatient care, are emphasised.[71]

Another issue that is emphasised is HIV/AIDS, since an increasing number of AIDS patients are surviving to old age. In addition, older persons can be at risk of HIV because they are typically not the subjects of information campaigns, prevention, and counselling. Diagnosis might be difficult because symptoms can be mistaken for other conditions that occur in older persons.[72]

The need for a gender perspective is mentioned in all framework documents. In the Madrid, Political Declaration Art 8, and in the European implementation of the MIPAA (RIS), commitment 8, governments are required to take measures to mainstream gender issues and to remove all obstacles to gender equality and, *inter alia*, to ensure equal access to, and equal treatment in, education, healthcare and other social fields (RIS, para. 82). Reasonable accommodation for differences between men and women must, however, in order to ensure substantial equality or equity, be an integrated part of equality as well as quality and acceptability measures.[73]

---

69 MIPAA, para. 69.

70 *Ibid*, para. 76. See also RIS, paras. 57–63, 72 and 73, stressing the need for a continuum of care, including primary healthcare, long-term care, palliative care, nursing homes and geriatric centres, treatment and rehabilitation programmes for persons with dementia, *etc.*

71 RIS, para. 60.

72 *Ibid.*, para. 62.

73 See Section 6.2.2, above and at the beginning of this section.

6.2.4. *Respect, protect, fulfil: recommendations for actions*

As a follow-up to the Berlin Ministerial Conference, and based upon the UNECE Member States' agreement to exchange information, experience and good practices between countries, the UNECE Population Unit (PAU) developed two questionnaires in October 2004 and June 2006 to collect information on the national follow-up on ageing issues. The submissions by the Member States were summarised in a draft report by PAU,[74] identifying some common patterns and five main topics of concern: welfare and well-being, healthcare, active ageing, lifestyle and image, and research.[75]

With regard to healthcare, the need for a holistic vision of healthcare provisions, encompassing supply and demand, as well as mechanisms to guarantee and improve them, were mentioned. The need for healthcare services designed for older persons with consideration of the age-specific issues were highlighted, as well as affordable, accessible and available services. Improved provisions for home care, better health insurance targeting older persons (e.g. care allowances and improved choices of healthcare provider), improved access to healthcare through financial measures (e.g. contribution free health insurance systems for older persons) were recommended. General reforms of the healthcare system to improve its efficiency and funding were also mentioned as important from the perspective of older persons. Responses from countries also showed that health promotion for the elderly is not narrowly dependent upon healthcare initiatives, but includes social services as well, in particular, at the local level. Countries having recently undergone, or in the process of undergoing, major health reforms (some former socialist countries) tended to focus on health as the main and overarching issue, while other countries particularly emphasised health as an integral part of the overall social protection system. The issue of accessibility, seen in the context of non-discrimination, human rights and dignity of the human being, was mentioned frequently as important.[76]

In order to respect, protect and fulfil the right to health effectively, states must avoid discriminatory laws and practices towards older persons, and must adopt legislation and other measures to ensure equal access with regard to healthcare and health-related services provided by third parties (e.g. private or public institutions). It is not acceptable that privatisation of the healthcare sector constitutes a barrier to availability, accessibility, acceptability and quality of health facilities, goods and services.[77]

Older people, despite a lack of income, pension or health insurance, must be provided with access to timely and adequate healthcare according to their needs.

---

74 Prepared for the Meeting of National Focal Points on Ageing, Segovia, Spain, 13–15 November 2006.

75 Draft summary report, p. 3

76 Draft summary report, p. 4.

77 General Comment No. 14, para. 35.

States must, through legislation, administrative measures, budgetary allocations, priority settings, *etc.*, facilitate, provide, and promote the right to health protection, e.g., through education and training of health personnel, health centres for older persons, research, social and financial support, and the monitoring of services and standards, *etc.*[78]

Awareness of the signs of dementia is limited in many countries, and the signs are often dismissed as a normal part of ageing. According to one study in the UK, 70 per cent of caregivers were unaware of the symptoms of dementia before diagnosis, and 58 per cent of caregivers believed the symptoms were a normal part of ageing.[79]

Therefore, knowledge, information and awareness in the general public is also essential in order to ensure access to healthcare and other services for older persons in need.

The monitoring of services, standards of care and conditions for care providers is important. In Norway, it has recently been documented that older patients, in particular, those with dementia, are in a vulnerable position in several areas: Diagnosis, identification of needs, and follow-up changes, cooperation problems among different levels of services, a lack of leadership and organisation, a lack of knowledge and competence, a lack of adequate routines for the distribution of medicines, and a lack of documentation (of diagnosis, medication and relevant observations made by health personnel). In many municipalities, too many healthcare workers are involved in the care for the same patient.[80]

A well-known problem is the risk of undernourishment. In Norway, despite the general awareness of this problem, 14 of 21 municipalities seem to lack sufficient measures to identify and follow-up relevant patients, partly due to a lack of competence-building among health providers. This could lead to serious health problems for fragile individuals.[81]

Without regular and systematic monitoring of the healthcare system, it could be hard to detect and change these weaknesses.

The MIPAA Guiding Framework and toolkit for practitioners and policy makers,[82] whose purpose is to assist countries to give effect to the MIPAA, provides, *inter alia*, practical recommendations based on national experiences, as well as guidance on how to 'mainstream' older persons concerns into all social fields, including healthcare and social services.[83]

---

78 Ssenyonjo, *Economic, Social and Cultural Rights in International Law*, p. 340.

79 UN Department of Economic and Social Affairs, Office of the High Commissioner for Human Rights, Current Status of the social situation, well-being, participation in development and rights of older persons worldwide, draft report of August 2010, p. 41.

80 Some patients have up to 26 different caretakers during one month

81 Report from the National Board of Health, 2010, pp. 5–7.

82 Document of 07/03/2008, prepared by R. Lane and F. Serour, the UN Department of Economic and Social Affairs, Division for Social Policy and Development.

83 *Ibid.*, pp. 12–16.

The recommendations by relevant actors mentioned or referred to above are all relevant with regard to the implementation of the right to health protection for older persons, and should be considered carefully. The governmental responsibility in the field of healthcare for vulnerable groups is crucial, since private actors may be more concerned with profits than with the human right of equitable access to appropriate healthcare for everyone.[84]

The WHO Europe recommends investing in public health systems, and, in particular, securing a strong primary care system as a way to ensure healthier populations, and also to meet the needs of vulnerable groups, including older people/persons with chronic and multiple health conditions.[85]

6.3. THE EUROPEAN SOCIAL CHARTER AND HEALTH PROTECTION FOR THE ELDERLY

6.3.1. General provisions: Article 11

While the Biomedicine Convention mainly focuses on equitable access to appropriate healthcare services, the (Revised) European Social Charter (ESC)[86] takes a wider approach to health protection. Article 11 ESC is titled '[t]he right to protection of health', indicating an individual rights perspective (which is in contrast to the Biomedicine Article 3), and stating that States Parties, with a view to ensuring the effective exercise of this right, must undertake, either directly or in cooperation with public or private organisations, to take appropriate measures designed, *inter alia*, 'to remove as far as possible the causes of ill-health' (paragraph 1), 'to provide advisory and educational facilities for the promotion of health and the encouragement of individual responsibility in matters of health' (paragraph 2), and finally, 'to prevent as far as possible epidemic, endemic and other diseases, as well as accidents (paragraph 3) (emphasis added).

This provision has a much broader perspective than the Biomedicine Convention, as it is not limited to healthcare services. States Parties are obligated to take effective measures in order to remove factors that affect health negatively. The wording in paragraph 1 indicates that not only a lack of appropriate healthcare, but also socioeconomic, environmental and hygienic factors, as well as anti-smoking measures and the prevention of alcohol and drug abuse, are relevant. The European Committee on Social Rights (ECSR) has mentioned a number of elements that States Parties should include, such as public health arrangements making generally available medical and paramedical practitioners

[84] Ssenyonjo, *Economic, Social and Cultural Rights in International Law*, pp. 340–341.

[85] The European Health Report 2009, pp. 114–157.

[86] There is an ESC and a revised ESC (see chapter 1). In the following, I am referring to the revised ESC, using the term ESC to keep it simple.

and adequate equipment, securing proper medical care for the whole population (all groups must be included) (see Section 6.2, above), and the prevention and diagnosis of disease and environmental measures. Special measures for vulnerable groups such as mothers, children and old people must be present.[87]

Older persons, as well as children, are more susceptible to various forms of environmental pollution than others, and thus protective measures could be urgent to prevent health damage.[88]

In addition, at least a substantial part of the costs of healthcare services must be financed by public or collective bodies.[89]

Paragraph 2 of Article 11 ESC is understood as requiring a system of health education, which includes proper budgeting for this purpose, health education and information directed to target groups, e.g. on health risks such as the dangers of tobacco (which most old people today are probably aware of). For old people, many need to be reminded about risky behaviours and encouraged to take personal responsibility for their own health, e.g. with regard to diet, exercise and smoking. In the Madrid International Action Plan on Ageing (MIPAA), it is pointed out that the leading causes of disease, disability and mortality in older persons can be alleviated through health promotion and disease prevention measures that focus, *inter alia*, on nutrition, physical activity and the cessation of smoking.[90]

Thus, information and advice on these issues are essential and should be implemented as public health measures geared towards the elderly population in general, and towards individuals in particular need.

Paragraph 3 of Article 11 (Revised) ESC[91] concerning prevention of diseases and accidents overlaps with paragraphs 1 and 2. With regard to the elderly, the prevention of accidents is of particular interest, since older persons are more prone to injuries from falling and other accidents than the average person. The general requirement is that while Member States may follow a policy of accident prevention, each state will be able to choose the adequate measures.[92]

6.3.2. General provision: Article 13

Article 13 ESC contains an individual right to social and medical assistance, obligating the States Parties to take effective measures to ensure 'any person who is without adequate resources and who is unable to secure such resources either

87 Harris and Darcy, *The European Social Charter*, p. 150.
88 Madrid International Action Plan on Ageing, para. 65.
89 *Ibid.*
90 Para. 65.
91 The only new element of Article 11 Revised ESC (compared to the 1961 Article 11 ESC) is the inclusion of "as well as accidents" (Harris and Darcy, The European Social Charter, p. 265).
92 Harris and Darcy, *The European Social Charter*, p. 265.

by his own efforts or from other sources ... be granted adequate assistance, and in case of sickness, the care necessitated by his condition' (paragraph 1, emphasis added). It is noteworthy that medical assistance in this paragraph does not refer to medical care or healthcare (cf. Article 11, above), but to financial aid for persons who cannot afford to purchase medical services or medicines, or to free healthcare.[93]

The individual rights perspective is crucial, aiming to move away from the stigma attached to state assistance and the notion of charity, also associated with imprecise and vague discretionary assessment criteria and available budgets.[94]

This provision obligates States Parties to take measures to secure necessary care, including healthcare and related services for everyone, and also to take different needs into account ('necessitated by his condition'). Considering whether the level of assistance is in accordance with the ESC, the ECSR has referred to 'the cost of living and/or a minimum level of subsistence fixed on a national level'.[95]

Social assistance could be in cash or kind, and all the various entitlements that could be claimed are relevant in order to assess the adequacy of state support.[96]

Of interest is also paragraph 3 of Article 13 ESC, obligating States Parties to ensure that 'everyone may receive by appropriate public or private services such advice and personal help as may be required to prevent, to remove, or to alleviate personal or family want' (emphasised here). Such personal assistance, including guidance, will often be urgent for older persons who experience increasing challenges in relation to health problems and reduced level of functioning. The ECSR has stressed the necessity of advice to enable persons in need to exercise their right to social and medical assistance effectively.[97]

It follows from Article 13 paragraph 4 ESC that only persons who have a lawful presence in the state ('lawfully within their territories') can claim social or medical assistance, implying that there is no requirement of lawful residence or work.[98]

This is a *lex specialis* provision, derogating from the general and narrower rule concerning the personal scope of the ESC, which is that it only protects nationals of other contracting states who have lawful residence, or who work regularly in the State Party concerned (see Appendix to the Revised European Social Charter). This derogation is relevant in respect of elderly persons moving

93 *Ibid.*, p. 167.
94 Harris and Darcy, *The European Social Charter*, pp. 165, 167.
95 *Ibid.*, p. 166, quoting the Committee (ECSR).
96 *Ibid.*
97 *Ibid.*, p. 173.
98 *Ibid.*, p. 174.

around and/or residing illegally in European countries, which is probably not too many.

6.3.3. *General provisions: Articles 14, 30 and 31*

According to Article 14 ESC, States Parties undertake 'to promote or provide services which, by using methods of social work, would contribute to the welfare and development of both individuals and groups in the community' (para. 1). Article 30 on protection against poverty and social exclusion provides that States Parties should take measures to ensure that at-risk persons have access to medical assistance.

Article 31 covers the right to housing, obligating states to ensure 'access to housing of an adequate standard', to prevent and reduce homelessness, and to make the price of housing accessible to those without adequate resources. The ECSR has stated that adequate housing under Article 31, paragraph 1 means 'a dwelling which is safe from a sanitary and health point of view, i.e. it must possess all basic amenities, such as water, heating, waste disposal, sanitation facilities and electricity and must also be structurally secure, not overcrowded and with secure tenure supported by the law.'[99]

These requirements are essential from a health perspective, also for old persons, e.g. in various forms of health or care institutions.

6.3.4. *Provisions directed towards older persons*

Article 23[100] Revised ESC concerning the right of elderly persons to social protection includes several provisions relevant to health protection:

> 'With a view to ensuring the effective exercise of the right of elderly persons to social protection, the Parties undertake to adopt or encourage, either directly or in co-operation with public or private organisations, appropriate measures designed in particular:
>
> to enable elderly persons to remain full members of society for as long as possible, by means of:
> - adequate resources enabling them to lead a decent life and play an active part in public, social and cultural life;
> - provision of information about services and facilities available for elderly persons and their opportunities to make use of them;

---

99 European Committee of Social Rights, Decision of 20 October 2009, para. 43.

100 This provision substitutes Article 4 of the Additional Protocol to the ESC of 1961, which was the first human rights treaty provision that specifically protects the elderly (D. Harris, *The European Social Charter*, 2nd edition, New York: Transnational Publishers 2001, p. 250). The 1961 ESC did not contain this provision.

- to enable elderly persons to choose their life-style freely and to lead independent lives in their familiar surroundings for as long as they wish and are able, by means of:
- provision of housing suited to their needs and their state of health or of adequate support for adapting their housing;
- the healthcare and the services necessitated by their state;
- to guarantee elderly persons living in institutions appropriate support, while respecting their privacy, and participation in decisions concerning living conditions in the institution' (emphasis added).

Many aspects of social protection are also important aspects of health protection, such as the provision of information, adequate housing, healthcare and social services, and participation in decision-making.[101]

As for healthcare and services, the formulation 'the health care and the services necessitated by their state' is similar to the formulation in Article 13 paragraph 1 ESC (see Section 6.3.2), emphasising necessity in light of individual needs ('his condition', 'their state'). The considerations of necessity will naturally also depend on the conditions and resources in different states, which must have a margin of appreciation to consider what is necessary. However, the margin of appreciation cannot be too wide, as the overall goal is, *inter alia*, to facilitate the further realisation of human rights and improved standards of living and well-being (cf. ESC preamble). The ECSR has been concerned that contracting parties report fully on the medical care that is available to the elderly. As for services, these should include home nursing and other domiciliary care or services provided in day centres, as well as contact services or recreational activities.[102]

The guidelines provided by the MIPAA should be followed in order to fulfil and fully realise the right to health protection for the elderly in Europe (see Section 6.1).

The overall goal of Article 23 is to enable older persons to remain full members of society by means of appropriate measures to this end. Contracting parties to the ESC must make focused and planned provision for older persons identified as a vulnerable part of the population with particular needs.[103]

Each of the mentioned measures cannot be elaborated on here, however, important is that health protection is part of social protection, and that healthcare services are just one among several measures that must be implemented in order for older people to be able to maintain a life in dignity and to be active members of society.

---

101 In Section 6.2 above, most of these aspects are mentioned.
102 *Ibid.*, p. 253.
103 Harris and Darcy, *The European Social Charter*, p. 251.

6.4. THE EU CHARTER OF FUNDAMENTAL RIGHTS AND THE RIGHT TO HEALTH PROTECTION

The Charter of Fundamental Rights (ECFR), Article 35 states:

> 'Everyone has the right of access to preventive health care and the right to benefit from medical treatment under the conditions established by national laws and practices. A high level of human health protection shall be ensured in the definition and implementation of all Union policies and activities' (emphasis added).[104]

While the first sentence of Article 35 of the Charter is formulated as an individual right (in contrast to the Biomedicine Convention) to preventive as well as curative healthcare, the second sentence expresses a 'mainstreaming' state obligation of health protection (see, also, Chapter 2). The first sentence puts forward an individual right perspective, signifying the notion that access to healthcare is a fundamental right of everyone. In particular, the rights perspective implies that unjustified discrimination is not acceptable. The general principle of non-discrimination in Article 21 of the Charter provides that '[a]ny discrimination based on any ground' such as sex, race, ethnic or social origin, *etc.*, and 'age', shall be prohibited. Thus, the right of everyone to equitable access to healthcare services (cf. above, in Section 6.2) – both preventive and curative – must be ensured.

However, the requirement of 'appropriate quality' as mentioned in the Biomedicine Convention Article 3 is not part of the ECFR Article 35. Rather, it is explicitly mentioned that it is 'the conditions established by national laws and practices' that determine the degree of healthcare quality and availability. This is a reference to the principle of subsidiarity, also mentioned in Article 51 and in the preamble of the EU Charter. However, the preamble states that the Charter 'reaffirms, with due regard for the powers and tasks of the Community and the Union ... the rights as they result, in particular, from the constitutional traditions and international obligations common to the Member States ...' Thus, although Article 35 of the ECFR (first sentence) is apparently limited to a quite strict non-discrimination principle with regard to access to healthcare services, the provision should be interpreted in light of common state obligations following from international law and human rights, including the ICESCR and the Biomedicine Convention. In addition, the non-discrimination principles developed by the ECtHR should be taken into account, including the requirement of reasonable accommodation for different needs (cf. above, in Section 6.2).

---

104 See Chapter 2 for more details on ECFR, Article 35.

A general policy of not prioritising appropriate healthcare for the elderly is not acceptable and would amount to discrimination against this group with regard to the right to health protection (cf. the duty to respect the right to such protection). Legislation and other measures to protect and fulfil the right to equitable access to healthcare services must be adopted (see above, in Section 6.2).[105]

The second sentence of ECFR Article 35 concerns Union policies and activities with regard to health. Member States are obligated to ensure a high level of 'human health protection' in the 'definition and implementation of all Union policies and activities.' The provision is based on the ESC, Article 11 (see Section 6.3.1, above) and the former EC Treaty, Article 152,[106] both focusing on human health protection.[107]

Chapter III of the Charter concerns equality, including Article 25, which is directed towards the elderly: 'The Union recognises and respects the rights of the elderly to lead a life of dignity and independence and to participate in social and cultural life.' This Article draws, *inter alia*, on Article 23 of the Revised ESC (see Section 6.3.4, above). However, it is far more limited in scope and detail, which signifies that the ESC is a more advanced and relevant document when it comes to health and social protection of the elderly.

7. FINAL REMARKS

Access to appropriate healthcare is a crucial issue for older persons, as disease and impairments are gradually becoming more common with old age. In addition, other factors of relevance to health are important to address in order to protect the health of older persons. The European legal system of health protection consists of several instruments of great significance to the health protection of older persons, both with regard to access to healthcare services and with regard to social rights and policies essential for health protection on a broader scale. As observed in the above discussions, the European legal framework is clearly interconnected with the international legal framework concerning health, in particular, the ICESCR Article 12 and the General Comment No. 14 (2000). It is important that the Biomedicine Convention and the European Social Charter, as well as the European Charter of Fundamental

[105] The non-discrimination principle is to be applied in compliance with, *inter alia*, Article 14 of the ECHR (Draft Charter of Fundamental Rights of the European Union, CHARTE 4473/00, p. 23).

[106] Article 152 is replaced by Article 168 of the Treaty of the functioning of the European Union.

[107] Draft Charter of Fundamental Rights of the European Union, CHARTE 4473/00, p. 32.

Rights, are interpreted in light of the international regime on health protection (in particular, Article 12 ICESCR and General Comment No. 14)). The Madrid International Plan of Action on Ageing (MIPAA), the related European instrument (RIS) and other international and regional framework documents should also be fully utilised by national governments in order to realise the right to health protection for the elderly across the European region.

The requirements of availability, accessibility, acceptability and good quality, which are internationally recognised criteria for ensuring health protection, must be addressed properly with regard to old people in all social fields relevant to health protection ('mainstreaming'). National measures must consider the particular challenges in their respective healthcare systems and socio-economic circumstances. Age, gender, ethnicity and socio-economic factors like level of education and income are all influencing on health outcomes for older persons. Thus, such factors must be taken into account when designing appropriate health programmes for different groups, including older persons belonging to various social and cultural strata. A high level of health of the population is both a central aim of development and a key promoter of economic growth and social development.[108]

For older persons, good health contributes to personal well-being, and enables them to participate in, and be active members of, social, cultural and political life in society.

---

108 UN Department of Economic and Social Affairs, Office of the High Commissioner for Human Rights, Current Status of the social situation, well-being, participation in development and rights of older persons worldwide, draft report of August 2010, p. 36. www.sparkpeople.com/resource/nutrition_articles.asp?id=869.

PART IV

CONCLUSIONS, CHALLENGES AND RECOMMENDATIONS